American Monetary Policy Adjustment and Its Impacts

Liu Weiping

American Monetary Policy Adjustment and Its Impacts

清華大學出版社
TSINGHUA UNIVERSITY PRESS

palgrave
macmillan

Liu Weiping
China Development Bank
Beijing, China

ISBN 978-981-99-7809-0 ISBN 978-981-99-7810-6 (eBook)
https://doi.org/10.1007/978-981-99-7810-6

Jointly published with Tsinghua University Press
The print edition is not for sale in China (Mainland). Customers from China (Mainland) please order the print book from: Tsinghua University Press

This Palgrave Macmillan imprint is published by the registered company Springer Nature Singapore Pte Ltd.
The registered company address is: 152 Beach Road, #21-01/04 Gateway East, Singapore 189721, Singapore

Paper in this product is recyclable.

Dr. Liu Weiping at Wuhan University

Comments for Professor Liu Weiping's book "American Monetary Policy Adjustment and Its Impacts"

China and the United Sates jointly drive global economic growth. While the US represents the largest economy in the world, China has contributed more to global economic growth in recent years, reflecting its much higher growth. The two largest economies are tightly connected through multiple channels. Any changes in economic or financial conditions in one economy could be felt in the other economy.

China and the US have been top trading partners of each other. A slowdown in US growth would reduce economic demand for Chinese goods and services, and thus slow China's economic growth, and vice versa. Besides the direct impact, there could be sizable indirect impact. For instance, China has large influence on emerging economies' growth. Slower growth in China would lead to slower growth in emerging economies and thus reduce total demand for US goods and services.

The two economies also interact with each other through financial linkages. Though the direct exposure of US assets to China is limited, any perceived shocks from China could lead to big movements in global investors' sentiment and thus large volatility in the US financial markets. This happened during the period of late 2015 when global investors were concerned about Chinese growth. On the other side, when US financial conditions change significantly it could generate large movements in China's capital flows and influence the value of RMB, which in turn influence China's financial conditions and economic growth.

China and the US differ in their growth trends and business cycles. Economic policies in these two economies, though mainly designed to counter negative shocks in their own economies, could impact the other country and the global economy as well. For instance, the 2007–2009 financial crisis was triggered by the collapse of the subprime mortgage market in the US, leading to a rapid growth decline in the US and then in other economies. In response, China launched a 4 trillion-yuan economic stimulus plan to bolster Chinese growth, which also helped stabilize global economic growth. As another example, during the COVID-19 pandemic of 2020, in response to the sharp rise of the unemployment rate and the expected large decline in output, the US government quickly launched a historical stimulus plan and lowered the interest rate to zero, which generated profound impact not only on the US but also the global economy.

In many aspects, the two economies also face similar challenges such as an aging population and geopolitical risks in other regions. In the US, the low labor force participation rate, especially after the large drop during the COVID-19 pandemic period, poses a big challenge for US economic growth while, in China, a stalled population and aging workforce may threaten future economic growth.

With all these connections, challenges, and risks, understanding how one country's economic policies may impact the other economy becomes crucially important. Professor Liu Weiping's book focuses on the impact of US monetary policy on China and China's policy responses. This is a great angle and an extremely important topic as US monetary policy not only impacts on US economic growth but also on financial conditions as well as on the strength of the US dollar, and thus can influence China and the global economy through all channels mentioned above—trade, growth, financial conditions, sentiment etc. Professor Liu starts from a careful review of the literature and provides detailed quantitative analysis using mainstream economic tools. Policy advice and insights are then shared based his thorough analysis. I expect Professor Liu's work to stimulate great interests and deep discussions from a wide range of readers regarding how to understand US monetary policy and how China should respond to it.

November 2023
Beijing, China

Nie Jun
Dean of Economics
and Management School
of Wuhan University, Professor

Foreword (Chen Jiyong) Mutual Benefit and Win-Win Results: China and the United States Need to Cooperate More Actively

In the post-financial crisis era, global economic imbalances and rebalancing are the primary issues facing the development of the world economy, and global economic rebalancing is impossible without the rebalancing of the Chinese and U.S. economies. As China opens up its economy further, the U.S. economy has become one of the most important international economic factors influencing China's macroeconomic development.

In view of the international financial crisis triggered by the U.S. subprime mortgage crisis, the current monetary policy framework has many defects and needs to be improved. The 2008 global financial crisis also reminds us that we should pay attention to the fact that virtual economies make up an increasing share of modern economies and are becoming increasingly important, and that virtual economies are a double-edged sword in that they both drive and destroy economic and social development, which requires the full attention of all countries when making monetary policy decisions. After the outbreak of the 2008 global financial crisis, the United States basically entered an "era of zero interest rates", and the conventional monetary policy with the federal funds rate as the tool no longer worked. Facts have proved that U.S. quantitative easing policy adjustments in 2008 played a pivotal role in the response to the financial crisis cycle.

Dr. Liu Weiping's monograph A Study of U.S. Monetary Policy Adjustments and Their Effects delves deep into U.S. monetary policy adjustments, their effects, and strategic choices for China's monetary policy from the perspective of the post-financial crisis era, and has important theoretical and practical implications. What is innovative about this study is that the author believes that the spillover effects of U.S. monetary policy adjustments differ significantly from one country or region to another, so it is necessary to demonstrate how such monetary policy adjustments affect different types of countries. To this end, this study selected more countries and regions as research samples, and conducted in-depth research on this issue based on a unified and comparable research framework. Second, this study expands the connotation of U.S. monetary policy adjustments to make them quantifiable and amenable to comparative analysis. Third, this study summarizes the operation and effectiveness of monetary policies of countries around the world in previous financial crises from the perspective of historical evolution with the hope of optimizing China's current monetary policy decision-making mechanism through academic research and policy research and enabling China's monetary policy decision-making and guidance mechanisms to make great progress in the process of effectively preventing and resolving financial crises, participating in international and regional financial cooperation, participating in the rebalancing of the global economy, participating in the reform of the international monetary system and pushing forward the internationalization of the RMB.

China is a large developing country. As a responsible major country and the world's second largest economy, China will make efforts to overcome uncertainties in global economic growth. On the basis of resolutely opposing trade protectionism, China will continue to push forward economic globalization and global economic governance and promote the sustainable development of the world economy. On China-U.S. economic cooperation, first, China and the United States are the two largest economies in the world, competition and complementarity coexist in China-U.S. economic and trade relations, and complementarity is greater than competition. The United States was China's second largest trading partner and largest export market in 2016, and there are broader prospects for economic and trade cooperation in the future. Second, China should take advantage of its ample foreign exchange reserves, industrial capacity, and experience in infrastructure development to actively invest in infrastructure in the United States and provide support for a new round of infrastructure development in the United States. Despite all the challenges and problems facing China-U.S. relations, it is of great significance to strengthen China-U.S. cooperation in economy, trade, and infrastructure in the face of the huge opportunities in infrastructure development in the United States. Third, there is a need for more active cooperation between China and the United States, especially strategic cooperation in the Asia-Pacific region under the Belt and Road Initiative, which will bring the world's two largest economies closer together, bring economic benefits while strengthening political trust, unimpeded trade and people-to-people exchanges between the two countries, and contribute to a stable and prosperous global economy.

May 2017
Beijing, China

Chen Jiyong
President of the China-U.S.
Economic Association
Director of the Institute for
the U.S. and Canadian Economies
of Wuhan University
Professor and Ph.D. Supervisor

Foreword (Song Min) Actively Respond to the Adjustment and Spillover Effects of U.S. Monetary Policy

Since the outbreak of the international financial crisis, U.S. monetary policy adjustments have had a great impact on other economies around the world. In order to stimulate the U.S. economy and stabilize financial markets, the Fed began to introduce quantitative easing (QE) in 2008, which led to a massive expansion of the Fed's balance sheet and eventually caused a flood of global liquidity. As the crisis receded, starting in 2015, the Fed began a series of nine interest rate hikes. In the wake of the COVID-19 outbreak in 2020, in order to solve the employment problem, the Fed once again unleashed unprecedented quantitative easing. As a result, U.S. dollar liquidity shifted from shortage to abundance, and the prices of financial assets hit new highs. As the most important international currency, the U.S. dollar facilitates international trade and investment to a certain extent, and promotes economic globalization and the prosperity and growth of the world economy. However, U.S. dollar hegemony will send global financial markets into turbulence in times of crisis, causing adverse effects on other economies.

As China further opens up its economy, U.S. policy adjustments have become one of the most important international factors affecting China's macroeconomic development. Changes in U.S. monetary policy have a profound impact on China's interest rates, foreign exchange market, capital flows, and commodities market. The world today is undergoing profound changes unseen in a century, and an unstable external environment will be one of the main features of China's new stage of development. In the context of global financial market integration, how will U.S. monetary policy affect China's macroeconomy? How should China choose economic and financial strategies to cope with the adverse impacts of external factors?

Starting from U.S. monetary policy, the book A Study of U.S. Monetary Policy Adjustments and Their Effects studies the spillover effects of U.S. monetary policy adjustments on emerging economies, as well as China's choice of monetary policies and the adjustment of its economic strategy from a post-financial crisis perspective; this book analyzes the choices and effects of monetary policies in various countries in the world in previous financial crises from a historical and forward-looking perspective, with a view to optimizing the decision-making and transmission mechanisms of China's monetary policy and effectively preventing and resolving financial risks. This study provides a new theoretical and empirical basis for understanding China's economic fluctuations and policy choices in the context of financial globalization.

First, this book elaborates on monetary policy theories, sorts out changes in U.S. monetary policy in different historical stages, focuses on examining the similarities and differences between conventional and unconventional monetary policy, and discusses the spillover effects of U.S. monetary policy on emerging economies in depth. The spillover effects of U.S. monetary policy adjustments differ significantly from one country or region to another. This study demonstrates in detail how U.S. monetary policy adjustments affect the macroeconomic situation of different types of countries.

Second, this book explores in-depth the spillover effects of U.S. monetary policy from both a theoretical and empirical perspective. At present, the United States is the world's most powerful country in terms of overall strength and most economically influential country. Its monetary policy not only plays a very important role in regulating its domestic economy, but also has a decisive impact on the development of countries around the world through various channels such as exchange rate fluctuations, international capital flows, and international trade. With the deepening of global value chains, the spillover effects of U.S. interest rate policy on China are becoming all the more noticeable. This book uses the VAR model, event studies, and other methods to analyze the effects of policy shocks on the economies of major countries around the world before and after the adjustment of U.S. monetary policy. This study shows that U.S. policy adjustments have a great impact on external capital markets, and the impact on different economies varies. The beggar-thy-neighbor effect of U.S. monetary policy adjustments in the post-financial crisis era combined with the impact of games and frictions between the two major powers of China and the United States has exerted significant external pressure on the steady development of China's economy. In addition, this book studies the impact of U.S. interest rate cuts and tariffs on China's macroeconomy under the DSGE framework, and analyzes the spillover effects of U.S. monetary policy in the context of dollarization. This study suggests that China should speed up economic restructuring, appropriately ease financing constraints for enterprises, and try to alleviate financing difficulties and liquidity shortages to cope with a deteriorating external environment, so as to prevent an exacerbation of economic volatility. On monetary policy, China should speed up the reform of its exchange rate regime, push forward the internationalization of the RMB, and flexibly use monetary policy tools.

Finally, this book expounds China's strategic choices in the context of global financial market integration. This study points out that China needs to adjust its economic growth pattern and foreign trade strategy to expand the space for growth, improve the quality of growth, and stimulate the vitality of development. At the same time, the crisis is also a good opportunity for the RMB to step onto the international stage. China should seize the opportunity to actively push forward the internationalization of the RMB, improve the ability to use the RMB as a means of settlement and payment by establishing and improving the mechanisms governing the circulation of the RMB in international trade payments, investment and financing, and capital markets, and actively promote the development of digital currency to create an international currency commensurate with its economic strength.

Professor Liu Weiping's book A Study of U.S. Monetary Policy Adjustments and Their Effects is complete in structure and substantial in content, and contains many of the authors' own insights. After more than 40 years of reform and opening-up, China has become a major economic power in the world, deeply integrated into the global economic system, and its influence on the world economy is growing. As a major surplus holder in international trade, China is an important force for rebalancing the global economy given its economic development and its image as a responsible major country. Internationally, in the coming period, the world economy may be caught up in a prolonged downturn, weak external demand may become the norm, various forms of protectionism will rise, and the external environment facing China's development will be more complicated. When devising a strategy to participate in the rebalancing of the global economy, China must follow the principles of taking China as the main player, giving consideration to both internal and external issues, actively participating, and achieving mutual benefit and win-win results, improve its ability to communicate openly on policies, and strengthen coordination and cooperation with other countries in the world.

May 2022
Beijing, China

Song Min
Dean of Economics
and Management School
of Wuhan University, Professor

PREFACE

Since 2007, the global financial crisis triggered by the U.S. subprime mortgage crisis has raised new questions for the world's theoretical study of monetary policy. The current world economy has entered a post-financial crisis era. Based on the perspective of post-financial crisis, this dissertation conducts an in-depth study of the Adjustment of American Monetary Policy and its impact.

An essential difference between global financial crisis beginning from 2007 to 2008 and the 1929 Great Depression is that the former hasn't triggered a disaster by virtue of measures endorsed by the governments and central banks of developed countries. Those measures successfully prevented the collapses of financial systems and created necessary liquidity to shun the breakdown of banking institutions. In comparison, the trend of open bank failure during the Great Depression once pushed the world economic toward the edge of crackup. After the outbreak of the global financial crisis in 2008, the United States stepped into the era of "zero rate." The common monetary policy based on the function of federal fund rate could not exert effects anymore. Federal Reserve Board immediately began to buy national debt and mortgage loan certificate on a large scale, which started quantitative easing monetary policy. It is proved that the adjustment of monetary policy adopted by America in 2008 has served a decisive function in coping with the life cycle of financial crisis. In the financial crisis caused by subprime mortgage crisis, the inappropriate monetary policy adopted by Federal Reserve at the early stage made the way to the explosion and expansion of the crisis. Theoretically, it is demanding to formulate mature rules to be followed for financial turmoil due to the nonlinear relationship between fictitious economy and real economy. Considering the timeliness, hysteresis, and uncontrollable intensity, the improper adjustment may lead to longer economic depression or even more hidden troubles, resulting in the selection of monetary policy more like a kind of balanced art instead of science when dealing with financial crisis. Therefore, decision on the selection of monetary policy as a resolution of financial crisis vitally matters. Rigorous monetary policy decision-making mechanism should be shaped to decide a framework of monetary policy so as to then control the expansion of crisis indirectly.

This study mainly discusses the following matters: to be started with, the dissertation introduces its background and research significance, and reviews the former research achievements including the overflow effect in America in post-financial crisis era. The dissertation illustrates the thoughts and methods of the former research and points out the innovations and shortcomings of them. Then this dissertation briefly summarizes theories of monetary policy, and explains the foundation and influence path of monetary policy in the aspects of money demand, money supply, and transmission mechanism of monetary policy. Besides, the dissertation reviews the effectiveness of monetary policy and the evolution of the foundation of United States' monetary policy theories since the Great Depression in the 1930s. Next, the dissertation illustrates the history course of the evolution of America's monetary policy, and analyzes the domestic and overseas background of the adjustments of the United States' monetary policy in post-financial crisis era. The dissertation discusses the main content of American monetary policy adjustments including common monetary policy and quantitative easing monetary policy in the aspects of monetary policy tool, international transmission mechanism and exit effects, etc. Afterward, this dissertation applies the model of VAR to do empirical research on the overflow effect on global economy by the adjustments of American monetary policy. The research mainly contains the effects of the adjustments of American monetary policy on the United States, developed economies, emerging markets, and developing economies. Then the dissertation studies the essential features and influence paths of conduction mechanism of monetary policy of the United States and the influence on global economic gains. With the combination of empirical research, the dissertation clarifies the impact of the adjustments of the monetary policy of the United States in the atmosphere of superpower games in multiple views and dimensions. Besides, the dissertation chooses comparatively more comprehensive data of China to deliver an empirical test of the overflow effect on China's economy by the adjustments of America's monetary policy. The results show that, in post-crisis era, there are some differences between the overflow effect of common monetary policy and quantitative easing monetary policy, and the latter's is more prominent. Then the dissertation demonstrates the pressure brought by those adjustments on China, which is experiencing the economic transformation period. The author believes that China needs to make strategic readjustment in the aspects of economic development pattern and foreign trade strategies. At last, the author summarizes the challenges that China's economy faces in post-crisis era, and provides China economy with related advice on how to face the adjustments of monetary policy of the United States in the aspects of economic development strategy and financial development strategy.

This study applies the model of VAR to do empirical research on the overflow effect on global economy by the adjustments of American monetary policy. The research mainly contains the effects of the adjustments of American monetary policy on the United States, developed economies, emerging markets, and developing economies. Then the study studies the essential features and influence paths of conduction mechanism of monetary policy of the United States and the influence on global economic gains. With the combination of empirical research, the study clarifies the impact of the adjustments of the monetary policy of the United States in the atmosphere of superpower games in multiple views and dimensions. Besides, the study chooses comparatively more comprehensive data of China to deliver an empirical test of the overflow effect on China's economy by the adjustments of America's monetary policy. The innovation of this research mainly has the following two points: first, most of the relevant literature mainly studies the spillover effect of the U.S. monetary policy to one or a few countries and regions (such as the BRICs), and less to expand at most. Second, the study of the United States monetary policy adjustment of the connotation of development, so that it can be quantified and compared.

It is of great practical significance to study the impact of U.S. monetary policy adjustment on China's economy in the post-financial crisis era. Based on U.S. conventional monetary policy, quantitative easing monetary policy, and monetary policy adjustment under the novel coronavirus pneumonia epidemic situation, this paper uses vector autoregressive model and event analysis method to study the impact of U.S. monetary policy adjustment on China's economy in the post-financial crisis era. The results are as follows. First, the rise of the U.S. federal funds rate has a strong positive spillover effect on China's economy in the quantitative easing monetary policy interval, but it has a negative impact in the normalization of the monetary policy. Interest rate shocks can explain more for the changes of China's economic variables in the quantitative easing monetary policy interval. Second, the implementation of U.S. quantitative easing monetary policy has a significant negative spillover effect on China's macro economy, which is manifested as the beggar-thy-neighbor effect. Third, compared with the emergency interest rate cuts and unlimited quantitative easing policy under the novel coronavirus pneumonia epidemic situation, the Fed's zero interest rate policy can have more extensive and significant impacts on China's stock market, bond market, and foreign exchange market, which ultimately led to complicated situations including a comprehensive decline in the stock market, a downward bond market and the devaluation of the RMB against the U.S. dollar. According to the results of the primary industry in the stock market, most industries, especially the information technology industry, are more vulnerable to the impact of U.S. monetary policy.

This paper examines the spillover effects of the U.S. monetary policy in the context of dollarization by constructing a DSGE model of small open economy with RMB asset liquidity constraint. At present, international trade is still settled in U.S. dollars, and the degree of RMB internationalization is not high, so domestic residents need to hold U.S. dollars to purchase foreign goods. The research shows that introducing the liquidity constraint of RMB in the international financial market can well reflect the characteristics of current economy in China. Dollarization will strengthen the international spillover effects of external shocks obviously and increase the domestic macroeconomic fluctuations in China. The market-oriented reform of exchange rate can effectively help to maintain financial and economic stability, greatly improve social welfare, and avoid the disadvantages of dollarization. This paper argues that it's benefit to reduce the dependence on the U.S. dollar, promote the internationalization of RMB, and persist in the reform of exchange rate system.

Liu Weiping

Contents

About the Author

Liu Weiping born in Changsha, Hunan province, is a Ph.D. holder, a Professor, and a Senior Research Fellow with China Development Bank. He holds a Ph.D. in law from the Department of Sociology, Tsinghua University, presides over Professor John L.Thornton's Global Leadership Program, and holds a M.A. in management; he holds a Ph.D. in Economics and a B.A. from and is a dual-employed professor of law and economics at the Department of World Economics, Wuhan University; he is a visiting scholar and researcher at the MIT Sloan School of Management and School of History. His main research interests include world economy, economy and society, international finance, and national strategies. He is the author of *Global Leadership*, *A Study on the American Monetary Policy Adjustment and China's Countermeasures*, *Social Trust: Informal Finance and Economic Transformation*, *China's Economy and Foreign Policy: A New Pattern of Open Economy in the Era of*

Competitive Cooperation and other works, as well as China-U.S. Infrastructure Cooperation Plan, Challenges Facing China-U.S. Economic and Trade Cooperation and Recommended Responses, Opening up Westward: Jointly Building the Silk Road Economic Belt and many other research reports. He has participated in and presided over major projects funded by the National Social Science Fund of China and major projects tackling hard-nut problems.

List of Figures

Chapter 4

Chapter 5

Chapter 6

Chapter 7

Chapter 8

List of Tables

Chapter 6

Chapter 8

PART I

Problems, Theories and Analyses

CHAPTER 1

Introduction

It is of great practical significance to study U.S. monetary policy adjustments, their effects and strategic choices for China's monetary policy and economic adjustment from a post-financial crisis perspective. The study summarized and studied the operation and effectiveness of monetary policies of countries around the world in previous financial crises from a historical and forward-looking perspective with the hope of optimizing the current monetary policy decision-making mechanism through academic research and policy research and enabling China's monetary policy decision-making and guidance mechanisms to make great progress in the process of effectively preventing and resolving financial crises, participating in international and regional financial cooperation and participating in the rebalancing of the global economy, and in the process of the reform of the international monetary system and the internationalization of the RMB.

1 Background and Significance of the Study

1.1 Background of the Study

As for the causes of the global financial crisis triggered by the U.S. subprime mortgage crisis in 2008, scholars from all over the world have given multiple interpretations and judgments from different perspectives. There are mainly the theory of excessive financial innovation, the theory of weak financial regulation, the theory of promotion by rating agencies,

L. Weiping, *American Monetary Policy Adjustment and Its Impacts*,
https://doi.org/10.1007/978-981-99-7810-6_1

and the theory of the ineffectiveness of international accounting standards. Generally speaking, these analyses of the causes of the financial crisis are generally one-sided, and abstractly summarize the causes of the financial crisis based on the reality of the outbreak of the financial crisis. Dialectically, there is some truth to all these theories, but in the absence of comprehensive and in-depth research, they fail to reveal the essence of the crisis.

It is widely believed that in the academic circles that global current account imbalances, the main cause of the global financial crisis, were caused by a global saving glut, which was closely related to China's monetary policy of suppressing the value of the RMB. In this study, a comprehensive and in-depth study was conducted on U.S. monetary policy adjustments and their effects along the two dimensions of theory and practice using qualitative and quantitative analysis methods. The study found that increases in China's current account surplus and the U.S. current account deficit from 2003 to 2008 were the result of an exogenous reversal of China's balance of payments, rather than declines in U.S. real interest rates and China's foreign exchange reserves. In fact, the macroeconomic policy of negative interest rates and the serious failure of regulators to regulate innovations in financial products were the two root causes of the global financial crisis. These two causes led to the problem of triangular debt on a global scale, which was unprecedented. The global triangular debt triggered by the global financial crisis mainly occurred between the United States, Europe and Japan, the world's three largest economies. The quantitative easing (QE) policy implemented by the United States was most representative of monetary policies around the world after the financial crisis. While effectively preventing the spread of the crisis and stimulating a gradual recovery of the U.S. economy, the policy had a huge impact on financial markets and economies around the world mainly in that it pushed up global asset prices sharply, with the stock markets of various countries and global commodity prices surging, and created asset bubbles and inflation in emerging markets.

There are essential differences between the 2007–2008 global financial crisis and the Great Depression which began in 1929. The 2007–2008 financial crisis did not trigger a disaster similar to the Great Depression which began in 1929, not least because the governments and central banks of developed countries responded with measures that effectively prevented the financial system from collapsing. At the same time, developed countries created the liquidity necessary to avoid the kind of open bank failures that brought the world economy to the brink of collapse during the Great Depression (Piketty 2014). This proves that during the 2007–2008 global financial crisis, the improper monetary policy implemented by the Fed in the early stage laid the groundwork for the outbreak of the financial crisis and the subsequent spread of the global economic crisis. Due to the nonlinear relationship between virtual economy and real economy, it is difficult to form proven rules to follow for financial turbulence in theory. When the United States needed to adjust its monetary policy to cope with the financial crisis, the monetary policy which was supposed to be a scientific instrument behaved more like the art of making trade-offs. This is because policy is time-sensitive and subject to lags, and its intensity is difficult to control. If not adjusted properly, it is likely to cause a long period of economic depression or sow the seeds of greater danger. Therefore, monetary policy decision-making is crucial to solving the problem of financial crises. A rigorous monetary decision-making mechanism should be developed to decide on a monetary policy framework and thus indirectly control the spread of the crisis. An ideal monetary policy framework should contain the gradual accumulation of risks and mitigate the economic trauma in the face of financial turbulence.

1.2 Significance of the Study

From the perspective of global development practice, the rise of Keynesianism after the Great Depression of the 1930s gave prominence to aggregate demand management policies and underscored government intervention in the macroeconomy. As a result, over a long time, governments preferred fiscal policy, and finally there was a global stagflation crisis in the 1970s. After the stagflation of the 1970s, monetarism gained popularity and the monetarist school of thought emerged in theoretical circles (Liu and Zhang 2012). Theoretically, both monetarism and new Keynesianism emphasized regulating the macroeconomy by monetary policy, so governments also preferred monetary policy. Since the 1980s, there has been no revolutionary progress in macroeconomics, making it difficult to meet the challenges posed by new situations. In particular, the prevalence of monetarism seems to be closely related to the current global financial crisis. Obviously, the outbreak of the current global financial and economic crisis inevitably calls for new macroeconomic theories.

As China further opens up its economy, the U.S. economy has become the most important international economic factor affecting China's macroeconomic development (Wang and Chen 2010). China's current monetary policy decision-making mechanism also needs to be improved. In view of the subprime crisis, the current monetary policy framework can hardly achieve this effect as it still has many defects and needs to be improved (Zhao 2013). The 2008 financial crisis also reminds us that the virtual economy is making up an increasing share of the modern social economy and is growing in importance. The virtual economy is an enormous force in both driving and destroying economic and social development, which requires full attention in monetary policy decision-making.

In early December 2008, based on the judgment of the international economic situation at that time, at the 2008 Central Economic Work Conference, China specifically put forward the requirement that monetary policy should play a role in countercyclical regulation and ensuring liquidity supply, so as to strengthen the concept and strategy of macro prudential management. Opportunities and challenges coexist in the post-financial crisis era. The global financial crisis triggered by the U.S. subprime crisis also exposed the defects of the dollar-based international monetary system. Therefore, at this crucial juncture, the world should draw on the lessons and experience to promote the reform of the international monetary system and build a new international financial order. The RMB is bound to become an important part of the reform of the international monetary system. In the post financial crisis era, the internationalization of the RMB also faces unprecedented opportunities. Therefore, we should actively create favorable conditions for internationalization, gradually and steadily advance the internationalization of the RMB (Chen and Wei 2010), and actively join the International Monetary Fund (IMF)'s Special Drawing Rights (SDR) basket.

2 Literature Review

2.1 Financial Crisis and Monetary Policy

The emergence of a financial crisis is not a simple accident of history, but is closely related to the economic cycle. Credit and asset prices also have their own cycles. So how do credit and asset prices relate to financial crises? The financial system is a whole. Although credit and asset prices are independent, they are still an integral part of the financial system. Therefore, when they fluctuate in cycles, the financial system will also fluctuate as a whole. Financial risks do not build up overnight. The emergence of a financial crisis and the financial risks behind it are actually related to the current monetary policy, which directly or indirectly promotes the accumulation of financial risks and thus leads to a financial crisis.

2.1.1 *Review of Relevant Literature*

There are pros and cons to economic globalization. Economic globalization not only promotes global economic development, but also globalizes financial risks. The U.S. subprime mortgage crisis of 2007 and the resulting global financial and economic crisis illustrate this point. In fact, financial crises are not as sudden as they appear to be, but always erupt for a reason. The financial crisis caused by the U.S. subprime mortgage crisis is similar to other financial crises in history. Confidence in prosperity leads to the growth of loans and the accumulation of financial risks. In the end, it takes only a single event to burst the bubble. Bordo and Jeanne (2002) believed that these factors were almost endogenous, and they were all in a "boom and bust cycle". The cycle coincides with the economic cycle: When the economy is booming, strong economic growth will cover up the transition phase of the cycle. Things will develop in the opposite direction when they become extreme. The transition phase is always likely to occur, but inertia tends to create a false illusion of prosperity. When the economy is no longer booming, the cycle will manifest itself in serious financial and economic problems: financial imbalance, economic deterioration, economic recession, etc. When these financial and economic problems get worse, devastating financial and economic crisis will arise. Reinhart (2008) showed through historical data and scientific analysis that before the financial crisis, there was a period of rapid growth in prices and credit, which was accompanied by an unprecedented increase in debt. This phenomenon is very similar to those observed during other financial crises in history. The occurrence of these financial crises is closely related to monetary policy, which is closely related to credit and price cycles, and credit and price cycles are closely related to financial cycles and economic cycles. Therefore, monetary policy is closely related to the occurrence of financial crises. These relationships can be described as "cyclical overdependence", a concept that encompasses economic ailments and financial imbalances caused by monetary policy. The financial bubbles behind a financial crisis are closely related to improper monetary policy. Improper monetary policy will lead to adverse consequences, such as credit expansion and asset price inflation, which in turn will lead to the excessive accumulation of financial risks and financial imbalances. Financial imbalances reflect a profound economic situation, that is, the contradiction between the real economy and the virtual economy. The overdevelopment of the virtual economy has led to the increasing dependence of economic and financial cycles on monetary policy.

Optimal policy under discretion in a Keynesian model should be the same. Kydland and Prescott (1977) found that optimal policies were not so trustworthy, because they were actually time-inconsistent, so he preferred rules over discretion. This view is supplemented and deepened by the following scholars: Barro and Gordon (1983) introduced the reputation mechanism; Rogoff and Walsh (1985–1995) et al. substantially revised and supplemented the views of their predecessors; the way in which rising inflation is achieved focuses on the importance of reputation. According to the optimal contract theory proposed by Walsh, a contract can be made, under which the specific authority to operate the monetary policy is independently exercised by the central bank, and the government will reward or punish the central bank depending on how it controls inflation. There are two key words for these macro-control methods, namely currency and interest rate. These two factors are specific operation methods, that is, to form a good monetary policy and operate on interest rates accordingly, the direct purpose of which is to stabilize prices. As long as prices are stable, specific flexible handling methods can be implemented. Of course, these regulation methods are always targeted at inflation, directly or indirectly (Ren 2008). By setting policy directives, economic development is incorporated into policy, so as to influence the short-term and long-term goals of economic activity. The reason why the United States had some outstanding achievements in inflation control during the Greenspan era lies in an inflation-targeted monetary policy operation framework. As far as economic development is concerned, monetary policy should be adapted to economic conditions. According to Taylor, when inflation keeps rising, you should implement a tight monetary policy, such as raising nominal interest rates, to reduce inflation; during a deflationary period, you should pursue an expansionary monetary policy, such as lowering nominal interest rates. Walsh believed that the optimal contract between the government and the central bank might reduce monetary authorities' preference for inflation while maintaining economic stability. Further analysis shows that the method of signing the contract only affects the independence of the central bank's policy tools, but not the independence of policy goals.

2.1.2 Monetary Policy Operation and Loan Reserve Policy

Although monetary policy has long occupied an important position in the West, after the outbreak of the subprime mortgage crisis in the United States in 2007, there was a major change: People no longer seem to believe that people should use monetary policy to stabilize prices when prices fluctuate or the market becomes unstable. Now, it is difficult to reach a consensus on this point. People just think that in times of financial and economic crisis, monetary policy should be used, but no one can give a convincing answer as to how to use it and intervene in economic development.

Some researchers believe that monetary policy should be used to intervene in the economy, but the thinking of these researchers is still confined to the existing framework of the original monetary policy. They still try to link inflation with asset prices, that is, they take asset prices and inflation as an organic whole. According to some views, traditional price indexes make a great contribution: Alchian and Klein (1973) constructed a current price index called the intertemporal cost index, which includes consumers' expected lifetime consumption. This is the beginning of a truly systematic interpretation and study of asset prices and inflation in the current structure including the consumer price index of consumer life expectancy. Pollack (1975) expanded the specific form of the intertemporal cost of living index; based on their research, Shibuya (1992) constructed a "dynamic equilibrium price index" that incorporates the asset price inflation factor; Bryan and Cecchetti (1993) constructed a core price index that incorporates asset price inflation; Goodhart and Hofmann (1995) put forward the broad price index, which includes property prices and stock prices in monetary policy. Goodhart and Hofmann (2001) put forward the financial conditions index. The real effective exchange rate, the weighted average real interest rate, and the real estate price and stock price index were used to construct a financial conditions index. Bryan and Ceccheui O'Sullivan (2002) used modern statistical techniques to put forward a dynamic factor index, the overall price level including three kinds of asset prices: stock prices, bond prices and property prices, and the concept of excluding commodity deviation, and used them to examine the effect of asset prices on changes in the overall price level. In 2001, Goodhart and Hofmann constructed a "financial conditions index" from the real effective exchange rate, the weighted average real interest rate, and the real estate price and stock price index (Huang 2009).

Theoretically, these attempts and propositions seem feasible. This is mainly because, in an economic activity, when the consumption factor dominates, that is, when consumption determines the value of assets, then asset prices which are in flux will have to be influenced by inflation and influence inflation. Asset prices contain a lot of information about future inflation, and future consumption can be predicted by asset prices. Therefore, in theory, the corresponding theory of inflation can be improved through prices. But the key problem is not theoretical predictability, but that market fluctuations cannot really be expected. If inflation occurs, can these monetary policies really regulate the economy?

2.2 Evolution of U.S. Monetary Policy

The development of U.S. monetary policy is closely related to the Fed's policy tools. With the change of the background of the times and macroeconomic conditions, the Fed has adjusted its monetary policy goals to achieve the policy effects of stabilizing prices, ensuring employment and promoting economic growth. Throughout the history of U.S. fiscal policy and monetary policy, U.S. monetary policy gradually came to the fore after World War II. For decades before that, including the Great Depression of the 1930s, U.S. macroeconomic policy relied heavily on expansionary fiscal policy to stimulate the economy by expanding government spending, i.e. Roosevelt's New Deal. Keynes' book The General Theory of Employment, Interest and Money is the theoretical cornerstone of this policy. Keynes (1936) believed that the low marginal efficiency of capital led to weak investment, resulting in insufficient effective demand, the sudden collapse of the marginal efficiency of capital was the main culprit for the outbreak of the Great Depression, and the effective solution to the crisis was for the government to actively intervene in the economy to stimulate consumption and increase investment through expansionary fiscal policy, and to promote the exponential growth of national income through the multiplier effect of investment. On the basis of Keynesian economic theory, Hicks (1937) proposed the analytical framework the IS-LM model, which gave a normative interpretation of Keynesian theory and explained the possible "liquidity trap" problem that could occur when the nominal interest rate was very low. After the end of World War II, the main problems facing the United States were unemployment and inflation, and expansionary fiscal policy helped to address the inflation problem. During this period, the Fed began to become independent from the Department of the Treasury and gradually increased its control over monetary policy. Drawing on previous studies, Hansen (1949, 1953) improved and proposed the now popular IS-LM model, whose conclusion supported monetary policy to play an active role in macroeconomic regulation. The conclusions drawn from the model were supportive of an active role of monetary policy in macroeconomic regulation and control. However, due to the powerful policy force of Keynesianism at that time, monetary policy was only used as an auxiliary tool of fiscal policy.

The timeline shows that for nearly 40 years from the 1930s to the 1960s Keynesian economic policy developed and prospered, and especially in the 1960s, the golden age of Keynesian economic policy, the scale and intensity of state intervention in the economy expanded to an unprecedented extent. Nevertheless, the Fed gradually began to stimulate economic growth through means such as interest rates and money supply, giving a boost to the role of monetary policy. An important basis for the effectiveness of traditional Keynesian policy is that the government can reduce unemployment at the expense of higher inflation, so as to effectively stimulate economic growth. According to the conclusion of a study by Phillips (1958) of the relation between unemployment and the rate of change of money wage rates in the United Kingdom from 1861 to 1957, unemployment and inflation were negatively correlated and did not go together. But this subtle relationship collapsed with the emergence of "stagflation". In the 1970s, the United States and other major developed countries in the West experienced the phenomenon of "stagflation", in which economic stagnation and inflation occurred at the same time. Traditional Keynesian theories were seriously challenged, the most influential of which were the monetarism pioneered by Friedman and the supply-side economics pioneered by Laffer, Feldstein and others. In his The Quantity Theory of Money: A Restatement (1956), Friedman reformulated the traditional quantity theory of money as the theory of demand for money, that is, the modern quantity theory of money, which holds that as long as the demand for money is stable, changes in money supply will cause changes in the price level, and the expansion of the actual size of cash holdings (the ratio of money supply to the price level) will increase aggregate output, thereby driving economic growth. Supply-side economics advocates shifting resources from consumption to investment, stimulating consumption mainly through tax cuts, and turning to tax cuts to stimulate investment. In other words, from the perspective of promoting economic growth, stimulating production supply in the economic equation is more effective than increasing consumer demand for goods and services. This school opposes state intervention in the economy and advocates a free enterprise system (Tang 1982). From the perspective of policy effect, monetarism maintains that fiscal policy is ineffective, and "stagflation" is a consequence of this policy. It advocates the implementation of "single rule" monetary policy, which controls the growth of money supply by means of interest rate adjustments. Meanwhile, the role of the Fed in regulating the U.S. economy was significantly strengthened. The important amendments to the Federal Reserve Act by the U.S. Congress in 1978 were an important sign. However, judging from the final result, the money supply of the United States grew rapidly from 1979 to 1982, but the inflation rate was abnormal. In 1979, the CPI rose 11.3% year-over-year, and in 1980, that figure reached 13.5%.[1] Monetary policy encountered considerable obstacles and challenges in practical application. At this time, supply-side economics took a unique approach, believing that only by solving aggregate supply issues such as the quantity, quality and efficiency of capital and labor input could economic vitality be effectively restored. They took aim at the serious tax burden problem at that time, because excessively high tax rates would inhibit people's creativity. After Reagan took office as President in 1981, he made tax reform as a core task based on the theories and policy recommendations of supply-side economics. The Economic Recovery Tax Act of 1981 and the Tax Reform Act of 1986 respectively lowered the top marginal business tax rate, which was eventually reduced to 28%. Faced with the twin dilemmas of hyperinflation and unemployment, then Fed Chairman Paul Volcker pointed out that the root cause of the scourge was an excess supply of dollars. The target of monetary policy shifted from the benchmark interest rate to the money supply, changes in interest rates were then determined by changes in the market money supply, and a high federal funds rate and monetary tightening measures were adopted to combat inflation. The federal funds rate hit 22% in early 1981, which pushed the economy further into recession, but inflation was eventually beaten. After Greenspan came to power, he made corresponding adjustments on the basis of Paul Volcker's monetary policy, with a focus on changing the intermediate target for monetary policy from the money

[1] Source: Wind.

supply to an index system centered on real interest rates and composed of a number of economic and financial variables, and adopted the Taylor rule. The Taylor rule was proposed by Taylor (1993), which is a rule applicable to short-term interest rates. Taylor pointed out that keeping the real short-term interest rate unchanged was a neutral monetary policy. When the output gap is positive and (or) inflation is above target, a premium will be applied to the interest rate, and vice versa (Peter 2013). The Taylor rule is the result of an empirical study of the actual monetary policy of the Federal Reserve System from 1987 to 1992 and can be expressed as follows:

$$i_t - \pi_t = R + \alpha(\pi_t - \pi^*) + \beta\left(\frac{Y_t - Y^*}{Y^*}\right)$$

where: $i_t - \pi_t$ refers to the real short-term interest rate, R refers to the average short-term real interest rate, $(\pi_t - \pi^*)$ refers to the deviation of inflation from the target, $\frac{Y_t - Y^*}{Y^*}$ refers to the output gap, and α and β reflect the weights of the deviation of inflation from the target and the impact of the output gap respectively. The Taylor rule states that the real short-term exchange rate must be equal to the average short-term real interest rate plus the portion reflecting the deviation of inflation from the target and the output gap. Taylor (1999) pointed out that simple policy rules performed much more robustly than complex rules in many models, and the basic conclusions of a single rule designed for the United States seemed to apply to other countries as well.

After the outbreak of the global financial crisis in 2008, the Fed injected liquidity into markets by purchasing state-guaranteed financial assets such as U.S. Treasury securities and mortgage-backed securities, ushering in the era of quantitative easing. A total of four rounds of quantitative easing were launched. The concept of "quantitative easing" was first formally proposed by Werner (1995), who believed that interest rate policy had little effect in the context of recession and deflation, and that it was a necessary measure for monetary authorities to improve the financial environment through open market operations. This provided a feasible operational idea for the implementation of quantitative easing in major developed economies in the future. Dai and Zhang (2012) pointed out that quantitative easing needed to meet the conditions of a deep recession, extremely low interest rates, a large increase in the monetary base, a substantial expansion of the balance sheet, and large-scale purchases of unconventional assets by the central bank, and gave a formal definition of quantitative easing: "If the central bank of a country that uses interest rates as a means of regulation has lowered interest rates to an extremely low level to counter recession and cannot stimulate the economy by further lowering interest rates, that is to say, when the interest rate transmission mechanism fails, it will inject money into the monetary base by purchasing long-term bonds and other unconventional assets on the secondary market in order to repair the interest rate transmission mechanism of monetary policy. This is called quantitative easing." The failure of the interest rate transmission mechanism has something to do with Keynes' liquidity trap theory. When interest rates fall below the normal interest rates in everyone's mind, even if the central bank increases the money supply, it cannot cut interest rates further. By then the public will hold on to cash, money in full, which will lead to the inability to convert savings into investment, serious recession of the economy, high unemployment and debt, and a significant erosion of public confidence, resulting in a series of vicious circles.

2.3 *Spillover Effects of U.S. Monetary Policy*

After the outbreak of the 2008 global financial crisis, U.S. monetary policy was substantially adjusted, with the federal funds rate falling to between 0 and 0.25%, and the Fed launched quantitative easing through massive purchases of Treasury and mortgage-backed securities. Chinese and foreign scholars have done a lot of research on the spillover effects of U.S. monetary policy adjustments, including effects at home and abroad.

2.3.1 *Foreign Research*

In terms of foreign research, research by Eichenbaum and Evans (1995) showed that a contractionary U.S. monetary policy shock (that is, a sudden tightening of monetary policy) would lead to a sustained depreciation of the dollar in both nominal and real terms, and this effect would last at least two years.

Neri and Nobili (2010) built a SVAR model including the federal funds rate, nominal M2, real GDP, GDP deflator and world commodity price index to study how changes in the federal funds rate by the Fed affect the eurozone economy. In the analysis, the international transmission mechanism works through the exchange rate, commodity prices, short-term interest rates and the trade balance.

Bernanke (2010) responded to public dissatisfaction with the rise in house prices after quantitative easing by the Fed by comparing historical data. He pointed out that U.S. house prices began to rise more rapidly in the late 1990s, prices grew at a 7–8% annual rate in 1998 and 1999, and in the 9–11% range from 2000 to 2003, the most rapid price gains were in 2004 and 2005, when the annual rate of house price appreciation was between 15 and 17%, monetary policy was highly accommodative to the housing market during the period of rising house prices, monetary policy did not contribute to price increases, and cross-country evidence showed no significant relationship between monetary policies and the pace of house price increases. He pointed out that the best response to the housing bubble would have been regulatory, not monetary.

Reis (2010) reviewed the unconventional U.S. monetary policy responses to the financial crises, divided into three groups: interest rate policy, quantitative policy, and credit policy. He believed that in a liquidity trap, in order to minimize the length and damage of the recession, the Fed needed to make a stronger commitment to low interest rates to change public expectations; for quantitative policy, the main challenge is the underlying inflation problem, which may affect the Fed's monetary policy independence; for credit policy, the results suggests that providing credit to traders in securities markets can restore liquidity with fewer government funds than extending credit to the originators of loans.

Curdia and Woodford (2010) believed that the Federal Reserve broke away from the Taylor rule when implementing monetary policies after the outbreak of the financial crisis, in which case the standard Taylor Rule should be adjusted. The authors believed that an adjustment for variations in credit spreads could improve upon the standard Taylor rule, but the optimal size of adjustment depended on the source of the variation in credit spreads, and a response to the quantity of credit was less likely to be helpful in the new situation.

Christiano et al. (2010) studied the link between monetary policy and stock market booms. Historical data and model simulations support the following conclusion. Inflation is low during stock market booms, so that an interest rate rule that is too narrowly focused on inflation destabilizes asset markets and the broader economy. Adjustments to the interest rate rule can remove this source of welfare-reducing instability. For example, allowing an independent role for credit growth (beyond its role in constructing the inflation forecast) would reduce the volatility of output and asset prices.

Gertler and Karadi (2011) developed a quantitative monetary DSGE model and used the model to evaluate the effects of the central bank using unconventional monetary policy to combat a simulated financial crisis. The results showed that the central bank was less efficient than private intermediaries at making loans but it had the advantage of being able to elastically obtain funds by issuing riskless government debt, because it was not balance sheet constrained, and the balance sheet constraints on private intermediaries were substantial and severe during a financial crisis.

Wright (2012) built a structural VAR model to examine the effects of monetary policy shocks on longer term interest rates when the federal funds rate is between 0 and 0.25% (zero lower bound). The author identified the VAR model using the following assumption: Monetary policy shocks are heteroskedastic, that is, monetary policy shocks have especially high variance on days of Federal Open Market Committee (FOMC) meetings and certain speeches, while there is otherwise nothing unusual about these days. The results suggested that monetary policy shocks lowered Treasury and corporate bond yields but the effects died off fairly fast. Studies conducted by Gagon et al. (2010) and Neely (2010) showed that quantitative easing in the United States lowered long-term interest rates in the United States and contributed to dollar depreciation.

Fratzscher et al. (2012) analyzed the effects of the Fed's unconventional monetary policy announcements and market operations on asset allocation and asset prices in 65 countries. The results showed that the effects of open market operations, such as the purchase of Treasury securities and mortgage-backed securities, on asset allocation and asset prices were much greater than those of announcements; from the perspective of the global economy, the effects of the Fed's policy on global asset prices were more significant than those of capital flows and asset allocation; meanwhile, the paper pointed out that the Fed's quantitative easing policy had indeed accelerated the flow of capital to emerging market economies, and even caused stock prices to rise and bond yields to fall worldwide.

Fawley and Neely (2013) summarized the course of quantitative easing in the United States, the euro area, the United Kingdom and Japan, pointing out that the policy initially attempted to alleviate financial market distress to improve credit markets, when the crisis deepened, the policy goal was expanded to include achieving inflation targets and stimulating the real economy, and the euro area policy also included easing the European debt crisis. Bekaert et al. (2013) built a VAR model to study the relationship between the Fed's monetary policy and market risk, in which monetary policy was represented by the federal funds rate and market risk was replaced by the VIX index. The results showed that a decline in the federal funds rate would lead to a lower VIX index, and lax monetary policy could reduce the volatility risk premium of stocks.

Ricci (2015) studied the impact of the ECB's monetary policy announcements on the stock price of large European banks. The results showed that banks were more sensitive to non-conventional measures than to interest rate decisions, and that the same type of intervention may have a different impact depending on the stage of the crisis; in addition, banks with weaker balance sheets and operating with high-risk were more sensitive to monetary policy interventions.

Bruno and Shin (2015) pointed out that the adjustment of bank leverage played a key role in the transmission mechanism of monetary policy, a contractionary U.S. monetary policy shock would lead to a decrease in cross-border bank capital flows and a decline in international bank leverage, and a decline in bank capital flows was closely related to dollar appreciation.

2.3.2 Domestic Research

After the outbreak of the financial crisis, Chinese scholars also conducted a lot of research on the spillover effects of U.S. monetary policy adjustments, especially quantitative easing. Wu and Liu (2009) studied the international transmission effect of U.S. monetary policy on China, the euro area, Japan, South Korea and Malaysia. The results showed that U.S. monetary policy had an international transmission effect on the output levels, net exports and prices in various countries, and the effect on prices in various countries was synchronous; and the United States could improve its balance of trade with little damage to its own development while negatively affecting the economic growth of other countries.

Xiao (2011) examined the channels of U.S. monetary policy shocks could transmit to six Asian economies with different exchange rate regimes. The results showed that most Asian economies responded to U.S. monetary policy shocks mainly through the interest rate channel and foreign exchange reserve channel. After the outbreak of the financial crisis, although U.S. quantitative easing might help to increase the economic output of Asia, it would lead to higher international commodity prices, inflows of hot money into emerging economies and worsening global economic imbalances.

Chen and Sun (2012) found that U.S. quantitative easing had a positive effect on output and prices in China, with the effect on the former greater than the latter, and in general, monetary policy effects transmitted through the financial market channel were stronger than those through the international trade channel.

Wei and Zou (2012) used an Ordered Probit model to study the independence of China's monetary policy relative to that of the United States and found that the relaxation of the RMB's trading band in the new period did not lead to the enhancement of China's monetary policy independence, and the relaxation of exchange rate controls could not enhance China's monetary policy independence. With the linkage in monetary policy between China and the United States as the research object, Xing and Tang (2011) used a SVAR model to analyze the spillover effects of U.S. monetary policy from three perspectives: interest rate, money supply and monetary policy independence, and concluded that U.S. monetary policy had spillover effects on China's monetary policy, indicating that China's monetary policy independence was affected by the externalities of U.S. monetary policy.

Du (2013) believed that quantitative easing by the Fed in the context of the financial crisis was biased towards the policy goal of maintaining financial market stability through the balance sheet channel, and modified the GOZ model (Gilchrist et al. 2009) by adding the signal effect of excess reserves, the portfolio rebalancing effect, and the coefficient of the elasticity of the financing premium in relation to corporate net worth to examine the effectiveness of quantitative easing.

Hu et al. (2013) analyzed the effects of quantitative easing by the Fed from the perspective of the transmission mechanism of monetary policy proposed by Tobin's Q theory. The results showed that the four rounds of quantitative easing by the Fed further maintained the financing function of capital markets, stimulated the financing of innovative enterprises, and played a role in restoring market confidence, reviving the property market, and promoting industrial restructuring and economic growth.

Huang (2014) studied the impact of the expansionary fiscal policy and monetary policy implemented in the United States from January 2008 to December 2011 on inflation in China. The results showed that China's best policy choice in the early stage of the crisis was to synchronize with the United States, the latter's policy would not have a direct impact on inflation in China, and inflation in China after the financial crisis was driven by fiscal policy.

Liu Lanbiao et al. (2014) analyzed the exit path of U.S. broad quantitative easing policy from the perspective of the central bank's balance sheet by using the shift-share analysis method. They believed that the exit path of the Federal Reserve was dominated by the withdrawal of liquidity tools, supplemented by repeated adjustments of securities holding tools, and with most of the structural effects withdrawn, the growth effect was still dominated by substantial increases in the reserve requirements for commercial banks. In order to cope with the spillover effects of the Fed's withdrawal of quantitative easing, the Chinese government should continue to strengthen its control over international capital flows and increase the room for adjustment of the RMB exchange rate.

Li (2014) believed that the Fed's quantitative easing policy mainly had a significant impact on emerging market countries through four channels: asset portfolio rebalancing channel, exchange rate channel, international trade channel, and passive monetary policy coordination channel, and had an impact on China's inflation level mainly through the exchange rate and international commodity price channels.

With the U.S. monetary base and the yields of medium to long-term Treasury securities as the proxy variables of the Fed's quantitative easing policy, Tang (2015) studied the impact of the policy on China's capital markets (including the stock market, bond market and credit market). The results showed that positive policy shocks had a "L-shaped" effect on China's stock market, the bond market responded positively and the credit market negatively. Structural variance decomposition suggested that changes in the U.S. monetary base had a greater impact on China's capital markets than Treasury yields.

With the 10-year-3-month Treasury yield spread as the proxy indicator of quantitative easing policy, and a total of 80 financial market variables including monetary market variables, stock and bond markets, foreign exchange markets and property markets as the affected variables, Yu et al. (2015) studied the impact of the U.S. exit from quantitative easing on U.S. and Chinese financial markets based on a FAVAR model. The results showed that the U.S. exit from quantitative easing would depress the stock and housing markets in the short term, while bond yields would rise sharply and the dollar would appreciate. For China, the stock market would be greatly negatively impacted in the short term, but the long-term negative impact would tend to disappear; the housing market would be subdued initially, but would not fall sharply; the RMB exchange rate would rise and foreign exchange reserves would decrease slightly, but the medium to long-term depreciation of the RMB would be limited and two-way fluctuations would intensify; the impact on the money and bond markets was not significant.

Nie and Jin (2015), based on China's industry-level export data, used a SVAR model to study the spillover effects of U.S. quantitative easing policy on China's industrial exports. The results showed that U.S. quantitative easing policy had a beggar-thy-neighbor effect on China's exports as a whole, but the impact on different industries was very different, with a weak positive spillover effect on low-tech industries and a negative spillover effect on medium- and high-tech industries to a certain extent. Variance decomposition showed that U.S. quantitative easing policy had certain explanatory power for fluctuations in exports in industries such as non-metallic mineral products, metal products, and machinery and equipment manufacturing.

With the monetary base and the scale of bond purchases by the Fed as the proxy indicators of quantitative easing policy, and the economic output, price level, import and export trade, exchange rates, capital market fluctuations and money supply of the BRICS countries as dependent variables, Ma and Yu (2015) used a PVAR model to study the spillover effects of U.S. quantitative easing policy on the BRICS countries. The results showed that the effects of policy shocks on the BRICS countries were sustained and stable, and that especially in the short term, would lead to an increase in the real economic output of the BRICS countries, push up their currencies, and promote the development of their stock markets.

Xiao (2015) pointed out that quantitative easing had a significant negative impact on the global economy in that it exacerbated the wealth gap worldwide to some extent, and had both positive and negative effects on China's economy, and after the withdrawal of quantitative easing, the Fed's monetary policy goals would be normalized.

To sum up, since the United States is a hegemon in the global economy, the spillover effects of U.S. monetary policy are very significant. Such effects are not only reflected in conventional monetary policy, but also in quantitative easing policy in the post-financial crisis era. The existing literature on the spillover effects of U.S. monetary policy adjustments can be improved as follows: First, select more countries and regions as research samples to more comprehensively study the impact of U.S. monetary policy adjustments on different types of countries, which is manifested in the heterogeneity of spillover effects; second, divide the research into the conventional monetary policy period and the quantitative easing policy period to demonstrate differences in spillover effects before and after the adjustment of the U.S. monetary policy, which is manifested in the spatiotemporal nature of spillover effects. Based on this, in this paper, we quantitatively analyze the heterogeneity and spatiotemporal nature of the spillover effects of U.S. monetary policy adjustments, and put forward targeted countermeasures and suggestions.

The theoretical basis and logical analysis of the impact of economic structure on macro governance lie in the relationship between economic development and economic structure, as well as the transmission mechanism of fiscal policy and monetary policy. This is also the main theoretical basis of this research project.

2.4 Effectiveness of Monetary Policy

From the two aspects of the effectiveness of monetary policy, we can draw the following conclusions: In the long run, monetary policy does not really affect prices, but it may have short-term effects. In theory, tight monetary policy is more conducive to achieving obvious results when it is implemented. However, although there have been many theoretical models and empirical studies, it is still difficult to reach a consensus.

To understand the effectiveness of monetary policy, different views and conceptual definitions can be adopted. As far as monetary policy is concerned, it generally refers to the central bank (or a similar institution) of a country influencing economic operations through money supply to achieve the corresponding economic goals. But what is the mode of money supply? It is difficult to agree on which way to achieve economic goals is more effectively, by influencing interest rates or by controlling the amount of money issued? But when it comes to economic problems, people seem to think that central banks should exert control over high-powered money. What are the goals we want to achieve through monetary policy, and to what extent can we finally achieve these goals? Monetary policy is often an emergency passive method, because, as mentioned earlier, it has little impact on long-term economic development, but it can achieve good results for short-term economic fluctuations. Short-term economic fluctuations often result in large price changes, and monetary policy plays an important role in stabilizing prices. Of course, price stability will help economic growth in the long run. In the longer term, monetary policy can help reduce economic volatility, which means it can better manage the impact of the economic cycle and respond to emergencies. Keynes had a similar view of monetary policy, arguing that monetary policy should promote employment and production, stimulate investment, and so on.

In the context of Chinese scholarship, there is a new interpretation of monetary policy. Ba (2000) believed that monetary policy was effective, if and only if in a specific financial context where good policies were put forward and implemented, the reality of and the way to realize the operation of the economy improved finance, and society ensured that economic resources were properly allocated and achieved their expected control goals. This view puts too much emphasis on the extent to which monetary policy is actually implemented, and thus tacitly acknowledges that monetary policy is effective. After all, ineffective policies are useless no matter how well they are implemented. But what kind of monetary policy is punctual and appropriate is another more complex question. Li (2003) believed that the effectiveness of monetary policy lied in the fact that changes in the total demand and total income of society were caused by changes in the money supply. More broadly, monetary policy, if effective, has a big impact on production and inflation. Wang (2003) put forward his own view. He believed that the effectiveness of monetary policy should be understood from two perspectives: First, it is a short-term economic issue, related to short-term economic fluctuations; second, what impact does monetary policy have on the real economy? Of course, if monetary policy is effective, there is a third question, that is, how to achieve effective monetary policy?

2.4.1 Effectiveness of Monetary Policy in Theory

Keynesian monetary policy is generally considered ineffective. In their view, monetary policy is extremely effective in influencing the real economy. When monetary policy is implemented, people's investments may change by changing interest rates, but only by accident. For predictable events, there is no change in output. When a real crisis arises, monetary policy only changes the flow of money. This may seem like a major change, but in fact it is only an illusion or a trap. Monetary policy is only truly effective if it boosts investment and real output, but this can only be achieved under unexpected circumstances. Monetary policy is theoretical monetary policy, so it has almost no practical effect in terms of its contribution to investment, production and employment, and is therefore ineffective in theory. When monetary policy produces practical effects in investment, production and employment under unexpected circumstances, it can be described by an "unexpected supply function".

The new Keynesian perspective on the effectiveness of monetary policy. In contrast to Keynesians, new Keynesians accept money-related opinions, a departure from their critical views. Their contribution to Keynesian monetary theory mainly lies in the fact that they believe that the money supply can play a critical or even substantial role in economic development. Unlike Keynesianism which holds that monetary policy can play a role by accident or under unexpected circumstances, new Keynesianism holds that monetary policy can be applied and influence economic development under normal circumstances. Changes in demand for money and prices are a process. The openness and incompleteness of the economic system lead to changes in wages and prices, which in turn influence economic development, because wages and interest rates are directly related to money. In this way, monetary policy will find an object to act upon. Especially for income: income has not changed much in relative terms, so monetary policy can be effective in theory.

The monetarist perspective on the effectiveness of monetary policy. Compared with Keynesians and new Keynesians, monetarists base their theories on the effectiveness of monetary policy on basic monetarist views, but sometimes they use different reasoning methods to draw similar conclusions. Because monetarists have different perspectives, their views on the effectiveness of monetary policy are more open. But they are generally more positive about the impact of monetary policy on the economy, both in terms of short-term and long-term economic development, than Keynesians and new Keynesians. In 1963 and 1970, Friedman, Schwartz, Tobin and others discovered the effects of the money supply on short-term economic development. Subsequently, in 1989 and 1992, studies by Stock, Watson, Cavor and others further corroborated this view. However, not all monetarists agree with the relevant views, but sometimes they hold a view similar to Keynesianism or new Keynesianism. For example, in 1995, McCandless and Weber found through empirical research that in the long run, there was no correlation between the money supply and the growth of output in the long run. The money supply directly affects prices not other factors, because the money supply is closely related to inflation.

The neoclassical synthesis' perspective on the effectiveness of monetary policy. The combination of new Keynesianism and neoclassical macroeconomics gave rise to a new school of economics, the neoclassical synthesis. This school combines rational expectations and dynamic general equilibrium analysis. From the perspective of the neoclassical synthesis, monetary policy is effective. Price change is a very key factor. Price change is manifested primarily as a slow adjustment, which is related to optimal pricing by manufacturers. Therefore, monetary policy can actually influence the economy by directly or indirectly influencing pricing by manufacturers. Since such influence is directly related to the real economy, monetary policy has a lasting influence on real economic variables.

2.4.2 Effectiveness of Monetary Policy Implementation

Summary of foreign research. Empirical research on the effectiveness of monetary policy in foreign countries is mainly related to practical work. Monetary policy has produced some effects in specific operations. The conclusion of foreign empirical research shows that: Tight monetary policy plays a role in economic development. In 1963, a study by Friedman and Schwartz showed that if the Federal Reserve Board had taken effective monetary measures before the Great Depression, the Federal Reserve Board could have mitigated the damage caused by the economic crisis. In 1989, Romer studied the effects of monetary policy on the performance of the economy over several periods. He found that the Federal Reserve Board would slow economic growth by tightening in order to reduce inflationary pressures, so monetary policy had an opposite effect on economic production and its output. In 1992, Mr. Benanke and Mr. Brand found that by adjusting the federal funds rate, bank deposits would change accordingly. In 1996, Stephen, Glenn, and Rudebush studied the effects of monetary policy on firms. They found that when the money supply was tightened, firms could reduce their investment and focus on their internal funds. Marvin (2005) argued that a tightening of the money supply directly led to the recession of 1981–1982.

Summary of domestic research. When it comes to the effectiveness of monetary policy and the corresponding research perspectives, unlike foreign scholars who pay more attention to empirical research, Chinese scholars, by contrast, pay more attention to the integration of research methods. In 2002, Zhou Yingzhang and Jiang Zhensheng conducted an empirical analysis of the transmission mechanism of China's monetary policy from 1993 to 2001 using a VAR model, a Granger causality test, variance decomposition and time series analysis. The results showed that China's monetary policy works by joint transmission through the credit channel and the monetary channel, mainly through the credit channel. According to a study by Zhou (2002), the currency had been characterized by "neutrality" since 1994, and monetary policy with "money supply" as the intermediate target could not achieve the desired effect. In 2002, Liu Bin found that money was in a neutral position in the process of economic development, and especially in the medium to long term, economic growth was influenced more by the development of the real sector than by monetary policy. In 2003, Chen Dewei studied China's monetary policy from 1993 to 2001 using the forecast error variance decomposition method. The results showed that monetary tightening could control economic growth, and was particularly helpful in preventing the economy from growing too fast; but monetary expansion did not have a positive effect on economic development, and could have a worsening effect on economic growth in different ways.

3 Research Ideas and Methods

3.1 Research Ideas

This study integrates progress in development practice and theory at home and abroad. Whether we are conducting research on economically developed countries or regions or exploring the development experience of emerging market countries or regions, we cannot avoid reflecting on and reviewing the development of monetary policy around the world and China's monetary policy after the global financial crisis. The main objective of this study is to study the impact and choice of China's economic and monetary policy in the context of the global crisis, starting with monetary policy. Based on an analysis of the problems in the monetary policy goal systems of typical market economy countries exposed by the global subprime mortgage crisis and the latest developments in research on monetary policy, this paper answers what are the shortcomings of China's existing monetary policy goal system? How to establish a monetary policy goal system based on global economic trends? For a particular end goal, such as the growth rate of output or the rate of inflation, what kind of intermediate target should we choose in order to regulate more effectively?

This paper is divided into three parts containing a total of 12 chapters: The first part is about problems, theory and analysis: Part I: Problems, Theories and Analyses, Chapter 1: Introduction (this chapter); Chapter 2:

Theories Related to Monetary Policy and Its Adjustment; Chapter 3: A Walk-Through and Analysis of U.S. Monetary Policy. Part II: Effects of U.S. Monetary Policy Adjustments. Chapter 4: Direct Effects of U.S. Monetary Policy Adjustments on International Monetary Policy; Chapter 5: Effects of U.S. Monetary Policy Adjustments on the World Economy; Chapter 6: Effects of U.S. Monetary Policy Adjustments on China's Economy; Chapter 7: Impact of U.S. Interest Rate Cuts and Tariffs on China's Economy; Chapter 8: Dollarization and Monetary Policy Spillovers; Chapter 9: Impact of Continued Interest Rate Hikes on the RMB Exchange Rate and China's Response Strategies;

3.1.1 Comparative Analysis

This study not only analyzes the macroeconomic background, system composition, operation mechanism, participants and credit expansion mechanism of China's monetary policy transmission mechanism, but also compares the relevant situations of monetary policy and transmission mechanisms in the United States, the European Union, Japan and other countries and regions, with a focus on examining the similarities and differences in the characteristics of monetary policy and transmission mechanisms between China and the United States, China and the European Union, and China and Japan. Meanwhile, this paper comprehensively examines similarities and differences in monetary policy between major economies from a global perspective, and puts forward more comprehensive and targeted suggestions on financial system reform and supporting mechanisms for strengthening China's monetary policy and transmission mechanism.

3.1.2 Combination of Qualitative and Quantitative Analysis

In addition to strengthening research on global and Chinese monetary policy, this paper employs a combination of qualitative and quantitative analysis methods, and uses traditional inductive and deductive methods to analyze and demonstrate monetary policy transmission mechanisms in terms of scale, type of institution, regional distribution, etc., and compare the relevant regulatory reform policies of the United States, the European Union, etc. horizontally and vertically, with a view to conducting systematic and in-depth research on the making of monetary policy and the development of monetary policy transmission mechanisms.

This paper analyzes the effects of monetary policy transmission mechanism tools on financial development. Representative macro-financial variables are selected and long-term trends between changes in the scale of the monetary policy transmission mechanism and macro-financial variables are tested through a VEC model. Then, representative indicators related to macro-financial variables and bank stability are selected, and the financial index is constructed by using the factor analysis method, the VAR model between changes in the monetary policy transmission mechanism and the financial index is established, and the impact of changes in the scale of the monetary policy transmission mechanism on finance is studied by using a Granger causality test, impulse response analysis and other methods.

3.1.3 Combination of Theory and Policy Analysis

Starting from the theories of monetary policy and its transmission mechanism, this paper presents a theoretical analysis of the emergence and transmission of international financial crisis. Meanwhile, combined with the previous theoretical analysis, this paper studies the intermediate target as the development strategy for China's monetary policy transmission mechanism, which adds practical significance to the theoretical research and policy connotation of this paper.

4 Innovation and Deficiencies

4.1 Innovation

There are the following two main points of innovation in this paper:

> First, most of the relevant literature mainly studies the spillover effects of U.S. monetary policy on one or a few countries and regions (such as the BRICS countries), and rarely extends to multiple countries. This study argues that the spillover effects of U.S. monetary policy adjustments differ significantly from one country or region to another, so it is necessary to demonstrate how such adjustments affect different types of countries. Therefore, this study selects more countries and regions as research samples, and conducts in-depth research on this issue based on a unified and comparable research framework.
>
> Second, this study expands the connotation of U.S. monetary policy adjustments to make them quantifiable and amenable to comparative analysis. In the post-financial crisis era, the most striking feature

of U.S. monetary policy adjustments is quantitative easing, but what is the difference between the spillover effects of the former and conventional monetary policy which also uses the federal funds rate as the intermediate tool? To answer this question, we selected January 2002 to June 2015 as the sample interval, and divided the entire interval into two sub-intervals: January 2002 to August 2008, and September 2008 to June 2015. The former is defined as the conventional U.S. monetary policy interval and the latter the U.S. quantitative easing (unconventional) policy interval. Thus, quantitative comparative analysis can be performed on the differences in the impact of policy shocks between the two stages.

4.2 Deficiencies

1. Data collection. At present, China's interest rate, credit, asset price and exchange rate transmission mechanisms are different from those of typical market economy countries, mainly because many aspects of China's economic and financial system are regulated. To compile data on the impact of global monetary policy on China in the post-financial crisis era into a rigorous article with a certain policy effect within a unified framework still requires very hard work.
2. Quantitative analysis. Statistical and information collection work for China's monetary policy and transmission mechanism is built on a weak foundation, and the financial data released by Chinese regulators is quite limited. As a result, there is a serious shortage of data samples for carrying out quantitative analysis using quantitative methods. Therefore, the lack of data samples also weakens the effect of data proof. This study is worth further deepening in the future, but it is still necessary to select more effective global economic and financial indicators for continuous consideration.

References

Bekaert G, Hoerova M, and Duca M L. Risk, Uncertainty and Monetary Policy. Journal of Monetary Economics, 2013, 60(7): 771–788.

Bernanke B S. Monetary Policy and the Housing Bubble. Speech at the Annual Meeting of the American Economic Association, Atlanta, Georgia. 2010a, 3.

Bernanke. Federal Reserve's Exit Strategy. Testimony before the Committee on Financial Services, U. S. House of Representatives, Washington, DC, February 10, 2010.

Bruno V, and Shin H S. Capital Flows and the Risk-Taking Channel of Monetary Policy. Journal of Monetary Economics, 2015, 71: 119–132.

Chen and Sun. An Analysis of the Impact of U.S. Quantitative Easing on China's Macroeconomy. Economic Science, 2012, (1): 12–26.

Chen and Wei. Analysis of the Benefits and Costs of RMB Internationalization, Friends of Accounting (Mid-Month Edition), September 15, 2010.

Christiano L J, Trabandt M, Walentin K. DSGE Models for Monetary Policy Analysis. Handbook of Monetary Economics, 2010, 3 (7): 285–367, edition 1.

Curdia V, and Woodford M. Credit Spreads and Monetary Policy. Journal of Money, Credit and Banking, 2010, 42(s1): 3–35.

Dai and Zhang. Quantitative Easing Around the World: When to Exit? Xiamen: Xiamen University Press, 2012.

Du. A Study of the Transmission Mechanism of U.S. Quantitative Easing Policy, Tianjin: Nankai University Press, 2013.

Fawley B W, Neely C J. Four stories of quantitative easing. Federal Reserve Bank of St. Louis Review, 2013, 95(January/February 2013).

Fratzscher M, Duca M L, and Straub R. Quantitative Easing, Portfolio Choice and International Capital Flows. Draft, European Central Bank, Frankfurt, 2012, 22.

Friedman M. The Quantity Theory of Money: A Restatement, University of Chicago, 1956, 4(2): 281–308.

Gertler M, and Karadi P. A Model of Unconventional Monetary Policy. Journal of Monetary Economics, 2011, 58(1): 17–34.

Gilchrist S, Ortiz A, and Zakrajsek E. Credit Risk and the Macroeconomy: Evidence from an Estimated DSGE Model. Unpublished Manuscript, Boston University, 2009.

Hansen A H. Monetary Theory and Fiscal Policy, 1949.

Hansen A H. Guide to Keynes, 1953.

Hicks J R. Mr. Keynes and the "Classics": A Suggested Interpretation. Econometrica: Journal of the Econometric Society, 1937: 147–159.

Hu, Wang, and Huang. The Effects of the Fed's Quantitative Easing Policy and Its Implications for China—A Perspective on the Transmission Mechanism of Monetary Policy Based on Tobin's Q Theory. Studies of International Finance, 2013, (12): 4–13.

Huang. Financial Crisis and Monetary Policy: A New Theoretical Framework. Financial Review, 2009, (1): 73–83.

Huang. The Impact of U.S. Expansionary Monetary and Fiscal Policy on China's Inflation, Changchun: Jilin University Press, 2014.

Keynes J M. The General Theory of Interest, Employment and Money, 1936.
Kydland F E, and Prescott E C. Rules Rather Than Discretion: The Inconsistency of Optimal Plans. The Journal of Political Economy, 1977: 473–491.
Li. A Study of the Theoretical Basis and Impact of U.S. Quantitative Easing Policy and the Strategy Adopted In Response to It, Tianjin: Nankai University Press, 2014.
Liu and Zhang. Progress in Research on and Insights into Monetary Policy and the Transmission Mechanism—From the Perspective of Contemporary Western Economics. Journal of Peking University (Philosophy and Social Sciences), January 2012, 49(1).
Ma and Yu. A Study of the Spillover Effects of U.S. Quantitative Easing Policy on BRICS Countries. Studies of International Finance, 2015, (3): 13–22.
Neely C J. The Large Scale Asset Purchases had Large International Effects. Federal Reserve Bank of St. Louis, Research Division, 2010.
Neri S, and Nobili A. The Transmission of US Monetary Policy to the Euro Area. International Finance, 2010, 13 (1): 55–78.
Nie and Jin. A Study of the Spillover Effects of U.S. Quantitative Easing Policy on the Exports of Chinese Industries, Studies of International Finance, 2015, (3).
Peter. Monetary Policy Goals, Institutions, Strategies, and Instruments, Beijing: China Renmin University Press, 2013.
Phillips A W. The Relation Between Unemployment and the Rate of Change of Money Wage Rates in the United Kingdom, 1861–1957. Economica, 1958, 25(100): 283–299.
Reis R. Interpreting the Unconventional US Monetary Policy of 2007–09. National Bureau of Economic Research, 2010.
Ren. An Empirical Analysis of Financial Asset Price Volatility and Inflation in China. Management and Fortune: Academic Edition, 2008, (12): 19–20.
Ricci O. The Impact of Monetary Policy Announcements on the Stock Price of Large European Banks During the Financial Crisis. Journal of Banking & Finance, 2015, 52: 245–255.
Tang. Feldstein and His "Supply-Side" Economic Theory. Economic Science, 1982, (1): 48–51.
Tang. A Study of the Impact of the Fed's Quantitative Easing Policy on China's Capital Markets. World Economy Study, 2015, (6): 12–23, 127.
Taylor J B. Discretion Versus Policy Rules in Practice. Carnegie-Rochester Conference Series on Public Policy, North-Holland, 1993, 39: 195–214.
Taylor J B. The Robustness and Efficiency of Monetary Policy Rules as Guidelines for Interest Rate Setting by the European Central Bank. Journal of Monetary Economics, 1999, 43(3): 655–679.
Tomales. Capital in the Twenty-First Century, Beijing, CITIC Press, 2014, pp. 486–487.

Wang and Chen. China-U.S. Economic Relations, Exchange Rate Regime and China's Exchange Rate Policy—An Empirical Analysis Based on the FAVAR Model. The Journal of Quantitative & Technical Economics, 2010, (1).

Wei and Zou. An Empirical Analysis of China's Monetary Policy Independence From U.S. Monetary Policy. Journal of International Trade, 2012, (7): 115–124.

Werner R A. How to Create a Recovery Through 'Quantitative Monetary Easing'. The Nihon Keizai Shinbun (Nikkei), 2 September 1995 (morning edition), 1995:26.

Wright J H. What does Monetary Policy do to Long-term Interest Rates at the Zero Lower Bound? The Economic Journal, 2012, 122(564): F447–F466.

Wu and Liu. An Empirical Study of the International Transmission of U.S. Monetary Policy and Its Impact. The Journal of Quantitative & Technical Economics, 2009, (6): 42–52.

Xiao. A Study of the International Transmission of U.S. Monetary Policy Shocks: An Empirical Analysis of Asian Economies. Studies of International Finance, 2011, (9): 18–29.

Xiao. The Impact of the U.S. Economic Recovery on the Global and Chinese Economies. International Trade, 2015, (2).

Xing and Tang. A Study of the Spillover Effects of U.S. Monetary Policy on China's Monetary Policy. Research on Financial and Economic Issues, 2011, (11): 50–55.

Yu, Zhang, and Wu. The Impact of the U.S. Exit from QE on the Financial Markets of China and the United States and China's Countermeasures—An Analysis Based on the FAVAR Model. World Economy Study, 2015, (4): 24–32; 127.

Zhao. Research on Monetary Policy Decision-Making from the Perspective of Financial Crisis, Doctoral Dissertation of Hunan University, October 24, 2013.

CHAPTER 2

Theories Related to Monetary Policy and Its Adjustment

Monetary policy is a collection of policies to control the money supply implemented by a country's government or central bank to achieve set economic development targets, and achieve the goals of stabilizing prices, full employment and promoting economic growth by regulating intermediate variable tools such as the intermediary interest rate, the monetary base, and the rate of inflation. Since the ultimate means of operation of monetary policy is mainly to regulate the money supply, the impact and objectives of monetary policy are different in the short and long run: In the short run, changes in the money supply have a direct impact on nominal variables, thus increasing short-term inflation and output growth; in the long run, monetary policy has no impact on real variables, which is manifested as the long-term neutrality of policy. The difference between long-term and short-term effects poses a challenge to the central bank's choice of policy objectives. Generally speaking, monetary policy should take stable nominal variables, such as output growth, inflation and employment as its short-term objectives, and price stability as its long-term objective (Peter 2013). Judging from U.S. monetary policy adjustments during the period from World War II to the subprime mortgage crisis, the Fed's policy behavior is consistent with these objectives (Cogley and Sargent 2005).

Traditional monetary policies have always played an important role in regulating the macroeconomy and achieving set economic targets.

L. Weiping, *American Monetary Policy Adjustment and Its Impacts*,
https://doi.org/10.1007/978-981-99-7810-6_2

However, since the 2008 global financial crisis, unconventional monetary policies, in particular quantitative easing, have been widely used by developed economies such as the United States, the euro area, the United Kingdom and Japan, due to the limited role of interest rates in the recovery from the crisis. The ultimate targets of monetary policy have changed, which is mainly reflected in getting out of deflation and stabilizing prices, repairing the market credit environment, and maintaining the stability of the financial system (Xu 2013). Although quantitative easing has injected some vitality into global economic recovery in the post-crisis era, it has met with a mixed response from countries. As the largest emerging market economy, China needs to make targeted policy adjustments to the implementation mechanism, transmission mechanism, spillover effects and exit effects of the policy.

There has been a lot of research on monetary policy. In order to fit this study, this chapter will explore the relevant theories from the following aspects: (1) briefly review the theoretical basis of monetary policy, and review it from three perspectives: money demand, money supply and monetary policy transmission mechanism; (2) sort out the process of U.S. monetary policy adjustment in different historical contexts; (3) examine the similarities and differences between traditional monetary policy and quantitative easing; (4) summarize the spillover effects of U.S. monetary policies at home and abroad, including both the effects of traditional monetary policies and the externalities of quantitative easing and covering the impact on China and other economies; (5) finally, summarize the theories studied.

Since monetary policy ultimately achieves the desired goal by regulating the money supply, its theories consist of four basic elements: theories of demand for money, theories of money supply, theories of the effectiveness of monetary policy and theories of monetary policy adjustments. By controlling the money supply, monetary authorities influence the demand for money based on certain policy transmission channels and then act on the real economy, thus constituting a complete chain of monetary policy implementation.

1 Theories of Demand for Money

Among theories of demand for money, the most influential ones are the quantity theory of money and the Keynesian theory of demand for money. Most of the theories of demand for money that were developed later are derived from these two theories. The quantity theory of money was the earliest theory to explain the demand for money, and its birth was marked by the transaction equation established by Fisher (1911)[1]:

$$MV_t \equiv P_t T$$

where M is the stock of money, P_t is the price level, T is the volume of trade, $P_t T$ is the value of all cash transactions, and V_t is the velocity of money. The accurate volume of trade T is often difficult to obtain. Proponents of the theory assume that T is equal to real GDP, expressed by Y. On this basis, the velocity of circulation V_t is assumed to be relatively stable and is regarded as exogenous. It is mainly determined by factors such as the characteristics of a country's payment system and residents' payment habits. If the velocity of circulation V_t is regarded as a constant $\overline{V}$, the quantity theory of money becomes the Cambridge cash balance theory, which was developed by the Cambridge economists Marshall (1923) and Pigou (1917), and can be expressed as follows:

$$M_d = \frac{1}{\overline{V}} PY$$

Since the reciprocal of the velocity of circulation $\overline{V}$ is Cambridge k, the above equation can be further expressed as:

$$M_d = kPY$$

This is the so-called Cambridge equation. This equation shows that the demand for money M_d is proportional to the actual number of transactions Y and proportional to the price level P. These two theories initially explained the function of money as a means of payment.

[1] Fisher Equation: It is an equation that reflects the relationship between nominal and real interest rates. Interest rates are divided into real and nominal interest rates. The nominal interest rate is the interest rate calculated on the basis of the promised value of money without taking inflation into account. The real interest rate is the nominal interest rate corrected for changes in the purchasing power of money. Since borrowers and lenders are more concerned with the real purchasing power of money than the nominal amount of money, the real interest rate is a more accurate measure of the costs and benefits of borrowing. The nominal interest rate is expressed in monetary terms, while the real interest rate is expressed in terms of a standardized basket of goods and services.

Friedman (1956, 1970) established the modern quantity theory of money, which was revised in 1970 and can be expressed as follows:

$$\frac{M_d}{P} = f\left\{Y_p, w, r_m, r_b, r_e, \frac{1}{P} \cdot \frac{dP^e}{dt}, u\right\}$$

where P is the price level, changes in P will change the real value of money, so the demand for money M_d is positively correlated with P; Y_p is permanent income, which can be viewed as an exponentially weighted moving average of historical and current income; w is the proportion of non-human wealth, which is negatively correlated with M_d; r_m is return on money, which is positively correlated with M_d; r_b and r_e are return on bonds and return on equity respectively, which are negatively correlated with M_d; $\frac{1}{P} \cdot \frac{dP^e}{dt}$ is the expected inflation rate, which is negatively correlated with M_d; u indicates other variables that affect monetary effects, such as consumer preferences, and its relationship with M_d is uncertain. Friedman's theory of demand for money suggests that monetary authorities adopt medium to long-term monetary rules to control the price level by setting the growth rate of the money supply. Although scholars have different views on the traditional and modern quantity theory of money, due to its relatively simple operation rules, the theory is still an important framework of reference for the economic development of developing countries, including China.

Unlike the quantity theory of money, the theory of demand for money proposed by Keynes in the General Theory of Employment, Interest and Money (1936) (hereinafter referred to as the "General Theory") studies the factors that affect the demand for money from the perspective of residents' motives for holding money. He divided the residents' motives for holding money into three types, the transactions, precautionary and speculative motives. Among them, the transaction motive and precautionary motive are related to current consumer expenditure, which is basically consistent with the quantity theory of money; the speculative motive is more complex, and it is related to actual bond yields, expectations of future bond yields, and the interest rate on the interest-bearing part of money. During the quantitative easing period, ultra-low interest rates led residents to hold a large amount of money, because residents believe that interest rates can only rise and bond prices can only fall in the future, resulting in insufficient savings, a sharp decline in investment, and further depression and recession in the economy. This is a feature of Keynes' liquidity preference theory in an ultra-low interest rate environment, namely the "liquidity" trap.

Scholars have conducted extensive research on the different motives for demanding money. The first is the transactions demand for money, for which the most famous theory is the inventory theoretic model proposed by Baumol (1952) and Tobin (1956),[2]which assumes that residents can switch between cash and bonds quickly. Therefore, the transmissions demand for money is negatively correlated with the yield of short-term bonds and positively correlated with the costs of switching between cash and bonds (or transaction costs). The transmissions demand for money can be expressed as follows:

$$M_T = \sqrt{\frac{Ya}{2r_b}}$$

where Y is monetary income, a is the costs of purchasing financial assets, and r_b is the annual yield of bonds. As can be seen from this equation, the growth rate of M_T is less than the growth rate of Y, , that is, under the condition that there is only the transmissions demand for money, there are returns to scale from holding money, which will also amplify the impact of the exogenous growth of the stock of money (determined by monetary authorities) on the operation of the economy. On this basis, Clower and Howitt (1978) studied a class of models of the demand for money that includes the Baumol-Tobin inventory theoretic model and found that many propositions of these theories could not withstand the test even if attempts were made to push the theories to the initial stage of generalization, so it was necessary to reconstruct the microfoundations of the relevant monetary theories. Some scholars explored the application of theory in practice. Frenkel (1977) measured expectations through observable data from the forward exchange market and used them to estimate the demand for money during the period of hyperinflation in Germany, and then analyzed the money supply process and the correlation between money and price. Field (1984) analyzed the trading data

[2] Baumol Model: The Baumol model, known as the "square-root rule," was created by American economist William Jack Baumol in 1952. A theoretical model of money demand obtained by introducing the interest rate factor into the analysis of the transactions demand for money, it proves the point that the transactions demand for money is affected by interest rates, thus correcting Keynes' view that the transactions demand for money is not sensitive to interest rates.

of the New York Stock Exchange from 1919 to 1929 and found that in addition to fluctuations in aggregate output and interest rates, fluctuations in monthly trading volume and turnover could also independently affect residents' transactions demand for money. In a recent study, Ragot (2014) found that financial adjustment costs in the Baumol-Tobin model could explain 78% of the total demand for money; Sunderam (2014) extended the theory to "money-like" short-term debt issued by shadow banks and explained why investors' demand for "money-like" debt was growing rapidly; Lucas and Nicolini (2015) studied the stability of money demand; Berensen et al. (2015) studied the extent to which financial innovations explained the breakdown of the relationship between money demand and interest rates since 1990.

The second is the precautionary demand for money, for which Whalen (1966) proposed the famous "cube root law",[3]which is expressed as follows:

$$M = \sqrt[3]{\frac{2s^2c}{r}}$$

where M is the precautionary demand for money, s is the standard deviation of a net payment distribution, c is the cost of illiquid money, and r is the opportunity cost rate of precautionary money, namely the interest rate. The Whalen model introduces the interest rate factor into the analysis of the precautionary demand for money. It can be seen from the above equation that there is an inverse relationship between the precautionary demand for money and interest rates, thus correcting Keynes' view that the precautionary demand for money is not sensitive to interest rates. Tsiang (1969) and Frenkel and Jovanovic (1978) expanded the theory from the inventory theoretic model and the model for unified analysis within the stochastic framework respectively in terms of transactions and precautionary demand for money.

Finally, speculative demand for money was studied by Tobin (1958) and Hicks (1962) based on the modern portfolio theory. The most famous theory is the Q theory proposed by Tobin (1969). Tobin's Q

[3] Whalen: An Overview of the Whalen Model. In 1966, American economist Whalen introduced the interest rate factor into the analysis of the precautionary demand for money and obtained the "cube root law" or Whalen model, which proves the point that the precautionary demand for money is affected by interest rates, thus correcting Keynes' view that the precautionary demand for money is not sensitive to interest rates.

theory provides a perspective linking stock prices and investment expenditure, and also reveals part of the transmission mechanism of monetary policy. The formula for calculating Q ratio is as follows: The formula for calculating the Q ratio is as follows[4]:

$$Q = \frac{\text{Market Value of Firm}}{\text{Assets}' \text{ replacement cost}}$$

When $Q > 1$, assets' replacement cost is relatively low, so investment demand will increase, and vice versa. This is reflected in the transmission of monetary policy. When the money supply increases, stock prices rise, leading to an increase in the Q ratio. Active investment by firms leads to an increase in aggregate output, which ultimately promotes the development of the national economy.

2 Theory of Money Supply

The money supply mechanism in a modern credit economy consists of two parts: first, the supply of base money by central banks; second, the creation of deposit money by commercial banks. The discussion on the root of money supply lies in research on the endogeneity and exogeneity of money. The so-called endogenous money means that the stock of money is created by actual economic activity, and is determined by the actual output, interest rates, price levels, etc. Correspondingly, exogenous money means that the stock of money is determined by monetary authorities who are external to the domestic production process. The former emphasizes that the demand for money determines the stock of money, while the latter emphasizes that monetary authorities determine the stock of money. Therefore, from the perspective of endogeneity and exogeneity of money, the theory of money supply can be divided into the theory of endogenous money supply and the theory of exogenous money supply.

The "currency in circulation argument" between monetarism and bankism in the mid-nineteenth century can be seen as the beginning of the theory of endogenous money supply. Bankism, pioneered by Tooke,

[4] Tobin's Q theory: Tobin's Q theory was proposed by Nobel laureate in economics James Tobin in 1969. James Tobin defined Tobin's Q as the ratio of the market value of a firm to the replacement cost of its capital stock.Its economic significance is to compare whether the market value of a firm as an economic agent is greater than the cost of capital that brings cash flow to the firm.

Wilson and Fullarton, maintains that the volume of currency in circulation is determined by the total volume of goods traded in society, and banks cannot arbitrarily decide the volume of banknotes. Marx pointed out in Capital that money is not determined by the central bank, but depends on the demand for money in production and circulation, which is a precursor to the modern theory of endogenous money supply. Tobin and Brainard (1963) and Tubin (1964) established an asset selection model to analyze the endogeneity of the money supply and the substitutability of assets in the transmission process. He believed that the money supply was subject to the public's asset preferences, which depended on the common activities of the whole social and economic sectors, rather than being directly controlled by monetary authorities. He also pointed out that the money multiplier was endogenous.

For the theory of exogenous money supply, the most commonly held views come from Keynes and Friedman. Keynes believed that the money supply was exogenously controlled by monetary authorities, and its changes affected the operation of the economy but were not constrained by economic factors. This theory pioneered the theory of exogenous money supply and gradually strengthened the role of monetary authorities in macro-control. Friedman and Schwartz deduced the famous money supply model in A Monetary History of the United States, 1867–1960, which can be expressed as follows[5]:

$$M = H \times \frac{\frac{D}{R}\left(1 + \frac{D}{C}\right)}{\frac{D}{R} + \frac{D}{C}}$$

where M is the stock of money, H is the monetary base, D is deposits in commercial banks, R is the reserve requirements for commercial banks, and C is money held by the public in the non-banking sector. Friedman and Schwartz believed that the money supply was jointly determined by H, $\frac{D}{R}$ and $\frac{D}{C}$, which provides theoretical support for monetary authorities to adjust money supply flexibly to intervene in the economy.

There are some differences between the theory of endogenous money supply and the theory of exogenous money supply. The former emphasizes that money is created in actual economic activity, and its theoretical hypothesis is a productive monetary economy; the theory of exogenous money supply assumes that money is exogenously given and exists in an

[5] Friedman, Schwartz: A Monetary History of the United States, 1867–1960.

exchange monetary economy. We can see that whether money can be created internally is the key to distinguishing the two theories. Obviously, the theory of exogenous money supply holds that the money creation process is an exogenous mode in which supply and savings determine credit, reserves, and money demand, while the theory of endogenous money holds that the money creation process is an endogenous mode in which reserves and credit determine savings and demand determines supply.

Differences in money creation mode also leads to monetary policies based on the two theories of money supply having different intermediate targets. Both Keynesianism and the monetarism pioneered by Friedman assume that the money supply is exogenous, but their intermediate targets are different. The former takes interest rates as the intermediate target, while the latter takes the money supply as the intermediate target. Keynesianism holds that money is a financial asset and there is a high level of substitutability between it and other financial assets. Since interest rates are relatively easy to observe, the central bank can adopt the necessary monetary policy according to the level of interest rates. For example, when the economy is overheating and interest rates are rising, the central bank should issue government bonds to reduce the money supply, thereby increasing interest rates; when the economy is too cold and interest rates are low, the central bank should buy government bonds to increase the money supply and further reduce interest rates. Friedman argued that due to the low interest rate elasticity of the demand for money, the money demand function is relatively stable. At the same time, he argued that the level of substitutability between monetary and non-monetary assets was low, changes in the money supply had little impact on financial markets, and the excess demand for money caused by the former would be directly transferred to the real economy, thus acting on the national economy through price adjustment mechanisms.

However, the above policy views were questioned by post-Keynesian theories of endogenous money supply, including the theory of horizontalism pioneered by Kaldor (1970, 1982) in the United Kingdom and Moore (1988, 1989) in the United States. They argued that the central bank wanted to maintain the stability of the financial system, so it must meet the demand of commercial banks for reserves, and interest rates were exogenously determined by the central bank (Wang 2008). According to the theory of horizontalism, credit money issued by the central bank is determined by the demand for money, and interest rates are the key to determining the demand for money. Specifically, when the economy is overheating, firms will force the central bank to issue more money, and when the economy is too cold, firms will cut back their demand for loans. So what is the role of the interest rate? It works mainly by changing the operating costs of firms. When interest rates fall, the marginal cost of firms will be lower than marginal revenue, firms will expand production and the demand for money will increase accordingly, and vice versa. It can be seen that according to the theory of horizontalism, the interest rate is a key variable in regulating the demand for money and thus the money supply, thus becoming an intermediate target for monetary policy. But in that case the central bank's control over the money supply will be greatly weakened. Meanwhile, the theoretical assumption that the demand for money is very sensitive to interest rates is not very effective during special periods, so it also has certain limitations in practical application.

3 Theory of Monetary Policy Adjustments

The reason why the monetary policy implemented by the central bank can have a direct or indirect impact on economic variables is closely related to the transmission channels of monetary policy adjustments. If transmission is obstructed, even if the monetary policy is perfect, it will not be able to effectively regulate economic activities. The so-called transmission mechanism of monetary policy adjustments refers to the process in which the central bank uses various monetary policy tools to regulate the money supply and total credit in the whole society, so that firms and residents can constantly adjust their economic behavior to bring the economy to a new equilibrium (Fan and Zhao 2005).There are two transmission mechanisms for traditional monetary policy, namely the interest rate transmission mechanism and the monetary transmission mechanism. Dai and Zhang (2012) gave more detailed monetary policy transmission mechanisms, as shown in Fig. 1.

In The General Theory, Keynes pioneered the transmission channel of monetary policy adjustments. This is manifested in the fact that if the central bank adopts an expansionary monetary policy, the money supply will rise, resulting in a decline in market interest rates, which stimulates an increase in investment spending, and according to the multiplier effect of investment, the aggregate output will eventually increase. This transmission process is also known as the interest rate channel transmission mechanism, which is based on the premise that the interest rate can play

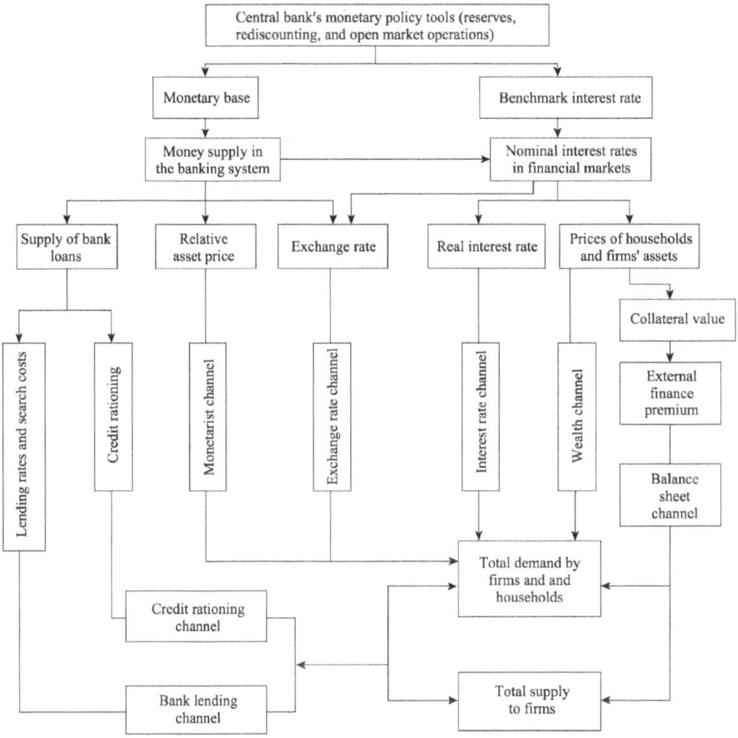

Fig. 1 Channels of monetary policy transmission (*Source* Dai, Zhang. Global quantitative easing: When will it end?, Xiamen, Xiamen University Press, 2012, p. 23)

an effective role. If the interest rate is low enough, it will fall into a "liquidity trap", at which time monetary policy will no longer be effective. However, Friedman, a representative of the monetarist school, believed that the interest rate played no key role in the transmission mechanism of monetary policy. He argued that an effective indicator of the effects of monetary policy was the nominal money supply, and residents' inflation expectations would gradually bring the interest rate back to the equilibrium level. This is known as the monetarist channel. Meltzer (1995) was also a proponent of the monetarist transmission mechanism. He argued that the interest rate was only one of the many relative asset prices, and the interest rate transmission channel with the interest rate as the core was somewhat biased.

The credit transmission channel has an important position in the relevant theories of monetary policy adjustment transmission mechanisms. Roosa (1951) pioneered the idea of credit transmission of monetary policy. Later, Bernanke and Blinder (1988), Bernanke and Gertler (1989), and Bernanke and Gertler (1995) defined the credit transmission mechanism in a narrow and broad sense. The credit transmission mechanism in its narrow sense does not consider the role of firms and residents, and mainly emphasizes the role of credit intermediaries such as banks in the market; the credit transmission channel in its broad sense, also known as the balance sheet channel, refers to the fact that monetary policy affects firms' ability to raise capital by affecting the net value, cash flows, liquid assets, etc. of firms in their balance sheets, which in turn affects their investment activities and eventually leads to changes in aggregate output (Zhang 2011). In the era of deepening economic globalization, the exchange rate channel has become increasingly important. Its transmission channel is as follows:

Money supply ↑→ Real interest rate ↓→ Currency depreciation
→ Net exports ↑→ Total output ↑

In other words, the interest rate and the exchange rate play a very important role in the transmission of monetary policy adjustments. Meanwhile, according to the Mundell-Fleming model, this poses certain challenges to monetary policy independence.

4 Brief Comments

In modern times, the effectiveness of both traditional monetary policy and quantitative easing policy is inextricably linked to the above-mentioned basic components. Due to the existence of the transactions, precautionary or speculative demand for money, people are using or demanding money all the time, but such demand is affected by income, preferences and other external circumstances. On the other hand, it is by influencing the money supply that the money supply side, namely the central bank, further regulates people's economic activities when it implements monetary policy. At this point, it is critical that the transmission channel of monetary policy is unobstructed. Just imagine, for economies with underdeveloped financial markets, the effectiveness of monetary policy will be greatly weakened, and policy lags will seriously restrict the realization of the means and objectives of government regulation. As the world's most powerful country economically, the United States is home to highly developed and highly globalized financial markets. When the Fed implements monetary policy, it will inevitably bring about two effects: the first is the domestic economic regulation effect and the second is the foreign policy spillover effect. Answering these questions is particularly important for understanding the effects of U.S. monetary policy adjustments.

This chapter summarizes the theoretical bases of monetary policy such as money demand, money supply, and monetary policy adjustment. Through this chapter, we cannot only see the transformation of the Fed's position since the Great Depression of the 1930s or the evolution of monetary policy tools and goals, but also have a general understanding of the background and theoretical basis of the implementation of U.S. quantitative easing policy after the outbreak of the 2008 financial crisis. From the literature review of the relevant theories of the spillover effects of U.S. monetary policy in Chapter 1, we can also see the externalities generated by U.S. monetary policy adjustments. Such effects were not confined to the United States, but also had a considerable impact on other countries, especially emerging market economies. These contents lay a solid foundation for the empirical part to systematically study the impact of U.S. monetary policy adjustments on the world economy and China's economy. Before that, it is necessary to analyze the background, policy tools, policy objectives and policy effects of U.S. monetary policy adjustments.

References

Baumol W J. The Transactions Demand for Cash: An Inventory Theoretic Approach. The Quarterly Journal of Economics, 1952: 545–556.

Bernanke B S, and Blinder A S. Credit, Money, and Aggregate Demand. American Economic Review, 1988, 78(2): 435–439.

Bernanke B, and Gertler M. Agency Costs, Net Worth, and Business Fluctuations. American Economic Review, 1989 (1): 14–31.

Bernanke B S, and Gertler M. Inside the Black Box: The Credit Channel of Monetary Policy Transmission. Journal of Economic Perspectives, 1995: 27–48.

Clower R W, and Howitt P W. The Transactions Theory of the Demand for Money: Are Consideration. The Journal of Political Economy, 1978: 449–466.
Cogley T, Sargent T J. Drifts and Volatilities: Monetary Policies and Outcomes in the Post WWII US[J]. Review of Economic Dynamics, 2005, 8(2): 262–302.
Dai and Zhang. Quantitative Easing Around the World: When to Exit? Xiamen: Xiamen University Press, 2012.
Fan and Zhao. Contemporary Monetary Policy: Theory and Practice, Shanghai: Shanghai Sanlian Bookstore, 2005.
Field A J. Asset Exchanges and the Transactions Demand for Money, 1919–29. The American Economic Review, 1984: 43–59.
Fisher I. The Purchasing Power of Money, Pickering & Chatto, 1911.
Frenkel J A. The Forward Exchange Rate, Expectations, and the Demand for Money: The German Hyperinflation. The American Economic Review, 1977: 653–670.
Friedman M. The Quantity Theory of Money: A Restatement, University of Chicago, 1956, 4(2): 281–308.
Friedman M. A Theoretical Framework for Monetary Analysis. The Journal of Political Economy, 1970: 193–238.
Hicks J R. Liquidity. The Economic Journal, 1962: 787–802.
Kaldor N. The new monetarism [J]. Lloyds Bank Review, 1970, 97(1): 18.
Kaldor N. The scourge of monetarism [M]. Oxford University Press, 1982.
Lucas R E, and Nicolini J P. On the Stability of Money Demand. Journal of Monetary Economics, 2015.
Marshall A. Money, Credit & Commerce, AM Kelley, Bookseller, 1923.
Meltzer A H. Monetary, Credit and (Other) Transmission Processes: A Monetarist Perspective. The Journal of Economic Perspectives, 1995: 49–72.
Moore B J. The endogenous money supply [J]. Journal of Post Keynesian Economics, 1988: 372–385.
Moore B J. The endogeneity of credit money [J]. Review of political Economy, 1989, 1(1): 65–93.
Peter. Monetary Policy Goals, Institutions, Strategies, and Instruments, Beijing: China Renmin University Press, 2013.
Pigou A C. The Value of Money. The Quarterly Journal of Economics, 1917: 38–65.
Ragot X. The Case for a Financial Approach to Money Demand. Journal of Monetary Economics, 2014, 62: 94–107.
Roosa R V. Interest Rates and the Central Bank. Money, Trade, and Economic Growth: Essays in Honor of John Henry Williams, 1951.
Sunderam A. Money Creation and the Shadow Banking System. Review of Financial Studies, 2014: hhu083.

Tobin J. The Interest-Elasticity of Transactions Demand for Cash. The Review of Economics and Statistics, 1956: 241–247.
Tobin J. Liquidity Preference as Behavior Towards Risk. The Review of Economic Studies, 1958, 25(2): 65–86.
Tobin J. Commercial Banks as Creators of "Money." Cowles Foundation for Research in Economics at Yale University, 1964.
Tobin J. A General Equilibrium Approach to Monetary Theory. Journal of money, credit and banking, 1969, 1(1): 15–29.
Tobin J, and Brainard W C. Financial Intermediaries and the Effectiveness of Monetary Controls. The American Economic Review, 1963:383–400.
Tsiang S C. The Precautionary Demand for Money: An Inventory Theoretical Analysis. The Journal of Political Economy, 1969: 99–117.
Wang. The Evolution of and Prospects for the Theory of Endogenous Money Supply. Shanghai Journal of Economics, 2008, (5): 3–11.
Xu. Research on the Theory, Practice and Effects of Quantitative Easing Policy, Beijing: Economic Press China, 1st edition, 2013.
Zhang. Monetary Policy Transmission Mechanism: Theoretical Development and Practical Choice. Chinese Review of Financial Studies, 2011, (1).

CHAPTER 3

A Walk-Through and Analysis of U.S. Monetary Policy

We take the Fed's monetary policy and the U.S. macroeconomy since the 1980s as the research object, and then derive the relationship between monetary policy and the macroeconomy. In the following studies, the adjustment of the federal funds rate is the main research index of monetary policy, and the inflation rate, unemployment rate and GDP are the main macroeconomic indicators. U.S. monetary policy from 1980 to 2020 can be divided into three stages by the intermediate target for monetary policy. The first stage is from 1980 to 1993, during which the ultimate target was to curb hyperinflation and the intermediary target was the money supply; the second stage is from 1993 to 2019, during which the intermediate target was changed from the money supply to an index system centered on real interest rates and composed of a number of economic and financial variables, and the Taylor rule was adopted; the third stage is U.S. monetary policy in the wake of the COVID-19 pandemic.

1 1980–1993

Keynesians had long focused only on fiscal expenditure and taxation and ignored the regulatory effects of monetary policy on the economy, and the Vietnam War and other government programs increased government spending and deficits, which coupled with the impact of external shocks such as the oil crisis gave rise to the phenomenon of "stagflation" in

L. Weiping, *American Monetary Policy Adjustment and Its Impacts*,
https://doi.org/10.1007/978-981-99-7810-6_3

the United States in the late 1960s and early 1970s, with unemployment and inflation rising to double digits. Faced with the twin dilemmas of hyperinflation and unemployment, then Fed Chairman Paul Volcker pointed out that the root cause of the scourge was an excess supply of dollars. The target of monetary policy shifted from the benchmark interest rate to the money supply, changes in interest rates were then determined by changes in the market money supply, and a high federal funds rate and monetary tightening measures were adopted to combat inflation. Although the Fed did not fully follow the "single rule" of monetarism, that is, to fix the growth rate of money supply at a level roughly consistent with the potential economic growth rate for a long time, the money supply officially replaced interest rates as the intermediate target of the Fed's monetary policy. An increase in the money supply helps to form the wealth effect, improve cash flow, and increase consumption and investment by households and firms through nominal perceived changes, which will influence changes in the price level. Investors and consumers will change their investment and consumption behavior based on their judgments about future prices, so as to achieve the ultimate target of influencing the direction of the economy. Starting in October, Volcker embarked on a determined effort to shrink the money supply and raise interest rates. The federal funds rate averaged 13.35% and 16.39% in 1980 and 1981, higher than the ten-year Treasury rate. Monetary policy operations with the money supply as the intermediate target succeeded in controlling inflation, but with the passage of time, the money supply was no longer closely connected to economic growth and the price level. This was mainly due to the relaxation of financial control and the acceleration of financial innovation, which had added many new factors to the money supply. Under such circumstances, the Fed constantly revised monetary aggregates according to the changing situation. For example, from 1971 to 1986, the Fed adjusted monetary aggregates six times. Still, given the many uncertainties, it was difficult for the Fed to define and collect statistics on monetary aggregates. Consequently, the Fed had to adjust the focus of money supply monitoring, and starting in 1987, it began to shift the focus of monitoring from M1 to M2 (Figs. 1 and 2).

Volcker's policy produced remarkable effects. CPI peaked at 13.6% in June 1980, then fell sharply and averaged 5.1% in 1984. The growth of M1 slowed sharply—8.3% in 1977 and 1978, 7.5% in 1979, and 7.3% in 1980, and down to 2.3% by 1981. The deceleration that began in late 1980 brought M1 below its four-quarter target range in the first

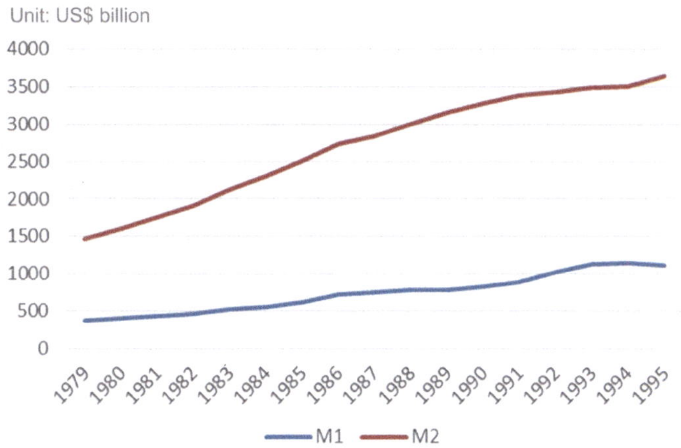

Fig. 1 M1 and M2, 1979–1995 (*Source* Wind)

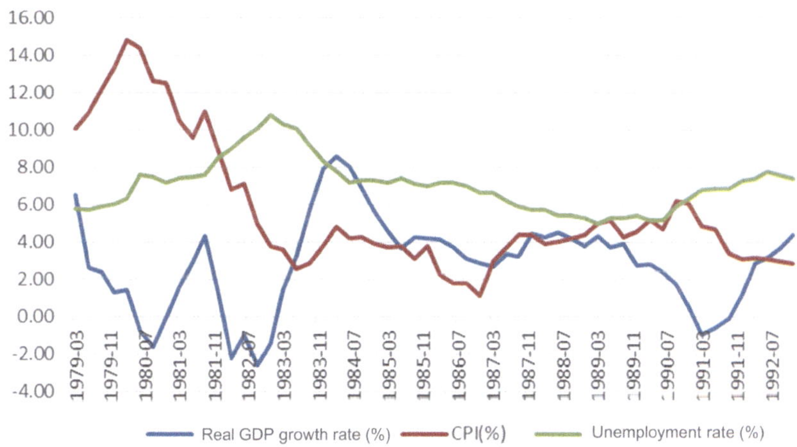

Fig. 2 Main macroeconomic indicators, 1979–1993 (*Source* Wind)

quarter of 1981. But measures to tighten the money supply correspondingly triggered a recession in 1980–1982. U.S. real GDP growth was 3.2% in 1979, fell to −0.2% in 1980, and was 2.6% in 1981 and −1.9% in

1982. Although monetary policy began to ease in July 1982, unemployment remained high at 10.8% in December 1982, the highest since the Great Depression. The Fed took action accordingly. In mid-July 1982, the FOMC began to lower the discount rate and raise the non-borrowed reserve target to push the federal funds rate down. From the end of June to the end of August, the federal funds rate fell from about 15–9%. At the same time, the growth of M1 was just within the target range. With a series of operations, the economy recovered, with GDP growth rising to 4.6% in 1983 and 7.3% in 1984. The United States recovered from the 1981–1982 recession much faster than other countries. In 1987, the Fed was again challenged by another wave of inflation fears under the Louvre Accord. When the dollar depreciated in 1986, oil prices were falling and the overall inflation level was decreasing. But by 1987, the effect of falling oil prices had faded and inflation began to rise, at which point the falling dollar reawakened inflation fears in the bond market. In response, in an adjustment between regular meetings, Volcker raised the federal funds rate to 6.5%. At the regular meeting on May 19, 1987, FOMC further raised the rate to 6.75%. Although the Louvre Accord triggered a moderate expansion-contraction policy cycle, the FOMC's overall efforts to keep track of inflation expectations ultimately created an environment of low inflation and economic stability.

In general, from 1980 to 1993, although Volcker, as chairman of the Federal Reserve, successfully curbed inflation by tightening the money supply, his policy led to two economic recessions, so Volcker's policy was too extreme, and the high interest rate policy stifled economic growth.

2 1993–2019

In the early 1990s, as the stable relationship between M2 and economic activity began to break down, the reality underpinning the use of the money supply as the intermediate target of monetary policy ceased to exist. On July 22, 1993, Federal Reserve Chairman Greenspan suddenly announced that the Fed had decided to abandon the monetary policy rule of regulating the operation of the economy by regulating the money supply that had been implemented for more than ten years, and to adjust real interest rates as the main means of macro control, which is now the "Taylor rule" in the U.S. financial sector. There are two main reasons for the transition from the "single rule" to the "Taylor rule". First, since the mid-1960s, a growing wave of "financial innovation" had made it increasingly difficult to define and collect statistics on the money supply. It was not surprising that the practice of taking the money supply as the intermediate target failed soon in the 1980s. The rise and fall of the price level will affect the opportunity cost of holding money. In a period of inflation, the opportunity cost of holding money is higher, and the velocity of money tends to accelerate; conversely, the velocity of money will decrease. For this reason, the same money supply will produce different levels of nominal demand at different stages of the economic cycle. Second, since the late 1970s, there had been a wave of financial liberalization around the world, led by offshore finance and cross-border banking. Compared with the 1970s, international capital flows had grown by leaps and bounds. In particular, short-term capital flows and foreign exchange transactions had grown more rapidly. These capital flows had brought great uncertainty to the implementation of various countries' monetary policies, and thus to the operation of the macroeconomy. It was for these reasons that the U.S. monetary authorities shifted from the "single rule" for stabilizing monetary growth to macro-control combining the "single rule" and the interest rate-guided "Taylor rule". Through the use of monetary policy tools, the Fed regulated the level of interest rates, thus guiding investment and consumption and influencing changes in national income. After the outbreak of the 2008 global financial crisis, the Fed injected liquidity into the market by purchasing state-guaranteed financial assets such as U.S. Treasury securities and mortgage-backed securities, ushering in the era of quantitative easing. A total of four rounds of quantitative easing were launched. The main channel to influence the economy through quantitative easing is the portfolio balance channel, that is, because different financial assets in the portfolio are not completely fungible, changes in the supply of different assets provided to private investors will affect the prices and returns of these assets. In other words, the Fed can use open market operations to change the relative supply of and demand for different assets in the market, and thus influence returns on different assets, so as to transmit monetary policy (Fig. 3).

According to the different ultimate targets of monetary policy, the post-1993 period can be divided into four stages: The first stage is from 1993 to the outbreak of the financial crisis, during which the U.S. economy was growing continuously and external system risks were stable, so the Fed mainly adopted the monetary policy of fine-tuning interest rates; the second stage is from the outbreak of the financial crisis to

Fig. 3 Federal funds rate, 1993–2007 (*Source* Wind)

2015, during which the Fed's monetary policy was primarily aimed at responding to the financial crisis and boosting the sluggish U.S. economy in the aftermath of the crisis, so the Fed mainly adopted multiple interest rate cuts and quantitative easing; the third stage is from 2015 to the present, during which the United States began to normalize monetary policy, constantly raising interest rates and shrinking the balance sheet, so that the federal funds rate gradually returned to normal. This stage can be subdivided into two parts: The United States exited from quantitative easing in 2015, and officially raised interest rates for the first time in August 2019. For this reason, the future of monetary policy was further analyzed.

3 1993–2007: Monetary Policy of Fine-Tuning Interest Rates

In 1994, indicators of resource stress were red across the board. The capacity utilization rate rose from slightly over 80% in the middle of 1993 to 85% at the end of 1994, and the supplier performance index rose from about 51 in 1993 to 65 at the end of 1994. The Fed was once again facing inflationary pressures, so the target for monetary policy at this stage was low inflation and moderate economic growth. In 1996, the United States entered a "new economic era," a long period of record prosperity, high growth, and even low inflation accompanied by low unemployment. From July 1999 to December 2000, the Fed raised interest rates several times in a year, raising the federal funds target rate from 5% to 6.5% and the discount rate from 4.5% to 6%. Beginning in June 2000, the growth of the real GDP growth in the United States began to slow down, and the inflation began to decline gradually, while unemployment began to rise gradually in 2001. This was consistent with the monetary policy transmission path of interest rate hikes leading to less investment and higher securities prices and thus leading to lower output levels and lower market prices, and therefore testified to the effectiveness of the Fed's monetary policy of constantly raising interest rates. During the period 2001–2004, the September 11 attacks and the wars in Afghanistan and Iraq led to increased downward pressure on the economy, steadily rising unemployment, rapidly falling inflation and deflation risk. In this context, the goal of the Fed's monetary policy for this stage was to stabilize prices, avoid inflation, reduce unemployment, and promote employment. As a result, during this period, the Fed pursued a prolonged accommodative monetary policy, slashed the federal funds target rate, which dropped from 5.5% in January 2001 to 1% in June 2003, and hovered around 2% until 2004. The federal funds rate also took a steep downward turn in 2001 and did not start to rise until June 2004. It can be seen that near the end of the period, the unemployment rate stabilized and began a downward trend, and since 2002, GDP growth had begun to pick up again, while the CPI had been fluctuating. This round of interest rate cuts worked well in easing the economic downturn, stimulating economic development, reducing unemployment, and staving off deflation. Successive interest rate cuts and cheap financing, on the one hand, stimulated investment, credit and consumption, which eased the economic downturn, but on the other hand, successive interest rate cuts led to a large number of asset bubbles in the economy (Figs. 4 and 5).

After experiencing an accommodative monetary policy environment in the previous stage, the U.S. federal fund interest rate was at a low level. Starting in 2002, the U.S. economy picked up steam and entered a stage of stable growth. An accommodative monetary policy was not conducive to economic development, nor to the adjustment of the Fed's monetary policy space, so the Fed announced its plans to raise interest rates to the market in advance in an effort to guide market expectations and carry out "countercyclical" regulation. Beginning in July 2004, the Fed adopted a gradual rate hike approach, raising interest rates for 14 times in a row,

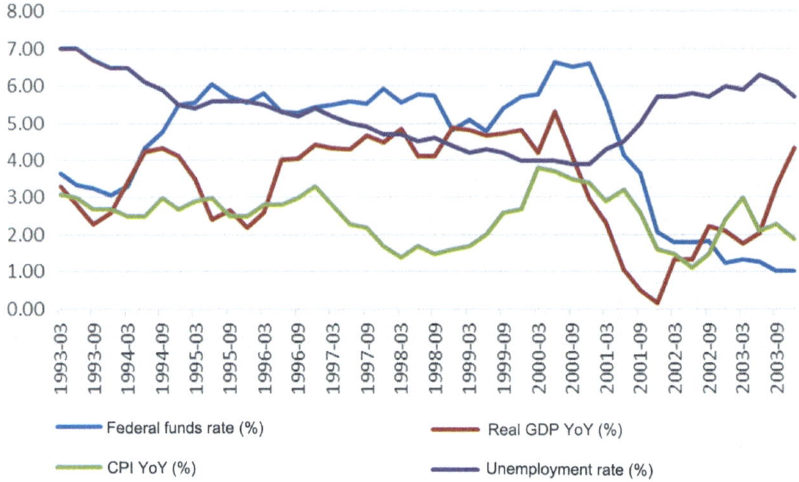

Fig. 4 Main economic indicators, 1993–2004 (*Source* Wind)

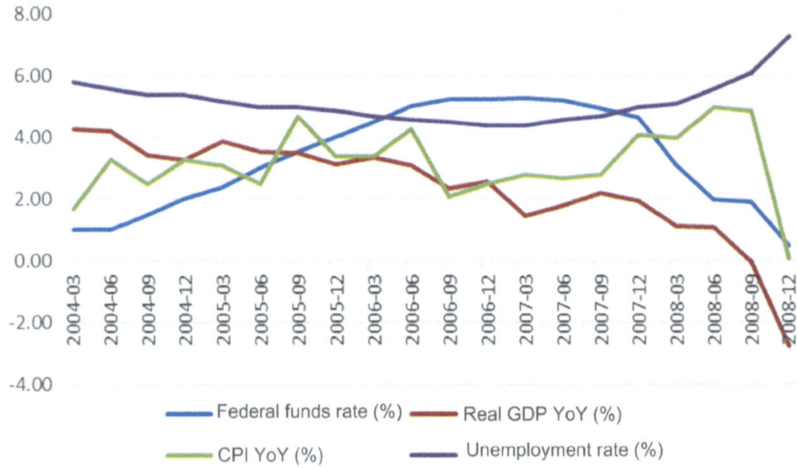

Fig. 5 Major economic indicators, 2004–2008 (*Source* Wind)

by 25 bp each time. The federal funds target rate was raised from 1% in June 2004 to 4.5% in January 2016, and the federal funds rate was raised from about 1% in June 2004 to about 5% in June 2006. As the Fed announced its plans to raise interest rates and inflation target in advance, the market formed reasonable expectations of the Fed's tightening monetary policy and inflation. With higher interest rates, economic growth was slightly weak. The year-over-year real GDP growth rate gradually declined from 4.30% in March 2004 to 1.48% in March 2007, while the inflation rate was relatively stable, fluctuating between 2% and 4%, and the unemployment rate declined somewhat.

During the implementation of the interest rate policy in this period, the Fed fine-tuned interest rates many times, but only small adjustments were made. The Fed not only actively controlled the intensity and scale of regulation through fine-tuning, but also paid attention to structured interest rate regulation, so as to create a relaxed environment for the operation of the economy and achieve the goal of preventing inflation. At the same time, efforts were made to improve the openness and transparency of policies and reasonably guide public expectations. The use of monetary policy tools mainly has the following characteristics: First, the Fed gradually lower the required reserve ratio and gradually reduced its use of this tool; second, the federal funds rate as the operational target was achieved through open market operations, which had become by far the most important and commonly used monetary policy tool; third, since the 1980s, the Fed had gradually reduced its use of the discount window, which mainly acted as a lender of last resort. Overall, from the 1990s until the start of the subprime mortgage crisis, monetary policy was successful in sustaining the development of the U.S. economy.

4 2007–2015: Ultra-Loose Monetary Policy

On February 13, 2007, New Century Financial issued a profit warning for the fourth quarter of 2006. Under pressure from Wall Street to pay off $17.4 billion in debt, New Century Financial, the second largest subprime mortgage company in the United States, announced on April 2, 2007 that it had filed for bankruptcy protection and laid off 54% of its workforce. On August 6, 2007, the 10th largest mortgage lender in the United States—American Home Mortgage Investment Corporation officially filed for bankruptcy protection in the court, becoming another large mortgage lender after New Century Financial in the United States to file for bankruptcy. On August 8, 2007, Bear Stearns, the fifth largest investment bank in the United States, announced the collapse of two of its funds, also due to the subprime mortgage crisis. Since then, the subprime mortgage crisis had begun to sweep the world, prompting the Fed to adopt an ultra-loose monetary policy. Monetary policy during the ultra-loose phase consisted of two parts, unprecedented ultra-low interest rates and a deteriorating Fed balance sheet. After September 2007, U.S. financial markets gradually tightened, with stock indexes falling to varying degrees since October, the credit market keeping tightening, liquidity in short-term funding markets seriously damaged, and bubbles in the property market bursting, increasing the risk of the U.S. economy sliding into a recession. As a result, the Fed cut interest rates three times in a row from September 2007 to December 2007. The federal funds target rate was lowered from 5.25% in September 2007 to 4.25% in December 2007, and then lowered to 0.25% in December 2008 in response to the worsening financial crisis. At the same time, the Fed launched the Term Auction Facility (TAF) in December 2007 and entered into reciprocal currency arrangements with the ECB to increase liquidity in financial markets and relieve rising pressures in dollar funding markets. Immediately after the collapse of Lehman Brothers in September 2008, the Fed launched a series of innovative monetary policy tools, including innovative tools for depository institutions, innovative tools for dealers and innovative tools for money markets. In March 2009, the Fed introduced a series of more aggressive policy measures to stimulate the economy and improve the availability of credit while keeping the federal funds rate at zero to 0.25%. Thus began the first round of quantitative easing (QE1): First, buy $300 billion of long-term Treasury securities over the next six months to support the federal government's bailout program. Second, provide liquidity support to the mortgage and housing markets through additional purchases of $750 billion of mortgage-backed securities and $100 billion of agency bonds. Through the first round of quantitative easing, the Fed created more than a trillion dollars in reserves, but the U.S. economy didn't get much better (Figs. 6 and 7).

The U.S. economy was in the doldrums after the financial crisis. Affected by a sharp drop in crude oil prices, inflation had fallen sharply since July 2008 and was below zero between March 2009 and October 2009. The core inflation rate also gradually declined and approached zero. Deflationary pressures on the U.S. economy increased dramatically. Meanwhile, the U.S. labor market was weak, with the unemployment rate

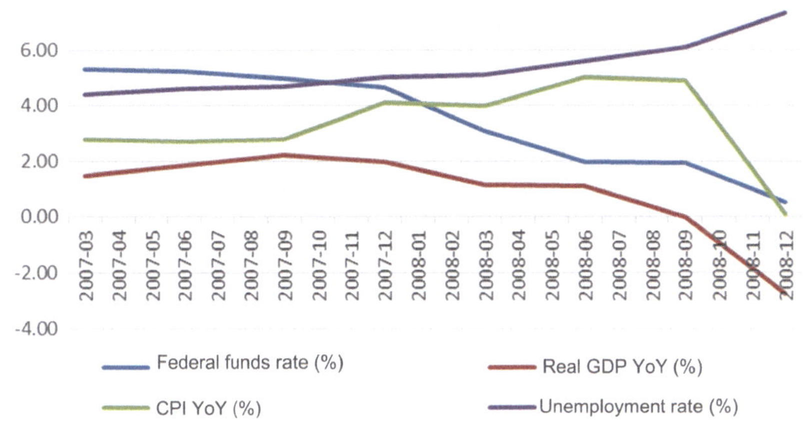

Fig. 6 Main economic indicators, 2007–2008 (*Source* Wind)

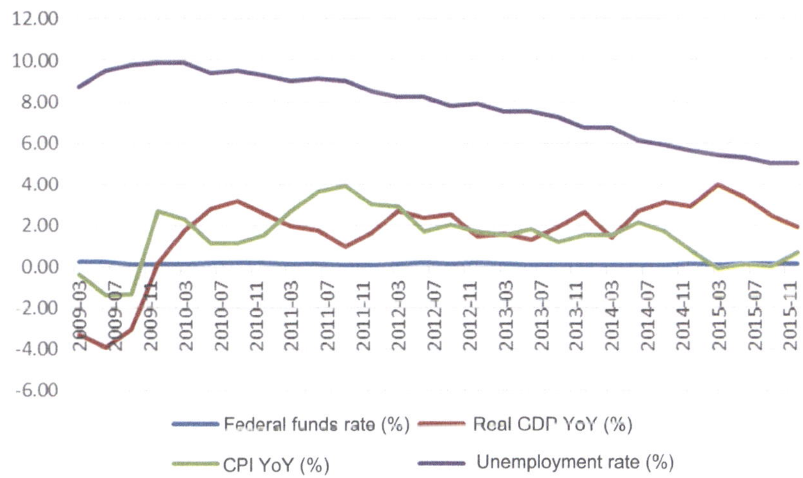

Fig. 7 Main economic indicators, 2009–2015 (*Source* Wind)

rising from 7.8% in January 2009 to 10% in October 2009. U.S. credit markets remained tight and household incomes and confidence remained depressed. In order to promote economic recovery and development, after lowering the federal funds target rate to the 0–0.25 percent range, the Fed mainly used non-traditional monetary policy tools—forward guidance and large-scale asset purchases—to achieve the monetary policy goals of maximizing employment and stabilizing prices. However, in 2010, the Fed believed that the pace of economic recovery in the United States was far from the policy goals of maximizing employment and stabilizing prices, the recovery of the U.S. real economy was slow, the willingness of firms to hire was low, and there was a risk of the European debt crisis spilling over to the U.S. economy. As a result, the Fed launched a second round of quantitative easing (QE2), announcing in November 2010 the purchase of $600 billion worth of long-term Treasury securities at a pace of $75 billion per month, with the aim of boosting the recovery of the real economy by driving down long-term bond yields and lowering borrowing costs. After August 2011, the inflation rate in the United States began to decline gradually, and the core inflation rate was only slightly lower than the policy target of 2%. Inflation was basically under control, and the policy goal of price stability had been basically achieved. However, although the U.S. labor market had improved since 2011, the unemployment rate remained high, reaching 8.3% in January 2012. In order to continue to stimulate the U.S. economy and reduce unemployment, on September 13, 2012, the Fed announced its third round of quantitative easing (QE3), with the expectation that the global low interest rate environment and abundant liquidity would continue for a longer period of time. But this could put inflationary pressures on emerging market countries. The Fed bought $40 billion worth of mortgage-backed securities every month. This round of quantitative easing was mainly aimed at maximizing employment. On December 12, 2012, the Fed announced a fourth round of quantitative easing (QE4), pledging to buy $45 billion worth of Treasury securities every month, which, combined with the monthly purchase of $40 billion worth of mortgage-backed securities in the third round of quantitative easing, brought the Fed's monthly purchase of assets to $85 billion. Quantitative indicators were used to determine periods of ultra-low interest rates. The policy objective was to further support economic recovery and the labor market. In December 2012, the Fed announced that it would expand its existing asset purchase program after Operation Twist expired at the end of 2012, and use quantitative indicators to determine periods of ultra-low interest rates. In addition to continuing to buy $40 billion worth of mortgage-backed securities, the Fed would buy about $45 billion worth of longer-term Treasury securities each month after Operation Twist, under which the Fed sold short-term Treasury securities and bought medium—and long-term ones, expired. Meanwhile, the Fed would continue to reinvest principal payments from maturing agency bonds and agency mortgage-backed securities. In addition, the Fed decided to keep the federal funds rate in the ultra-low range of 0–0.25% as long as the unemployment rate was above 6.5% and inflation was expected to be no more than 0.5% points above its long-run target of 2% over the next one to two years. If the outlook for the job market did not improve significantly, the Fed would continue to buy Treasury securities and mortgage-backed securities, and make appropriate use of other policy tools.

Quantitative easing injected liquidity into financial markets in time, easing the pressure brought about by the credit crunch, and stabilizing sentiment in financial markets to a certain extent. Against the policy background of quantitative easing, the U.S. economy recovered slowly, and the real GDP growth rate turned from negative to positive in 2010, reaching 3.01% in 2014; employment continued to improve, with the unemployment rate falling from 10% in October 2009 to 6.6% in January 2014; meanwhile, the United States staved off the risk of deflation in 2009, and the core inflation rate moved slowly but steadily towards the long-run policy target of 2% from 2009 to 2014. Despite the slow recovery of the U.S. economy, the long-term loose monetary policy had timely slowed risk spillovers from other economies to the United States and ensured the steady and stable operation of the U.S. economy.

5 2015–2019: Normalization Phase

The period from July 2015 when the Fed announced adjustments to its monetary policy objectives to the present is the normalization phase. Monetary policy normalization refers to the process of shifting monetary policy from responding to crises to a normal state and gradually withdrawing unconventional policy measures. Quantitatively, exit quantitative easing and shrink the monetary authority's balance sheet; price-wise, continue to raise the short-term policy rate, that is, the federal funds rate, to gradually restore it to a normal level. In December 2015, the Fed raised the federal funds rate, signaling the official start of the monetary policy normalization phase. The monetary policy normalization process had been continuously strengthened through the operations of raising interest rates first and then shrinking the balance sheet, and raising interest rates quickly and shrinking the balance sheet slowly.

First, changes in the federal funds rate and the size of the Fed's balance sheet during the ultra-loose phase. At the end of 2006, the federal funds rate was still at a high of 5.17%. Since September 2007, after ten cuts, the federal funds rate had dropped precipitously. At the end of 2008, it fell to an all-time low of 0.14%, effectively entering the zero interest rate phase, which lasted for seven years. After the implementation of quantitative easing policy, the Fed's balance sheet ballooned. For a long time, the annual growth rate of the Fed's assets had remained at about 2%. However, in 2008 there was an unprecedented increase in the Fed's assets, which soared by 150.73% in one year. Since then, the three rounds of quantitative easing had been continuously ramped up, and the size of the Fed's balance sheet had kept rising, reaching a high of $4.49 trillion at the end of 2015, a four-fold increase over 2007.

Second, changes in the federal funds rate and the size of the Fed's balance sheet during the normalization phase. Starting in 2014, the Fed continuously signaled rate hikes. In December 2015, the Fed started a new cycle of interest rate hikes. After nine rate hikes, the federal funds rate rose again to 2.4% by the end of 2018. While ending its zero interest rate policy, the Fed had repeatedly signaled it would reduce its balance sheet, but it wasn't until October 2017 that it officially started implementation. After 14 months of continuous balance sheet reduction, by December 2018, the Fed's assets shrank to $4.08 trillion.

6 2019–2020

In 2019, the global economy was under increasing downward pressure due to trade frictions. U.S. economic growth had also slowed compared to 2018, with real GDP growing at 2.3% and 2.1% year-over-year in the second and third quarters of 2019. Compared with the 2.9% real GDP growth rate in 2018, U.S. economic growth was moderating from high levels. Against this backdrop, on July 31, the Fed announced its first interest rate cut in 10 years, decided to lower the target range for the federal funds rate by 25 bp, and said that it would end its balance sheet reduction early. After that, the Fed lowered the federal funds rate twice on September 19 and October 31 to 1.5 1.75%. The Fed's statement on balance sheet expansion also came as scheduled. Starting on October 15, the Fed would purchase short-term Treasury securities at a pace of $60 billion per month.

In late 2019, economic conditions in the United States began to improve. In October, the U.S. unemployment rate fell further to 3.5%, its lowest level since 1969. The year-over-year growth rate of the core CPI in the United States also remained unchanged from September to November, at just 2.3%. With the change of the U.S. economic situation, the direction of U.S. monetary policy had also begun to change. At the December FOMC meeting, members voted unanimously to leave the target range for the federal funds rate unchanged, marking the Fed's shift to a "wait and see mode".

As 2020 began, the strong performance of the U.S. labor market continued unabated, and the Fed maintained its "raise-and-hold" strategy. In its monetary policy report to the U.S. Congress on February 7, the Fed said downside risks to the U.S. economy appeared to have receded. Fed Chairman Jerome Powell even said they would gradually transition away from repo operations. The U.S. economy appeared to be well on its way to recovery.

However, the good times did not last long. As COVID-19 spread further, people were increasingly worried about the pandemic. The panic began in the stock market: On February 24 and 25, the S&P 500 and the Dow Jones Industrial average began to fall, down 6.3% and 6.6% respectively in the two days. In response to the risks posed by the pandemic, **the Fed cut the federal funds rate by 50 bp on March 3 to 1.0–1.25%.** The rate cut was not only the biggest since the financial crisis, but also the only fourth emergency rate cut in U.S. history. U.S. stock markets tumbled in response, with the S&P 500 and the Dow Jones Industrial Average falling by 3.4% and 3.6% respectively on that day. Meanwhile, the 10-year Treasury yield had been drifting lower, hitting a record low of 0.318%.

On March 13, the United States declared a "national emergency." U.S. public health policy had been slow in responding to a growing COVID-19 pandemic, forcing the Fed to take increasingly aggressive measures to ease immediate concerns. To address the liquidity crisis and stabilize financial markets, the Fed not only injected $1.5 trillion of short-term funds into 24 large banks on March 12, but also **made another emergency cut to interest rates on March 15, lowering the target range for the fed funds rate by 100 bp to the "zero lower bound" in 2018,** which meant that the interest rate policy space accumulated by the United

Fig. 8 Federal funds target range—lower limit federal funds target range—upper limit (*Source* FRED)

States since 2015 had been exhausted. In addition, the Fed announced a massive quantitative easing program of at least $700 billion (Fig. 8).

U.S. stock markets were going through a shake-up at the time: Between March 9 and March 18, U.S. stock markets had four circuit breakers. The S&P 500 and the Dow Jones Industrial Average fell 19.3% and 23.1%, respectively, over a 10-day period, which was unprecedented in the history of U.S. stocks. On March 23, the Fed held another emergency meeting and announced its second round of massive bailouts, including the launch of unlimited quantitative easing and a program to lend to small and medium-sized businesses, and increased the pace of asset purchases to $125 billion per day. U.S. stocks had since rebounded sharply.

7 Dynamics and Interpretation of U.S. Monetary Policy in 2021

7.1 Monetary Policy Background

Since 2020, in response to the impact of the pandemic, the Fed has adopted unprecedented monetary easing policies, not only ushering in an era of unlimited quantitative easing, but even revising its monetary policy framework in August 2020 in an effort to restore employment and restructure the U.S. economy. The advent of this monetary framework also had a decisive impact on the Fed's subsequent monetary policies. The Fed's monetary policy in 2021 was a continuation of the policy in 2020, but it was different. The changing landscape of the U.S. economy and the pandemic mandated that more factors be taken into account in the Fed's monetary policy.

7.2 Main Monetary Policies and Interpretations

In the first quarter of 2021, the Fed's monetary policy remained on hold. However, the situation had changed a lot since 2020. The $1.9 trillion fiscal stimulus was starting to have an effect and the pace of vaccination was very promising, which meant that the U.S. economy might grow more than expected in 2021. A dilemma was beginning to unfold before the Fed. On the one hand, a looming shortage of up to 10 million jobs requires the Fed to keep policy easy for a long time. On the other hand, the upward pressure on inflation could not be ignored as the economy recovered rapidly. If the Fed tightened monetary policy ahead of time to rein in inflation, it would be difficult to achieve its long-term employment target.

This question was carried over to the second quarter of 2021 before it was answered. The CPI rose by 2.6% year-over-year in March, and the rapid rise in inflation caused concern in the market. At first, the Fed took a cavalier approach to inflation. At the April FOMC meeting, the Fed argued that "rising inflation was transitory and inflation would not exceed 2% in the long run". The Fed's high tolerance for inflation was well documented. The new monetary policy framework, introduced in August 2020, allowed the Fed not to respond to short-term deviations of inflation from the target. For the Fed, inflation was increasingly taking a back seat to employment, and the Fed still had plenty of room to tolerate inflation.

However, the U.S. core CPI rose 3.8% and the core PCE rose 3.4% year on year in May. There were indications that the high inflation in the United States was not temporary but would persist for a longer period. The Fed had to start taking inflation seriously. At the June FOMC meeting, the Fed signaled a shift in monetary policy for the first time since the start of the pandemic, formally putting discussions on the taper (tapering QE bond purchases) on the agenda and raising its inflation expectations. With the recovery of U.S. manufacturing and services, the Fed was almost ready to taper, but the timing was still open to debate. To taper early would be detrimental to the recovery of the labor market, but too long a delay would result in excessive inflationary pressures and excess liquidity in financial markets.

Tapering became the focal point of the Fed's monetary policy at subsequent FOMC meetings. At the July FOMC meeting, the Fed did not adjust the size of asset purchases, but quietly set up two monetary policy tools to prepare for the future tapering process. By August, the U.S. unemployment rate had fallen to 5.2% and "clear progress" had been made towards the Fed's cherished employment target, which provided a good foundation for the start of tapering. At the August FOMC meeting, Powell made it clear for the first time that tapering could start in 2021. At the September FOMC meeting, Powell was more determined, saying a taper would be announced at the next meeting if the economy developed as expected.

At the November FOMC meeting, the Fed started the taper as scheduled, announcing a $10 billion reduction in its monthly purchases of Treasury securities and $5 billion in MBS (mortgage-backed securities). At the same time, the Fed said it would hold off on raising interest rates, citing a mismatch between supply and demand as the cause of high inflation—while the demand side had recovered strongly, the supply side was still constrained by the pandemic and the recovery was weak. In the long run, the problems of tight supply chains and labor shortages in the United States would be alleviated in the future, and a rush to control inflation by raising interest rates at the moment could disrupt the pace of economic recovery. Therefore, the Fed was taking a "wait and see" approach to inflation, waiting for supply chain issues to be resolved before considering raising rates.

At the December FOMC meeting, the Fed sped up the taper, doubling the pace of its purchases from $10 billion a month in Treasury securities and $5 billion in MBS to $20 billion a month in Treasury securities and $10 billion in MBS. At this pace, the current round of quantitative easing would end around March next year. Elevated inflation expectations were the main reason the Fed sped up the taper. At the meeting, the Fed revised its "transitory inflation" description, acknowledging that "Inflation has been running above the 2% inflation target for some time". This means that the Fed might have misjudged the direction of inflation, and that the supply shortage had been deeper and longer than the Fed

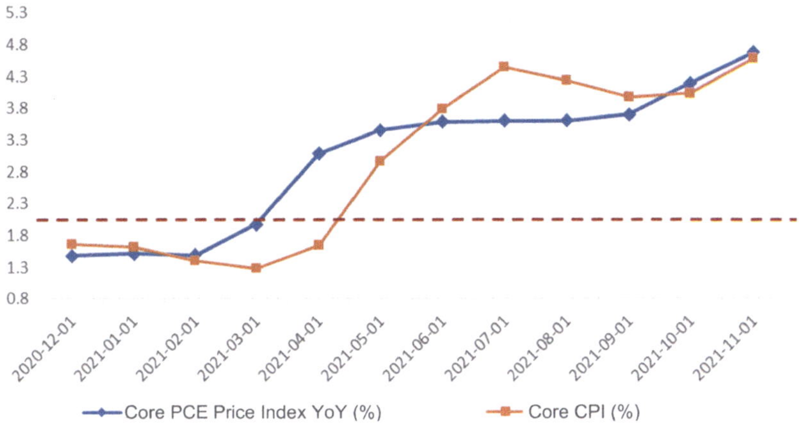

Fig. 9 U.S. core PCE and core CPI in 2021 (*Source* FRED)

expected. Nevertheless, the Fed still believed inflation would fall back to near 2% by the end of next year (Fig. 9).

7.3 Policy Effects

2021 was the year when the Fed's monetary policy began to shift. Over the past year, the U.S. economy had continued to grow, with consumption performing well and the job market recovering rapidly, spurred by loose monetary and fiscal policy. On this basis, a shift in the Fed's monetary policy was inevitable.

On the one hand, the pandemic remained an important factor influencing the Fed's monetary policy. With global vaccination rates rising, the negative impact of the pandemic had been mitigated. Thanks to a huge fiscal stimulus and relentless quantitative easing by the Fed, the U.S. unemployment rate fell quickly, to 4.2% in November 2021, close to pre-pandemic levels. However, the adverse impact of the pandemic on the job market had not completely subsided, as shown by the slow recovery of the U.S. labor force participation rate and large numbers of people dropping out of the labor market. Meanwhile, the newly discovered Omicron variant had sown fears for the global pandemic, and dark clouds still loomed over the U.S. response to the pandemic. The pandemic would remain the bane of U.S. monetary policy for the foreseeable future.

On the other hand, as the U.S. economy recovered, inflation in the United States was rising. The slow recovery of the supply side was the underlying cause of inflation, and the Fed's high tolerance for inflation under the new monetary policy framework was the main cause. By December 2021, however, inflation had already long exceeded the Fed's inflation target, with the CPI rising 6.8% in November from a year earlier, the biggest increase since 1982. Such inflationary pressures were bound to dampen domestic demand, which would force the Fed to face up to inflation and take relevant measures.

The Fed's attitude towards tapering was closely watched around the world. In the second quarter of 2021, as the U.S. economic recovery picked up speed, the Fed was virtually ready to taper. Yet memories remained of the taper tantrum of 2013, when all kinds of asset became extremely sensitive to taper signals, triggering volatility in global asset prices. As a result, the Fed had been treading carefully on the taper, with Powell even saying to reporters that "we are discussing whether to start talking about the taper" for fear of causing market panic. Thus, the Fed cautiously sent a taper signal, waited for markets to digest it, and then sent more signals. The effort paid off—In November 2021, everything was ready, the taper arrived on schedule, market shocks were limited, and taper tantrum, which the Fed had labeled as a dreadful monster, did not happen.

In the medium to long term, the general direction of monetary policy tightening by the Fed had been set. On the one hand, with an increase in vaccination rates and the implementation of fiscal stimulus, the economy continued to strengthen, so maintaining an overly loose monetary policy was no longer necessary. On the other hand, a rapid economic upswing and production bottlenecks spurred higher inflation, making monetary tightening more urgent. At the December FOMC meeting, the Fed not only sped up tapering of its debt purchases, but also sent a message through its dot plot that it could raise rates three times in 2022. The Fed could begin preparing to raise rates as soon as the taper was completed in March 2022 (Fig. 10).

In April, the negative impact of the pandemic followed. The U.S. real GDP grew by just 0.3% in the first quarter of 2020, and the unemployment rate rose to 14.7% in April. On April 9, the Fed took further easing steps, providing up to $2.3 trillion in financing to businesses and local governments and including some junk bonds in its asset-purchase program. U.S. fiscal policy kept pace, with a $2.2 trillion fiscal stimulus

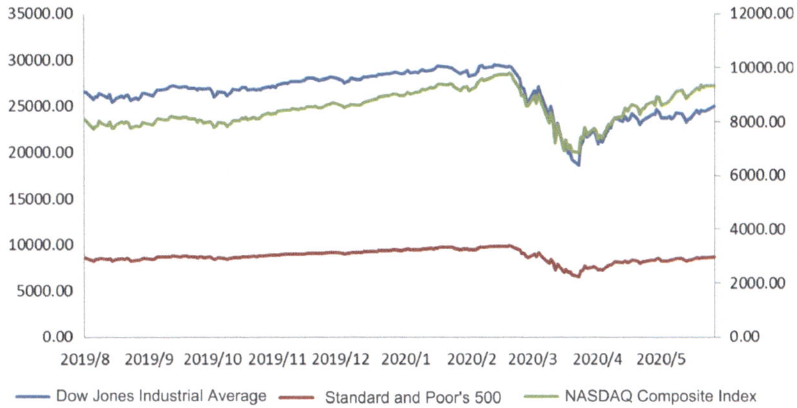

Fig. 10 Main stock market indexes since the U.S. interest rate cut (*Source* FRED)

package and a $484 billion relief bill passed on March 27 and April 23, respectively. The LIBOR-OIS spread, a measure of credit stress, gradually narrowed in April as liquidity pressures finally began to ease amid extremely aggressive monetary and fiscal policy in the United States. On May 12, the Fed began buying corporate-bond ETFs.

Meanwhile, in order to reserve space for monetary policy, the Federal Reserve began to gradually reduce the daily pace of its purchases of Treasury securities. The subsequent monetary policy of the United States was still inextricably linked to the development of the pandemic.

8 Analysis of Tapering's Impact

8.1 Promulgation of the Policy of Unlimited Quantitative Easing

8.1.1 Impact of the Pandemic on the U.S. Economy

The pandemic has had a huge impact on the U.S. economy, with "lockdowns" and flights suspended in many places, and work and production stopped in many industries. The U.S. economy has suffered the biggest impact since the Great Depression of the 1930s. The pandemic has halted the sustained expansion of the U.S. economy. The National Bureau of Economic Research determined that the U.S. economy officially entered recession in February 2020, ending more than 10 years of economic expansion. U.S. GDP shrank by 3.5% in 2020, the biggest contraction since World War II, as the pandemic dampened consumer spending and business investment, pushing millions of Americans out of work and into poverty.

8.1.2 *The Introduction of Quantitative Easing Policy*

The pandemic affected the global economy and trade, which in turn impacted liquidity in U.S. financial markets. The Fed introduced a policy combining "a zero interest rate and quantitative easing" for the first time in 12 years since 2008 to ease liquidity strains and resist the strong impact of the spread of the pandemic on the fundamentals of the economy. In March 2021, the Biden administration decided to implement a $1.9 trillion stimulus package and a $2 trillion infrastructure plan. The Fed lowered the target range for the federal funds rate by 100 bp to 0–0.25% at an extraordinary meeting on March 15. On March 23, the Fed announced an open-ended asset purchase program, under which it would buy $75 billion worth of Treasury securities and $50 billion in agency mortgage-backed securities every day that week, initiating unlimited quantitative easing. The main new features of unlimited quantitative easing are as follows: First, purchase government bonds every month according to the plan, without setting any limits on how much to buy and when to buy; second, buy mortgage-backed securities (MBS) in addition to Treasury securities; third, provide assistance and loans directly to institutions, businesses and individuals.

Compared with the historical background of the last round of quantitative easing, which began in 2008, this round of easing began not with a crisis in financial institutions, but with the impact of COVID-19 on the real economy. As far as policy is concerned, quantitative easing launched by the Fed in response to the 2008 financial crisis was different from that in response to the pandemic. The four rounds of quantitative easing at that time were limited in amount, but quantitative easing under the impact of the pandemic was not limited in amount and therefore not "quantified" (Table 1).

8.2 *Fed Tapering*

8.2.1 *Review of the Previous Tapering of Asset Purchases*

After nearly five years of quantitative easing following the 2008 financial crisis, the Federal Reserve officially started tapering in December 2013.

Table 1 Quantitative easing in the United States from 2008 to 2014

	Time	*Policy content*	*Impact*
First round of quantitative easing	December 2008–April 2010	Bought a total of $1.25 trillion worth of mortgage-backed securities guaranteed by Fannie Mae and Freddie Mac, along with $175 billion in agency securities and $300 billion in Treasury securities	Eventually pushed down mortgage rates and boosted the housing market
Second round of quantitative easing	November 2010–June 2011	Bought $600 billion worth of long-term Treasury securities	The main objective was to lower interest rates on long-term bonds in order to expand domestic investment spending. Stimulated economic growth
Third round of quantitative easing	September 15, 2012–December 13, 2012	Bought $40 billion worth of MBS each month	Expansion of assets under management
Fourth round of quantitative easing	December 13, 2012–December 19, 2012	Bought $45 billion worth of Treasury securities and $40 billion in MBS each month	Expansion of assets under management

This was the first time in the Fed's history that tapering was used. The Fed officially announced tapering at the FOMC meeting held on December 18, 2013, reducing the monthly pace of its asset purchases from $85 to $75 billion. Since then, the pace of its purchases of Treasury securities had been slowing, culminating in a complete exit from QE in October 2014.

The U.S. exit from quantitative easing put pressure on the RMB. China's central bank stepped in to keep the Chinese yuan from weakening. The Chinese stock market crashed in the summer of 2015. The RMB depreciated rapidly, and the flow of foreign capital into the Chinese market slowed down. China's central bank carried out exchange rate reform. From 2014 to 2018, the central bank introduced measures such as adding a counter-cyclical factor to the central parity formation mechanism, increasing the issuance of central bank bills in offshore markets, and raising the risk reserve ratio for forward FX sales (see Table 2).

The impact of the previous tapering on the economy was transmitted and manifested in the following three aspects.

1. Changes in the overall interest rate level and the spread. Interest rates continued to rise after the previous tapering was signaled, then briefly fluctuated downward and stabilized, and rose again immediately prior to the official start of tapering. The main reason for the rise in U.S. Treasury yields during this period was that the U.S. economy was improving and real interest rates were rising. It is worth noting that the adjustment of U.S. Treasury yields in the first stage after tapering was signaled preceded the adjustment of Chinese government bond yields. The time lag between the adjustments led to a sharp narrowing of the China-U.S. yield spread between May and July 2013.
2. Risk appetite. The U.S. economy was in a sustained repair phase when the previous tapering was signaled, while the economic growth of emerging markets was under great downward pressure, so the overall risk appetite of market participants decreased.
3. U.S. dollar index. During the previous tapering, the U.S. dollar index gradually strengthened. The Fed's exit from quantitative easing (including balance sheet shrinkage, rate hike, etc.) generally led to an upswing in yields on dollar assets and the strengthening of the dollar. This attracted capital from outside the United States back to the United States and other hot money to the United States, resulting in financial turmoil in emerging markets. Each round of dollar repatriation was often accompanied by turmoil in the financial sector of emerging markets, especially those economies with large external debt and high financial leverage, such as Brazil, Argentina, Mexico, Turkey, etc.

Under the above three transmission factors, during the previous tapering, capital flows as a share of GDP in emerging economies over the same period fell sharply in 2013–2014, resulting in capital outflows. China saw a slowdown in capital inflows and then a net outflow of capital.

Table 2 The Fed's exit from quantitative easing that lasted from 2008 to 2013 and the response of China's Central Bank

Landmark event	*Time*	*Content*	*Policy choice of the People's Bank of China in the same period*
1. Scaled back purchases of Treasury securities for the first time	January 2014	Reduced MBS purchases by $5 billion; reduced purchases of Treasury securities by $5 billion	Cut interest rates and the reserve requirement ratio
2. Raised interest rates for the first time	December 2015	The FOMC announced a 25 bp interest rate hike, raising the target range for the federal funds rate range to 0.2–0.50%	Carried out exchange rate reform and devalued the RMB rapidly; cut interest rates and the reserve requirement ratio
3. Shrank the balance sheet for the first time	October 2017	Reduced reinvestment in Treasury securities by $6 billion and reinvestment in MBS by $4 billion each month	Stopped adjusting benchmark interest rates and raised the MLF rate
4. Raised interest rates for the last time	September 2018	The FOMC announced a 25 bp interest rate hike, raising the target range for the federal funds rate range to 2–2.25%	Stopped adjusting benchmark interest rates, raised the MLF rate, raised the counter-cyclical factor, and increased the issuance of central bank bills

8.2.2 *The Current Tapering of Asset Purchases*

The Fed implemented loose economic policy to boost the U.S. economy during the COVID-19 pandemic, buying Treasury securities and asset-backed securities on a large scale to provide a highly liquid development environment for financial markets. Although this move promoted the development of the U.S. economy, it also brought about extremely serious inflation, causing the value of the dollar to fall sharply, so tapering was a very important measure.

The Fed officially announced the tapering plan at its November 2021 meeting. The timing and the intensity of tapering were basically in line with market expectations. The Fed announced it would keep its benchmark interest rate unchanged and reduce the monthly pace of its Treasury purchases by $10 billion from the current $80 billion and its MBS purchases by $5 billion from the current $40 billion in November and December, and said it would adjust the pace of tapering appropriately as the economic outlook changed. This marks the beginning of the final phase of QE and the start of monetary policy normalization.

This time, the Fed provided sufficient guidance on expectations. Specifically, the journey to tapering can be divided into several stages: not mentioning tapering (April 2021 and before), discussing when to start talking about tapering (June), starting talking about tapering (July), giving advance notice on tapering (September), and officially announcing tapering (November). It took nearly half a year from the mention of tapering to its official implementation. The overall performance of U.S. financial markets was stable in this process.

What makes the current tapering special?

First, the current tapering started on a bigger scale and tapered faster. The tapering of 2013 started at reducing the monthly pace of securities purchases by $45 billion for Treasury securities and $40 billion for MBS, and the current tapering started at $80 billion for Treasury securities and $40 billion for MBS. According to the tapering roadmap set out at the November 3 meeting, the current tapering would reduce the monthly pace of purchases by an amount $5 billion higher than the previous tapering, and take eight months to complete, three months shorter than the previous tapering. According to the current tapering roadmap, when QE ends in June 2022, the Fed's asset holdings will expand to $9 trillion, twice as much as when the last round of QE ended.

Second, the causes of financial shocks are different. Unlike the financial and debt crises centered around the United States and Europe that started in 2008, the COVID-19 pandemic had a worldwide impact and mainly affected the operation of manufacturing and service industries, so it was not a financial crisis in a specific market. As a result, despite unprecedented easing in the United States, the risk of capital outflows from emerging markets was relatively small as the impact was worldwide and had not triggered large-scale capital inflows into emerging market countries. But there had been a massive flow of cheap money into U.S. stocks and commodities. Commodity prices had been rising on the back of supply chain bottlenecks and futures speculation, bringing inflation into most countries. This prompted many countries to tighten monetary policy earlier than the United States.

Third, the current tapering caused less disturbance to market sentiment, and has not yet caused any large fluctuations. Judging by the performance of capital markets after the previous tapering, the impact of the tapering phase on assets is less than that of the signaling phase.

Fourth, the current tapering may be further accelerated. With the arrival of COVID-19 medications, the threat of COVID-19 will be significantly reduced. This could be followed by an explosion of spending on services and a normalization of supply chains. The economy will improve significantly and inflationary pressures will rise again in the short term. Against this background, tapering is likely to accelerate further.

8.3 A Shift in U.S. Monetary Policy Will Bring About Serious Spillovers Around the World

The recovery of the U.S. economy, the world's largest economy, is undoubtedly conducive to global economic recovery, but the global spillovers brought about by a shift in its monetary policy cycle cannot be ignored.

First, global liquidity has tightened, and the recovery of the real economy is facing shocks. At present, global economic recovery is fragmented and not built on a solid foundation. The rise in inflation is not due to economic overheating, but more due to the delayed recovery of supply, excess liquidity and the diminishing marginal effect of stimulus. In the future, the Fed will make a shift in monetary policy and major central banks will follow suit, which will lead to a contraction in global liquidity, worsening financing conditions and active or passive deleveraging in various sectors. In this process, the refinancing cost of small and medium-sized businesses and low-rated firms will increase, which will put them at greater risk of default and bankruptcy; deficit financing will be under great pressure, and expansionary fiscal policy will be constrained; countries that have been hit hard by COVID-19 and economically fragile countries will face severe shocks. Historically, the Fed's interest rate hikes have repeatedly become the cause of financial and economic crises in other countries. A shift in U.S. monetary policy will shift adjustment costs to the world and financial risks will spill over to the real sector, which will make global economic recovery more difficult and fragmented.

Second, interest rates will rise and global financial markets are poised for a bumpy ride. With a shift in U.S. monetary policy, global liquidity has gradually gone from "extremely abundant" to "abundant" or "neutral". This is conducive to controlling inflation and asset price bubbles in the long run, but in the short term, interest rates will move upward, and global financial markets will face major adjustments and even turbulence. U.S. Treasury yields have risen rapidly since 2021, so the securities market has reacted in advance and absorbed expectations of a monetary policy shift. As there is still some way to go before a rate hike takes place, interest rates at the short end will be suppressed, while rates at the long end will rise again, and the yield curve of Treasury securities will go from "flat" to "steep". As far as the foreign exchange market is concerned, during the previous round of monetary policy normalization, the U.S. dollar index rose briefly in the taper discussion and forward guidance stage, but it was difficult to change the weakening trend. With the further confirmation of interest rate hikes, the U.S. dollar index is expected to embrace cyclical reversal opportunities, and non-U.S. currencies will be under pressure to pull back. As far as the stock market is concerned, U.S. stocks may undergo larger and longer adjustments. After a hawkish signal from the June 2021 FOMC meeting, the three major U.S. stock indexes fell, with more than 70% of stocks in the S&P 500 falling, reflecting widespread concerns among investors. In the short term, declines in U.S. stocks are relatively controllable, but as monetary policy normalization proceeds to the interest rate hike and balance sheet reduction stage, stock market risk may be sharply amplified. As far as the commodities market is concerned, a shift in U.S. monetary policy is generally bearish for commodity prices. The prices of commodities with strong financial attributes, such as gold, face the risk of substantial adjustment.

Third, international capital flows have changed direction and the "taper tantrum" may return to some emerging markets. Since April 2020, emerging markets have experienced a financial overheating driven by short-term capital inflows, currency appreciation, and rising asset prices and leverage as the United States unleashed liquidity, with cumulative net inflows into portfolio investments reaching $634.9 billion (as of May 2021). Although many emerging economies have learned the lessons of 2013 and adopted measures such as early interest rate hikes to stabilize markets as expectations of a shift in U.S. monetary policy heat up, they will inevitably face the "taper tantrum" challenges of capital outflows, currency depreciation, asset sell-offs, increased external debt pressure, and rapid deleveraging. In particular, some emerging economies, such as Argentina, Turkey and Peru, face prominent internal vulnerabilities and COVID-19 resurgences, which may increase risks and even trigger local financial crises.

8.4 Impact of the Current Tapering on China

China's economy is steadily recovering. The prudent monetary policy is flexible, precise, reasonable and appropriate, and financial risks are effectively prevented and controlled. All these have greatly enhanced the ability and resilience of China's economy to respond to the Fed's policy shift.

When the Fed exited quantitative easing during the previous tapering, China was in the stage of superposition of three periods. The size of debt and real estate bubbles were strictly controlled, and there was certain pressure on economic growth. After a rapid rise in the U.S. dollar index, China, which was pursuing exchange rate reform, also saw a depreciation of the RMB and an outflow of capital. At present, the money flowing into China during the pandemic is mainly through the purchase of yuan-denominated bonds, and is long-term funds rather than hot money. In addition, China's stable supply chain constitutes an advantage in global production and trade during the pandemic. In the case of a reduced trade deficit in services and an increase in the trade surplus, the possibility of a depreciation of the RMB and an outflow of capital is very small. Even China's success in controlling COVID-19 will attract more long-term capital inflows. Since October, the U.S. dollar index has risen above 94, but the yuan has strengthened against the trend.

On the whole, the impact of a shift in U.S. monetary policy on China's economic and financial system is limited, but a rise in international interest rates and a tightening in dollar liquidity will increase volatility and risks in China's financial markets.

First, the RMB has entered a two-way fluctuation stage following a strong performance cycle. The strong performance of the RMB exchange rate (a relative price) since May 2020 is more due to divergence between China and the rest of the world in COVID-19 control, economic recovery, monetary policy trends, and return on assets. In the future, with a shift in U.S. monetary policy, the flood of dollar liquidity will be restrained, the U.S. dollar index will rebound at a low level, the upward trend in the RMB exchange rate will moderate significantly, and two-way fluctuations will increase, so the foreign exchange management policy should be "promoting a balanced flow in both directions".

Second, cross-border capital inflows have slowed or even turned into outflows. During the previous round of monetary policy normalization by the Fed, domestic market players accelerated overseas asset allocation, direct investment in the United States surged, and enterprises adjusted their asset-liability structure by repaying dollar loans early, increasing advance payments for imports percentage-wise, etc. As a result, China saw a net capital outflow for three consecutive years, with net capital outflow from non-reserve financial accounts exceeding $410 billion in both 2015 and 2016, and the balance of foreign exchange reserves falling from a high of $4 trillion to around $3 trillion. Since the start of the pandemic, China's balance of payments has been generally stable, with large capital inflows into portfolio investments Capital inflows into portfolio investments are comprised mostly of short-term capital. With the change of monetary policy cycle, the China-U.S. yield spread has narrowed and capital inflows have slowed. This poses the risk of a short-term capital outflow, increasing volatility in China's capital markets.

Third, the cost of foreign debt is rising, and risks in the market for U.S.-dollar denominated bonds issued by Chinese-funded enterprises cannot be ignored. In recent years, with China's deep integration into global markets and capital account liberalization, the scale of foreign debt has expanded constantly. As of the first quarter of 2021, the balance of China's foreign debt stood at $2.53 trillion, of which about 48% was denominated in U.S. dollars. In particular, under the influence of such factors as interest rates, exchange rates and regulation in China and the United States, the market for U.S.-dollar denominated bonds issued by Chinese-funded enterprises has become increasingly active, and is characterized by short maturities, dominance by the real estate industry, and polarized ratings. Against the backdrop of a tightening financing environment at home, debt repayment peaks abroad, and rising financing costs, most bond issuing enterprises rely on the "borrow new funds to repay old debts" model, and the capital chains of some weak enterprises will become strained. Many holders of U.S.-dollar denominated bonds issued by Chinese-funded enterprises are also issuers of U.S.-dollar denominated bonds issued by Chinese-funded enterprises. Various institutions are connected by an intricate chain of debt, resulting in systemic debt risks.

Fourth, the impact of the shift in U.S. monetary policy on various sectors of China's macroeconomy is different. In terms of investment, the Fed's policy shift has led to the return of some capital, increased the financing costs of Chinese-funded enterprises, and intensified the game of major powers, which may adversely affect China's investment and industrial development. In terms of consumption, the Fed's shift in monetary policy has led to an increase in the price of imported goods, which has curbed household consumption to a certain extent, but a strengthening dollar has led to a relative decline in commodity prices, which will partially reduce imported inflationary pressure. In terms of exports, the Fed's policy shift means that the U.S. economy is recovering well, and its demand will drive the growth of China's foreign trade, so the overall impact is positive.

PART II

Impact of U.S. Monetary Policy Adjustments

CHAPTER 4

Direct Impact of U.S. Monetary Policy Adjustments on International Monetary Policy

From the perspective of global development practice, the rise of Keynesianism after the Great Depression of the 1930s gave prominence to aggregate demand management policies and underscored government intervention in the macroeconomy. As a result, over a long time, governments preferred fiscal policy, and finally there was a global stagflation crisis in the 1970s. After the stagflation of the 1970s, monetarism gained popularity and the monetarist school of thought emerged in theoretical circles (Liu and Zhang 2012). Theoretically, both monetarism and new Keynesianism emphasized regulating the macroeconomy by monetary policy, so governments also preferred monetary policy. Since the 1980s, there has been no revolutionary progress in macroeconomics, making it difficult to meet the challenges posed by new situations. In particular, the prevalence of monetarism seems to be closely related to the current global financial crisis. Obviously, the outbreak of the global financial and economic crisis triggered by the subprime mortgage crisis in the United States in 2007 inevitably calls for new macroeconomic theories.

L. Weiping, *American Monetary Policy Adjustment and Its Impacts*,
https://doi.org/10.1007/978-981-99-7810-6_4

1 Prominent Issues Concerning and Domestic and International Context of the Adjustment of U.S. Quantitative Easing Policy

1.1 Global Financial Crisis and Prominent Monetary Policy Issues

After the outbreak of the 2008 financial crisis in the United States, it quickly spread around the world. In order to resist the impact of the financial crisis, countries adopted strong fiscal and monetary policy measures. After July 2008, China stopped appreciating the RMB, the exchange rate remained basically stable, and the inflation rate dropped significantly. China launched a 4 trillion yuan stimulus package in late 2008 in response to the global financial crisis triggered by the U.S. subprime mortgage crisis. The move led to a dramatic expansion of credit in China in early 2009. Fiscal policy and foreign exchange policy are important tools used by China to regulate economic development. So what is the root cause of this financial crisis, how should we deal with it, and what role China's foreign exchange policy and fiscal expansion plan will play? This is one of the important studies we are facing at present.

Like many other macroeconomic policy issues in China, the inefficiency or even ineffectiveness of monetary policy at the macro level is closely related to system and mechanism problems at the meso and micro levels. Under the current market economy model, China's monetary policy system has been gradually established after years of development, and is being applied to monetary policy objectives at multiple levels, and monetary policy tools are becoming more varied, but there are still many problems and defects in the operation of the current monetary policy system.

Judging from the current implementation of China's monetary policy, not only the operation of China's monetary policy system produces very different results from the operation of the monetary policy systems of typical market economy countries, but the results of the implementation of the Chinese central bank's monetary policy are often quite different from the results expected by financial markets. This also shows that the transmission mechanism behind the operation of China's monetary policy is significantly different from the transmission mechanism that a mature market economy should have as discussed in the theory of monetary economics.

1.2 Domestic Context of the Adjustment of U.S. Quantitative Easing Policy

After the 2008 financial crisis, the U.S. economy fell into recession. The banking sector suffered a major blow and was overwhelmed, resulting in a sharp decline in credit activities, a significant reduction in financial support for the real economy, a high CPI index, a plunge in the Dow Jones Industrial Average, and even negative GDP growth in the third quarter of that year. In response to this bad situation, the Fed implemented a series of monetary policies to increase market liquidity in various ways, so as to stimulate economic recovery, stabilize the market and repair the banking system.

1.2.1 Launch of U.S. Quantitative Easing Policy

Due to the financial crisis caused by the subprime mortgage crisis, a large number of small and medium-sized businesses in the United States went bankrupt or were on the verge of collapse, which had a huge impact on the real economy of the United States. But traditional monetary policy was not the way out of the crisis as it could not cause changes in the real economy. In order to prevent the crisis from eroding the real economy and save enterprises from liquidity difficulties, the Fed made bold innovations in monetary policy: New monetary policy tools expanded the list of recipients of bailout funds from the Fed to include businesses. As a result, businesses could obtain funds directly from the Fed, thus shorten the time lag of monetary policy, improving efficiency and avoiding greater losses. In this way, monetary policy played an important role in rebuilding market confidence.

1.2.2 The Implementation of Stimulative Monetary Policy in the United States

Since 2008, the U.S. government had introduced a series of bailout measures, including increasing spending, cutting taxes, increasing transfer payments, and strengthening social safety nets; the Federal Reserve Board had introduced various forms of monetary easing, including reducing the federal funds rate to 0–0.25%, expanding asset purchases (QE series), and adjusting monetary policy targets.

Since 2008, the U.S. government had introduced a series of bailout measures, including increasing spending (including transfer payments), cutting taxes, and strengthening social safety nets; the Fed had introduced various forms of monetary easing, including reducing the federal funds rate to 0–0.25%, expanding asset purchases (QE series), and adjusting monetary policy targets. All but the richest 20% of Americans benefited from these policies. Among them, the poorest 60% of the population saw their share of total income change from a decline in 1999–2007 to an increase, while the income share of the richest 20% of the population shifted from an increase to a decrease.

Obviously, the coordination of fiscal policy and monetary policy is very conducive to narrowing disparities in income and wealth. Since distributive disparities are usually addressed only as a social problem, a successful inclusion in the target list of economic governance would probably require significant advances in economic theory unless the distributive problem is so severe that it matches or exceeds, for example, the situation in the Great Depression of 1929 (Table 1).

U.S. monetary policy, in fact, did not play a substantial role in 2007–2008: In 2008, U.S. GDP growth was only 0.4%, the CPI was 0.1%, and the unemployment rate at the beginning of the year was 4.9%. The unemployment rate rose to 7.2% at the end of 2008. The employment situation was very grim (Zhang and Song 2011). Undoubtedly, this marked the official start of quantitative easing by the Federal Reserve, and next more aggressive financial measures and monetary policy measures would follow.

March 2009, the Dow Jones Industrial Average bottomed out. In the four quarters, U.S. GDP grew at an annualized pace of −6.4%, −0.7%, 2.2% and 5.7% respectively, and the CPI rose −0.4%, indicating that signs of economic recovery in the United States were beginning to appear, but U.S. GDP growth for the whole year was −2.4%. The unemployment rate continued to rise to 9.3% (Cheng 2011). Quantitative easing led to more obvious signs of economic recovery in 2010 in the United States. The CPI rose 1.5% and GDP grew by 2.9% in 2009. Innovative monetary policy proved to be a key factor in finding a way out of the subprime mortgage crisis.

1.3 International Context of the Adjustment of U.S. Quantitative Easing Policy

1.3.1 Japan's Monetary Policy

The global financial crisis triggered by the U.S. subprime mortgage crisis affected the Japanese economy mainly through the credit and trade channels. In the face of the grim situation of the financial crisis, since 2007, the

Table 1 Monetary policy tools of the Federal Reserve in 2007–2008

Name	*Start time*	*End time*	*Object*	*Content*
Term Auction Facility (TAF)	2007.12.12	2010.3.8	Depository institutions	Under a single-price auction system for loans, banks bidding above the stop-out rate would receive all Fed loans
Primary Dealer Credit Facility (PDCF)	2008.3.17	2010.2.1	Primary dealers	Allow them to borrow from the Federal Reserve through the discount window
Asset-Backed Commercial Paper Money Market Fund (AMLF)	2008.9.19	–	Depository institutions and bank holding companies	Extend non-recourse loans at the discount rate to them to finance their purchases of commercial paper from money market mutual funds
Money Market Investor Funding Facility (MMIFF)	2008.9.22	2010.2.1	Money market mutual funds and other investors	Inject liquidity into shrinking money markets
Commercial Paper Funding Facility (CPFF)	2008.10.27	2010.2.1	Commercial banks, large enterprises and other businesses	The CPFF purchased commercial paper directly from eligible issuers of commercial paper, thus restoring the financing function of the commercial paper market
Term Asset-Backed Securities Loan Facility (TALF)	2008.11.25	–	Holders of asset-backed securities backed by consumer loans and small business loans	Financial institutions applied to the Federal Reserve for loans on securities backed by newly and recently originated consumer or small and medium-sized business loans

Source Zhang and Song (2011)

Bank of Japan had announced a large-scale monetary policy with targeted relief measures.

Inject massive amounts of cash into the financial system through multiple channels to make it more resilient to crises. First, capital injection through open market operations. On October 9, 2008, the Bank of Japan made a capital injection of 4 trillion yen. Second, innovation in monetary policy. First, the Bank of Japan tried to prevent the spread of the credit crunch by subscribing for subprime loans or subordinated bonds issued by financial institutions since the start of financial crisis to directly provide capital to banking financial institutions, which strengthened the core capital and supplementary capital of Japanese financial institutions through capital injections. Second, by acquiring shares of Japanese companies in which the Bank of Japan had a large shareholding, the bank's capital adequacy ratio would decline in the event of a sharp decline in corporate yields.

Adjust financing relations to avoid a vicious cycle between banks, financial institutions and enterprises. There was a stable and close relationship between Japanese companies and banks. Japanese companies were heavily dependent on Japanese banks for both indirect and direct financing. Banks not only provided loans to companies, but also held large amounts of commercial paper and corporate stock, so when the liquidity of Japanese banks was insufficient, companies would be unable to obtain funds from banking and financial institutions. Accordingly, the Bank of Japan implemented the following monetary policy.

Since January 2009, the Bank of Japan (BOJ) had acquired a large number of corporate notes from companies rated A or above to directly provide funds to companies, so as to meet the financing needs of companies. In February of the same year, the Bank of Japan announced a relaxation of the guarantee conditions for corporate bonds and asset-backed corporate notes.

The balance of Japan's M2 increased by 3.24% year-over-year after innovation in monetary policy. GDP grew by 4.22% year-over-year in the first quarter of 2010, breaking through the awkward situation of negative growth that had lasted for seven consecutive quarters. But the price index continued to fall as deflation had been plaguing the Japanese economy, which remained weak and lacked momentum for growth.

1.3.2 Monetary Policy in the Euro Area

On October 15, 2008, the ECB issued an emergency "unlimited capital injection plan" to ease the liquidity strains in financial markets. On the same day, the Bank of England, the ECB and the Swiss National Bank announced that they would jointly inject \$254 billion into European countries and major financial institutions. Meanwhile, the ECB provided \$170.9 billion in refinancing loans with seven-day maturities at an interest rate of 2.277% to banking institutions. The ECB also adopted other monetary policies to inject liquidity into the market (Zhang and Song 2011).

Cut interest rates and inject liquidity into the market through open market operations and secondary financing. Since the ECB had been cautious in its interest rate policy and had long pursued a prudent monetary policy with the primary goal of controlling inflation, it did not immediately cut interest rates after the outbreak of the financial crisis. However, as pressure from the crisis intensified, in May 2009, the ECB introduced a low interest rate policy of 1%, which lasted until September of the same year when the European economy improved slightly. But the 16 countries in the euro area still maintained a low interest rate policy. In terms of open market operations and refinancing, the ECB moderately extended the average maturity of open market operations and added longer-term refinancing operations with a maturity of three months and six months to stabilize market interest rates and increase the supply of market liquidity.

Innovate new policy tools and strengthen international coordination of monetary policies. After the subprime mortgage crisis occurred, in addition to traditional monetary policy measures, the ECB also tried innovative monetary policy transmission tools. The ECB and the Federal Reserve jointly conducted a 7-day and 28-day TAF auction and swap respectively. This move not only provided sufficient liquidity support to European banking and financial institutions, but also defused the first recession in the euro area since its creation by innovating in monetary policy. However, due to interference from a conservative interest rate policy, the effect of the new policy was not significant.

In order to avoid excessive inflation, the ECB was cautious about lowering the interest rate. In July 2008, the ECB raised the refinancing rate again. The CPI index rose first and then fell, the Financial Times 100 Index plunged, and year-over-year GDP growth was negative. Year-over-year GDP growth in the four quarters of 2009 was −5.18%, −4.91%, −

4.09% and −2.11%, respectively, and it was only in the first quarter of 2010 that the GDP of the euro area finally achieved a positive growth of 0.64%. Overall, the euro area economy remained in a slow recovery.

1.3.3 China's Monetary Policy

As can be seen from the specific policies of the United States, the euro area and Japan, they all adopted active monetary policies, but their priorities were different. The United States prioritized innovation in monetary policy tools, Japan had a monetary policy based primarily on the close relationship between banks and companies, and the euro area focused on international coordination of monetary policies. China's monetary policy was still based on the use of traditional policy tools to increase market liquidity. Since 2000, the global economy had recovered in an all-round way. China's economy was developing well and the U.S. economy was recovering actively, but the economies of the euro area and Japan were still recovering slowly. It can be seen that the implementation of monetary policy should be based on national realities, the level of economic development, regional differences, and the level of development of financial markets. China should learn from other countries' innovations in monetary policy and at the same time follow the path of monetary policy with Chinese characteristics.

2 Transmission Mechanism of U.S. Monetary Policy Adjustments and Its Impact on International Monetary Policy

2.1 Choice of Tools and Transmission Mechanism of U.S. Monetary Policy

The intermediate target of monetary policy refers to the part that the central bank first influences when implementing monetary policy, such as interest rates or the supply of money. By influencing these variables, the central bank's policy indirectly influences the ultimate target variables such as output, employment, prices, and balance of payments. For convenience of presentation, unless otherwise specified, monetary policy targets and tools hereinafter refer to intermediate targets and tools for monetary policy.

2.1.1 *The Choice of Monetary Policy Tools Under the Financial Structure of the United States in Different Periods*

Interest rate targets were achieved through open market operations in the period from the 1940s to the early 1950s. In 1941, in order to finance the war effort, the Fed basically adopted a loose monetary policy. Although the target tool was to keep interest rates steady and low, this was done primarily through open market operations. This choice of monetary policy was related to the level of financial development in the United States at that time. Open market operations become the most realistic and effective influence tool.

Back then, the three-month Treasury bill rate was 0.375% and the long-term Treasury bond rate was 2.4%. Whenever rates rose above that level and Treasury prices fell, the Fed would make open market purchases to force rates down. Although this policy had some success, inflation occurred in the United States after the outbreak of the Korean War in 1950. In March 1951, the Fed and the Treasury reached a "unanimous agreement" to abolish the practice of pegging interest rates, and the Fed promised not to let interest rates rise sharply (Zhang 2001).

Money supply control for target changes in the period from the 1950s to the 1970s. During this period, with the development of U.S. financial markets, the U.S. monetary authorities began to look for other monetary policy targets. In the 1950s, the Fed used intermediate targets such as net free reserves, the three-month Treasury bill rate, and monetary aggregate M1, and decided the importance of target controls in this order. The results show that the Fed controlled the first two targets well, and its control over the monetary aggregate began to weaken. Failure in monetary management led to three economic crises in the first 10 years.

Monetary policy dominated by interest rate policy in the period from 1980 to 2008. This period was a period of prosperity in which U.S. financial markets were thriving, with the rapid expansion of financial assets and frequent innovation in financial institutions and financial instruments. After the 1980s, the development of U.S. financial markets, especially the deregulation of emerging financial institutions, led to the gradual rise of investment-oriented financial institutions as dominant players in the financial markets. Such institutions often used leverage to make money by constantly creating new financial derivatives. This made them very sensitive to interest rates. In line with this, the Fed has refocused its policy options on interest rates, this time not as a target but as a tool of regulation. Interest rates and Treasury prices became the benchmark variables of all financial instruments. The effectiveness of interest rate policy was unprecedentedly unleashed at this stage.

Low interest rates combined with quantitative easing were used in the period from 2008 to the present. With the development of U.S. financial markets, due to the high credit ratings of U.S. Treasury securities, robust liquidity in the Treasury market, and the abundance of derivative financial products related to U.S. Treasury securities, U.S. Treasury yields had come to be seen by market participants as risk-free benchmark interest rates and had developed into pricing benchmarks in the financial markets. In its response to the financial crisis, the Fed not only continued to use its proven interest rate tool, but also carried out bold unconventional operations—quantitative easing and Operation Twist—on Treasury securities that affected the level of long-term interest rates. These policy tools were designed to increase the monetary base, inject liquidity and encourage lending by buying back Treasury securities or changing the term structure for Treasury securities.

2.1.2 Monetary Policy Transmission Under the U.S. Financial Structure in Different Periods

Monetary policy in the United States comprises mainly three magic weapons: adjusting the required reserve ratio, rediscount policy and open market operations. While the United States hasn't finally abandoned the required reserve ratio so far, the Fed has largely abandoned it as a policy tool. After the creation of the Fed in 1913, discount window lending was the main tool to help member banks respond to emergencies and implement monetary policy, primarily by discounting commercial paper. By adjusting the rediscount rate, it could affect how much commercial banks paid to borrow from the Fed, and thus the total amount of credit in the economy. Now, instead of lending to banks through rediscounting, the Fed lends directly to banks. Open market operations have become the Fed's primary monetary policy tool. When the economy overheats and inflationary pressure increases, the Fed will sell bonds through open market operations to push down bond prices and raise interest rates to curb the overheated economy.

The transmission mechanism of monetary policy determines the intermediate target and operational target of monetary policy. The practice of monetary policy in the United States for more than 60 years has proved that the transmission mechanism of the Fed's monetary policy has gone through the process from conducting open market operations

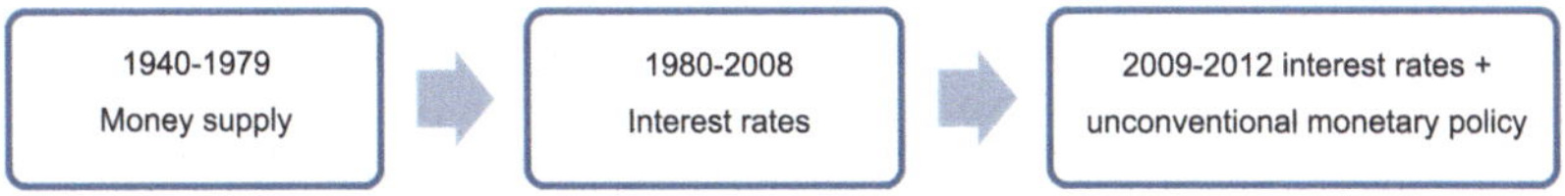

Fig. 1 Evolution of U.S. monetary policy tools (*Source* Compiled and produced by the author based on data relating to the choice of monetary policy tools under the U.S. financial structure in different periods)

to control the money supply, to interest rate adjustment, and finally to interest rates and unconventional money supply. Accordingly, the objectives of monetary policy have changed. At present, U.S. monetary policy mainly affects the demand for goods and services by businesses and individuals by affecting real interest rates, which in turn changes the demand for goods and services by businesses and individuals, ultimately affecting spending, employment, and inflation (Peng and Shi 2007) (Fig. 1).

The Fed's choice of monetary policy transmission mechanism in different periods was restricted by the economic conditions at that time, especially by the financial market conditions at that time. Before the 1980s, the financial markets were underdeveloped and financial innovation was rare, so the money supply became the most effective policy tool choice, and interest rate adjustments could hardly have an effect (Zhang 2001). After the 1980s, massive financial innovation and financial markets with greater depth and breadth not only made the money supply difficult to control, but also made financial markets more sensitive to interest rate policies, so interest rate adjustments could play a bigger role.

Basically, every transmission mechanism of monetary policy cannot work without the support of the U.S. financial structure (financial institutions, financial markets and financial instruments) during the same period.

Exchange rate levels can change through the influence of monetary policy and further affect export and import performance. However, as the dollar establishes itself as an international safe-haven asset, the direction of such influence is often influenced by other factors. Generally speaking, expansionary monetary policy devalues the currency and effectively improves the current account, generating net exports and stimulating foreign consumption and domestic production and investment.

An increase in the money supply will help create wealth effects, improve business cash flow, and increase consumption and investment by households and firms through changes in nominal perception. Changes in the money supply will also lead to changes in the price level. Investors and consumers will change their investment and consumption behavior according to their judgment on future prices. In this way, the ultimate target of influencing the direction of the economy is achieved.

The theory of the credit school holds that monetary policy can play a role by influencing the lending behavior of banks and the asset and liability position of businesses. Bank credit works mainly by influencing the financing behavior of large and medium-sized businesses. For example, under an expansionary monetary policy, an increase in bank lending will lead to an increase in business investment activity; under an expansionary monetary policy, improvements to balance sheets will lead to an increase in investment demand.

2.2 *Spillovers of the U.S. Exit from QE and Characteristics of the Mechanism for the Transmission Thereof*

The impact of the U.S. exit from QE on the global economy is mainly felt at the level of the real economy and finance. At the level of the real economy: First, the condition for the United States to exit quantitative easing was the steady recovery of the U.S. economy, and the rise in U.S. demand was conducive to the growth of other countries' foreign trade. Second, the exit from QE would reduce the supply of U.S. dollars, or trigger a decline in the price of international commodities denominated in U.S. dollars, which would ease global imported inflationary pressure. At the level of finance: First, the exit from QE would reduce the supply of U.S. dollars, and countries (other than the United States) would face certain depreciation pressure and capital outflow pressure. Second, judging from the current situation, with the steady recovery of the U.S. economy, it was highly likely that the Federal Reserve would raise interest rates in 2015; a narrowing of yield spreads between the United States and other countries would intensify the downward pressure on non-U.S. dollar currencies and capital outflow pressure, thus increasing liquidity pressure in global financial markets and making it more difficult for monetary authorities in various countries to regulate in the process of economic restructuring (Fig. 2).

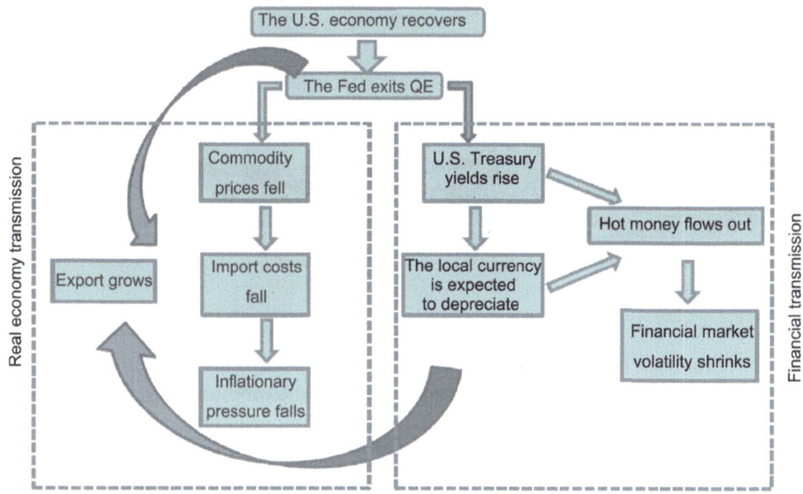

Fig. 2 Spillovers of the exit from QE—transmission mechanism (*Source* Compiled and produced by the author based on data relating to the characteristics of the mechanism for the transmission of the spillovers of the U.S. exit from QE 2008–2015)

2.2.1 *Spillovers of the Exit from QE—Affecting the Stability of Emerging Market Currencies*

The currencies of some emerging economies depreciated significantly against the U.S. dollar. When the Fed launched QE in 2008, it caused huge disruption to the exchange rates of emerging market currencies against the U.S. dollar (Fig. 3).

After 2011, the dollar gradually strengthened as the U.S. economy recovered. In May 2013, Bernanke, former chairman of the Federal Reserve, signaled withdrawal from QE, and the exchange rates of emerging market currencies against the U.S. dollar fluctuated sharply again. In early 2014, the Fed's tapering kicked off, and emerging market currencies depreciated sharply again in January. The U.S. dollar index had weakened since February, and emerging market currencies had rebounded against the U.S. dollar (Fig. 4).

From an objective point of view, there were many factors that led to fluctuations in the exchange rates of emerging market currencies, such as structural contradictions in the economy and rising downside risks to the economy. Changes in the Fed's monetary policy were only one of the factors.

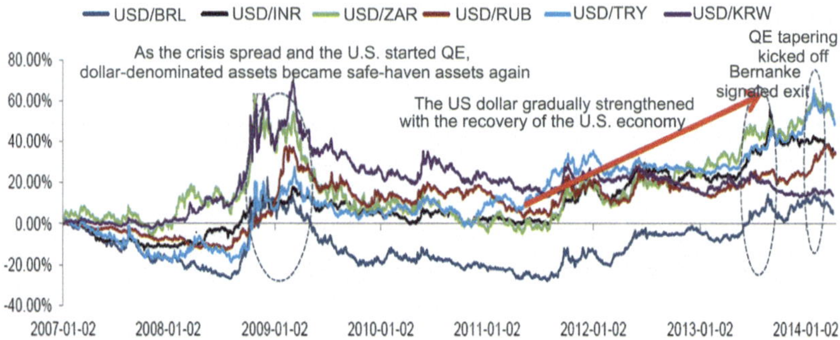

Fig. 3 Changes in the exchange rates of some emerging market currencies (with January 2, 2007 as the benchmark) (*Source* Compiled and produced by the author based on data relating to changes in the exchange rates of emerging market currencies against the U.S. dollar after the Fed launched QE in 2008)

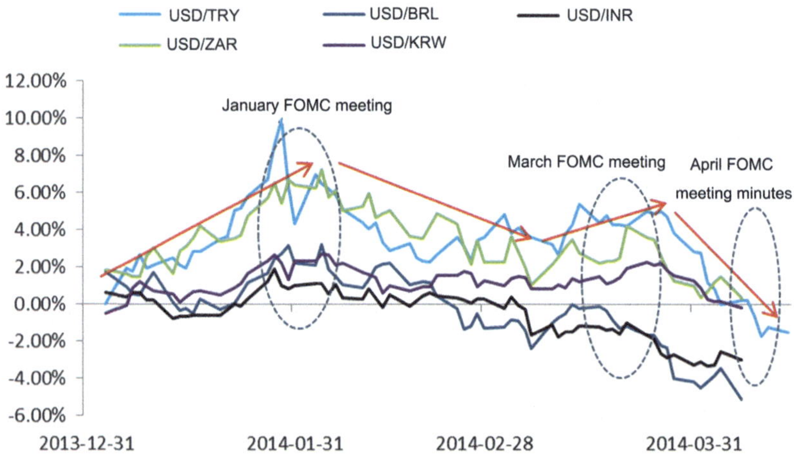

Fig. 4 Changes in the exchange rates of some emerging market currencies (with December 31, 2013 as the benchmark) (*Source* Compiled and produced by the author based on data relating to changes in the exchange rates of emerging market currencies against the U.S. dollar after the Fed launched QE 2013–2014)

2.2.2 *Spillovers of the Exit from QE—Affecting Sharp Fluctuations in Commodity Prices*

The launch and end of QE at each stage have been accompanied by fluctuations in commodity prices. The launch of QE by the Fed and the significant increase in fiscal deficits after the financial crisis have increased the supply of dollars worldwide. Commodities are priced in dollars, and the supply of dollars has actually grown faster than the production of commodities, so commodity prices have risen.

There are many factors affecting commodity prices. In recent years, rising demand for commodities from emerging markets and other factors have also had a great impact on commodity prices. The launch and end of previous QE programs have been accompanied by a significant rise or fall in commodity prices (Fig. 5). The reduction in Treasury purchases under QE3 has also led to a decline in commodity prices. The analysis shows that the quantitative easing policy and fiscal policy of the United States are important factors affecting international commodity prices.

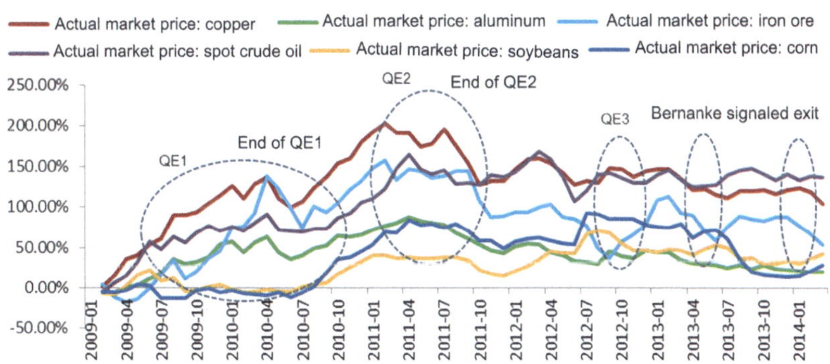

Fig. 5 IMF actual market prices of commodities (*Source* Compiled and produced by the author based on IMF data on the impact of the Fed's QE on commodity price fluctuations from 2009 to 2014)

3 Effects of U.S. Quantitative Easing Policy Adjustments on International Monetary Policy

3.1 Effects of U.S. Quantitative Easing Policy Adjustments on Global Financial Markets

The most typical example of the evolution of the transmission mechanism of global monetary policy under the financial crisis is the quantitative easing (QE) policy implemented by the United States. Since November 2008, the Fed has launched three rounds of quantitative easing (QE) and one Operation Twist, which effectively prevented the crisis from spreading and stimulated the recovery of the U.S. economy, but also caused a huge impact on global financial markets. The impact was reflected in a surge in asset prices around the world, with stock and commodity prices rising sharply around the world, and asset bubbles and inflation created in emerging markets.

3.1.1 Implementation and Effect of QE Policy Since November 2008

The background of the Fed's QE policy. In 2008, the subprime mortgage crisis broke out in the United States. The financial markets of Europe, the United States and other developed countries fluctuated sharply. Liquidity in global financial markets dried up rapidly. A large number of financial institutions including Lehman Brothers collapsed. The U.S. subprime crisis morphed into a global financial crisis and economic crisis. In response to the crisis, Bernanke, then chairman of the Federal Reserve, launched a series of extraordinary monetary policies, including an emergency move to cut interest rates to zero, three rounds of quantitative easing (QE), and Operation Twist (OT) (Table 2).

1. Chronicle of the Fed's QE and OT

See Table 3.

2. QE had a huge impact on global financial markets

Stock markets in developed countries rose sharply, and stock markets in emerging markets were indirectly affected. The massive amount of money released by QE and improved economic expectations greatly boosted stock markets in the United States, Europe, Japan and other developed countries. During the three rounds of QE, stock markets in developed countries rose sharply, with U.S. stocks hitting record highs. Emerging market countries performed strongly in the crisis. In the early stages

Table 2 The Fed's extraordinary implementation of three consecutive rounds of Quantitative Easing (QE)

Time	*Event*
QE1 2008.11–2010.3	Over 17 months, the Fed bought $1,425 trillion in mortgage-backed securities and $300 billion in long-term Treasury securities, injecting $1,725 trillion in liquidity. It effectively contained the spread and expansion of systemic risks
QE2 2010.11–2011.6	Half a year after QE1 ended, the U.S. economy did not pick up, although financial markets stabilized. In response, the Fed decided to buy $75 billion in assets every month for a total of $600 billion over an 8-month period
Operation Twist 2011.9–2012.12	With inflation rising and the economy sluggish, the Fed decided to buy long-term Treasury securities to replace short-term ones, so as to inject liquidity without adding to the money supply. A total of $667 billion were "twisted"
QE3 2012.9–2014.11	To further stimulate economic growth, the Fed had bought $85 billion in assets a month since September 2012, including $40 billion in MBS and $45 billion in Treasury securities. The purchase ended in December 2013, lasting for 15 months

Source Compiled and produced by the author based on data relating to the time and events of the Fed's unconventional implementation of three consecutive rounds of QE

of QE (first and second rounds), a large amount of dollars flowed into emerging market countries, causing their stock markets to rise sharply. But since Operation Twist and the third round of QE, as the structural problems of emerging markets were exposed, their stock markets had begun to decline.

3.1.2 The Course and Impact of the Exit from QE Since June 2013

With the U.S. economy recovering, unemployment falling below 7% and inflation moderating, Bernanke first mooted the idea of unwinding QE in June 2013, throwing markets into turmoil. Affected by global capital flows into European and U.S. markets, emerging market stocks fell even more. In July of the same year, Bernanke said there was no timetable for ending QE, which soothed markets.[1]

[1] Source: Wall Street Pay Raise Not Equivalent to U.S. Economic Recovery, People's Daily, March 19, 2014. http://news.xinhuanet.com/2014-03/19/c126285464.htm.

Table 3 Chronicle of the Fed's QE and OT

Time	*Event*
2008/11/25	The Fed announced the purchase of \$100 billion of agency debt and \$500 billion of MBS
2009/3/18	The Fed announced that it would expand its MBS purchases to \$1.25 trillion, raise the cap for agency debt to \$200 billion, and purchase up to \$300 billion of long-term Treasury securities
2010/3/21	QE1 ended
2010/8/27	Bernanke floated possibility of QE2
2010/11/3	The Fed announced the \$600 billion QE2
2011/6/30	QE2 ended
2011/9/21	The Fed announced Operation Twist which ran through the second quarter of 2012
2012/6/20	The Fed announced an extension of Operation Twist through the end of 2012
2012/9/13	The Fed announced the \$40 billion per month QE3, and continued Operation Twist through the end of the year
2012/12/12	The Fed announced that after Operation Twist expired, it would expand asset purchases to maintain total asset purchases at \$85 billion per month

Source Compiled and produced by the author based on data relating to the time and events of the chronicle of the Fed's QE and OT

Six months later, the Fed decided to cut its monthly asset purchases under QE3 on December 19, 2013, and then the Fed double the pace of tapering on January 29 and March 19, 2014, respectively. The Fed's three cuts, which reduced its monthly asset purchases from \$85 billion to \$55 billion, caused significant fluctuations in global financial markets.[2]

[2] Source: Review of the Federal Reserve's Quantitative Easing Policy, financial.net.cn, December 19, 2013. http://forex.xinhua08.com/a/20131219/1286967.shtml?f=arelated.

In terms of the impact on markets, the day the exit plan was first announced, European, American, Japanese and emerging market stocks fell sharply. Affected by expectations, the impact of the second and third exits was significantly smaller than the first.

As a result of the QE exit, global liquidity tightened, resulting in higher interest rates and bond yields. When Bernanke first proposed withdrawing QE, long-term bond yields in Europe, the United States, Japan and emerging markets rose sharply. When QE was substantially withdrawn, bond yields did not rise significantly. The news of the QE exit had no significant impact on LIBOR, but it had a psychological impact on SHIBOR.

Affected by QE withdrawal, the U.S. dollar index rose significantly, while gold and oil prices fell sharply. Exchange rates fluctuated widely. Affected by capital outflows, exchange rates in the "Fragile Five" (Brazil, Indonesia, India, Turkey and South Africa) and countries such as Argentina and Turkey fell sharply, causing severe turmoil in markets.

Analysis of the conditions for the Fed's QE exit: the only "threshold" for the Fed to taper QE3 asset purchases was unemployment falling to 7%, the "threshold" of the Fed's zero interest rate policy. The Fed's forward guidance on interest rates included: unemployment falling to 6.5%, and a 2% inflation target (the CPI is 2% with a margin of error of plus or minus 0.5%). The March 2014 FOMC meeting adjusted the Fed's forward guidance on interest rates: from anchoring the 6.5% unemployment rate to anchoring qualitative guidance that took into account multiple economic indicators such as employment, inflation and financial conditions.

The market consensus was that the stance of monetary policy prior to Yellen's appointment was dovish. The March FOMC meeting adjusted the forward guidance on short-term interest rates, a move that was supposed to be dovish, until Yellen said at a press conference that if the economy performed as the Fed expected, the Fed would buy debt in the fall, perhaps in about six months. The expression exceeded market expectations and the market reacted. Fed Chair Janet Yellen followed in the footsteps of former Fed Chair Ben Bernanke. We believe that if the U.S. economy continues its recovery, it is highly likely that the Fed will continue to cut QE by $10 billion per FOMC meeting. The QE3 asset purchase program may end in 2014.

3.1.3 *Review of the Background of the Fed's Exit from QE*

As the effects of the financial crisis faded and the U.S. economy entered a substantial recovery phase, the Fed had repeatedly signaled to markets that it would start to consider an exit from its unconventional monetary policy. As early as 2012, markets expected the Fed to exit QE when the economy picked up, but due to the subsequent sluggish economic growth in the United States, the Fed decided to extend OT and launch QE3 in 2012.

It was not until June 19, 2013 that Bernanke put forward a timetable for ending QE for the first time after the FOMC meeting (the withdrawal of QE could begin as early as the second half of 2013 when the unemployment rate was close to 7%). This move caused big swings in markets. Then on July 10 Bernanke reassured markets by publicly stating that there was no timetable for ending QE.

On December 19, 2013, the FOMC meeting unexpectedly decided to cut QE by $10 billion beginning in January 2014, officially starting the exit from QE (Table 4).

3.1.4 *Progress of the Fed's Exit from QE and the Whole Process of the QE Exit*

In May 2013, the former chairman of the Federal Reserve signaled an exit; the December 2013 FOMC Meeting decided to reduce bond purchases by $$10 billion to $75 billion/month, beginning in January 2014; the January FOMC meeting decided to further reduce bond purchases by $10 billion to $65 billion/month; the March 2014 FOMC meeting decided to further reduce bond purchases by $10 billion to $55 billion/month.[3]

3.1.5 *Preparation and Incremental Exit Phase*

Preparation for exit (May 2013–December 2013): From May 2013, when former Fed Chairman Ben Bernanke gave the first exit signal, to December 2014, when the FOMC meeting finally decided to taper the asset purchase program QE3, the Fed gave markets sufficient preparation time to build up expectations of QE reduction through information transmission and communication.

Incremental exit (January 2014 to the third and fourth quarters of 2014): As the employment situation improved, former Fed Chairman Ben Bernanke said that there was about an 80% chance that the FOMC

[3] Relevant data on the Federal Reserve's website.

Table 4 Review of the background of the Fed's exit from QE

Background	*Review*
Background 1 The U.S. economy had recovered substantially	In 2013, the U.S. economy continued to recover, with GDP increasing 1.9% for the full year and at an annual rate of 4.1% in the third quarter, showing strong momentum. The PMI remained above 50%. Economic recovery set the stage for a QE exit
Background 2 Employment improved	Since 2011, the employment situation in the United States had been improving, with the unemployment rate falling from 10% in 2009 to below 7% at present, in line with the Fed's policy target, thus starting the exit from QE
Background 3 Inflation was stable	QE succeeded in pulling the United States out of deflation in 2009, and kept inflation moderate except for the high inflation before Operation Twist in 2011, ensuring that the Fed could exit QE smoothly while keeping interest rates near zero
Background 4 The Fed's balance sheet could not expand indefinitely	Since the crisis began in 2007, the Fed had expanded its balance sheet by 4.8 times through a series of bailouts and QE. The Fed could not expand its balance sheet forever and needed to exit QE in due course

Source Compiled and produced based on data relating to the review of the background of the Fed's exit from QE

meeting would begin tapering the asset purchase program by the end of 2013. The U.S. unemployment rate fell to 7% in November 2013. In January 2014, the Fed announced it would reduce its asset purchases to $10 billion a month. As of April 2014, the Fed's asset purchase program was buying $55 billion in long-term Treasury securities and asset-backed securities each month. If the Fed's future U.S. economic data come in line with expectations, the Fed could end asset purchases by the end of 2014.

3.1.6 Reverse Operation and Stock Exit Stage

Reverse operation (late 2014 or early 2015 to mid-2015): Before the QE stock exit, the Fed will likely reverse QE2 by selling some of its holdings of long-term Treasury bonds and buying an equal amount of short-term Treasury bonds. The reverse operation should occur in the fourth quarter of 2014 or the first quarter of 2015 and last for no more than six months.

Stock exit and interest rate hikes (after the third quarter of 2015): After the reverse operation, if the U.S. economic recovery shows no obvious signs of slowing down, employment is relatively full and credit growth is still high, we believe that the Fed will first raise the required reserve ratio to achieve a mild monetary tightening, and finally, the Fed will raise the federal funds rate and gradually sell off some of its holdings of Treasury securities and MBS. The Fed is likely to suffer losses from falling prices in the sale process. Given the large amount of Treasuries and MBS currently held by the Fed, we expect the Fed to sell only a portion of the bonds and hold the rest to maturity. That would lessen the impact on the bond market, but it would also protect the Fed from excessive losses. The pace of Fed rate hikes and bond sales depends heavily on the stability of the U.S. economic recovery, employment and inflation.

3.2 Impact of the U.S. Exit from Quantitative Easing on Global Financial Markets

See Table 5.

3.2.1 Impact of the Fed's Exit from QE on Global Stock Markets

Developed countries. In the short term, the QE exit will reduce the supply of funds in markets, leading to declines in European and U.S. stock markets. This was particularly evident when Bernanke first put forward a timetable for ending QE in June 2013 and bond purchases were scaled back for the first time in December 2013. In the long run, the QE exit will push up U.S. dollar exchange rates and interest rates, causing global funds to flow back to U.S. markets, which has a positive effect on pushing up U.S. stock markets; European stock markets are highly correlated with U.S. stock markets, and the growth of the U.S. economy will also have an income effect on the European economy, so the QE exit will also have a positive effect on European stock markets in the long run. Judging from the date when the news of QE was released, there was uncertainty about the degree and direction of volatility in European and U.S. stock

Table 5 Impact of the QE exit on global financial markets

QE exit event	*Impact on global financial markets*
1. Global stock markets fluctuated sharply	The news of the QE exit pushed global stock markets down sharply, while Bernanke's reassurance to markets pushed stock markets back up. Stock markets in developed countries rebounded as a whole, while emerging markets fluctuated downward (except India)
2. Global foreign exchange markets fluctuated sharply	The news of the QE exit caused a tightening of funds, which pushed up bond yields on the day Pushed global interest rates up
3. The commodities bull market and the gold bull market ended	Prices plunged sharply, oil prices fluctuated sharply, and mineral prices faced downward pressure
4. Global foreign exchange markets fluctuated sharply	The news of the QE exit caused sharp fluctuations in the exchange rates of various currencies. The U.S. dollar index surged, the euro and the yen fell accordingly, emerging market countries were in financial turmoil, and countries like Argentina, Turkey, Ukraine and Indonesia saw a rapid devaluation of their currencies

Source Compiled and produced by the author based on data relating to the impact of the Fed's exit from QE on global financial markets

markets. This was because developed European and American markets had a more rational expectation mechanism, and the different strength of policy launches and the direction of deviation from expectations determined stock market volatility on that day. After the launch of Abenomics, the Japanese stock market developed independently of European and U.S. stock markets. The impact of the QE exit on the Japanese stock market was indirect or covered by Japan's own QE policy changes.

Emerging markets. The QE exit will lead to an acceleration of capital outflows from emerging markets, which coupled with certain bubble factors in the early stage will trigger a sharp decline in emerging market stocks. This was evident when Bernanke first put forward a timetable for ending QE and bond purchases were scaled back for the first time. The economic recovery in Europe and the United States has a positive effect on emerging markets, but in the short to medium term, the negative effects of capital outflows are negligible. Performance varies greatly across emerging market stocks. There are many emerging economies, facing different political and economic environments. Some have serious economic structural problems, some have "double deficits", some are politically unstable, and some still maintain high competitiveness. Their stock markets also head in different directions. The impact of the U.S. exit from QE on the Chinese stock market is more psychological. The announcement of the QE exit will not immediately lead to capital outflows, but it still causes significant fluctuations in A-shares.

3.2.2 Spillovers of the QE Exit—International Capital Flows

International capital flows and the prices of other currencies against the U.S. dollar are two sides of the coin. At the end of 2013, by observing the capital flows in three emerging markets, India, China Taiwan and South Korea, it was found that after Fed Chairman Bernanke announced the exit signal, capital outflows from the three countries/regions accelerated. In early 2014, after the Fed started QE3 tapering, the negative impact on the above countries/regions eased (Fig. 6).

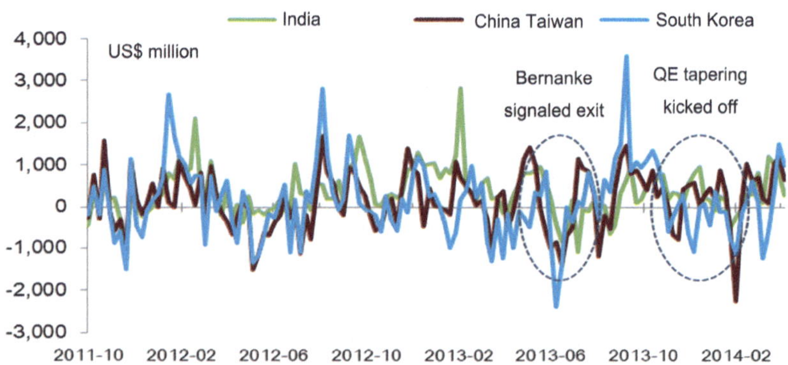

Fig. 6 Capital flows in some emerging markets (*Source* Compiled and produced by the author based on data relating to the impact of the Fed's exit from QE [October 2011–February 2014] on global financial markets)

3.3 *Impact of U.S. Quantitative Easing on the Monetary Policy of Typical Market Economy Countries*

After the outbreak of the subprime mortgage crisis, many Chinese and foreign scholars attributed the crisis to the Fed's low interest rate policy. By canvassing the Fed's monetary policy from 2001 to 2008, this study draws the following conclusions: The Fed is "helpless", and under the Fed's existing monetary policy target system, the Fed is unable to make a better choice. In a monetary policy system with a single operational target (the federal funds rate) such as the Federal Reserve, it is difficult to balance the ultimate targets of boosting output growth and curbing inflation. Even if the two ultimate targets of output growth and inflation are considered at the same time, the targets of financial assets and property prices have to be ignored.

The Fed's monetary policy can be divided into two stages with June 2004 as the dividing point. The first stage: The U.S. economy was at a low ebb throughout this period. The Fed's low interest rate policy was a reasonable response to real economic fluctuations. From the beginning of 2001 to June 2004, the Fed reduced the federal funds rate from 6.50% to 1.00%. By 2004, the U.S. economy was beginning to show signs of recovery. It was also in 2004 that the housing and subordinated debt bubbles just started to expand. The second stage: During this period, U.S. housing prices and subordinated debt prices soared to their peaks, and GDP growth continued but slowed. From June 2004 to June 2006, the Fed raised the federal funds rate from 1% all the way up to 5.25% to cope with rising inflation. This fact shows that the Fed effectively reduced inflation at the expense of a small amount of GDP growth, but was no longer able to cope with soaring asset prices. If the benchmark interest rate is raised significantly in response to asset price bubbles, the result will inevitably be that output growth is subdued.

There is a view that if the Fed raised the benchmark interest rate earlier, it might have curbed the housing bubble. Through a simulation study, economist Taylor (2007) found that if the Fed started raising the benchmark interest rate in June 2002, it could curb the housing bubble. But Taylor also believed that starting raising the benchmark interest rate in June 2002 was likely to hit the real economy of the United States hard. As we know, from 2001 to 2003, the U.S. economy suffered a series of blows, such as the bursting of the stock market bubble, the 911 incident, and the rise in world oil prices. If the Fed started raising the benchmark interest rate in 2001, it is likely that the U.S. economy would get stuck in prolonged deflation like Japan in the 1990s. The above argument points to the fact that the three ultimate targets of monetary policy (output growth rate, inflation rate, and financial market volatility) do not move in the same direction, and that it is difficult to reconcile the three ultimate targets that do not move in the same direction with a single operational target.

"We are against the Fed using any certain rule as a guideline to guide its monetary policy" is the monetary policy philosophy that Federal Reserve Chairman Alan Greenspan once publicly stated. His view is that monetary policy should be a risk management mechanism. If there are multiple risks in the economy, such as the risk of a decline in output, inflationary risk and the risk of financial market volatility, whichever of these risks is the greatest at a given time should be the main transmission target of monetary policy. If the risk of a decline in output is greater than the risk of financial market volatility, the main target should be the risk of a decline in output, and vice versa.

Greenspan's monetary policy philosophy works on the premise that the effect of monetary policy transmission on the above risks is in the same cycle and direction: When the central bank implements a tight monetary policy to reduce the risk of financial market volatility and inflationary risk, the risk of a decline in output will not increase; similarly, when the central bank implements an expansionary monetary policy to reduce the risk of a decline in output, the risk of financial market volatility and inflationary risk will not increase. However, when this premise is false, the actual effect of implementing monetary policy according to Greenspan's philosophy will be "solving one problem only to find another cropping up". During Greenspan's time at the helm of the Fed (1987–2006), the real economic situation in the United States was relatively good, with stable economic growth and low inflation, but during this period, the United States experienced several financial crises, including the stock market bubble crisis of 2001 and the subprime mortgage crisis of 2007. There is no doubt that the U.S. subprime mortgage crisis was related to the monetary policy advocated by Greenspan. Was it because the benchmark interest rate set by Greenspan was improper? Greenspan's limitations lie mainly in the fact that he had only one operational target of monetary policy—the federal funds rate, but he wanted to achieve multiple ultimate targets.

According to the analysis, the U.S. subprime mortgage crisis of 2007 not only challenged the Fed's monetary policy practice, but also questioned the inflation targeting system based on the Taylor rule that is currently popular in major Western countries. From Keynesianism to monetarism, and then to neoclassical macroeconomic theory and new Keynesianism, thoughts on monetary policy in contemporary macroeconomic theories are mainly concentrated on the so-called Taylor rule (Taylor 1993). The Taylor rule states that the policy interest rate should be flexibly adjusted according to a linear combination of the deviation of the actual growth rate of output from the potential growth rate (output gap) and the deviation of the actual inflation rate from the inflation target.

From the theory and practice of monetary policy in the United States and other typical Western market economy countries, we can draw three inspirations: (1) Contrary to what theoretical economists believe, the monetary policy practiced by central banks is aimed at achieving multiple ultimate targets, including output, the rate of inflation, the growth rate, the employment rate, the balance of payments, and even asset price volatility; (2) Although academics have long believed that "rule-based" monetary policy should be implemented due to dynamic inconsistencies, in practice, most central banks implement "discretionary" monetary policy; (3) Obviously, a single operational or intermediate target of monetary policy is overstretched in dealing with multiple ultimate targets, and multiple intermediate or operational targets are necessary. This shows that to improve China's monetary policy is by no means to change it to a monetary policy with a single operational or intermediate target like that of a typical market economy country, but rather to reorganize the current monetary policy target system and retain truly effective intermediate targets of monetary policy.

3.4 *Effects of Global Monetary Policy Adjustments on RMB Exchange Rates*

Since the adjustment of the U.S. QE policy in 2008, the monetary policy of major economies in the world has also been adjusted accordingly, and the main content of the adjustment has had a significant impact on the RMB exchange rate. For the whole of 2014, the RMB depreciated by 0.36% against the U.S. dollar, the first annual depreciation since the resumption of foreign exchange rate reform in 2010. At the same time, the RMB generally strengthened against the currencies of major trading partners, and the nominal and real effective exchange rate indices compiled by the Bank for International Settlements reached record highs, appreciating by 6.4% and 6.2% respectively throughout the year. A important reason why the RMB had fallen against the U.S. dollar and risen against other currencies was that the Federal Reserve began to unwind quantitative easing (QE) in January 2014.

In 2015, in order to prevent deflation, the ECB, which had been cautious about quantitative easing, announced the official start of the European version of QE from March 9, that is, to purchase 60 billion euros worth of assets per month until September 2016. The ECB's quantitative easing program is a major watershed event in current global monetary policy. After the ECB announced the implementation of QE, Sweden, Denmark, Poland, Switzerland, Egypt, Israel, Russia, Turkey and other countries with close ties to the European economy successively lowered their benchmark interest rates, and India, Indonesia, Thailand, Canada, Peru and Australia also cut interest rates to varying degrees. This paper analyzes and compares the impact of quantitative easing in the United States, Japan and Europe after the 2008 financial crisis on the RMB exchange rate, so as to make a brief judgment on the impact of the new round of quantitative easing and future trends in the RMB exchange rate.

3.4.1 *Impact of U.S. Quantitative Easing on RMB Exchange Rates*

In response to the 2008 financial crisis and to stimulate economic growth, the United States had launched three rounds of quantitative easing, whose implementation and withdrawal had an important impact on the global financial system. The main content of quantitative easing in the United States is divided into five stages (as shown in Table 6). After three rounds of quantitative easing (QE3 is divided into two stages), the Fed's assets expanded from $2,075.8 billion in early November 2008 to $4,486.8 billion at the end of October 2014. The size of the Fed's balance sheet expanded 1.2 times in six years (Fig. 7).

The impact of quantitative easing in the United States on the RMB exchange rate was very obvious. As can be seen from Fig. 8, during or even before each round of QE (because announcement was earlier than implementation or the market's expectation), the dollar depreciated continuously against the yuan (since China re-pegged the yuan to the dollar from the second half of 2008 to June 2010, a sustained

Table 6 Five stages of quantitative easing in the United States

Stage	*Time*	*Scale of bond purchases*	*Interest rate*
Stage 1: QE1	November 2008–April 2010	On November 25, 2008, the Fed began to implement quantitative easing (QE1) (the Fed directly purchased agency bonds and mortgage-backed securities issued by Freddie Mac, Fannie Mae, and the Federal Home Loan Banks).By April 2010, the Fed had expanded the monetary base by $1.725 trillion	On December 17, 2008, the Federal Open Market Committee (FOMC) announced a reduction in the federal funds rate from 1% to 0–0.25%
Stage 2: QE2	November 2010–June 2011	On November 4, 2011, the Fed announced the implementation of the second round of quantitative easing (QE2). From November 2010 to June 2011, the Fed purchased $600 billion in long-term Treasury securities at a monthly pace of $75 billion	Keep the federal funds rate unchanged at the ultra-low level of 0–0.25%

(continued)

Table 6 (continued)

Stage	*Time*	*Scale of bond purchases*	*Interest rate*
Stage 3: QE3 with Operation Twist	September 2012–December 2012	On September 15, 2012, the Fed launched a third round of quantitative easing (QE3), under which $40 billion of mortgage-backed securities (MBS) would be bought on a monthly basis. Meanwhile, the Fed continued to perform Operation Twist, its program of selling short-term Treasury securities and purchasing long-term Treasuries	Keep the federal funds rate unchanged at the ultra-low level of 0–0.25%
Stage 4 QE3 without Operation Twist	January 2013–October 2013	On December 12, 2012, the Fed announced that starting in January 2013, it would purchase $45 billion of Treasury securities every month to replace Operation Twist, which combined with its monthly purchases of $40 billion in MBS brought the Fed's monthly asset purchases to $85 billion	Keep the federal funds rate unchanged at the ultra-low level of 0–0.25%
Stage 5: QE exit	January 2014–October 2014	On October 29, 2013, the Federal Reserve announced a gradual exit from quantitative easing. Starting in January 2014, the Fed would reduce its monthly pace of asset purchases by $10 billion	Keep the federal funds rate unchanged at the ultra-low level of 0–0.25%

Source Compiled and produced by the author based on data relating to the five stages of quantitative easing in the United States

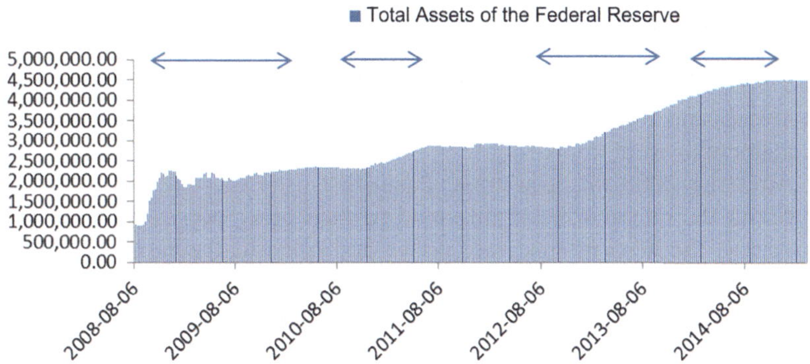

Fig. 7 Total assets of the Federal Reserve (US$ million) (*Source* Wind)

Fig. 8 USD/CNY (central parity rate) (*Source* Wind)

depreciation of the dollar only appeared in the first half of 2008 during QE1).

It should be noted that the U.S. exit from quantitative easing did not mean the Fed would shrink its balance sheet, but rather stabilize it at around $4.5 trillion. From this point of view, the QE exit would not boost the dollar significantly against the yuan.

3.4.2 *Impact of Japan's Quantitative Easing on RMB Exchange Rates*

In March 2001, Japan became the first country in the world to implement quantitative easing, which consisted mainly of: First, supplying ample liquidity by maintaining a high level of current account balances (CAB) held by commercial banks at the central bank; second, increasing open market operations, shifting from the traditional purchase of short-term government bonds to the purchase of long-term government bonds, and even the purchase of bank equity for a time, and exiting quantitative easing in March 2006 amid signs that Japan's macroeconomic fundamentals were improving.

After the 2008 financial crisis, Japan first used the interest rate tool, lowering the rate at which banks lend to each other overnight, and then restarting the zero interest rate policy and quantitative easing, and the Bank of Japan's balance sheet expanded. The truly massive expansion of the Bank of Japan's balance sheet came after the election of Shinzo Abe as Prime Minister and the appointment of Haruhiko Kuroda as governor of the Bank of Japan. The total assets of the Bank of Japan more than doubled from 158 trillion yen in early 2013 to 320 trillion yen in March 2015 (Table 7; Figs. 9 and 10).

In the first and second stages when the balance sheet was not expanded or expanded slowly, the yen appreciated slightly against the yuan. It was not until the Abe government introduced qualitative and quantitative easing policy, which rapidly and substantially expanded the central bank's balance sheet that the yen began to enter a channel of rapid depreciation. This shows that when there is quantitative easing on a larger scale involving another currency (U.S. dollar), quantitative easing on a small scale cannot achieve the effect of currency depreciation. Further quantitative easing on a larger scale will mean a "beggar thy neighbor" currency war. At present, there is no timetable for the withdrawal of Japan's quantitative easing, and there is still room for the yen to fall against the yuan.

3.4.3 Impact of Major European Monetary Policy Tools on RMB Exchange Rates

Interest rate. The ECB had slashed interest rates since the outbreak of the financial crisis. In June 2014, the ECB cut the interest rate on commercial banks' deposits at the central bank below zero to disincentivize commercial banks from channeling liquidity back to the central bank.

Long term refinancing operation (LTRO), very long term refinancing operation (VLTRO), and targeted longer-term refinancing operation (TLTRO). From 2008 to 2009, the ECB offered liquidity provision at three months, six months and one year multiple times. In October 2011, the ECB restarted its 12-month long term refinancing

Table 7 Three stages of Japan's quantitative easing after the financial crisis

Stage	*Time*	*Scale of bond purchases*	*Interest rate*
Stage 1: conventional monetary policy	October 2008–October 2010	The Bank of Japan decided to buy one trillion yen of corporate bonds with one year or less remaining to maturity from January to September 30, 2009; from mid-February 2009 to the end of April 2010, the Bank of Japan would spend up to one trillion yen to restart buying shares held by financial institutions; starting in March 2009, the Bank of Japan would provide one trillion yen in subprime loans to big banks	The rate at which banks lend to each other overnight was cut twice, from 0.5% to 0.1%
Stage 2: unconventional monetary policy	October 2010–December 2012	On October 28, 2010, the Bank of Japan began to implement a 35 trillion yen asset purchase program. Since then, the Bank of Japan had expanded its asset purchase program eight times, eventually increasing it to 101 trillion yen	On October 5, 2010, the rate at which banks lend to each other overnight was reduced to 0–0.1%, and the zero interest rate policy was reintroduced

(continued)

Table 7 (continued)

Stage	*Time*		*Scale of bond purchases*	*Interest rate*
Stage 3: qualitative and quantitative easing (QQE)	January 2013–present	April 2013–October 2014	The Bank of Japan planned to increase the money supply at an annual rate of about 60–70 trillion yen over two years, nearly doubling the monetary base, from 138 trillion yen at the end of 2012 to 270 trillion yen at the end of 2014. The measures included an increase in the central bank's purchases of Japanese government bonds to 50 trillion yen a year, which is expected to double the national debt in two years, from 89 trillion yen at the end of 2012 to 190 trillion yen at the end of 2014	The zero interest rate policy was maintained

Stage	*Time*	*Scale of bond purchases*	*Interest rate*
	October 31, 2014–March 31, 2015	The Bank of Japan expanded the annual pace of increase in the monetary base from the current 60–70 trillion yen to 80 trillion yen; the Bank of Japan further increased its purchases of government bonds, from 50 trillion yen to 80 trillion yen a year. Meanwhile, the Bank of Japan extended the duration of its holdings of government bonds and increased its purchases of risky stock exchange-linked funds. It would buy three trillion yen of exchange-traded funds (ETFs) and 90 billion yen of real estate investment trusts (REITs) in the coming year	

Source Compiled and produced by the author based on data relating to the three stages of quantitative easing in Japan after the financial crisis

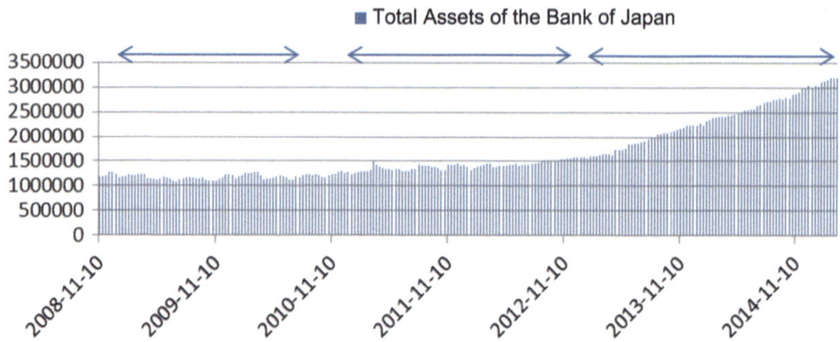

Fig. 9 Total assets of the Bank of Japan (billion yen) (*Source* Wind)

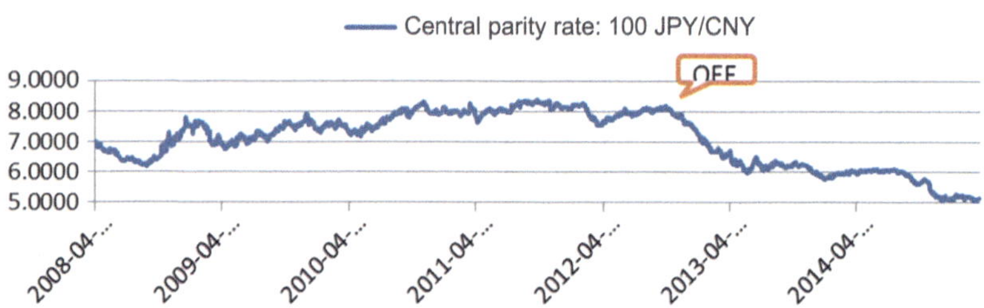

Fig. 10 100 JPY/CNY (central parity rate) (*Source* Wind)

operations. As the debt crisis worsened and bank liquidity tightened, the ECB launched two rounds of three-year long term refinancing operations on December 21, 2011 and February 29, 2012 respectively, and lowered the mortgage and margin requirements for eurozone banks to ensure the availability of liquidity to banks.

Securities Markets Programme (SMP). On 14 May 2010, the ECB launched the Securities Markets Programme, which allows the ECB to purchase bonds directly in the primary and secondary markets in accordance with relevant regulations. As of 5 March 2012, the ECB's bond holdings stood at 219.5 billion euros.

Outright Monetary Transactions (OMT). On September 6, 2012, the ECB launched Outright Monetary Transactions (OMT) and suspended the Securities Markets Programme. OMT is a program under which the ECB can make unlimited purchases in the secondary market, under certain conditions, of government bonds issued by euro area member states when the debt crisis of euro area member states reaches a certain level. OMT has not yet been activated since its launch.

The main task of the ECB was to prevent inflation, so the ECB had been cautious about balance sheet expansion. As can be seen from Fig. 11, the total assets of the ECB peaked between 2012 and 2013, which was caused by the two rounds of LTROs launched by the ECB around 2012. The total assets of the ECB gradually fell after 2013, while the two rounds of LTROs had a three-year term, which showed that eurozone banks had no urgent demand for long-term liquidity as most of them had made early repayments, and the mechanism through which the ECB tried to transmit liquidity to the real economy through eurozone banks was not smooth enough. This may be one of the reasons why the ECB finally opted for quantitative easing by buying securities in the secondary market.

On January 22, 2015, ECB President Mario Draghi announced the official launch of the European version of QE: Starting in March 2015, the ECB would buy investment grade securities issued by eurozone member states, agencies and supranational institutions in the secondary market at a pace of 60 billion euros per month. Purchases might be continued until September 2016 and were expected to bring in a total of 1.14 trillion euros and newly add 950 billion euros. The main purpose of the European version of QE was to bring inflation back to 2%, so September 2016 was only a preliminary plan, not a definite exit time.

There had been no material change in the ECB's balance sheet, but as can be seen from Fig. 12, the depreciation of the euro against the

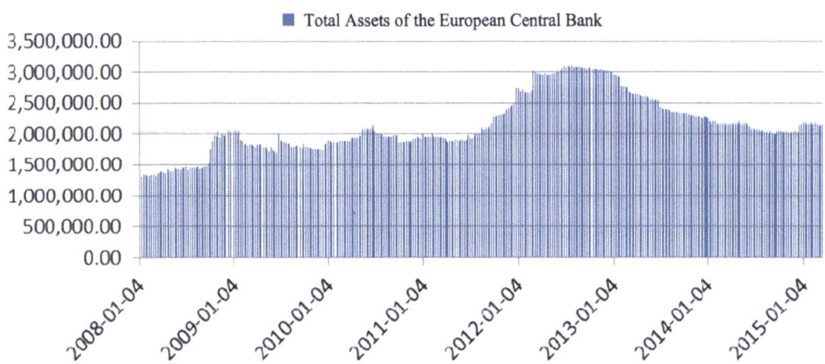

Fig. 11 Total assets of the European Central Bank (million euros) (*Source* Wind)

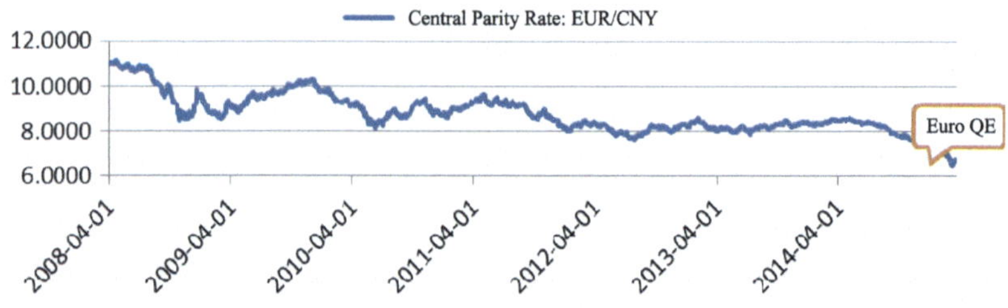

Fig. 12 EUR/CNY (central parity rate) (*Source* Wind)

yuan was much earlier than the announcement of the QE program by the ECB. This was because the Ukraine crisis dragged down the European economic recovery in 2014, the inflation rate fell into negative territory, and markets widely expected that the European Central Bank would have to implement QE. Thus, when quantitative easing is implemented, the impact of expectations on exchange rates could not be ignored.

4 Dollar Hegemony from the Perspective of the Fed's Monetary Policy Adjustments

The super economic power of the United States has established the current hegemony of the U.S. dollar in the international monetary system. The outbreak of COVID-19 in 2020 has had a huge impact on the U.S. economy. For this reason, the Fed has returned to the zero interest rates seen in the aftermath of the 2008 financial crisis in addition to pursuing unlimited quantitative easing. The release of huge liquidity has flooded the foreign exchange market with dollars, and the U.S. dollar index has depreciated by more than 10%, thus weakening the global hegemony of the U.S. dollar. In response, China should make full use of its institutional advantages to consolidate achievements in the fight against COVID-19 and continuously enhance its economic strength. At the same time, China should adopt appropriate monetary policy and proactive fiscal policy, deepen financial market reform and steadily advance the pace of RMB internationalization.

As the COVID-19 pandemic was escalating around the world, the Federal Reserve cut the federal funds rate directly by 100 bp to a range of 0–0.25% on March 15, 2020, and said it would buy \$700 billion in Treasury securities and mortgage-backed securities. The easing was the largest bailout in the Fed's history, the rate cut came just 12 days after the last emergency rate cut, and the scale of the action was unprecedented. The last time the Fed hit the zero lower bound was during the 2008 financial crisis, and the rate cut exceeded the largest single rate cut of 75 bp at that time. While the Fed's move drew rare praise from President Donald Trump, U.S. markets did not buy it. Just after the Fed announced a massive "bailout", fears spiked in the U.S. stock market, with all three major U.S. stock index future contracts hitting their circuit breaker and the Dow closing down about 3,000 points, its biggest one-day point loss on record. It can be seen that the signs of weakness in the U.S. economy since 2019, combined with the unexpected impact of the COVID-19 pandemic, are bound to fundamentally reverse the trend of the U.S. dollar strengthening, which may shake the hegemony of the U.S. dollar in the world (Liu and Liu 2020).

4.1 Manifestations of Dollar Hegemony

After World War II, the United States became the most economically powerful country in the world. In the international monetary system led by the United States, the U.S. dollar had a special status as an equivalent to gold, which laid the economic foundation for the hegemony of the U.S. dollar. The subsequent dollar crisis led to the collapse of the Bretton Woods system, but did not fundamentally affect the hegemony of the U.S. dollar in the global economy, which was mainly manifested as follows:

1. International settlement. As the global currency, the U.S. dollar has seen its dominance weakened in recent years by the trend towards de-dollarization, but it is still the dominant currency. By 2019, the U.S. dollar remained the most widely used currency, accounting for around 40% of global trade. In recent years, the international status of the RMB has been rising, but it only accounts for about 2% of global trade, ranking only as the fifth most active currency for global payments by value.
2. International reserves. The U.S. dollar dominates the global composition of official foreign exchange reserves, making up more than 60% of foreign exchange reserves. The euro, yen and pound combined account for only about 30% of foreign exchange reserves. By the third quarter of 2019, the share of global foreign exchange

reserves denominated in yuan reached a record high since the IMF began releasing data on the yuan, but was just above 2%.

3. International capital markets. According to a report by the Bank for International Settlements, the U.S. dollar accounted for 88.3% of global forex trades in April 2019, with trades averaging $5.82 trillion per day, up 31% from April 2016. Special Drawing Rights (SDRs) are an important book asset. The value of a SDR is jointly determined by the most important currencies in the world. The RMB was not officially added to the SDR basket until October 1, 2016. Now value of a SDR is jointly determined by a basket of five currencies including the U.S. dollar, the euro, the RMB, the Japanese yen and the British pound. The weighting of the U.S. dollar is 41.73%, while that of the RMB is only 10.92%. In global forex trades, the RMB is far behind the U.S. dollar, ranking only eighth, with a share of only 4.3%.

4.2 *Reasons and Basis for the Formation of Dollar Hegemony*

1. The great economic power of the United States is a fundamental pillar of dollar hegemony. The United States possesses extraordinary economic power, especially in high-technology industries. After the 2008 global financial crisis, the United States was the first developed country to come out of the trough and usher in economic recovery and development. In 2018, its GDP growth rate reached 2.9%, far higher than the growth rate of about 1% in Japan, Europe and other major developed countries. Despite the huge impact of COVID-19 on the U.S. economy, the economy has rebounded significantly with new President Joe Biden's emphasis on COVID-19 control, as well as broader policy support and faster vaccine supply. In the World Economic Outlook released by the International Monetary Fund (IMF) in early 2021, the growth rate of the U.S. in 2021 was significantly raised by 2 percentage points to 5.1%, while that of the euro area was lowered by 1 percentage point to 4.2%. Gita Gopinath, the IMF's economic counsellor and director of the research department, also noted that "the U.S. is expected to surpass its pre-pandemic levels this year, much better than the euro area". Although China's economy is expected to grow by 8.1% in 2021, China is still far from the forefront of high-tech manufacturing. In fact, in export

markets for computers, automobiles and biotechnology, China is almost insignificant. Chinese exports often compete on low prices, and their quality needs to be further improved.

2. SWIFT is the main driver of dollar hegemony. SWIFT (Society for Worldwide Interbank Financial Telecommunication) connects financial institutions around the world and provides secure messaging services to financial institutions around the world. It now provides transaction services to more than 11,000 banks, securities institutions, businesses and customers in more than 200 countries and territories. Payments and settlements via SWIFT are based on the U.S. dollar, making SWIFT an important vehicle for the United States to implement the hegemony of the U.S. dollar. All countries and enterprises engaged in international trade basically need to use the system for money transfers and settlements, which makes many countries become path-dependent. In this way, the United States can use SWIFT to exercise long-arm jurisdiction over all countries in the world and implement relevant financial sanctions. For example, U.S. sanctions against Iran prohibit foreign financial institutions that conduct major financial transactions with Iranian financial institutions from opening or maintaining accounts in the United States, cut off the payment and settlement channels between the outside world and Iran, and completely isolate Iran financially from the rest of the world, resulting in heavy damage to Iran's economy. At present, the fact that global trade settlements are dominated by the U.S. dollar, and SWIFT is controlled by the United States further strengthens the global hegemony of the U.S. dollar.
3. Petrodollars perpetuate the hegemony of the U.S. dollar under the current international monetary system. Although the collapse of the Bretton Woods system broke the link between the dollar and gold, the petrodollar became a new vehicle for the continuation of dollar hegemony. Since the United States and Saudi Arabia reached a petrodollar deal in 1974, all oil trade has been conducted in dollars. Oil as the world's most traded commodity and the requirement to buy oil in dollars enable the United States to indirectly influence and control world oil trade through U.S. dollar exchange rates. Petrodollars in the world economy provide a favorable guarantee for the United States to "shear wool from the world", perpetuating the global hegemony of the U.S. dollar.

4.3 The Fed's Monetary Policy Adjustment Process

The Fed's monetary policy adjustments since 2020 can be roughly divided into three stages:

1. The Fed kept monetary policy on hold (2020.1–2020.2).

   In August 2019, the Fed announced its first interest rate cut in 10 years, saying that it would end its balance sheet reduction early. At the same time, the U.S. economy was gradually improving, with U.S. real GDP growing by 2.34% year-over-year in the fourth quarter of 2019, and the unemployment rate returning to a record low of 3.5% in December. Against this backdrop, the Fed played wait and see with monetary policy by keeping it on hold. At the December 2019 FOMC meeting, members voted unanimously to leave the target range for the federal funds rate unchanged. Since then, the Fed's monetary policy had been in a wait-and-see mode.

   At the start of 2020, the employment situation in the United States was improving, with the unemployment rate remaining at 3.5% in January. The year-over-year growth rate of the industrial production index rose to −0.2% from −0.8% in December 2019. The strong performance of the U.S. labor market had given the Fed a shot in the arm, with signs that the Fed's 2019 interest rate cut policy was beginning to pay off, which made the Fed's monetary policy start to sound like it was winding down. In its semi-annual monetary policy report, released on February 7, the Fed concluded that interest rates are now at the right level to support economic growth and employment. On February 11, Fed Chairman Jerome Powell even said publicly that he would phase out the repurchase program.

   The Fed's monetary policy at this stage was mainly based on optimistic expectations for the recovery of the U.S. economy. The good performance of the U.S. economy reinforced the Fed's optimistic expectations. On this basis, the Fed basically continued its previous monetary policy. Not only did the Fed not take further easing measures, but even considered winding down and planned to slow down the pace of its bond purchases.
2. Rescue measures after the COVID-19 outbreak (2020.3–2020.8).

   However, the good times did not last long. As the COVID-19 pandemic spread further overseas, U.S. financial markets were rocked, triggering four consecutive circuit breakers in March. From February 20 to March 23, the Dow Jones Industrial Average and the S&P 500 fell by a staggering 38% and 34%. Risk aversion among investors was pushed to the highest level, U.S. Treasuries were dumped, and a liquidity crisis in financial markets was imminent.

In order to mitigate the impact of the pandemic, the Fed was forced to adopt unprecedented easing measures to address immediate needs. The Fed's two consecutive emergency rate cuts in March brought interest rates back to the zero lower bound. Meanwhile, the Fed launched a massive $700 billion quantitative easing program and injected $1.5 trillion of short-term money into 24 large banks. On March 23, the Federal Reserve struck again with unlimited quantitative easing and the Main Street Lending Program, which provided loans to small and medium-sized businesses, and announced that it would buy unlimited amounts of Treasuries and MBS.

In April, the negative impact of the pandemic followed. U.S. real GDP growth in the first quarter of 2020 was only 0.3%, the industrial production index fell by 16.3% year-over-year, and the unemployment rate rose to 14.8% in April. In an effort to jump-start the economy as quickly as possible, the Fed took further easing steps on April 9, providing up to $2.3 trillion in financing to businesses and local governments and including some junk bonds in its asset purchase program. U.S. fiscal policy kept pace, with a $2.2 trillion fiscal stimulus package and a $484 billion relief bill passed on March 27 and April 23, respectively. Massive quantitative easing had led to a rapid expansion of the Fed's balance sheet, with total assets reaching an unprecedented $7.2 trillion on June 10. Since then, as financial markets had gradually improved, the pace of the Fed's asset purchases had stabilized. Thereafter, the Fed announced that it would hold interest rates at the zero lower bound and said it would not reduce the pace of its asset purchases.

Affected by the COVID-19 pandemic, the direction of U.S. monetary policy was fundamentally reversed at this stage, and unprecedented easing was adopted to solve the liquidity crisis in markets and stimulate economic recovery. The reasons for the Fed's aggressive bailout measures can be summarized in three points: First, the Fed announced a massive corporate bond purchase program in an attempt to avert a debt crisis; second, through the Paycheck

Protection Program Liquidity Facility (PPPLF), the Main Street Lending Program (MSLP), and the Medium-Term Lending Facility (MLF), the Fed provided credit support to small businesses to maintain normal production and prevent a sharp rise in unemployment; third, the Federal Reserve used a number of liquidity facilities designed to reduce liquidity risk in markets and restore the effective operation of markets.

3. The Fed's New Monetary Policy Framework (2020.8–early 2021). In June 2020, a second surge of the COVID-19 pandemic hit the United States, with shutdowns and large-scale corporate bankruptcies leading to sluggish consumer spending and employment, and the reopening of the U.S. economy stalled again. Minutes from the Fed's August meeting suggested the economy might not recover as quickly as expected, leading to a drop in market sentiment. At this critical juncture, the Federal Open Market Committee announced that it had completed its review of the monetary policy framework and issued a new monetary policy guidance document. The advent of the Fed's new monetary policy framework marked the beginning of a new phase in the Fed's monetary policy.

   The Fed's new monetary policy framework comes with the following two major changes: First, more attention is paid to the employment goal of monetary policy. The new policy framework document prioritizes the "employment" goal of monetary policy over the "inflation" goal, suggesting that "maximum employment" has replaced "stable prices" as the primary goal of the Fed's monetary policy. Meanwhile, the new monetary policy framework replaces the "deviation" from the maximum level of employment in the employment assessment criteria with a one-way "gap", suggesting that monetary policy may not have to respond to an overheated job market. Second, there is a shift from inflation targeting to average inflation targeting. In the new monetary policy framework, symmetric inflation targeting is replaced by average inflation targeting, which means that even if the current inflation rate exceeds 2%, as long as the average inflation rate remains within a reasonable range, the Fed may not have to adjust its loose monetary policy.

   Concerns about a "low growth, low inflation and low interest rates" environment were the main factors that prompted the Fed to change its monetary policy framework. Although the Fed's loose monetary policy in the early stage mitigated the negative impact of the pandemic to a certain extent, it was difficult to reverse the slump in consumer spending and the downturn in the labor market. Against this backdrop, the introduction of the new monetary policy framework will give the Fed more flexibility in monetary policy and enable it to adopt more aggressive easing measures.

After the January 27, 2021 FOMC meeting, the Fed announced that it would keep interest rates unchanged at 0–0.25% and reiterated its commitment to its asset purchase program under which it would buy at least $120 billion of treasuries per month until the economy grew substantially. If the COVID-19 pandemic continues to weigh on economic activity and pose considerable risks to the economic outlook, the Fed will be committed to using a variety of tools to support the economic recovery and maintaining its long-term accommodative policy under the new monetary policy framework.

4.4 *Impact of the Fed's Monetary Policy on Dollar Hegemony*

1. The Fed's loose monetary policy will lead to a depreciation of the dollar. Big Fed rate cuts and unlimited quantitative easing released huge amounts of dollars, flooding foreign exchange markets with dollars. The U.S. dollar index plummeted by more than 10%, from a high of 102 in March 2020 to under 90 in January 2021. In recent years, the European Union and Japan have not completely recovered from the impact of the financial crisis, and their interest rates have been at the zero lower bound, or they have adopted a negative interest rate policy, which greatly limits the room for interest rate adjustment. The Fed's zero interest rate policy has essentially eliminated yield spreads between the United States and the rest of the developed world, adding to downward pressure on the dollar. In addition, the end of the OPEC+ agreement to reduce production has sent oil prices tumbling, a trend exacerbated by falling oil demand due to the COVID-19 pandemic. The decline in oil prices, on the one hand, might hit the U.S. shale oil market and, on the other hand, reduce the demand for petrodollars in the world market, and eventually lead to the end of the petrodollar.
2. Sharp rate cuts are likely to cause market panic and affect investor confidence. In the face of huge external uncertainties, a series of

sharp rate cuts will only add to market panic rather than counteract shocks in markets. The three major U.S. stock index futures contracts fell sharply after the Fed cut interest rates, triggering a trading halt. The Dow Jones Industrial Average also hit its daily downside limit and closed down about 3,000 points, its biggest single-day point drop ever. The Fed's rock-bottom interest rate policy failed to stabilize the economy and restore investor confidence. Instead, it reduced the space for monetary policy adjustment, increased the negative image of the United States as irresponsible, and shook the foundation of dollar hegemony.

3. Rate cuts may lead to global financial turmoil and harm long-term economic growth. The zero interest rate policy of the United States may have a great impact on the stability of international financial markets, increase irregularities in currency competition, and thus set off turmoil in global financial markets. Interest rate cuts will make U.S. dollars chase higher returns and flow to the financial markets of other countries around the world, which will have an impact on the monetary policies of other countries around the world. In order to reduce financial losses and ensure financial stability, countries will race to cut interest rates to follow up quantitative easing, which will form a new wave of exchange rate competition and competitive devaluation, posing a serious threat to the global economy. The closer interest rates get to the zero lower bound, the more limited monetary policy's ability to stimulate the economy. In this way, global financial turmoil, interest rate policy restrictions and the global spread of the COVID-19 pandemic are likely to plunge the world economy into another crisis.

4.5 China's Response Policies and Measures

1. Enhance China's own economic power. All schemes are useless in the face of absolute power. The key to breaking dollar hegemony is to enhance our own economic power. China has acted decisively and taken effective measures to fight the pandemic, fully highlighting its institutional advantages. Although in the short term, these efforts entailed huge economic costs, they have contributed significantly to a rapid economic recovery. On the other hand, the United States has been ineffective and slow in its response to the pandemic, and

the second wave of COVID-19 is unfolding, which will have a negative impact on its economic development. Instead of achieving the desired effect of economic regulation, aggressive monetary policy added to market panic, as evidenced by the three major U.S. stock index future contracts hitting their circuit breaker. While doing a good job in its fight against COVID-19, China has completed the orderly resumption of work across the country and put its domestic production capacity back on track. In the context of the global spread of the pandemic, China should further show its image as a responsible major country, make China a haven for world economic development, attract more capital and technology inflows with a favorable international environment, and seize the opportunity to vigorously develop the economy and narrow the economic power gap between China and the United States.

2. Adopt a moderate monetary policy and complement it with a proactive fiscal policy. By no means can China resort to short-term stimulus policies and adjustments in its response to the impact of the pandemic. Although the RMB 4 trillion stimulus package in 2008 played a key role in China's economic recovery, it also brought about a series of negative effects such as overcapacity and a buildup of financial risks. After all, monetary policy is a total-based policy. Appropriate easing in the short term can alleviate the current problem of insufficient liquidity, but in the long run, it may drive money out of the real economy and into the virtual economy, exacerbating the risk of a buildup of financial bubbles. Therefore, while maintaining overall liquidity at an appropriate level, we should increase the introduction of a variety of innovative policies such as the inclusive loan repayment extension support tool for micro and small enterprises to guide funds more accurately to micro and small enterprises and private enterprises, pay more attention to the flexibility, moderation and precision of monetary policy, remove obstructions to the financing process, and improve the efficiency of enterprise production funds. In addition, we should complement monetary policy with a proactive fiscal policy. Even as the state is promoting investment in new infrastructure construction, we should guide and encourage private capital to invest in new infrastructure construction We should lower barriers to entry into the relevant industries, effectively promote the reform of state-owned enterprises, and use market mechanisms to foster momentum for

economic development, so as to achieve high-quality and sustainable economic development.

3. Strive to change the existing international trade settlement system and strengthen cooperation with EU countries. In order to wean ourselves off over-reliance on SWIFT, we should improve our ability to use the RMB as a means of settlement and payment, and accelerate the upgrade of the Cross-Border Interbank Payment System (CIPS). We should encourage the Export–Import Bank of China to provide more financial facilities for importers and exporters who choose to settle in RMB, and encourage commercial banks to provide more financial innovation tools for cross-border trade settlement in RMB, lower the threshold for cross-border trade financing in RMB, and lower the cost of cross-border trade settlement in RMB. We should further improve CIPS, accelerate the upgrade of CIPS, and actively promote the application and development of Digital Currency Electronic Payment (DCEP). DCEP is essentially the digitalization of RMB, which is equivalent to the digitalization of banknotes. Combined with the traceability and tamper resistance of blockchain technology, DCEP can effectively strengthen financial regulation and deeply integrate with big data, and therefore is more helpful to the implementation of economic regulation and control. In fact, in order to evade U.S. coercion and bypass the U.S. dollar payment system to continue trade with Iran, the EU planned in 2018 to create a special purpose vehicle (SPV) as a viable alternative to SWIFT for the international community. Although the SPV settlement mechanism is still a long way off, it reflects the EU's desire to challenge the global hegemony of the U.S. dollar. In the face of COVID-19 outbreaks in Europe, China and the United States showed two very different attitudes, which undoubtedly brought the relationship between China and Europe closer. We should take advantage of this opportunity to strengthen cooperation and exchanges with the EU. Developing a settlement system independent of SWIFT is no longer an unattainable dream.
4. Steadily advance the internationalization of the RMB, and expand the influence and role of the RMB through the Belt and Road Initiative and the Regional Comprehensive Economic Partnership (RCEP). The internationalization of the RMB is the most direct means of breaking the hegemony of the U.S. dollar. The better China's economic development, the more conducive it will be to

advancing the internationalization of the RMB. In recent years, positive progress has been made in the use of the RMB in neighboring countries and countries along the Belt and Road. By the end of 2019, China had signed currency swap agreements with 21 countries along the Belt and Road, and established RMB clearing arrangements in eight countries along the Belt and Road. We should continue to optimize the cross-border RMB policy framework, and promote the sustainable development of cross-border RMB investment and financing around major national strategies such as the Belt and Road Initiative and international capacity cooperation. Meanwhile, The Belt and Road Initiative can drive DCEP reform, greatly improve the operational efficiency of the industrial chain, and promote the overall development of China's economy and society.

5. Optimize cross-border RMB policies, promote the two-way opening-up of capital markets, and improve the RMB exchange rate formation mechanism. We should raise the level of cross-border RMB business, further open up financial markets, improve macroprudential measures, and steadily advance market-oriented reform of the RMB exchange rate regime. We should help enterprises save on exchange costs, avoid exchange rate risks, simplify settlement procedures and speed up capital turnover in cross-border trade and settlement, and expand cross-border use of the RMB even as enterprises "go global".

References

Cheng. The U.S. Economy: A Bumpy Recovery. China Business News, August 4, 2011.

Liu and Liu. The Hegemony of the U.S. Dollar from the Perspective of the Adjustment of the Federal Reserve's Monetary Policy. Economic Daily—Special Report on Information, 2020, (31).

Liu and Zhang. Progress in Research on and Insights into Monetary Policy and the Transmission Mechanism—From the Perspective of Contemporary Western Economics. Journal of Peking University (Philosophy and Social Sciences), January 2012, 49(1).

Peng and Shi. The Basic Direction of Bernanke's Change—On the Evolution of U.S. Monetary Policy. International Economic Review, May 27, 2007.

Taylor J B. Discretion Versus Policy Rules in Practice. Carnegie-Rochester Conference Series on Public Policy, North-Holland, 1993, 39: 195–214.

Zhang. The Historical Development and Theoretical Evolution of the Monetary Policy Transmission Mechanism in the United States. Economic Review, September 30, 2001.

Zhang Xueyong and Song Xuenan. Monetary Policy and Its Effects During a Financial Crisis: From the Perspective of International Comparison. Studies of International Finance, September 12, 2011, (9).

CHAPTER 5

Effects of U.S. Monetary Policy Adjustments on the World Economy

With the outbreak of the global financial crisis as the dividing line and the federal funds rate and the reserve balances of depository institutions at Federal Reserve Banks as the characterization indicators of the Fed's conventional monetary policy and quantitative easing policy respectively, this chapter uses a VAR model to empirically study the impact of shocks from relevant policy variables on the economic variables of major countries and China before and after the adjustment of U.S. monetary policy. This paper mainly analyzes the impact of policy adjustments on China, advanced economies and emerging market and developing economies; this paper examines the basic characteristics of the transmission mechanism of U.S. monetary policy, its influence path and its impact on world economic growth, and uses empirical research to clarify the multi-dimensional and multi-level impact brought about by U.S. monetary policy adjustments in the context of games among major powers. This paper argues that China needs to make strategic adjustments to its economic growth pattern and foreign trade strategy. There are the following two main points of innovation in this paper: First, most of the relevant literature mainly studies the spillover effects of U.S. monetary policy on one or a few countries and regions (such as the BRICS countries), and rarely extends to multiple countries. Second, this study expands the connotation of U.S. monetary policy adjustments to make them quantifiable and amenable to comparative analysis (Liu, 2018).

L. Weiping, *American Monetary Policy Adjustment and Its Impacts*,
https://doi.org/10.1007/978-981-99-7810-6_5

1 Research Background

As the world's largest and most influential economy, the United States can have a significant impact on the world economy through a sign of trouble in its economic development. With the advancement of economic globalization and liberalization, countries and regions around the world have gradually become a community with a shared future. The economic disorders of major developed countries, the United States in particular, have a tendency to affect the whole world. The global financial turmoil triggered by the U.S. subprime mortgage crisis of 2008 is a typical example. After the outbreak of the financial crisis, the real economy of the United States suffered a heavy setback, and the credit base was damaged, resulting in a serious decline in the money supply, investment and consumer spending, and a sharp increase in unemployment in the United States. The devastation that occurred to the U.S. economy triggered a global economic recession. Countries and regions around the world entered an economic winter one after another. Domestic consumer demand was insufficient, investment and trade were sluggish, and the job market faced a severe test, thus forming a temporary vicious circle. As can be seen from Fig. 1, from 2008 to 2009, the world's major economies experienced a decline in GDP growth, or even negative growth, and were in recession.

According to modern macroeconomic theory, in order to effectively respond to a financial crisis, the government should adopt expansionary

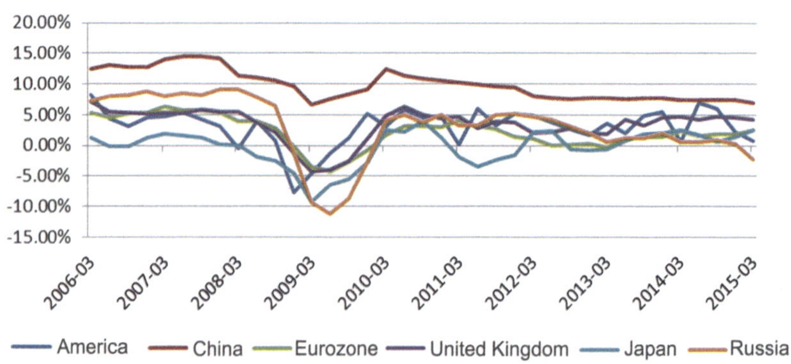

Fig. 1 Changes in GDP Growth in major economies before and after the financial crisis (*Source* compiled and produced by the author based on empirical results obtained using Eviews 8.0)

fiscal and monetary policy in an effort to provide market liquidity and boost the confidence of market participants, so as to provide a solid foundation for preventing the crisis from spreading and promoting economic recovery. In general, expansionary fiscal policy mainly stimulates aggregate demand and reduces unemployment by issuing government bonds, increasing fiscal spending and reducing tax revenue; expansionary monetary policy drives the growth of aggregate demand by increasing the money supply, and is often used in tandem with tools such as interest rates and open market operations. In the face of a once-in-a-century financial crisis, the Fed works with the Treasury and other regulators to advance the goals of financial stability, economic recovery, and job creation. What exactly led the Fed to finally resort to the unconventional policy of quantitative easing?

First, if the U.S. Department of the Treasury pursued expansionary fiscal policy by issuing government bonds, then who should buy government bonds in order for fiscal policy to have a real effect? Obviously, at that time, domestic financial institutions could not play a fundamental role by buying government bonds, because banks and other financial institutions were generally suffering from a credit contraction and a lack of credit, and them buying government bonds was more likely to lead to market liquidity freezing further, high interest rates and severely weak investment. Fiscal policy could only be effective if the buyers were the central banks or financial institutions of other countries. But the reality was that the gross external debt of the United States in the fourth quarter of 2008 was 94.5% of GDP,[1] close to the threshold of 100%, and other economies were also facing economic downturns, so the U.S. government could not get the policy effect of turning the tide by bringing in foreign investment. Under both internal and external pressures, it was the Fed that ultimately bought government bonds. That is, the Fed injected liquidity into markets by purchasing state-guaranteed financial assets such as U.S. Treasury securities and mortgage-backed securities in an effort to boost financial markets and rebuild the credit base.

Second, what role would the Fed's interest rate tool play? In June 2007, the U.S. real estate industry gradually showed signs of deterioration, and the market risks caused by falling house prices and rising mortgage delinquency rates were intensifying, resulting in exposure to

[1] Source: Wind.

financial market risks. In September 2007, the Fed started the process of reducing the federal funds rate, which saw the federal funds rate lowered 10 times from 5.25% to 0% to 0.25%, ushering in the era of "zero interest rates" in the history of U.S. monetary policy. Figure 2 shows changes in the federal funds rate before and after the financial crisis. It can be seen that the Fed cut rates at an unprecedented pace, and the federal funds rate approached zero at the end of 2008 in just over a year.

According to the IS-LM analysis framework, when the interest rate is very low, the LM curve is approximately horizontal, at which point the government cannot cut the interest rate further as it has to increase the money supply through expansionary monetary policy, nor can it increase national income, so monetary policy becomes ineffective. This scenario is the "liquidity trap" postulated by Keynes. Under such circumstances, interest rates are so accommodative that the Fed can no longer use this tool effectively to achieve its policy objectives.

Third, in the above context, when conventional expansionary fiscal and monetary policies failed to work, the Fed began to resort to quantitative easing, and by intervening in the market, the Fed improved the credit environment and fundamentally restored the normal operation of the financial system, thereby raising aggregate demand. Bernanke (2009) pointed out that the primary cause of the financial crisis was the real

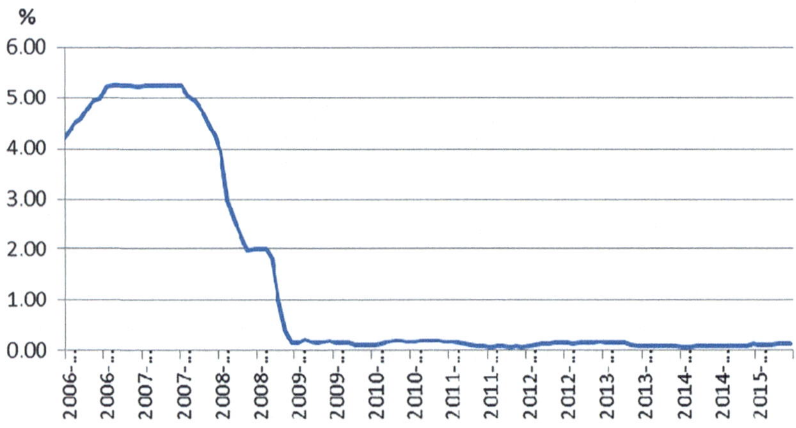

Fig. 2 Federal funds rate (*Source* compiled and produced by the author based on empirical results obtained using Eviews 8.0)

estate cycle and related subprime mortgage defaults, which substantially increased the operating pressure on many financial institutions and hit investor confidence in the credit market, and unlike conventional monetary policy, quantitative easing was implemented in response to the rapid deterioration of domestic credit conditions, the enormous survival stress faced by financial institutions and other practical problems. Under the huge impact of the financial crisis, the Fed shifted from conventional monetary policy to quantitative easing policy, which immediately had wide-ranging global implications. The euro area, the United Kingdom and Japan followed suit. Emerging market economies drew great interest from international capital because of their relatively strong growth potential. Hot money poured in, causing severe imported inflation. So what impact will U.S. monetary policy adjustments after the financial crisis have on the world economy and China's economy? Compared with traditional monetary policy that uses a money supply or interest rate target, what different impact will quantitative easing have on the development of the global economy and major economies? How to respond to and protect against these external shocks? These issues are to be studied and solved in the empirical part of this paper.

2 Research Methods and Data Selection

2.1 Research Methods

When studying the dynamic effects of changes in one variable on other variables, traditional linear regression models or simultaneous equation models cannot sensitively capture the dynamic mechanism behind such effects. The regression coefficients obtained from these models reflect the equilibrium between variables over a period of time. In order to deal with the analysis and prediction of various economic indicators, Sims (1980) proposed VAR models, which use each variable in the system as a function of all lagged variables to build a model, thus promoting the application and development of the dynamic analysis of economic systems. In addition, univariate time series models mainly predict each variable individually, while VAR models have the advantage that they take all variables as a system to predict the impact of shocks on the system, which makes predictions consistent with each other and very convenient and practical in practice.

According to Chen (2014) and Gao (2014), two time series vectors $\{y_{1t}, y_{2t}\}$ are considered, and these two variables and their lags are used as response and explanatory variables in the simultaneous regression model, respectively, to form a binary VAR (p) system:

$$\begin{aligned} y_{1t} &= \beta_{10} + \beta_{11} y_{1,t-1} + \cdots + \beta_{1p} y_{1,t-p} + \gamma_{11} y_{2,t-1} \\ &+ \cdots + \gamma_{1p} y_{2,t-p} + \varepsilon_{1t} \\ y_{2t} &= \beta_{20} + \beta_{21} y_{1,t-1} + \cdots + \beta_{2p} y_{1,t-p} + \gamma_{21} y_{2,t-1} \\ &+ \cdots + \gamma_{2p} y_{2,t-p} + \varepsilon_{2t} \end{aligned}$$

where $\{\varepsilon_{1t}\}$ and $\{\varepsilon_{2t}\}$ are both white noise processes, and a contemporaneous correlation is allowed between the disturbance terms in the two equations. By combining the above two equations in matrix form, we get:

$$\begin{pmatrix} y_{1t} \\ y_{2t} \end{pmatrix} = \begin{pmatrix} \beta_{10} \\ \beta_{20} \end{pmatrix} + \begin{pmatrix} \beta_{11} & \gamma_{11} \\ \beta_{21} & \gamma_{21} \end{pmatrix} \begin{pmatrix} y_{1,t-1} \\ y_{2,t-1} \end{pmatrix} + \cdots + \begin{pmatrix} \beta_{1p} & \gamma_{1p} \\ \beta_{2p} & \gamma_{2p} \end{pmatrix} \begin{pmatrix} y_{1,t-p} \\ y_{2,t-p} \end{pmatrix} + \begin{pmatrix} \varepsilon_{1t} \\ \varepsilon_{2t} \end{pmatrix}$$

We can simplify the above equation as follows.

$$y_t = \begin{pmatrix} y_{1t} \\ y_{2t} \end{pmatrix}, \ \Phi_0 = \begin{pmatrix} \beta_{10} \\ \beta_{20} \end{pmatrix}, \ \Phi_1 = \begin{pmatrix} \beta_{11} & \gamma_{11} \\ \beta_{21} & \gamma_{21} \end{pmatrix}, \cdots, \ \Phi_p = \begin{pmatrix} \beta_{1p} & \gamma_{1p} \\ \beta_{2p} & \gamma_{2p} \end{pmatrix}, \ \varepsilon_t = \begin{pmatrix} \varepsilon_{1t} \\ \varepsilon_{2t} \end{pmatrix}$$

So the VAR (p) model expressed in matrix form is as follows:

$$y_t = \Phi_0 + \Phi_1 y_{t-1} + \cdots + \Phi_p y_{t-p} + \varepsilon_t$$

When the VAR model does not contain exogenous variables, the unrestricted VAR model can be further expressed as follows:

$$\Phi(L) y_t = \varepsilon_t$$

If the roots of the determinant $\det[\Phi(L)]$ are all inside the unit circle, that is, its modulus is less than 1, then the model satisfies the stability condition, which is an important basis for us to test whether the empirical part of the model system is stable. After the VAR model is established, it is necessary to determine the lag order of variables. In actual selection, it is necessary to find a find an equilibrium point between a sufficient number of lags and a sufficient number of degrees of freedom. There are the following six test methods for determining the lag order by Eviews, namely LogL, LR, FPE, AIC, SC and HQ. Among them, the likelihood ratio (LR), the Akaike information criterion (AIC) and the Schwarz Criterion (SC) are commonly used test criteria, and the latter two are mainly introduced here.

The vector white noise process$\{\varepsilon_t\}$ is a weakly stationary random process, which satisfies the following conditions:

$$E(\varepsilon_t) = 0,\ E(\varepsilon_t \varepsilon_t') = \Sigma,\ E(\varepsilon_t \varepsilon_s') = 0$$

where Σ is the positive definite matrix. The matrix Σ can be estimated according to the residual $\widehat{\varepsilon_t}$, denoted by, whose (i, j) element is $\widehat{\Sigma}_{ij} = \frac{1}{T}\sum_{t=1}^{T} \widehat{\varepsilon}_{it}\widehat{\varepsilon}_{jt}$. T is the sample size. Then AIC and SC are given by the following equations:

$$AIC(p) = \ln\left|\widehat{\Sigma}\right| + n\ (np + 1)\frac{2}{T}$$

$$SC(p) = \ln\left|\widehat{\Sigma}\right| + n(np + 1)\frac{\ln T}{T}$$

Here, n is the number of variables in the VAR model, p is the lag order, and $n(np + 1)$ is the number of coefficients to be estimated in the model. AIC and SC require that the smaller the value of the above equations is, the better. Similarly, six criteria are provided according to Eviews and the lag order satisfying the greatest number of criteria is selected as the final lag order of the model.

After determining the lag order of the VAR model, it is necessary to re-check the stability of the model, that is, to check whether the AR roots are inside the unit circle, which is a necessary condition for determining the convergence of the impulse response function of the model, because divergent functions are of substantive significance in guiding actual research and forecasting. If these conditions are satisfied, the impulse response function of the VAR model can be further studied.

The VAR model in practical application is a non-theoretical model, which does not require any prior constraints on variables, and the economic significance of model parameters is difficult to explain. It mainly provides guidance in a statistical sense. In analysis using a VAR model, the effects of changes in one variable on another variable are often not analyzed, but the dynamic effect of a one-standard deviation positive shock to an endogenous variable on the whole system was analyzed. This is the pulse response function analysis method.

The above VAR (p) model $y_t = \Phi_0 + \Phi_1 y_{t-1} + \cdots + \Phi_p y_{t-p} + \varepsilon_t$ is written in Vector Moving Average (VMA) form by using the lag operator:

$$(I - \Phi_1 L - \cdots - \Phi_p L^p) y_t = \Phi_0 + \varepsilon_t$$

$$\Phi(L) y_t = \Phi_0 + \varepsilon_t$$

where $\Phi(L) = I - \Phi_1 L - \cdots - \Phi_p L^p$. By multiplying both sides of this equation by $\Phi(L)^{-1}$, we get

$$y_t = \Phi(L)^{-1}\Phi_0 + \Phi(L)^{-1}\varepsilon_t$$

Let $\Phi(L)^{-1} \equiv \varphi(L) = \varphi_0 + \varphi_1 L + \varphi_2 L^2 + \cdots$, $\varphi(L)^{-1}\varphi_0 \equiv \alpha$,then the VMA representation of VAR model is as follows:

$$y_t = \alpha + \varphi_0 \varepsilon_t + \varphi_1 \varepsilon_{t-1} + \varphi_2 \varepsilon_{t-2} + \cdots = \alpha + \sum_{i=0}^{\infty} \varphi_i \varepsilon_{t-i}$$

According to the law of vector differentiation,

$$\frac{\partial y_{t+s}}{\partial \varepsilon_{t'}} = \varphi_s$$

Here $\left({}^{\partial y_{t+s}}/_{\partial \varepsilon_{t'}}\right)$ means that the partial derivative of the n-dimensional column vector y_{t+s} with respect to the n-dimensional row vector $\varepsilon_{t'}$ gives you a square matrix φ_s of order n, in which the element in the ith row and the jth column is $(\partial y_{i,t+s} / \partial \varepsilon_{jt})$. It represents the impact on the shock on the value $y_{i,t+s}$ of the ith variable in the period $(t + s)$ when the disturbance term ε_{jt} of the jth variable increases by one unit in the period t, while other variables and the disturbance terms for other periods remain unchanged. $(\partial y_{i,t+s} / \partial \varepsilon_{jt})$ is the impulse response function of the VAR model, which is regarded as a function on an interval s.

2.2 Data Selection

In order to study the economic effects of U.S. monetary policy adjustments, we need to first select representative variables that accurately measure the Fed's monetary policy. After the outbreak of the 2008 financial crisis, the U.S. monetary policy shifted from conventional monetary policy to the unconventional policy of quantitative easing. The latter was launched with the Fed announcing for the first time in November 2008 that it would purchase agency bonds and Mortgage-Backed Securities (MBS) and was officially withdrawn in October 2014 The six-year policy had been rolled out four times to continuously boost the U.S. economy and job market. The end of quantitative easing in the United States coincided with increasing discussion of a rate hike by the Fed, and international markets were keeping a constant and sensitive eye on it.

U.S. monetary policy adjustments include not only the transition from conventional to unconventional monetary policy, but also the impact of the withdrawal of quantitative easing and rate hike expectations, that is, the transition from unconventional to conventional monetary policy. When simulating these scenarios, a VAR model can predict Representative variables in the form of a one-standard deviation positive shock. Therefore, in this paper, the selection of the representative variables of the Fed's monetary policy is divided into two steps: (1) The federal funds rate was used to measure conventional monetary policy. In the 1990s, the Fed changed the intermediate target of monetary policy from the money supply to an index system centered on real interest rates and composed of a number of economic and financial variables. In July 1993, Alan Greenspan, then Fed Chairman Alan Greenspan announced that from now on the real interest rate would be used as the main means of macroeconomic regulation, mainly because changes in the pattern of investment in the United States had greatly weakened the correlation between money supply and economic growth. The typical indicator of the real interest rate was the federal funds rate. (2) The reserve balances of U.S. depository institutions at Federal Reserve Banks were used as the proxy indicator of quantitative easing. The Fed made large-scale purchases of Treasury securities and mortgage-backed securities during quantitative easing, and most of these financial assets were the assets of commercial banks or depository institutions, and the reserve balances of the latter at Federal Reserve Banks were used to pay for the Fed's large-scale bond purchases (Zhu, 2014). Figure 3 shows the federal funds rate, the reserve balances of depository institutions at Federal Reserve Banks, and the volume of bond purchases from January 2003 to June 2015, of which the volume of bond purchases is derived from the Fed's combined holdings of Treasury securities and mortgage-backed securities.[2]

As can be seen from Fig. 3, around 2008, reserve balances and the volume of the Fed's bond purchases moved in an almost opposite direction of the federal fund interest rate. Influenced by quantitative easing, the Fed made large-scale purchases of Treasury securities and mortgage-backed securities. The reserve balances of depository institutions at Federal Reserve Banks increased rapidly. At the same time, the federal funds rate was extremely low, between 0% and 0.25%. The main

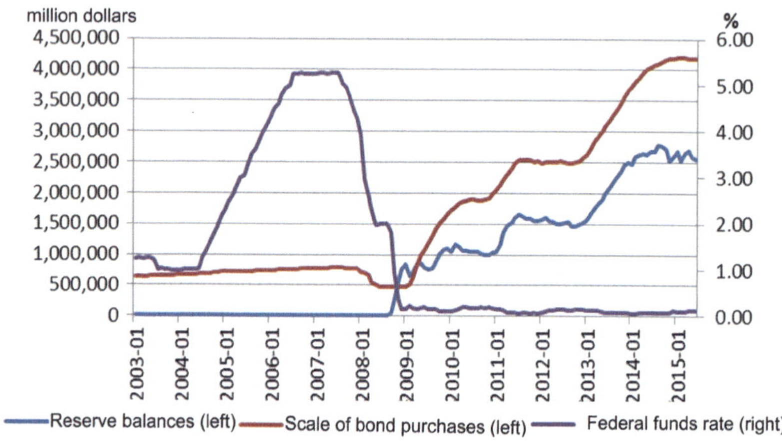

Fig. 3 Reserve balances of U.S. depository institutions at federal reserve banks, the volume of the fed's bond purchases, and the Federal Funds Rate (*Source* compiled and produced by the author based on empirical results obtained using Eviews 8.0)

[2] During the U.S. financial crisis, the U.S. economy was gradually made to recover steadily through the adjustment of monetary policy. The Federal Reserve began to raise interest rates in 2015. A narrowing of yield spreads between the United States and other countries would intensify the downward pressure on non-U.S. dollar currencies and capital outflow pressure, thus increasing liquidity pressure in global financial markets and making it more difficult for monetary authorities in various countries to regulate in the process of economic restructuring. Data selection and analysis after the rate hike are not described here.

considerations for choosing the reserve balances of U.S. depository institutions at Federal Reserve Banks as the proxy indicator of quantitative easing are as follows: The financial crisis was marked by the bankruptcy of Lehman Brothers in September 2008, and the Federal Reserve started the first round of quantitative easing in November of the same year. According to the data, the reserve balances of U.S. depository institutions at Federal Reserve Banks began to increase substantially in October 2008, while the Fed's bond purchases began to increase substantially in March 2009. Therefore, this paper maintains that the former is more forward-looking and sensitive in measuring quantitative easing, while the latter is subject to policy lags.

In empirical research in this chapter and the next chapter, this paper will analyze the impact of U.S. monetary policy adjustments on the world economy and China's economy. When studying the former, for the sake of representativeness and data availability, we selected 14 countries and regions, including the United States, Germany, France, the United Kingdom, Italy, Japan, Canada, China, Russia, India, Brazil, South Africa, Australia, and the euro area. The first seven countries are G7 members, the middle five are BRICS countries, Australia is the representative of Oceanian countries, and the euro area was studied as a whole. The sample countries include developed market economies and emerging market economies, as well as representative countries in Asia, Europe, North America, South America, Africa and Oceania. World Bank statistics show that the combined GDP of the sample member countries accounted for 69.6% of global GDP in current U.S. dollars in 2014, so they are very representative. Since China officially became a member of the World Trade Organization on December 11, 2001, in order to unify the research interval as much as possible and for China, in this paper, we choose January 2002 to June 2015 as the sample interval, consisting of a total of 162 sets of monthly data. In addition, since the bankruptcy of Lehman Brothers in September 2008 marked the outbreak of the financial crisis and was also a key point that led to the adjustment of U.S. monetary policy, the whole range was divided into two sub-ranges: January 2002 to August 2008 and from September 2008 to June 2015. The former was defined as the conventional U.S. monetary policy interval, and the latter the U.S. (unconventional) quantitative easing policy interval, consisting of 80 and 82 sets of monthly data respectively.

It should be pointed out that research on the world economy and China's economy both involves China. This paper holds that, when demonstrating the impact of U.S. monetary policy adjustments on the world economy, because the data series of all sample member countries are not as available as China's, a unified and simplified model framework should be constructed here for analysis, and conclusions should be drawn concerning the impact of U.S. monetary policy adjustments on the world economy by analyzing all sample countries separately and then summarizing the shock features. The results of studies conducted by Ma and Yu (2015), Zhu (2014), Xiao (2011), Frztzscher et al. (2012), Neri and Nobili (2010), Cogley and Sargent (2005), et al. were consulted when selecting model variables. This paper mainly considers from the four perspectives of trade, inflation, exchange rates and capital markets. In order to enhance comparability, data were processed as follows: (1) All trade deficit data are adjusted by exchange rates and expressed in millions of U.S. dollars; (2) Year-over-year data are used for the CPI. As the CPI in Australia is a quarterly indicator, this paper uses the cubic-match last interpolation method to convert it into a monthly indicator; (3) The data sample period for South Africa is from January 2004 to June 2015, and the sample period is divided into January 2004 to August 2008 and September 2008 to June 2015. This is because the South Africa Stock Market Index began to update in January 2003, and South Africa began to run a trade deficit in January 2004; (4) The data sample period for Italy is from January 2003 to June 2015. In line with the data processing method for South Africa, the sample period is divided into January 2003 to August 2008 and 2008 ember to June 2015.

The names, meanings and data sources of variables selected in the empirical part of this paper are shown in Table 1.

3 Empirical Analysis and Results

The most important point in the application of a VAR model is to ensure the stability of the model, that is, the impulse response function converges in the long run, because the divergent responses obtained by an unstable model are not helpful for research, analysis and practical reference. From the perspective of proxy indicators, the adjustment of U.S. monetary policy is reflected in two main features: the rapid decline of the federal funds rate to between 0% and 0.25% and the substantial and rapid growth of the reserve balances of U.S. depository institutions at Federal Reserve Banks after the outbreak of the financial crisis. Abnormal fluctuations in raw data pose a challenge to the application of the VAR model. In order

Table 1 Description of empirical data

Data name	*Abbreviation*	*Meaning and purpose*	*Source*	*Processing method*
Federal funds rate	FFR	Represent conventional U.S. monetary policy	Federal Reserve	Monthly average
Reserve balances with Federal Reserve Banks	RB	Represent quantitative easing policy	Federal Reserve	Monthly average
Balance of trade	NE	Represent the net exports of a country; for studying the impact of policy adjustments on imports and exports	Wind	All denominated in U.S. dollars
Consumer Price Index	CPI	Represent price changes in commodity markets; for studying the impact of policy adjustments on inflation	Wind	Year-over-year
Real effective exchange rate	REE	Represent changes in the real exchange rate of a country's currency	Bank for International Settlements	Adjusted for inflation
Stock market index	SI	Represent changes in a country's capital markets	Wind	Closing price in the month

Source compiled and produced by the author based on empirical results obtained using Eviews 8.0

to overcome these difficulties and use a unified framework to study the impact of U.S. monetary policy adjustments on 13 sample countries and regions, the original indicators are preliminarily processed as follows: The federal funds rate, trade deficits and the CPI are directly processed by the first-order difference operation; reserve balances, the real effective exchange rate and the stock market index are processed by the first-order difference operation after logarithms are taken, and the processed federal funds rate, reserve balances, trade deficit, CPI, real effective exchange rate and stock market index are abbreviated as dffr, dlnrb, dne, dcpi, dlnree and dlnsi, respectively. The first-order difference sequence has significant economic implications and mainly measures fluctuations in an economic variable. The ADF test showed that the model variables of all sample countries and regions were stationary in the three time intervals, meeting the conditions of stationarity and comparability of the VAR model.

In the specific operation, the federal funds rate and reserve balances were added into the VAR model, and the variable vectors are $(dffr, dne, dcpi, d\ln ree, d\ln si)$ and $(d\ln rb, dne, dcpi, d\ln ree, d\ln si)$ respectively. Then model estimation was performed on the 14 countries and regions in three time intervals, for a total of 84 models. In the model estimation, 84 models were estimated and proofread respectively in terms of lag orders, AR root tests, cointegration tests, impulse response functions, etc.,[3] in order to comparatively analyze the impact of U.S. monetary policy adjustments on the sample countries and even the world economy.

The findings of this chapter are presented and analyzed in the following three parts: First, the domestic effects of U.S. monetary policy adjustments, that is, the impact on the U.S. economy; second, the study of the spillover effects of U.S. monetary policy adjustments abroad, which can be further studied at the two levels of developed economies and emerging market and developing economies. According to the World Economic Outlook (April 2015) released by the IMF, in this paper, we divide the sample countries and regions except the United States into: (1) developed economies, including eight economies, namely Germany, France, the United Kingdom, Italy, Japan, Canada, the euro area and Australia; (2) emerging market and developing economies, including Brazil, Russia, India, China and South Africa, known as the BRICS countries.

3.1 Domestic Effects of U.S. Monetary Policy Adjustments

In response to the financial turmoil caused by the subprime mortgage crisis, the Fed shifted from the conventional monetary policy adopted since 1993 with real interest rates as the main regulatory tool to quantitative easing policies such as the zero interest rate policy and the purchase

[3] Due to the large amount of data, it is impossible to present them all here. The main results will be organized and compiled in this paper.

of government bonds. But in the final analysis, monetary policy adjustments were intended to ease the U.S. economic, financial and job market woes, so we first analyze the domestic effects of such adjustments, and from there extend to external markets.

3.1.1 Impact on Trade

After sorting out the empirical results, Fig. 4 shows the impulse response function of fluctuations in the trade deficit caused by a one-standard deviation positive shock to the proxy variable of U.S. monetary policy.

First, analyze the impact of conventional monetary policy on trade. As can be seen from the figure above, in the face of a one-standard deviation positive shock to fluctuations in the federal funds rate, fluctuations in the trade deficit fluctuation gave a relatively significant and close positive response in the first period, and the responses in the three time periods were \$431 million, \$547 million and \$487 million, respectively. However, in the second period, the situation reversed, and the negative response reached the maximum, reaching −\$761 million, −\$541 million and −\$1.486 billion, respectively. After that, the absolute value of the response decreased continuously, was significant for about 9 months, and finally converged to 0. The overall response in time period 1 and time period

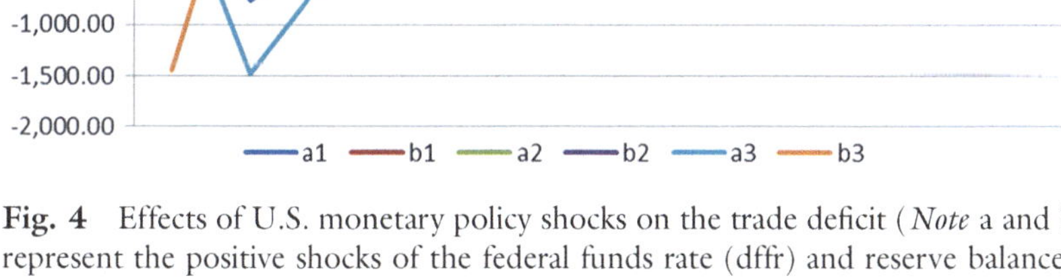

Fig. 4 Effects of U.S. monetary policy shocks on the trade deficit (*Note* a and b represent the positive shocks of the federal funds rate (dffr) and reserve balances (dlnrb) respectively; 1, 2 and 3 refer to the three time periods from January 2002 to June 2015, January 2002 to August 2008 and September 2008 to June 2015, respectively. Unless otherwise noted, this marking regime is used in the following sections of this chapter *Source* compiled and produced by the author based on empirical results obtained using Eviews 8.0)

3 was negative, and the cumulative 12-month response was −$1.162 billion and −$2.596 billion. The cumulative 12-month response in period 2 was $408 million, suggesting that a positive shock to fluctuations in the federal funds rate during the financial crisis would have a more significant negative impact on trade.

Let's look at the impact of quantitative easing on trade. According to Fig. 4, the responses of samples b1 and b3 were the opposite of the effect of conventional monetary policy shocks, and the response of sample b2 was weak. Take the samples after September 2008 as an example. In the face of a one-standard deviation positive shock to reserve balances, the trade deficit gave a maximum negative response of −$1.445 billion in the first period, but then in the second period, the response became $1.043 billion, and in all subsequent periods, the cumulative 12-month response was $905 million. The results show that the rapid growth of the reserve balances of U.S. depository institutions at Federal Reserve Banks caused by the Fed's quantitative easing ultimately contributed to an improvement in the trade deficit, resulting in a boost to the economic recovery.

3.1.2 *Impact on Inflation*

Statistics from the U.S. Department of Labor show that after the outbreak of the financial crisis, the United States faced deflationary pressure for nearly a year, and the CPI registered a negative year-over-year growth. In order to examine the statistical correlation between U.S. monetary policy adjustments and the CPI, Fig. 5 shows the impulse response function of fluctuations in inflation caused by a one-standard deviation positive shock to the proxy variable of U.S. monetary policy.

Across the sampling interval, fluctuations in inflation responded differently to a one-standard deviation positive shock to conventional monetary policy and quantitative easing policy, with the former giving a sustained positive response, i.e. tending to increase fluctuations in inflation, and the latter giving a more pronounced negative response, that is, the larger the reserve balances of U.S. deposit institutions at Federal Reserve Banks, the greater the deflationary pressure. This statistical feature was more pronounced during quantitative easing, that is, when interest rates are close to zero, rising interest rates can ease deflation; on the other hand, the Fed injected liquidity into the market by purchasing Treasury bonds and agency bonds. Due to the extreme severity of the financial crisis at its outset, the market did not immediately warm up. Moreover, scholars

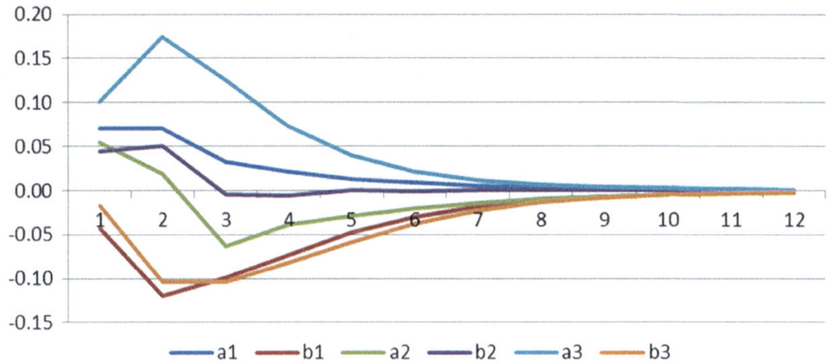

Fig. 5 Impact of U.S. monetary policy shocks on inflatsion (*Source* compiled and produced by the author based on empirical results obtained using Eviews 8.0)

generally believed that U.S. quantitative easing had brought greater imported inflation to external economies.

3.1.3 *Impact on the Real Effective Exchange Rate of the U.S. Dollar*

The current real effective exchange rate data released by the Bank for International Settlements is 2010 data, which is used to reflect the appreciation or depreciation of a country's currency. Appreciation occurs when its value increases, and vice versa. Figure 6 shows the impulse response function of fluctuations in the real effective exchange rate caused by a one-standard deviation positive shock to the proxy variable of U.S. monetary policy.

It can be seen from Fig. 6 that the real effective exchange rate of the U.S. dollar responded completely differently to the positive shocks of the two kinds of monetary policy in time periods 1 and 3. During the conventional monetary policy period from 2002 to August 2008, fluctuations in the federal funds rate and reserve balances increased the exchange rate to varying degrees. During this period, the macroeconomy was in normal operation. An increase in reserve balances reflected an increase in demand for the dollar, and an increase in the federal funds rate led to an inflow of international capital, which in turn led to an appreciation of the dollar. However, after September 2008, the financial crisis broke this impact mechanism, which was mainly manifested in the fact that a one-standard

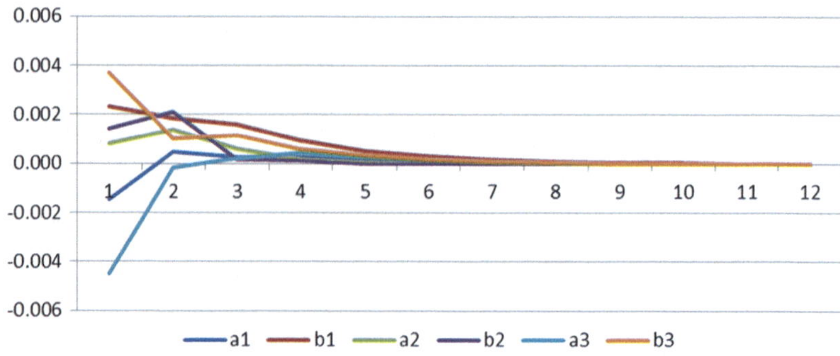

Fig. 6 Impact of U.S. monetary policy shocks on the real effective exchange rate of the U.S. Dollar (*Source* compiled and produced by the author based on empirical results obtained using Eviews 8.0)

deviation positive shock to the federal funds rate tended to devalue the dollar, while a one-standard deviation positive shock to reserve balances pushed the dollar higher. The effect of the initial shock lasted for about 8 months, and then the response function gradually converged to 0. This suggests that in the post-financial crisis era, the role of the federal funds rate in economic recovery and boosting confidence in the currency has been greatly diminished, while quantitative easing, expressed in reserve balances, can have a positive effect.

3.1.4 *Impact on the Stock Market*

Using the S&P 500 index to represent the U.S. stock market, Fig. 7 shows the impulse response function of stock market fluctuations caused by a one-standard deviation positive shock to the proxy variable of U.S. monetary policy.

We mainly analyze the impact of quantitative easing on stock market fluctuations in September 2008. As can be seen from Fig. 7, sample a3 and b3 responded differently to a one-standard deviation positive shock to the federal funds rate and reserve balances respectively. Sample a3 gave the most significant positive response in the first period, reaching 0.0167, and then the response gradually decreased. The response of sample b3 was initially negative, reached a maximum negative value of -0.0098 in the second period, and then gradually weakened to 0. This paper holds that after the outbreak of the financial crisis, the federal funds rate was

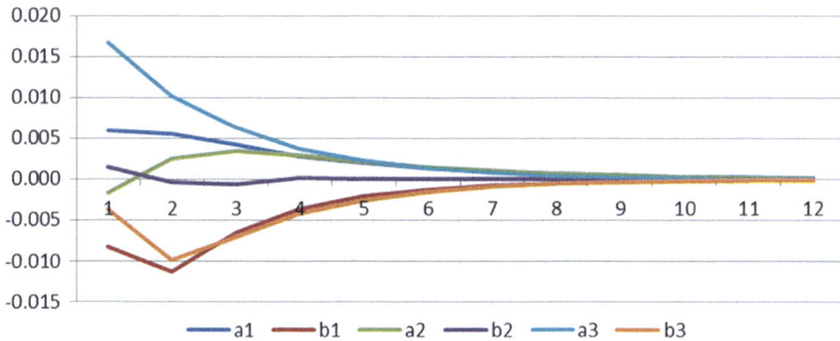

Fig. 7 Impact of U.S. monetary policy shocks on stock market fluctuations (*Source* compiled and produced by the author based on empirical results obtained using Eviews 8.0)

close to zero, the interest rate tool was almost useless, but an increase in the simulated interest rates can be seen as a signal of a boost to the market. The role of reserve balances was different. After a significant increase in the reserve balances of U.S. depository institutions at Federal Reserve Banks in September 2008, the U.S. stock market did not improve significantly within a year, but went from bad to worse with the collapse of market confidence. Reserve balances were a precursor to the crisis. The resulting increase in fluctuations in reserve balance weighed down the stock market, a statistical feature that lasted about eight months, as seen in the chart above.

3.1.5 Summary

Next, this paper summarizes the above responses In order to be more targeted, the impulse responses to a one-standard deviation positive shock to fluctuations in the federal funds rate during the conventional monetary policy period and a one-standard deviation positive shock to fluctuations in reserve balances during the quantitative easing policy period are compared and statistically analyzed in Table 2.

Judging from the responses in different periods, the effects of the Fed's conventional and unconventional monetary policy shocks were different: On the one hand, in the first period, trade and the CPI responded completely differently to the two kinds of monetary policy shocks, while the exchange rate and the stock market responded the same way. On the other hand, the maximum response of variables to monetary policy

Table 2 Impulse response characteristics of U.S. monetary policy shocks

		1	*2*	*3*	*4*	*5*	*6*	*Cumulative (12 periods)*
Conventional monetary policy (a2)	Trade	**547.00**	−541.06	147.96	59.36	63.04	43.11	408.36
	CPI	0.0540	0.0186	**−0.0636**	−0.0383	−0.0290	−0.0199	−0.1182
	Exchange rate	0.0008	**0.0014**	0.0006	0.0002	0.0001	0.0000	0.0031
	Stock market	−0.0017	0.0025	**0.0035**	0.0029	0.0021	0.0015	0.0139
Quantitative easing policy (b3)	Trade	**−1444.86**	1043.36	321.90	406.48	206.70	157.39	905.08
	CPI	−0.0164	−0.1030	**−0.1032**	−0.0818	−0.0578	−0.0371	−0.4522
	Exchange rate	**0.0037**	0.0010	0.0012	0.0006	0.0004	0.0002	0.0072
	Stock market	−0.0037	**−0.0098**	−0.0070	−0.0042	−0.0026	−0.0015	−0.0310

Note Figures in bold indicate the largest absolute values of responses. Trade is measured in millions of U.S. dollars, the CPI is measured in percentages, and the exchange rate and stock market are measured in 1

Source compiled and produced by the author based on empirical results obtained using Eviews 8.0

shocks occurred in different periods, and trade and the stock market responded completely differently. However, there are similarities between the two. From the exchange rate point of view, both kinds of monetary policy shocks contributed to boosting confidence in the currency. But the current inhibitory effect of currency appreciation on exports in the current period was also obvious, as can be seen from the responses of the exchange rate and trade in the second period under conventional monetary policy: 0.0014 and −541.06, and the responses of the exchange rate and trade in the first period under quantitative easing policy: 0.0037 and −1444.86. According to the 12-period cumulative impulse response, the cumulative response characteristics of trade, the CPI and the exchange rate were consistent, and the stock market was an exception in that it responded completely differently to monetary policy shocks.

4 Impact of U.S. Monetary Policy Adjustments on Major Economic Variables in Developed Economies

The developed economies defined in this paper include Germany, France, the United Kingdom, Italy, Japan, Canada, the euro area and Australia. From the perspective of model design, there are six submodels, a1, a2, a3, b1, b2 and b3, each submodel contains four effect variables per country (excluding the proxy variable of monetary policy), and each shock contains at least six periods, so the simplified empirical results for the eight economies contain at least 1152 pieces of data. Due to the large amount of data, in order to make the analysis more targeted and necessarily simplified, this part only comparatively analyzes the impulse responses of the sample variables of eight economies to a one-standard deviation positive shock to fluctuations in the federal funds rate during the conventional monetary policy period and a one-standard deviation positive shock to fluctuations in reserve balances during the quantitative easing policy period, which are represented by a2 and b3 respectively. See Table 3 for the relevant summary.

Next, this paper analyzes Europe, Asia, North America and Oceania from the perspective of the continents to which developed countries and regions belong.

First, sample economies in Europe. First, so far as the euro area as a whole is concerned, during the conventional U.S. monetary policy period,

Table 3 Summary of main pulse responses to U.S. monetary policy shocks to sample developed economies

Developed economies	*Response variables*		*1*	*2*	*3*	*4*	*5*	*6*	*Cumulative (12 periods)*
Germany	a2	Trade	**−162.06**	−106.66	57.22	−18.24	16.45	−3.33	−208.18
		CPI	0.0385	**−0.0493**	−0.0046	−0.0104	−0.0057	−0.0045	−0.0452
		Exchange rate	**0.0019**	−0.0012	−0.0008	−0.0005	−0.0004	−0.0003	−0.0019
		Stock market	−0.0034	0.0068	**0.0071**	0.0050	0.0034	0.0025	0.0266
	b3	Trade	334.70	**−440.70**	−4.88	−116.02	−35.18	−41.40	−369.86
		CPI	0.0022	**−0.0371**	−0.0339	−0.0238	−0.0164	−0.0113	−0.1421
		Exchange rate	**−0.0018**	−0.0001	0.0001	0.0001	0.0001	0.0000	−0.0016
		Stock market	0.0000	−0.0040	**−0.0078**	−0.0040	−0.0033	−0.0021	−0.0254
France	a2	Trade	**−113.69**	**113.69**	−69.54	21.40	−19.97	3.34	−76.13
		CPI	−0.0197	**−0.0494**	−0.0287	−0.0187	−0.0139	−0.0097	−0.1622
		Exchange rate	**0.0008**	−0.0007	−0.0006	−0.0005	−0.0004	−0.0003	−0.0024
		Stock market	−0.0046	**0.0073**	0.0061	0.0041	0.0031	0.0022	0.0234
	b3	Trade	−32.52	**54.05**	38.31	29.52	16.75	11.92	137.34
		CPI	0.0120	**−0.0448**	−0.0414	−0.0301	−0.0205	−0.0137	−0.1622
		Exchange rate	**−0.0008**	−0.0001	0.0000	0.0001	0.0001	0.0001	−0.0006
		Stock market	0.0002	**−0.0075**	−0.0054	−0.0034	−0.0022	−0.0014	−0.0223

Developed economies	*Response variables*		*1*	*2*	*3*	*4*	*5*	*6*	*Cumulative (12 periods)*
United Kingdom	a2	Trade	−49.53	**63.09**	17.86	28.26	16.03	12.79	115.80
		CPI	−0.0107	−0.0088	**−0.0261**	−0.0223	−0.0169	−0.0121	−0.1236
		Exchange rate	0.0007	**0.0027**	0.0017	0.0012	0.0008	0.0006	0.0091
		Stock market	−0.0022	**0.0065**	0.0040	0.0030	0.0021	0.0015	0.0183
	b3	Trade	28.00	**54.52**	22.84	23.37	10.47	9.04	160.89
		CPI	**−0.0661**	−0.0443	−0.0252	−0.0154	−0.0098	−0.0062	−0.1771
		Exchange rate	0.0010	**−0.0031**	−0.0025	−0.0016	−0.0010	−0.0007	−0.0090
		Stock market	**−0.0029**	−0.0027	−0.0027	−0.0019	−0.0012	−0.0008	−0.0134
Italy	a2	Trade	−54.73	**−219.19**	58.61	−97.43	−4.35	−34.84	−418.51
		CPI	0.0055	**−0.0530**	−0.0246	−0.0230	−0.0179	−0.0140	−0.1678
		Exchange rate	**0.0011**	−0.0009	−0.0003	−0.0004	−0.0003	−0.0002	−0.0017
		Stock market	0.0013	**0.0091**	0.0056	0.0046	0.0036	0.0029	0.0353
	b3	Trade	**308.84**	−130.15	84.67	−26.71	23.35	−6.76	259.26
		CPI	−0.0002	−0.0274	**−0.0330**	−0.0292	−0.0215	−0.0155	−0.1547
		Exchange rate	**−0.0010**	−0.0001	0.0001	0.0001	0.0002	0.0001	−0.0003
		Stock market	−0.0002	**−0.0081**	−0.0062	−0.0038	−0.0022	−0.0013	−0.0235

(continued)

Table 3 (continued)

Developed economies	*Response variables*		*1*	*2*	*3*	*4*	*5*	*6*	*Cumulative (12 periods)*
Japan	a2	Trade	169.85	**−327.12**	26.00	−105.78	−24.00	−43.26	−383.70
		CPI	**−0.0320**	−0.0150	−0.0197	−0.0115	−0.0096	−0.0068	−0.1117
		Exchange rate	**−0.0025**	−0.0012	−0.0016	−0.0010	−0.0008	−0.0006	−0.0093
		Stock market	−0.0052	**0.0072**	0.0059	0.0045	0.0034	0.0025	0.0244
	b3	Trade	**546.35**	−386.75	27.94	−104.26	4.19	−30.24	39.12
		CPI	0.0321	−0.0314	**−0.0390**	−0.0310	−0.0206	−0.0134	−0.1247
		Exchange rate	0.0055	**0.0071**	0.0045	0.0027	0.0017	0.0010	0.0242
		Stock market	**−0.0207**	−0.0097	−0.0057	−0.0036	−0.0023	−0.0014	−0.0456
Canada	a2	Trade	**−133.76**	−81.26	−44.75	−41.22	−28.38	−21.12	−395.55
		CPI	**−0.0201**	0.0096	0.0012	−0.0030	−0.0029	−0.0024	−0.0230
		Exchange rate	**−0.0022**	0.0012	0.0018	0.0015	0.0011	0.0008	0.0060
		Stock market	**−0.0037**	0.0014	0.0009	0.0007	0.0005	0.0004	0.0009
	b3	Trade	−78.48	**−164.58**	−64.18	−53.95	−37.30	−24.58	−469.51
		CPI	**−0.0563**	−0.0527	−0.0264	−0.0197	−0.0136	−0.0091	−0.1950
		Exchange rate	**−0.0065**	−0.0017	−0.0014	−0.0012	−0.0008	−0.0005	−0.0131

Developed economies	*Response variables*		*1*	*2*	*3*	*4*	*5*	*6*	*Cumulative (12 periods)*
		Stock market	−0.0062	**−0.0065**	−0.0051	−0.0033	−0.0023	−0.0016	−0.0278
Eurozone	a2	Trade	**880.12**	−29.39	152.57	58.11	53.31	34.91	1, 222.21
		CPI	**−0.1606**	−0.0509	−0.0331	−0.0211	−0.0154	−0.0108	−0.3138
		Exchange rate	**−0.0022**	−0.0001	−0.0003	−0.0002	−0.0002	−0.0001	−0.0033
		Stock market	−0.0101	**0.0164**	0.0152	0.0106	0.0076	0.0052	0.0556
	b3	Trade	**1, 829.06**	−800.93	399.58	−12.09	47.37	22.11	1, 524.30
		CPI	−0.0014	−0.0407	**−0.0423**	−0.0300	−0.0195	−0.0129	−0.1684
		Exchange rate	**−0.0025**	−0.0002	0.0000	0.0001	0.0001	0.0001	−0.0024
		Stock market	**0.0224**	−0.0110	−0.0163	−0.0035	−0.0043	−0.0024	−0.0192
Australia	a2	Trade	**110.10**	−43.23	17.82	−4.43	3.02	−1.13	79.00
		CPI	−0.0039	−0.0046	−0.0048	**−0.0059**	**−0.0059**	−0.0058	−0.0567
		Exchange rate	**−0.0030**	−0.0016	0.0006	0.0002	0.0002	0.0001	−0.0028
		Stock market	−0.0025	**0.0066**	0.0036	0.0027	0.0019	0.0015	0.0177
	b3	Trade	**109.14**	−27.16	6.86	−20.24	−19.35	−24.03	−86.30
		CPI	−0.0106	−0.0284	−0.0399	−0.0447	**−0.0453**	−0.0430	−0.3746
		Exchange rate	**−0.0090**	−0.0040	−0.0030	−0.0014	−0.0004	0.0003	−0.0119
		Stock market	−0.0016	**−0.0089**	−0.0042	−0.0028	−0.0012	−0.0003	−0.0135

Note Figures in bold indicate the largest absolute values of responses. Trade is measured in millions of U.S. dollars, the CPI is measured in percentages, and the exchange rate and stock market are measured in 1

Source compiled and produced by the author based on empirical results obtained using Eviews 8.0

in response to a one-standard deviation positive shock to the federal funds rate, the balance of trade in the euro area gave the maximum positive response at the beginning, reaching \$880 million. Although the response in the second period was negative, it was only \$29 million. After that, the response function remained above the X-axis and finally converged to 0. During the U.S. quantitative easing policy period, a sudden increase in the reserve balances of U.S. depository institutions at Federal Reserve Banks would significantly promote the foreign trade of the euro area in the current period, but the duration was short. So far as the cumulative response function is concerned, the 12-period cumulative response was \$1.524 billion, which was greater than the conventional monetary policy shock of \$1.222 billion, so the quantitative easing policy adopted by the Fed after the outbreak of the financial crisis contributed to the recovery and development of the foreign trade of the euro area to some extent. So far as inflation and the exchange rate are concerned, the adjustment of U.S. monetary policy had brought certain deflationary and depreciatory pressure to the euro area. Although euro area stock markets (represented by the Euro STOXX 50 Index) gave the maximum positive response to the shock to reserve balances at the beginning, the 12-period cumulative response was negative, in the medium to long term, U.S. quantitative easing policy had an inhibitory effect on euro area stock markets.

Germany, France, the United Kingdom, and Italy are all representatives of European countries. We mainly examine the differences in the impact of U.S. monetary policy adjustments on the four sample European countries. For easy comparison, this paper analyzes the cumulative response function, and the response values and maximum values of each period are clearly identified in the table. During the conventional U.S. monetary policy period, when a one-standard deviation positive shock was applied to the federal funds rate, Germany, France and Italy gave a negative cumulative response, with Italy giving the largest response, reaching −\$419 million, followed by Germany and France. Although the United Kingdom gave a negative response at the beginning and a small response during each period, the 12-period cumulative response was \$116 million. Similarly, when the shock to the federal funds rate was negative, the corresponding results were just the opposite. An increase in the federal funds rate had an inhibitory effect on inflation in all four sample countries, which could reduce the real effective exchange rates of Germany, France and Italy, but tended to drive the pound higher. It should be noted that although Germany, France and Italy are all eurozone countries that use the euro as an invoicing or settlement currency, the real effective exchange rate released by the Bank for International Settlements is weighted by 2008–2010 trade data and adjusted for each country's consumer price index, which will lead to inconsistencies in the real effective exchange rate of the euro in different eurozone countries. During the U.S. quantitative easing policy period, a one-standard deviation positive shock to the reserve balances of U.S. depository institutions at Federal Reserve Banks impacted the four sample countries differently, which was mainly manifested in the fact that the impact adversely affected Germany's foreign trade, but relatively improved the trade situation of France, Germany and Italy. In terms of inflation, the exchange rate and the stock market, the impact of the shock on the four member countries was relatively consistent, characterized by easing inflation or bringing deflationary pressure, exacerbating the tendency for currency depreciation, and depressing stock markets in the sample countries.

Second, Asia (here it refers to Japan). From 2002 to the outbreak of the financial crisis, an increase in the federal funds rate might worsen Japan's balance of trade and lead to the unfavorable situation of deflationary pressure and exchange rate devaluation, but it would give a boost to the stock market, while a sharp drop in the federal funds rate will work the other way around. In the quantitative easing period, a one-standard deviation positive shock to the reserve balances of U.S. depository institutions at Federal Reserve Banks significantly improved Japan's trade position in the current period, but the situation reversed in the second period, and the 12-period cumulative value was only $39 million, which had a weak impact. The shock might bring about potential deflationary pressure. Japan's inflation rate had been negative since 2009, which was only eased by the quantitative stimulus of "Abenomics". Unlike in the case of the euro area, the shock stimulated the appreciation of the yen and reached a maximum of 0.0071 in the second period, in line with the actual situation. In the stock market, the quantitative easing policy implemented in response to the crisis put a lot of pressure on the Japanese stock market, and the response reached a maximum negative value of -0.0207 in the current period.

Third, North America (here it refers to Canada). Except for the effect on exchange rates, the effects of conventional U.S. monetary policy shocks on Canada is similar to those on Japan. A one-standard deviation positive shock to policy gave the Canadian dollar a boost, but the response reached a maximum negative value of -0.0022 at the beginning.

After that, the response remained positive. U.S. quantitative easing policy had a serious impact on neighboring Canada: it had the potential for reducing the size of the trade surplus and even causing a trade deficit; it lowered Canada's inflation rate but ushered in an era of austerity; Lower the real effective exchange rate of the Canadian dollar and dampened the performance of the stock market. It can be said that, in a statistical sense, U.S. quantitative easing policy smacked of "beggar thy neighbor" manipulation, and the negative impact of policy spillovers on Canada left no room for optimism.

Fourth, Oceania (here it refers to Australia). During the conventional U.S. monetary policy period, a one-standard deviation positive shock to the federal funds rate would promote or improve Australia's trade and stock market to some extent, but it might lead to signs of a decline in inflation and the real effective exchange rate. During the U.S. quantitative easing policy period, Australia, which is in the middle of the ocean, still could not escape the negative externalities brought by Fed monetary policy shocks, which would cause potential adverse effects such as worsening trade, falling inflation, damaged confidence in the currency, and sluggish stock market performance. Unlike in the case of Canada, the increase in reserve balances significantly improved Australia's trade position during the period, reaching a maximum positive value of $109 million.

In summary, the impact of U.S. monetary policy on the sample developed economies varied. Relatively speaking, U.S. quantitative easing policy contributed to improving the trade position of the euro area (except Germany) and Japan, while it had a potential negative effect on Germany, Canada and Australia. Policy shocks had an inhibitory effect on inflation rates in developed economies and even brought deflationary pressure, which was directly related to the decline in demand caused by the financial crisis. In terms of exchange rates, monetary policy shocks contributed to the appreciation of the yen, and put a lot of downward pressure on the exchange rates of the sample developed economies except Japan. This indicated that U.S. policy exerted strong pressure on the exchange rate of the yen after the outbreak of the financial crisis, which was somewhat correlated with the "Abenomics" policies put forward by the Abe administration to push the yen down after it came into power. In terms of stock markets, all the sample developed economies gave a negative cumulative response to the sudden implementation of U.S. quantitative easing policy, which was consistent with the overall macro environment at that time, and also indicated the huge impact of the adjustment of the Fed's monetary policy on external capital markets in a statistical sense.

5 Impact of U.S. Monetary Policy Adjustments on the Variables of Emerging Market and Developing Economies

The emerging market and developing economies defined in this paper include China, Brazil, Russia, India and South Africa, known as the BRICS countries. As representatives of emerging market economies, the BRICS countries account for 29.6% of the world's land area and 42.6% of the world's population. Over the past decade, the BRICS countries have contributed more than 50% of global economic growth.[4] For this reason, in this paper, we choose the BRICS countries to study the spillover effects of U.S. monetary policy adjustments on emerging market and developing economies, as they are good examples from which lessons can be drawn.

First, examine the impact of U.S. monetary policy adjustments on China's economy. First, during the conventional U.S. monetary policy period, in response to a one-standard deviation positive shock to the federal funds rate, China's balance of trade gave the maximum positive response in the current period, reaching $880 million. In the second period, the response fell back into negative territory at −$29 million, and in the third period, it was $153 million. After that, the range of fluctuations gradually narrowed, and the 12-period cumulative response reached $1.222 billion. That is to say, while tightening credit conditions in the United States, an increase in the federal funds rate would leave some room for growth in China's foreign trade statistically, provided that the influence of other factors is not considered. However, during the quantitative easing policy period, an increase in the federal funds rate would have an inhibitory effect on China's trade, and even the surplus in the current period decreased by $2.555 billion, so the impact was significant. In addition, policy shocks during the conventional monetary policy period might lead to lower inflation and exchange rate devaluation, but they were not good for the stock market. During the quantitative easing

[4] Source: Review of the Outcomes of BRICS Summits, Economic Information Daily, July 10, 2015.

policy period, the effect of a one-standard deviation positive shock to the reserve balances of U.S. depository institutions at Federal Reserve Banks on China's economy was not exactly the same as that on other sample countries. The response of the balance of trade to the shock in the first three periods was \$617 million, −\$710 million and \$825 million respectively. That was quite a roller-coaster ride. The 12-period cumulative response was \$1.548 billion, and the overall response was positive. The response of the CPI to the shock in the first period was 0.1851, indicating a tendency toward an increase in inflation, but after that, it kept a small negative response. The 12-period cumulative response was – 0.1144, which meant that in the medium term, U.S. quantitative easing might lead to a decline in China's inflation rate. The impact of policy shocks on the real effective exchange rate of RMB is similar to that on the yen, i.e., an increase in reserve balances tended to raise the exchange rate of the RMB, pushing the currency higher, which was consistent with reality. Similarly, policy shocks were not conducive to the normal operation of China's stock market. The 12-period cumulative response was – 0.0478, indicating a significant negative impact.

In Brazil, a one-standard deviation positive shock to fluctuations in the federal funds rate during the conventional U.S. monetary policy period would provide a small boost to trade and have a significant inhibitory effect on inflation. In addition, a sudden increase in interest rates would help strengthen the Brazilian real and boost the stock market. During the quantitative easing policy period, foreign trade always gave a negative but small response to a one-standard deviation positive shock to reserve balances, with the maximum response being −\$34 million. The 12-period cumulative response was −\$128 million, which was not significant overall. The impact of U.S. quantitative easing policy on Brazil's inflation is worthy of attention. The CPI gave the strongest negative response of 0.0504 in the current period, and the 12-period cumulative response was 0.0363, indicating that U.S. monetary policy shocks might raise the overall price level in Brazil. In terms of the exchange rate and stock market, U.S. policy adjustments might lead to a bad situation in which Brazil's currency depreciated and the stock market was sluggish.

In Russia, conventional U.S. monetary policy shocks might lead to worsening foreign trade, lower inflation, currency depreciation and a downturn in the stock market. The impact of U.S. quantitative easing policy was alarming. Unlike in the case of China and Brazil, the positive shock to reserve balances had a long-term negative and significant impact on Russia's trade. Specifically, the response of trade in the first four periods was −$49 million, −$366 million, −$125 million and −$133 million respectively, and the 12-period cumulative response reached −$880 million, so U.S. quantitative easing policy undoubtedly had a big impact on Russia's foreign trade. Quantitative easing policy had a negative impact on Russia's CPI and stock market, but it might lead to a higher exchange rate of the ruble. As can be seen from Table 4, the response of the exchange rate reached a maximum of 0.0054 in the first period, and the cumulative response was 0.0019, so U.S. quantitative easing policy affected the exchange rate of the ruble as it did the exchange rate of the RMB.

The impact of U.S. monetary policy adjustments on India and South Africa was to some extent consistent with that on other sample countries, but one thing to note is the impact of U.S. quantitative easing policy on India's CPI. The results show that the CPI gave a maximum positive response of 0.0676 to a one-standard deviation positive shock to the reserve balances of U.S. depository institutions at Federal Reserve Banks in the current period, and the 12-period cumulative response was 0.1299. The impact was more significant than that on Brazil's CPI. In summary, there is reason to believe that U.S. quantitative easing policy might have the spillover effects of imported inflation (as in the case of China in the current period, Brazil, and India) and exchange rate appreciation (as in the case of China and Russia) on emerging market and developing economies. Table 5 shows the direction in which U.S. quantitative easing policy shocks acted on the economies of the BRICS countries, taking the 12-period cumulative response as an example.

6 Summary and Policy Recommendations

6.1 Summary

With the outbreak of the global financial crisis as the dividing line and the federal funds rate and the reserve balances of depository institutions at Federal Reserve Banks as the characterization indicators of the Fed's conventional monetary policy and quantitative easing policy respectively, this section uses a VAR model to empirically study the impact of shocks from relevant policy variables on the economic variables of major countries and China before and after the adjustment of U.S. monetary policy. In order to quantitatively analyze the spillover effects of U.S. monetary

Table 4 Summary of main pulse responses to U.S. monetary policy shocks to sample emerging market and developing economies

Emerging market and developing economies	*Response variables*		*1*	*2*	*3*	*4*	*5*	*6*	*Cumulative (12 periods)*
China	a2	Trade	**880.12**	−29.39	152.57	58.11	53.31	34.91	1, 222.21
		CPI	**−0.1606**	−0.0509	−0.0331	−0.0211	−0.0154	−0.0108	−0.3138
		Exchange rate	**−0.0022**	−0.0001	−0.0003	−0.0002	−0.0002	−0.0001	−0.0033
		Stock market	−0.0101	**0.0164**	0.0152	0.0106	0.0076	0.0052	0.0556
	b3	Trade	617.25	−709.97	**825.19**	190.33	252.71	115.24	1, 548.06
		CPI	**0.1851**	−0.0836	−0.0592	−0.0514	−0.0333	−0.0244	−0.1144
		Exchange rate	**0.0020**	0.0011	0.0007	0.0006	0.0004	0.0003	0.0058
		Stock market	**−0.0284**	−0.0067	−0.0040	−0.0030	−0.0019	−0.0013	−0.0478
Brazil	a2	Trade	**216.08**	−118.43	28.88	−25.16	3.07	−5.23	99.87
		CPI	0.0109	−0.0246	−0.0470	−0.0582	**−0.0587**	−0.0538	−0.4058
		Exchange rate	−0.0008	**0.0025**	0.0011	0.0007	0.0000	−0.0002	0.0015
		Stock market	0.0031	**−0.0036**	0.0009	−0.0005	0.0004	0.0001	0.0015
	b3	Trade	−27.97	**−33.69**	−12.94	−16.59	−9.88	−8.88	−128.02
		CPI	**0.0504**	0.0141	0.0004	−0.0046	−0.0056	−0.0051	0.0363

Emerging market and developing economies	*Response variables*		*1*	*2*	*3*	*4*	*5*	*6*	*Cumulative (12 periods)*
		Exchange rate	**−0.0107**	−0.0058	−0.0032	−0.0020	−0.0013	−0.0008	−0.0254
		Stock market	**−0.0202**	−0.0092	−0.0059	−0.0039	−0.0026	−0.0017	−0.0468
Russia	a2	Trade	**−384.55**	−104.06	31.94	−51.03	−22.02	−16.27	−597.35
		CPI	0.0025	**−0.0340**	−0.0166	−0.0130	−0.0104	−0.0081	−0.1024
		Exchange rate	0.0012	**−0.0015**	−0.0011	−0.0009	−0.0007	−0.0006	−0.0053
		Stock market	−0.0680	**−0.0085**	−0.0065	−0.0054	−0.0052	−0.0035	−0.1075
	b3	Trade	−48.99	**−365.60**	−124.64	−132.56	−65.54	−50.84	−879.62
		CPI	−0.0967	**−0.1197**	−0.0952	−0.0604	−0.0284	−0.0076	−0.3904
		Exchange rate	**0.0054**	0.0025	−0.0002	−0.0014	−0.0016	−0.0013	0.0019
		Stock market	**−0.0225**	−0.0181	−0.0145	−0.0104	−0.0075	−0.0051	−0.0870
India	a2	Trade	**−46.10**	25.04	19.10	13.88	8.96	6.37	40.19
		CPI	**0.0571**	−0.0422	−0.0384	−0.0271	−0.0193	−0.0135	−0.1108
		Exchange rate	0.0003	**0.0016**	0.0012	0.0009	0.0006	0.0004	0.0058

(continued)

Table 4 (continued)

Emerging market and developing economies		*Response variables*	*1*	*2*	*3*	*4*	*5*	*6*	*Cumulative (12 periods)*
		Stock market	−0.0037	**0.0119**	0.0073	0.0051	0.0035	0.0025	0.0316
	b3	Trade	70.59	**240.25**	62.01	61.95	34.34	24.16	533.01
		CPI	**0.0676**	0.0256	0.0098	0.0101	0.0060	0.0040	0.1299
		Exchange rate	**−0.0015**	−0.0005	0.0003	0.0002	0.0002	0.0001	−0.0011
		Stock market	**−0.0165**	−0.0106	−0.0065	−0.0044	−0.0028	−0.0018	−0.0457
South Africa	a2	Trade	61.01	**−100.85**	34.49	−46.79	0.00	−20.24	−106.49
		CPI	−0.0180	**−0.0680**	−0.0485	−0.0333	−0.0261	−0.0200	−0.2736
		Exchange rate	**0.0117**	0.0047	0.0020	0.0014	0.0010	0.0008	0.0241
		Stock market	**−0.0129**	0.0072	0.0048	0.0039	0.0033	0.0025	0.0163
	b3	Trade	**−29.34**	15.13	−17.79	−0.42	−5.86	−1.43	−44.24
		CPI	**−0.0274**	−0.0092	−0.0231	−0.0234	−0.0189	−0.0139	−0.1422
		Exchange rate	**−0.0122**	−0.0037	−0.0022	−0.0013	−0.0008	−0.0005	−0.0213
		Stock market	**−0.0086**	−0.0051	−0.0028	−0.0022	−0.0014	−0.0009	−0.0226

Note Figures in bold indicate the largest absolute values of responses. Trade is measured in millions of U.S. dollars, the CPI is measured in percentages, and the exchange rate and stock market are measured in 1

Source compiled and produced by the author based on empirical results obtained using Eviews 8.0

Table 5 Direction in which U.S. quantitative easing policy shocks acted on the economies of the BRICS countries

	Trade	*CPI*	*Exchange rate*	*Stock market*
China	+	–	+	–
Brazil	–	+	–	–
Russia	–	–	+	–
India	+	+	–	–
South Africa	–	–	–	–

Note " + " indicates that the response is positive, and "–" negative
Source Compiled and produced by the author based on empirical results obtained using Eviews 8.0

policy adjustments, we selected January 2002 to June 2015 as the sample interval, and divided the entire interval into two sub-intervals: January 2002 to August 2008, and September 2008 to June 2015. The former is defined as the conventional U.S. monetary policy interval and the latter the U.S. quantitative easing (unconventional) policy interval. Thus, the differences in the impact of policy shocks between the two stages can be comparatively analyzed. The main empirical results of this paper are as follows:

1. Shocks to the federal funds rate and reserve balances before and after the adjustment of U.S. monetary policy. By comparing the impulse response functions, it can be found that the latter (i.e., quantitative easing policy) had a more significant impact;
2. A study of 14 sample countries and regions based on a unified analysis framework with the balance of trade, consumer price index, real effective exchange rate and stock market index as response variables shows that the impact of U.S. quantitative easing policy on the sample countries was different. The main difference was that policy shocks might cause deflationary pressure and currency depreciation in most of the sample developed economies, and the spillover effects of imported inflation (as in the case of China in the current period, Brazil, and India) and exchange rate appreciation (as in the case of China, Russia and India in later periods) in emerging market and developing economies.

3. When considering interest rates, the size of foreign exchange reserves and property prices, we can be found that in the post-financial crisis era, U.S. quantitative easing policy may have multiple impacts on China, such as a year-over-year decline in industrial value-added, an increase in net exports, a decrease in cumulative price level but a significant increase in the price level over the same period, currency appreciation, a decline in long-term interest rates, a sluggish stock market, a decrease in foreign exchange reserves and a rise in property prices.
4. This study also gives a statistically significant answer to the expectation of an interest rate hike caused by the withdrawal of quantitative easing policy. If the Fed hikes interest rates, the rate hike may lead to a depreciation in the RMB exchange rate and a decrease in foreign exchange reserves, but it will help further promote China's economic development and curb property prices.

6.2 Policy Recommendations

According to the results obtained by SVAR, the policy recommendations include the following: (1) Expanding domestic demand, implementing the national policy of expanding domestic demand and investment-driven, and expanding the field of support from major national projects to urban infrastructure have played an important role in promoting the development of China's urbanization. Expanding the field of financial support to urban infrastructure, taking developing the real economy as a solid foundation, accelerating reform and innovation as a strong driving force, and ensuring and improving people's well-being as the fundamental purpose, coordinating the current and long-term development, paying more attention to expanding the space for growth, paying more attention to improving the quality of growth, paying more attention to stimulating development vitality, paying more attention to sharing the fruits of development, focusing on solving problems in economic and social development, promoting stable and rapid economic development, and maintaining social harmony and stability is one of the important strategic tasks of China's economic development since the 17th National Congress of the Communist Party of China. (2) In terms of money supply, the impact of U.S. monetary policy had a tightening effect on China's money supply in the first two periods, but the direction changed fundamentally in the third period and after that, and the response was positive for a long time, indicating that quantitative easing policy promoted the expansion of China's monetary policy to some extent. Increase the independence of monetary policy; (3) The spillover effects of U.S. policy shocks are manifested in a slight stimulus to savings and disincentive to investment. It is suggested that existing resources be put to good use to promote the Belt and Road Initiative and achieve common development.

Based on the above empirical results, this paper proposes the following relevant countermeasures: First, China should accelerate economic restructuring, make economic development (expressed in terms of industrial value-added) less responsive to U.S. monetary policy shocks, and reduce its dependence on exports; second, speed up the reform of the exchange rate regime, improve the RMB exchange rate formation mechanism, enhance exchange rate flexibility, and advance the internationalization of the RMB, so as to minimize the adverse impact of U.S. monetary policy adjustments on China; third, in the post-financial crisis era, monetary authorities should make flexible use of monetary policy tools, pay attention to changes in economic variables such as price levels, exchange rates, and long-term interest rates in an effort to counteract the spillover effects of U.S. monetary policy shocks in time; fourth, strengthen the management of foreign exchange reserves and reduce unnecessary losses on reserves caused by the adjustment of U.S. monetary policy; Fifth, Although loosening capital controls is a direction of current development, they still cannot be completely lifted at this stage, as the empirical results show that property prices and stock market operation are more vulnerable to external shocks, and complete capital account liberalization carries certain risks. The conclusions and recommendations set forth in this paper offer a valuable frame of reference for dealing with the unconventional monetary policies of the United Kingdom, the euro area, Japan and other countries and regions.

References

Liu. The Impact of U.S. Monetary Policy Adjustment on the World Economy, Development Finance Research, No.5, 2018, No.21 in total.

Bernanke and Reinhart. Conducting Monetary Policy at Very Low Short-term Interest Rates. The American Economic Review, 2004, 94.

Chen. Advanced Econometrics and Stata Applications (Second Edition), Beijing: Higher Education Press, 2014.

Cogley T, and Sargent T J. Drifts and Volatilities: Monetary Policies and Outcomes in the Post WWII US. Review of Economic Dynamics, 2005, 8(2): 262–302.

Fratzscher M, Duca M L, and Straub R. Quantitative Easing, Portfolio Choice and International Capital Flows. Draft, European Central Bank, Frankfurt, 2012, 22.

Gao. Econometric Analysis Methods and Modeling: Views Applications and Examples, Beijing: Tsinghua University Press, 2014.

Ma and Yu. A Study of the Spillover Effects of U.S. Quantitative Easing Policy on BRICS Countries. Studies of International Finance, 2015, (3): 13–22.

Neri S, and Nobili A. The Transmission of US Monetary Policy to the Euro Area. International Finance, 2010, 13 (1): 55–78.

Sims C A. Macroeconomics and Reality. Econometrica: Journal of the Econometric Society, 1980: 1–48.

Xiao. A Study of the International Transmission of U.S. Monetary Policy Shocks: An Empirical Analysis of Asian Economies. Studies of International Finance, 2011, (9): 18–29.

Zhu. The Mechanism by Which U.S. Monetary Policy Affects China's Economy, PhD thesis, Changchun: Jilin University Press, 2014.

CHAPTER 6

Impact of U.S. Monetary Policy Adjustments on China's Economy

By using a combination of the VAR model and the event study method to systematically study the impact of U.S. monetary policy adjustments on China's economy in the post-financial crisis period based on the three aspects of conventional U.S. monetary policy, U.S. quantitative easing policy and U.S. monetary policy adjustments in the context of the COVID-19 pandemic, we can find that: An increase in the federal funds rate had a strong positive spillover effect on China's economy in the quantitative easing policy interval, and a negative effect in the monetary policy normalization interval; the implementation of U.S. quantitative easing policy had a significant negative spillover effect on China's macroeconomy as a whole, manifested as a beggar thy neighbor effect; in the context of the COVID-19 pandemic, the Fed's zero interest rate policy had a more extensive and significant impact on China's stock market, bond market and foreign exchange market than emergency rate cuts and unlimited quantitative easing, and ultimately led to a complex situation where China's stock market fell across the board, China's bond market was down, and the RMB depreciated against the U.S. dollar.

1 Introduction

Since the start of the 2008 global financial crisis, in response to changes in the economic situation and the impact of emergencies, U.S. monetary policy has generally undergone three stages of adjustment: In the

L. Weiping, *American Monetary Policy Adjustment and Its Impacts*,
https://doi.org/10.1007/978-981-99-7810-6_6

first stage, the Federal Reserve System (hereinafter referred to as the "Fed") launched quantitative easing and the zero interest rate policy respectively in November and December 2008, implementing a combination of unconventional monetary policies; in the second stage, with the Fed announcing the end of its asset purchase program in October 2014 and beginning raising interest rates in December 2015, U.S. monetary policy gradually started to normalize; in the third stage, in March 2020, in response to the huge impact of the COVID-19 pandemic, the Fed reintroduced the zero interest rate policy and started unlimited quantitative easing. Studies show that with the deepening of China's economic opening-up, the U.S. economy has become the main international economic factor affecting China's macroeconomic development. Changes in U.S. monetary policy not only affect its own economy, but also have certain spillover effects on the economies of other countries, and China's economy will inevitably be affected. Therefore, it is of great policy value and practical significance to systematically study the impact of U.S. monetary policy adjustments on China's economy in the post-financial crisis era (Liu and Ma, 2020).

2 Literature Review

After the outbreak of the global financial crisis in 2008, the U.S. monetary policy went through the roller-coaster adjustment of "unconventional monetary policy - monetary policy normalization—unconventional monetary policy in the context of the COVID-19 pandemic". The United States is the world's largest economy, so the adjustment of its monetary policy is bound to cause certain spillover effects on other economies. The following is a summary of the spillover effects of unconventional U.S. monetary policy and U.S. monetary policy normalization.

2.1 Spillover Effects of Unconventional U.S. Monetary Policy

Unconventional U.S. monetary policy mainly includes the zero interest rate policy and quantitative easing policy. With regard to the zero interest rate policy, Pan and Yan (2012) conducted an empirical analysis of the macroeconomic effects of the Fed's "zero interest rate commitment". The results showed that the zero interest rate commitment could accelerate the financial markets' positive response to changes in the benchmark interest rate, helped boost consumer confidence and curb deflation, and had a more significant impact on the real economy than on the financial markets. McKinnon and Liu (2013) believed that the zero interest rate policy of the United States would lead to an influx of international hot money into emerging market economies, bringing the adverse effects of rapid currency appreciation and imported inflation to these economies. Ho et al. (2018) believed that a decrease in the U.S. policy interest rate would lead to an increase in China's investment in property development and the Shanghai Composite Index, which was partly related to the substantial inflow of hot money into China; moreover, an increase in U.S. policy uncertainty would negatively affect the Chinese stock and property markets in normal years, but not at the zero lower bound.

As for the quantitative easing policy, a large number of studies have shown that U.S. quantitative easing policy has spillover effects on other economies to varying degrees through various channels. A study by Qi et al. (2013) showed that U.S. quantitative easing policy would put more upward pressure on the RMB, that is, it would impact China's macroeconomy through the exchange rate channel. Li and Zhang (2013) believed that U.S. quantitative easing policy had a significant impact on price levels in China through international commodity prices and the exchange rate channel. Liu and Han (2014) pointed out that the quantitative easing policy of developed economies, the United States in particular, would cause a global liquidity expansion, which would lead to an increase in the money supply of China and Brazil, and have spillover effects on asset bubbles in their stock markets, indicating that the policy channel and asset price channel of quantitative easing policy were significant. Ma and Yu (2015) used a PVAR model to study the spillover effects of U.S. quantitative easing policy on the BRICS countries. The results showed that the policy would lead to an increase in the real economic output of the BRICS countries, push up their currencies, and bring a booming virtual economy to them. Neely (2015) believed that U.S. quantitative easing policy had a significant impact on the international community mainly by lowering the yield of international long-term bonds and the value of the dollar. Lu and Fang pointed out that U.S. quantitative easing policy had an impact on short-term capital flows in China through the exchange rate and interest rate channels. A study conducted by Nie and Jin (2015) based on China's industry-level export data showed that U.S. quantitative easing policy inhibited China's industrial exports through the trade channel, and the negative spillover effect on the medium and high-tech industry was large. Chen and Ma (2016) found that U.S. quantitative easing policy affected China's macroeconomy mainly through the trade channel and imported inflation. Chen et al. (2016) believed that U.S. quantitative easing policy had contributed to the economic recovery after the financial crisis in some emerging market economies such as China and Brazil, and was also an important external factor for overheating in these economies in 2010–2011. In addition, U.S. quantitative easing policy could act on the economic and financial indicators of emerging market economies through the international capital flow channel and affect their credit cycles and corporate credit conditions, and had a volatility spillover effect on the financial markets of other economies.

2.2 *Spillover Effects of U.S. Monetary Policy Normalization*

At the end of October 2014, the Fed announced the end of its asset purchase program, temporarily ending its six-year quantitative easing policy, and then entered a slow process of monetary policy normalization, mainly through Fed balance sheet reduction and interest rate hikes.

Li and Li (2017) believed that Fed balance sheet reduction would further strengthen the strong dollar cycle established by interest rate hikes, triggering a return of dollars from international financial markets, which would have a huge impact on the global economy, especially emerging economies. Xiao and Lan (2017) studied the spillover effects of the normalization of the Fed's monetary policy. The results showed that the Fed's rate hikes and balance sheet reduction had a significant impact on commodity prices, output, property prices and stock prices in China through the capital flow, exchange rate and interest rate channels. A simulation analysis conducted by Yu et al. (2015) showed that the U.S. exit from quantitative easing would negatively impact China's stock market and property market in the short term, and would also lead to a rise in the exchange rate of the RMB and a slight decline in foreign exchange reserves, but the impact on the money market and bond market was not significant. Sun and Zhang (2016) used a TVP-VAR model to study the time-varying characteristics of the impact of the Fed's rate hikes on China's output. The results showed that combined with the adverse effects of capital flight and falling U.S. demand for imports, the impact of the Fed's rate hikes in 2015 on China's output was negative. Liu et al. (2016) research believes that the Fed's rate hikes would have a negative impact on the Chinese stock market through the exchange rate channel, but the impact would not last long. A study by

Caceres et al. (2016) showed that interest rate changes as part of U.S. monetary policy normalization would have spillover effects on interest rates in other countries, and the response of short-term interest rates in other countries was moderate, while that of long-term interest rates was more significant; in addition, unexpected changes in interest rates had a stronger spillover effect than expected changes in interest rates. Fu (2017) built a two-economy DSGE model to analyze the impact of the Fed's rate hikes on the exchange rate of the RMB and related prices. The results showed that the Fed's rate hikes would lower China's inflation rate and stock prices and promote a depreciation in the RMB exchange rate, but the depreciation would not necessarily lead to an increase in exports. A study conducted by Goes et al. (2017) based on the data of Brazil and Mexico showed that the 10-year Treasury yield was a core factor affecting the sovereign bond yields of these two countries, and U.S. monetary policy normalization had the potential spillover effects of raising interest rates and exacerbating market volatility. Li and Gao (2019) used a PVAR model to study the impact of U.S. monetary policy normalization on emerging economies and developed economies. The results showed that the impact on emerging economies was greater than that on developed economies, and U.S. monetary policy normalization had significant spillover effects on the output, commodity prices, and balance of trade of emerging economies, mainly through capital markets and foreign exchange markets. Wu et al. (2019) found that the Fed's rate hikes had led to the unfavorable situations of capital outflows and asset depreciation in most emerging market economies. Further analysis showed that countries with good infrastructure, sound banking systems and strong economic growth were better positioned to deal with the negative impact of the Fed's rate hikes. Kalu et al. (2020) found that in the process of monetary policy normalization, a rise in the 10-year Treasury yield and Treasury bill rates would negatively impact African stock markets, but shocks to the S&P 500 would have a positive impact.

3 Summary

Table 1 summarizes the research methods and variables of part of the relevant literature. It can be found that most of the existing literature on the spillover effects of U.S. monetary policy adopts the VAR model and its extensions, and mainly selects variables from areas such as macroeconomics, finance, and asset prices. This provides important research support for the subsequent parts of this paper. Based on existing literature, this paper mainly makes improvements in the following aspects: First, in terms of research design, the adjustment of U.S. monetary policy in the post-financial crisis era was divided into three stages: unconventional monetary policy, monetary policy normalization and unconventional monetary policy in the context of the COVID-19 pandemic. In addition, 12 indicators, divided into two groups, namely macroeconomic indicators and financial and asset price indicators, were selected to characterize China's economy, with a view to comparatively analyzing the differences between the spillover effects of the adjustment of conventional and unconventional monetary policy in the United States on China's economy along multiple dimensions. Second, in view of the Fed's policy adjustment measures such as "emergency rate cut", "zero interest rate" and "unlimited quantitative easing" in the context of the COVID-19 pandemic, the short-term impact of such events on China's financial markets, including the stock market, bond market and foreign exchange market, was quantitatively studied using the event study method. This series of studies helps to clearly understand the external challenges facing China's economy in the post-financial crisis era, and provides a policy-making basis for China's response to U.S. monetary policy adjustments in terms of economic development strategy and financial development strategy.

4 Empirical Comparison of the Spillover Effects of Conventional U.S. Monetary Policy and U.S. Quantitative Easing Policy on China's Economy

After the outbreak of the financial crisis, China played an irreplaceable role in the recovery of the world economy, and its contribution to the world economy was universally recognized. But at the same time, thanks to global integration, China's strong growth momentum and potential in the post-financial crisis era attracted a strong injection of international capital, which coupled with significant international yield spreads led to very severe imported inflationary pressure. For example, China's CPI grew 6% year-over-year in the first half of 2011. In the process of the internationalization of the RMB, the value of the RMB also became the object of the game for developed economies. The RMB faced continued pressure from pubic opinion to appreciate, a trend that only weakened

Table 1 Relevant literature research information

Author (year)	*Research methods*	*Variables*
Li and Zhang (2013) [7]	SVAR model	Size of the Fed's balance sheet, international commodity price index, nominal effective exchange rate of the RMB, consumer price index, and industrial producer price index
Ma and Yu (2015) [9]	PVAR model	Size of the Fed's bond purchases, monetary base, balance of trade, price level, year-over-year growth in gross industrial production, stock index, exchange rate, and money supply
Lu and Fang (2015) [11]	VAR model	Short-term capital inflows into China, China-U.S. yield spread, USD/CNY real exchange rate index, quantitative indicators of U.S. quantitative easing policy (U.S. nominal M2 growth rate QoQ - U.S. GDP growth rate QoQ),and China's Manufacturing Purchasing Managers Index
Yu et al. (2015) [22]	FAVAR model	Money market variables, stock and bond market variables, foreign exchange market variables, and property market variables
Chen and Ma (2016) [13]	PVAR model	Size of the Fed's bond purchases, federal funds rate, total imports and exports, price level, real effective exchange rate, and stock market index
Sun and Zhang (2016)[23]	TVP-VAR model	U.S. interest rates, China's interest rates, U.S. real GDP, China's real GDP, and real effective exchange rate of the RMB
Tillmann (2016) [15]	Qual VAR model	proxy variable of U.S. quantitative easing policy, industrial production growth rate, 10-year Treasury yield, capital flows, EMBI spread, MSCI Emerging Markets Index, and exchange rate
Liu (2017) [31]	VAR model	Year-over-year growth in industrial value-added, balance of trade, CPI, real effective exchange rate, 10-year Treasury yield, stock market index, foreign exchange reserves, and property prices
Xiao and Lan (2017) [21]	TVP-VAR model	Federal funds rate, size of the Fed's balance sheet, capital flow indicators, exchange rate, yield spread between Chinese 10-year bonds and comparable Treasuries, CPI, year-over-year changes in industrial value-added, new housing price index YoY for 70 large and medium-sized cities, and Shanghai Composite Index

(continued)

Table 1 (continued)

Author (year)	*Research methods*	*Variables*
Li and Gao (2019)[28]	PVAR model	Federal funds rate, macroeconomic indicators (monthly gross industrial production, CPI and net exports), and financial indicators (yield spread between Chinese 10-year bonds and comparable Treasuries and stock price index)
Kolasa and Wesołowski (2020) [32]	DSGE model	Capital flows, term spread, exchange rate, output, inflation, etc

in August 2015 when the RMB exchange rate hit its largest single-day decline in history. Interest rate and exchange rate are the most important factors affecting international hot money and can directly or indirectly affect many aspects of China's real economy. Meanwhile, these two indicators are also directly affected by the adjustment of U.S. monetary policy. Next, we will use the vector autoregression (VAR) model to compare the differences between conventional and unconventional U.S. monetary policy in terms of the impact of their adjustments on China's economic dynamics.

4.1 Variable Selection

With the filing for bankruptcy protection by Lehman Brothers in September 2008 as the starting point, we set a research interval from September 2008 to February 2020 to study the spillover effects of U.S. monetary policy adjustments on China's economy in the post-financial crisis era. In this paper, the proxy variable of U.S. monetary policy is selected primarily based on two points. First, the federal funds rate was used to measure conventional monetary policy. In the 1990s, the Fed changed the intermediate target of monetary policy from the money supply to an index system centered on real interest rates and composed of a number of economic and financial variables. A typical example of real interest rates is the federal funds rate. Second, the reserve balances of U.S. depository institutions at Federal Reserve Banks were used as the proxy indicator of quantitative easing. The Fed made large-scale purchases of Treasury securities and mortgage-backed securities during quantitative easing, and most of these financial assets were the assets of commercial banks or depository institutions, and the reserve balances of the latter at Federal Reserve Banks were used to pay for the Fed's large-scale bond purchases [33]. In order to comprehensively analyze the impact of U.S. monetary policy adjustments on China's economy, 12 indicators were selected to describe China's economy from two aspects: macroeconomics, finance, and asset prices. In order to comprehensively analyze the impact of U.S. monetary policy adjustment on China's economy, 12 indicators, divided into two groups, namely macroeconomic indicators and financial and asset price indicators, were selected to characterize China's economy, with data from Wind and the Bank for International Settlements. The relevant data are shown in Table 2. Since the Fed ended quantitative easing in October 2014, in this paper, we further divide the entire sample interval into two time periods, September 2008 to October 2014 and November 2014 to February 2020, corresponding to the quantitative easing policy interval and the monetary policy normalization interval. In order to reduce heteroscedasticity, natural logarithms are taken of reserve balances, the purchasing managers' index, the retail sales of consumer goods, foreign direct investment, the real effective exchange rate and the stock market index. The stability of variables varies across time intervals. For the sake of the stability of the model and the comparability of the results, first-order differencing is performed for all variables.

First, all the processed data were tested for stationarity. The relevant results are shown in Table 3. It should be noted that, in order to avoid redundancy, we only show the results of the stationary test of the variables in the entire sample interval.

The results in Table 3 show that all first-order difference sequences are stationary, and this property is also valid in the two subintervals, which will ensure the stability and consistency of the VAR model. In order to study the impact of the adjustment of conventional U.S. monetary policy on China's economy, the federal funds rate was selected as the impact variable of the VAR model, and two variables, one containing macroeconomic variables and the other financial and asset price variables, were constructed. Correspondingly, in order to study the impact of the adjustment of U.S. quantitative easing policy on China's economy, the reserve balances of U.S. depository institutions at Federal Reserve Banks were added to the VAR model system, and two model variables, one containing macroeconomic variables and the other financial and asset price variables, were constructed. On this basis, the spillover effects of different U.S.

Table 2 Variable Selection and meanings

Type	*Data name*	*Abbreviation*	*Variable description*
Policy variables	Federal funds rate	FFR	Represent conventional U.S. monetary policy; the monthly average is taken
	Reserve balances of U.S. depository institutions at Federal Reserve Banks	RB	Represent U.S. quantitative easing policy; the monthly average is taken
Macroeconomic indicators	Year-over-year growth in industrial value-added	IVA	Reflect changes in the real economy
	Balance of trade	NE	Represents the net exports of a country; for studying the impact of policy adjustments on imports and exports
	Consumer price index	CPI	Represent price changes in commodity markets; for studying the impact of policy adjustments on inflation
	Purchasing managers' index	PMI	An internationally accepted leading index for monitoring macroeconomic trends
	Retail sales of social consumer goods	CS	Represent a country's household consumption in dollars; seasonally adjusted using X12
	Foreign direct investment	FDI	Measured by the actual amount of foreign capital used; for studying the impact of monetary policy adjustments on foreign capital inflows; seasonally adjusted using X12

Type	Data name	Abbreviation	Variable description
Financial and asset price indicators	Capital flows	CF	Measured by "hot money = increase in foreign exchange reserves - FDI - trade surplus"
	Real effective exchange rate	ER	Represent the actual appreciation or depreciation of the RMB
	China-U.S. yield spread	IRS	Measured by the yield spread between Chinese 10-year bonds and comparable Treasuries
	Money supply growth rate	M2	Represent a change in the money supply, which can indicate the monetary policy of the central bank
	Stock market index	SI	Closing price of the CSI 300 Index
	Property prices	RE	Before January 2011, the new housing price index for 70 large and medium-sized cities was used; after that, the new commodity housing price index for 70 large and medium-sized cities was used

Table 3 Stationarity test

Variable	*Test form(c, t, q)*	*ADF statistics*	*1% threshold*	*5% threshold*	*10% threshold*	*Conclusion*
DFFR	(0, 0, 3)	−7.7427	−2.5823	−1.9432	−1.6151	Stationary
DlnRB	(0, 0, 0)	−8.1325	−2.5820	−1.9432	−1.6152	Stationary
DIVA	(0, 0, 1)	−10.0702	−2.5821	−1.9432	−1.6152	Stationary
DNE	(0, 0, 2)	−9.1498	−2.5822	−1.9432	−1.6151	Stationary
DCPI	(0, 0, 2)	−5.0405	−2.5822	−1.9432	−1.6151	Stationary
DlnPMI	(0, 0, 0)	−6.1040	−2.5820	−1.9432	−1.6152	Stationary
DlnCS	(0, 0, 2)	−2.9750	−2.5822	−1.9432	−1.6151	Stationary
DlnFDI	(0, 0, 1)	−12.7938	−2.5821	−1.9432	−1.6152	Stationary
DCF	(0, 0, 1)	−13.2503	−2.5821	−1.9432	−1.6152	Stationary
DlnER	(0, 0, 0)	−7.8269	−2.5820	−1.9432	−1.6152	Stationary
DIRS	(0, 0, 0)	−9.9252	−2.5820	−1.9432	−1.6152	Stationary
DM2	(0, 0, 0)	−10.4896	−2.5820	−1.9432	−1.6152	Stationary
DlnSI	(0, 0, 0)	−11.0353	−2.5820	−1.9432	−1.6152	Stationary
DRE	(0, 0, 1)	−3.7864	−2.5821	−1.9432	−1.6152	Stationary

Note D represents the first-order difference, and the test forms c, t and q represent the constant term, time trend term and lag order in the unit root test equation respectively

monetary policy adjustments on China's economy in different intervals were compared along multiple dimensions.

4.2 *Result Analysis*

The lag order of the model was selected according to rules such as AIC, SC, LR and HQ, and then the stability of the model was determined by an AR root test. The results showed that the modulus of all unit roots was less than 1, indicating that the VAR model was stable. After obtaining a stable VAR model, we need to further study the effects of shocks to an endogenous variable on other variables in the current period. Different from the regression coefficient in a traditional OLS regression model, the impulse response function of a VAR model can analyze the dynamic effect of a one-standard deviation positive shock on the variable system, rather than the fitting coefficient or long-term equilibrium relationship between variables. In principle, the impulse response function is a tool of signal science and generally refers to the output response of the system when inputting the unit shock function. In the VAR model, a shock to any endogenous variable can be selected as the input signal, and the response function corresponding to other variables is the output.

4.2.1 Spillover Effects of Conventional U.S. Monetary Policy on China's Economy

For a one-standard deviation positive shock to the federal funds rate, the relevant results are shown in Fig. 1–2.

In the quantitative easing policy interval, the federal funds rate basically remained between 0% and 0.25% for a long period. Interest rates fluctuations narrowed significantly, at which point the impulse response function for shocks to interest rates changed somewhat. According to Fig. 1, judging from the response in the current period, a shock to U.S. interest rates would reduce the balance of trade, and increase the inflation rate, the purchasing managers' index and the scale of foreign direct investment. Judging from the 12-period cumulative impulse response, the Fed's rate hikes had a negative impact on China's industrial value-added, balance of trade and consumer spending, the exchange rate of the RMB, the China-U.S. yield spread and the stock market index, and had a positive impact on other economic variables. Overall, an increase in the federal funds rate during the quantitative easing period would dampen any rise in China's industrial production, trade surplus, consumer spending and property prices, but the signal of a move away from the zero interest rate policy sent by a rate hike would lead to the good performance of the economy on the leading indicators, namely the purchasing managers' index and the stock market index.

The Fed's rate hikes were an important sign of U.S. monetary policy normalization. As can be seen from Fig. 2, in the monetary policy normalization interval, in the face of a one-standard deviation positive shock to the federal funds rate, the industrial value-added, the balance of trade, the purchasing managers' index and property prices gave a positive response to varying degrees in the current period, and unfavorable situations such as lower inflation rates, sluggish consumer spending and foreign direct investment, short-term capital flight, the depreciation of the RMB and a decline in the stock market index occurred. Judging from the 12-period cumulative impulse response, the Fed's rate hikes had a positive impact on China's industrial value-added, consumer spending, capital inflows and property prices, and a negative spillover effect on other economic variables.

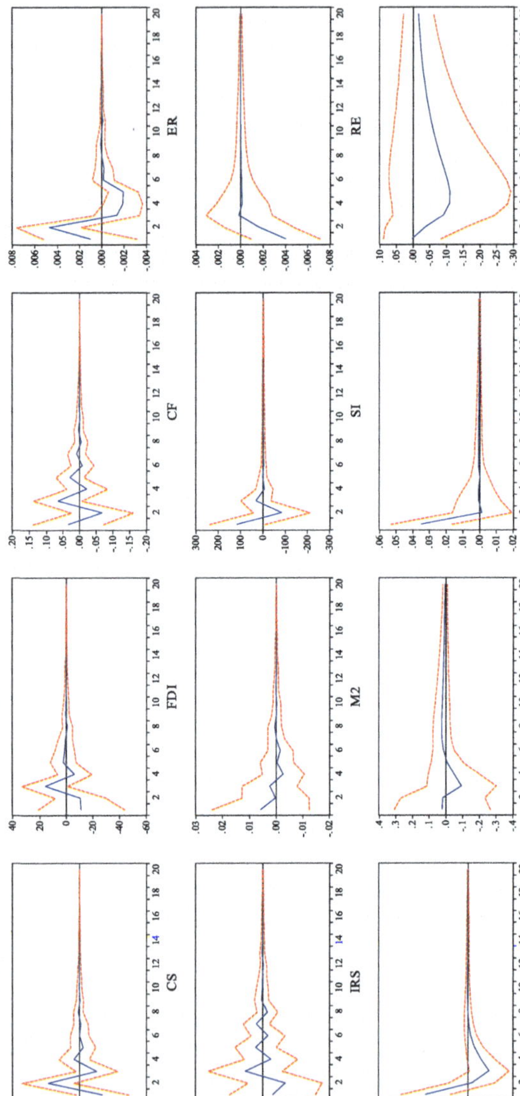

Fig. 1 A shock to the federal funds rate—quantitative easing policy interval

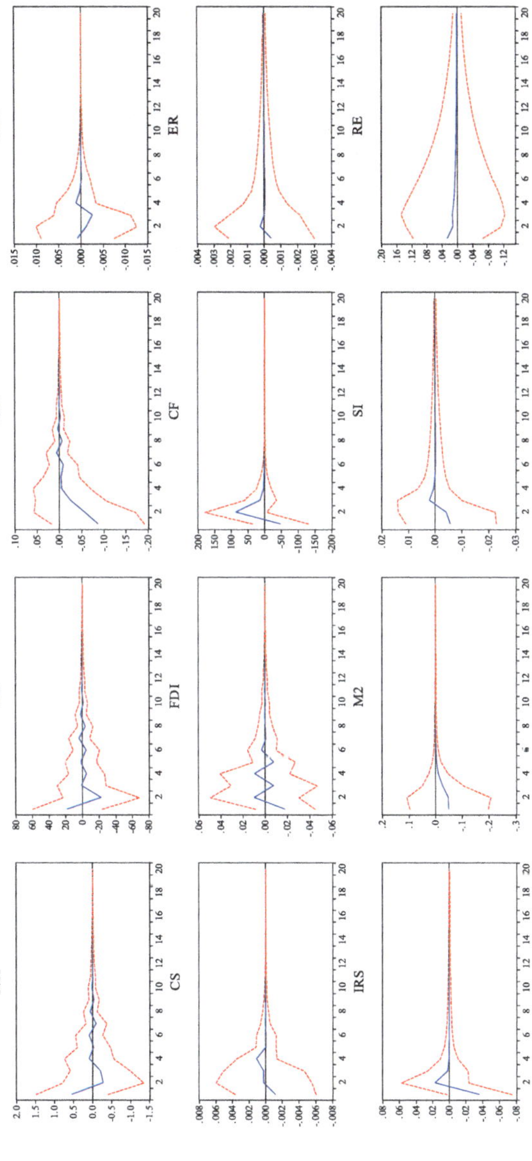

Fig. 2 A shock to the federal funds rate—monetary policy normalization interval

4.2.2 *Spillover Effects of U.S. Quantitative Easing Policy on China's Economy*

The impulse responses to a one-standard deviation positive shock to the reserve balances of U.S. depository institutions at Federal Reserve Banks in different intervals are shown in Fig. 3.

Figure 3 shows that in the quantitative easing policy interval, a shock to reserve balances had a negative impact on industrial value-added, the balance of trade, the purchasing managers' index, foreign direct investment and the real effective exchange rate of RMB. Judging from the 12-period cumulative pulse response, the negative impact also affected capital flows and the China-U.S. yield spread. Overall, although U.S. quantitative easing policy could boost the operation of China's consumer market and stock market to varying degrees, its adverse shocks were wider in scope, covering industrial output, trade, inflation rates, capital flows, exchange rates and property prices. It is thus clear that U.S. monetary policy adjustments in this interval had greater negative spillover effects on China's economy, posing a great challenge for China in its effort to actively respond to the relevant adverse effects.

According to Fig. 4, in the monetary policy normalization interval, China's consumer spending, foreign direct investment and capital flows, the China-U.S. yield spread and the stock market index would respond positively to a one-standard deviation positive shock to reserve balances in the current period; judging from the 12-period cumulative pulse response, a shock to reserve balances had a sustained negative impact on all variables except for foreign direct investment, capital flows, the U.S.-China yield spread and the stock market index, on which it had a long-term positive impact. In the normalization process of the Fed's monetary policy, interest rate hikes and tapering occurred concurrently. At this stage, if the Fed did exactly the opposite by adopting expansionary measures, that would have a broad negative impact on China's economy; correspondingly, if the Fed stepped up its tapering efforts, that would send a signal that the economy was picking up speed, thus bringing about significant positive spillover effects on China's economy.

For easy analysis and comparison, Table 4 comprehensively presents the 12-period cumulative impulse responses to a one-standard deviation positive shock to the federal funds rate and a one-standard deviation positive shock to the reserve balances of U.S. depository institutions at Federal Reserve Banks and the variance decompositions.

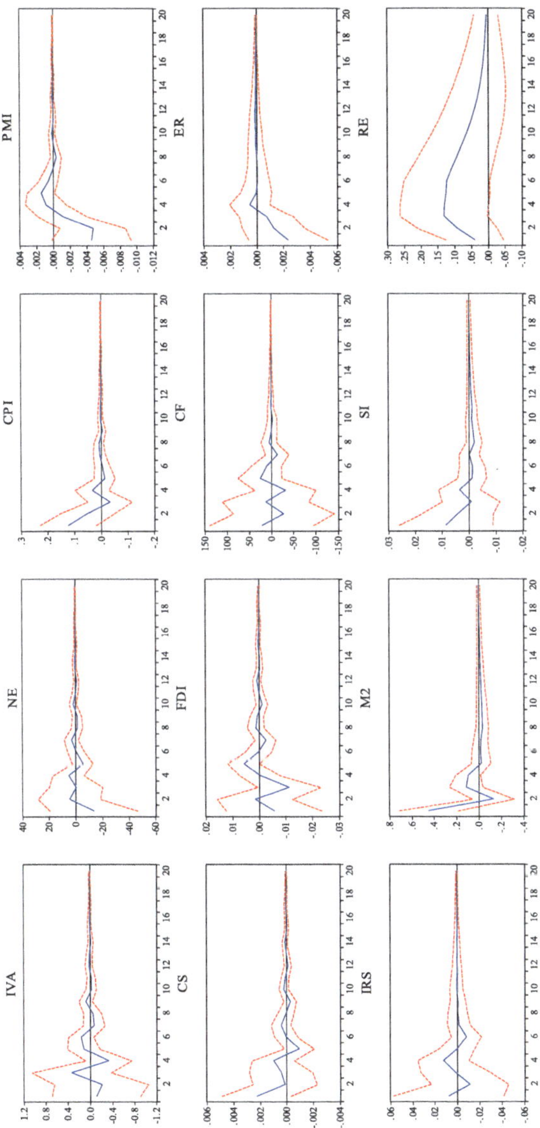

Fig. 3 A shock to reserve balances—quantitative easing policy interval

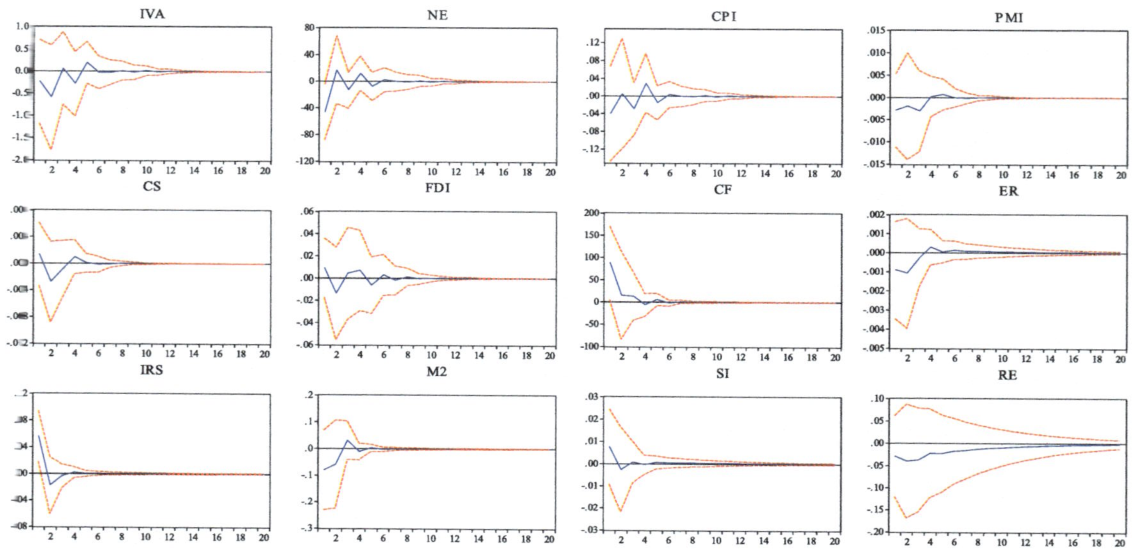

Fig. 4 A shock to reserve balances—monetary policy normalization interval

Table 4 12-Period cumulative impulse responses to A shock to the federal funds rate and reserve balances and variance decompositions

	Shock to interest rates				*Shock to reserve balances*			
	Quantitative easing		*Monetary policy normalization*		*Quantitative easing*		*Monetary policy normalization*	
	Impulse response	*Variance decomposition*	*Impulse response*	*Variance decomposition*	*Impulse response*	*Variance decomposition*	*Impulse response*	*Variance decomposition*
IVA	−0.2213	6.3295	0.1624	1.8062	−0.1510	1.2556	−0.8647	2.0740
NE	−8.0580	2.0002	−7.9374	1.9790	−9.5332	1.0373	−35.6881	6.0755
CPI	0.0397	2.7112	−0.1826	4.1393	0.1676	4.7837	−0.0464	1.4493
PMI	0.0002	6.3684	−0.0017	0.4421	−0.0082	7.0686	−0.0070	1.0226
CS	−0.0011	1.3853	0.0004	0.4360	0.0030	2.5853	−0.0013	2.0186
FDI	0.0044	0.5194	−0.0114	1.3502	−0.0113	2.1738	0.0026	0.9011
CF	48.7779	5.5006	59.4984	6.5697	−4.9857	0.8008	116.3804	5.4327
ER	−0.0060	8.0001	−0.0005	0.1786	−0.0036	3.4284	−0.0014	1.5937
IRS	−0.0116	17.7276	−0.0170	5.7696	−0.0035	0.7605	0.0403	12.5830
M2	0.0292	0.8895	−0.1383	1.3237	0.3029	15.2957	−0.1201	2.6612
SI	0.0383	15.6452	−0.0080	0.9791	0.0050	1.6471	0.0087	1.2024
RE	−0.8550	7.0199	0.0966	0.2504	1.0712	8.3824	−0.2340	1.1474

The results show that: (1) The cumulative impulse response to a shock to the federal funds rate and the degree to which it explains variations in economic variables in China vary depending the interval. Compared with impulse responses, a rise in interest rates in the quantitative easing policy interval had strong positive spillover effects on China's economy, while it had a more negative impact in the monetary policy normalization interval. Judging from the results from variance decompositions, in the quantitative easing policy interval, shocks to interest rates had great explanatory power for the China-U.S. yield spread, the securities index, exchange rates, property prices, the purchasing managers' index and industrial value-added; in the monetary policy normalization interval, shocks to interest rates mainly explained changes in capital flows, the China-U.S. yield spread and inflation rates, and generally explained economic variables in China to a lower degree than in the quantitative easing policy interval. (2) In the quantitative easing policy interval, a rise in reserve balances had a negative impact on China's industrial output, balance of trade, purchasing managers' index, capital flows, etc. to varying degrees, and would also lead to an increase in the money supply and imported inflation, indicating that shocks had significant negative spillover effects on China's economy; according to the results from variance decompositions, shocks to reserve balances in this interval mainly explained changes in China's money supply, property prices, purchasing managers' index, inflation rate, etc. In the monetary policy normalization interval, a rise in reserve balances would be detrimental to the improvement of China's industrial output, balance of trade, purchasing managers' index and other indicators, and would also cause a decline in the money supply and deflation; judging from the results from variance decompositions, shocks to reserve balances had great explanatory power for changes in the China-U.S. yield spread, the balance of trade, capital flows, etc.

5 Impact of U.S. Monetary Policy Adjustments on China's Financial Markets in the Context of COVID-19

At the end of 2019, the COVID-19 pandemic broke out and gradually spread around the world, causing a wide range of negative shocks to the world economy and financial stability. In response, the Fed adjusted its monetary policy beyond expectations in an effort to offset the impact of the pandemic. On March 3, 2020, the Fed made an emergency rate cut, lowering the target range for the federal funds rate by 50 bp. On March 15, 2020, the Fed announced its interest rate decision (i.e. to lower the target range for the federal funds rate by 100 bp to the "zero lower bound") three days earlier than scheduled, and at the same time launched a new quantitative easing program of at least $700 billion. On March 23, 2020, in order to achieve the goal of promoting maximum employment and stable prices, the Fed announced that it would purchase unlimited quantities of Treasury securities and agency mortgage-backed securities, officially launching unlimited quantitative easing. The financial markets were highly sensitive and responsive to such information. Next, based on event study methods, we will focus on analyzing the impact of U.S. monetary policy adjustments on China's financial markets, including the stock market, bond market and foreign exchange market, in the context of the pandemic.

5.1 Research Design

Drawing on the research ideas of Guo et al. (2016) and Fang et al. (2019), with major adjustments in U.S. monetary policy after March 2020 as external shock events, we used the event study method to analyze their spillover effects on the operation of China's financial markets. The event study method is often used to study the impact of a specific type of event on the target variable. The method, centered on the point in time when the event occurs, measures the significance of the cumulative abnormal return of the target variable before and after the event. The specific research process is as follows:

First, define the events, event dates, event windows, and estimation windows. As mentioned earlier, in this paper, we select the Fed's monetary policy adjustment plans adopted on March 3, 2020, March 15, 2020 and March 23, 2020 as research events, which are respectively recorded as "emergency rate cut", "zero interest rate" and "unlimited quantitative easing". Considering that most of China's financial markets were closed or trading did not take place on the days when the Fed announced its monetary policy decisions, the first trading days after the days, namely March 4, 2020, March 16, 2020 and March 24, 2020, were defined as time 0. [−1, 1], [−2, 2], [−3, 3], [−4, 4] and [−5, 5] were selected as the event window periods. In order to avoid overlap between the estimation windows and event windows, the estimation windows were set to be 150 to 10 trading days before the event windows.

Second, select research samples. In this part, the stock market, bond market and foreign exchange market are respectively represented by the CSI 300 index, the CSI Aggregate Bond Index and the central exchange rate of the RMB against the U.S. dollar. In order to examine the impact of U.S. monetary policy adjustments on different sectors in China, listed companies were divided into 11 first-level sectors according to Wind's industries classification standard: energy, materials, industrial, consumer discretionary, consumer staples, healthcare, finance, information technology, telecommunications services, utilities and real estate. The formula for calculating returns in each market is, where, is the closing price of the financial indicator i in the period t. The relevant data are from Wind.

Third, estimate normal and abnormal returns. Normal returns can be estimated using the constant mean return model, the market model, the market-adjusted model, the Fama–French three-factor model, the Carhart four-factor model, etc. Given that most of the target variables are the returns of stock market indexes, the constant mean return model was chosen to estimate normal returns by drawing on the treatment methods developed by Kaketsis and Sarantis (2006) and Guo et al. (2016). The idea behind the model is to take the average return of the target variable of the estimation window as the normal return of the target variable of the event window. An abnormal return is the difference between the actual return and the normal return of the target variable in the event window, and the cumulative abnormal return is the sum total of abnormal returns in any time period over the event window. Finally, we test the statistical significance of the cumulative abnormal return to determine whether the occurrence of the event has a significant effect on the target variable.

5.2 *Result Analysis*

This part uses the event study method to examine the impact of major adjustments in U.S. monetary policy on China's financial markets since March 2020. The empirical results are shown in Table 5–7.

Table 5 Results of the analysis of the "emergency rate cut" event

	[−1, 1]	*[−2, 2]*	*[−3, 3]*	*[−4, 4]*	*[−5, 5]*
Stock market	3.17%	4.72%*	−2.36%	−0.04%	−2.72%
Bond market	0.02%	0.09%	0.47%***	0.41%**	0.36%*
Foreign exchange market	−0.62%**	−1.11%***	−1.46%***	−1.17%**	−1.03%*
Energy	3.08%	5.78%**	0.16%	0.14%	−0.39%
Materials	2.94%	7.11%**	−1.95%	−0.54%	−3.62%
Industry	3.15%	7.29%**	−0.82%	1.97%	0.47%
Consumer discretionary	3.53%	5.67%*	−2.69%	−0.65%	−2.85%
Consumer staples	7.17%***	8.58%***	1.58%	4.77%	3.82%
Healthcare	3.55%	6.11%**	1.50%	1.12%	−3.25%
Finance	4.21%**	4.82%*	−1.92%	0.15%	−1.89%
Information technology	−0.80%	1.47%	−11.31%**	−6.99%	−15.87%**
Telecommunications services	1.19%	3.86%	−3.51%	−0.06%	−2.65%
Utilities	3.61%**	5.43%**	0.86%	2.62%	2.51%
Real estate	4.41%*	6.46%**	1.86%	2.03%	3.74%

Note * * *, * * and * indicate significance at the 1%, 5% and 10% levels respectively, the same below

5.2.1 *Impact of the "Emergency Rate Cut" Event on China's Financial Markets*

Table 5 shows that for the Fed's "emergency rate cut" event on March 3, 2020, the cumulative abnormal returns of the China's stock market over the event windows [−1, 1] and [−2, 2] were 3.17% and 4.72% respectively, and the latter was significant at the 10% level; the cumulative abnormal returns of the stock market over the remaining event windows were negative and statistically insignificant, indicating that the "emergency irate cut" event had a short-term stimulating effect on China's stock market, but due to the impact of the pandemic, the stock market quickly reversed course to the downside. The cumulative abnormal returns of China's bond market over the five event windows were all positive, and were most significant in the event window [−3, 3], indicating that the "emergency rate cut" event was conducive to boosting the bond market. The cumulative abnormal returns of the foreign exchange market over the five event windows were significantly negative, that is, the "emergency rate cut" event reduced the central parity rate of the RMB against the U.S. dollar. Since the exchange rate of the RMB against the U.S. dollar is quoted directly, the event led to a passive appreciation of the RMB.

Judging from the results for first-level sectors in China's stock market, the event window [−2, 2] accounts for a significantly higher proportion of cumulative abnormal returns, which is consistent with the empirical results for the stock market. Over the event window [−2,2], the cumulative abnormal returns of sectors such as consumer discretionary, industry, materials, real estate and healthcare were high, and the cumulative abnormal return of the information technology sector was the lowest. Over the event windows [−3, 3] and [−5, 5], it can be found that the cumulative abnormal returns of the information technology sector were −11.31% and −15.87%, respectively, and were significant at the 5% level, indicating that the high-tech sector bore the brunt of the increasing competition and friction between China and the United States in the new era.

5.2.2 *Impact of the "Zero Interest Rate" Event on China's Financial Markets*

As can be seen from Table 6, the Fed's "zero interest rate" event on March 15, 2020 had a broad and significant impact on China's financial markets. The cumulative abnormal returns of China's stock market over the five event windows were all negative, and were significant at the 5% level, indicating that the "zero interest rate" event had a significant negative impact on China's stock market. China's bond market did not extend its performance in the "emergency rate cut" event, and also suffered a significant short-term setback. The empirical results for the foreign exchange market were unexpected. The central parity rate of the RMB against the U.S. dollar did not fall but rose, that is, the RMB was under pressure to depreciate against the U.S. dollar, which can be explained from the following two aspects: On the one hand, the Fed's adoption of a zero interest rate policy and launch of a new round of quantitative easing caused panic in the U.S. and global markets, and although the Fed printed money like crazy to pump massive amounts of liquidity into the banking system, commercial banks did not put the money into the credit market as the Fed hoped, resulting in a continued shortage of dollar-denominated assets, as evidenced by a decrease in the M2 money multiplier from 4.47 in February 2020 to 4.17 in March and 3.56 in April. On the other hand, the CFETS RMB exchange rate index was 93.57 and 95.73 on March 13

Table 6 Results of the analysis of the "zero interest rate" event

	[−1, 1]	*[−2, 2]*	*[−3, 3]*	*[−4, 4]*	*[−5, 5]*
Stock market	−6.32%***	−10.31%***	−13.03%***	−9.18%**	−16.05%***
Bond market	−0.20%*	−0.31%**	−0.41%**	−0.50%**	−0.09%
Foreign exchange market	0.62%**	0.98%**	1.55%***	2.47%***	2.18%***
Energy	−3.48%	−7.23%***	−9.91%***	−8.10%**	−13.33%***
Materials	−6.70%***	−10.48%***	−12.15%***	−9.23%**	−17.36%***
Industry	−5.36%**	−9.42%***	−10.42%***	−6.82%	−14.08%***
Consumer discretionary	−7.15%***	−10.95%***	−12.93%***	−9.37%**	−18.10%***
Consumer staples	−6.52%***	−10.63%***	−11.83%***	−7.40%*	−13.15%***
Healthcare	−5.80%**	−9.87%***	−12.60%***	−10.59%**	−13.93%***
Finance	−5.03%**	−8.62%***	−11.86%***	−8.21%**	−14.07%***
Information technology	−7.12%**	−10.94%**	−11.52%**	−6.94%	−19.18%***
Telecommunications services	−8.02%**	−12.27%***	−13.37%**	−8.78%	−15.63%**
Utilities	−3.08%*	−5.04%**	−6.12%**	−3.74%	−6.83%**
Real estate	−5.22%**	−10.32%***	−13.14%***	−9.43%**	−16.61%***

and 20, 2020, respectively, indicating that the RMB appreciated against a basket of currencies after the Fed's "zero interest rate" event, despite a depreciation of the RMB against the U.S. dollar.

According to the empirical results for the first-level sectors in China's stock market, affected by the Fed's "zero interest rate" event, the cumulative abnormal returns of most sectors were significantly negative. Take the event window [−5, 5] as an example. The cumulative abnormal returns of all sectors except utilities were less than −10%, and the cumulative abnormal returns of information technology, consumer discretionary, materials and real estate were even below −15%. Thus, it can be seen that the Fed's new round of quantitative easing had a huge impact on the market performance of various sectors in China.

5.2.3 *Impact of the "Unlimited Quantitative Easing" Event on China's Financial Markets*

Table 7 shows that the overall impact of the "unlimited quantitative easing" event was not significant due to the proximity of the Federal Reserve's announcement of the formal launch of unlimited quantitative easing on March 23, 2020 in time to the "zero interest rate" event, and

Table 7 Results of the Analysis of the "Unlimited Quantitative Easing" Event

	[−1, 1]	*[−2, 2]*	*[−3, 3]*	*[−4, 4]*	*[−5, 5]*
Stock market	1.73%	2.67%	1.51%	−1.62%	−1.97%
Bond market	0.12%	0.18%	0.17%	0.11%	0.05%
Foreign exchange market	−0.42%	0.27%	0.19%	0.56%	1.26%**
Energy	0.73%	1.07%	−0.58%	−3.32%	−4.02%
Materials	0.27%	0.35%	0.00%	−3.41%	−3.69%
Industry	0.03%	−0.42%	−0.42%	−3.61%	−3.96%
Consumer discretionary	1.06%	1.11%	0.17%	−3.60%	−4.85%
Consumer staples	2.87%	5.45%*	4.76%	3.12%	6.04%
Healthcare	3.37%	7.62%**	5.30%	2.64%	2.32%
Finance	1.43%	2.88%	1.25%	−2.16%	−2.90%
Information technology	−2.50%	−4.92%	−4.54%	−10.66%	−11.45%
Telecommunications services	0.90%	−0.06%	−0.68%	−4.88%	−6.66%
Utilities	1.41%	1.56%	1.15%	−0.26%	0.12%
Real estate	2.09%	3.28%	2.10%	−3.03%	−5.23%

the strong reaction of China's financial markets to the latter. The cumulative abnormal returns of China's stock market over the event windows [−1, 1], [−2, 2] and [−3, 3] were positive but statistically insignificant, and the cumulative abnormal returns over the other two event windows were negative, that is, the "unlimited quantitative easing" event had a short-term stimulating effect on the stock market, and the impact was temporary. The cumulative abnormal returns of China's bond market over the five event windows were positive but statistically insignificant, and had a limited effect when it comes to boosting the bond market. The result for China's foreign exchange market over the event window [−1, 1] was negative, and the results over other event windows were positive, of which the result over the event window [−5, 5] was significant at the 5% level, indicating that the "unlimited quantitative easing" event pushed the RMB higher in the short term, but the status quo of a strong dollar remained unchanged over an enlarged event window.

According to the results for first-level sectors in China's stock market, the cumulative abnormal returns of the consumer staples and healthcare industry sectors over the five event windows were all positive, of which the result over the event window [−2,2] was relatively significant, indicating that in the context of the pandemic, the "unlimited quantitative easing" event was conducive to boosting the consumer goods and healthcare sectors; in contrast, other sectors were negatively impacted by the event, especially the information technology sector.

6 Conclusions and Policy Recommendations

This paper systematically studies the impact of U.S. monetary policy adjustments on China's economy in the post-financial crisis era using a combination of the VAR model and the event study method, focusing on the three aspects of conventional U.S. monetary policy, U.S. quantitative easing policy and U.S. monetary policy adjustments in the context of the COVID-19 pandemic. The main conclusions are as follows: First, an increase in the federal funds rate had a strong positive spillover effect on China's economy in the quantitative easing policy interval, and a negative effect in the monetary policy normalization interval; shocks to interest rates generally explained economic variables in China to a higher degree in the quantitative easing policy interval than in the monetary policy normalization interval. Second, an increase in the reserve balances of U.S. depository institutions at Federal Reserve Banks was detrimental to the improvement of China's industrial output, balance of trade, purchasing managers' index and other indicators in both the quantitative easing policy interval and the monetary policy normalization interval, indicating that U.S. quantitative easing policy had a significant negative spillover effect on China's macroeconomy, manifested as a beggar-thy-neighbor effect. Third, with regard to the emergency rate cut, zero interest rate and unlimited quantitative easing policies adopted by the Fed in the context of the COVID-19 pandemic, the results show that the zero interest rate policy had a more extensive and significant impact on China's financial markets than other policies, as evidenced by a complex situation where China's stock market fell across the board, China's bond market was down, and the central parity rate of the RMB against the U.S. dollar did not fall but rose; judging from the results for the first-level sectors in the stock market, different industries were affected differently, but the cumulative abnormal returns of the information technology sectors in the three events, especially the zero interest rate event, were mostly negative, indicating that China's high-technology sector was vulnerable to the negative impact of the shocks of the Fed's new round of unconventional monetary policy.

Based on the research conclusions of this chapter, the following insights can be obtained: First, the beggar-thy-neighbor effect of U.S. monetary policy adjustments in the post-financial crisis era combined with the impact of games and frictions between the two major powers of China and the United States has exerted significant external pressure on the steady development of China's economy, which underscores the practical significance of China's efforts to achieve internal high-quality development through expanding domestic demand in order to improve economic resilience and competitiveness. Second, in terms of economic development strategy, on the one hand, China needs to further expand its opening-up to the outside world to counteract the adverse impact of U.S. monetary adjustments on trade activities, and on the other hand, it needs to vigorously develop the real economy to improve the potential and competitiveness of industrial output and high-tech industries. It can be seen that, faced with the potential spillover effects of U.S. monetary policy adjustments, the most important thing for China is to put its own house in order, tap the potential of economic development, and better cultivate and utilize domestic and international markets. Third, in terms of financial development strategy, in view of the complex impact of U.S. monetary policy adjustments on China's financial markets, the real estate sector and other sectors of the virtual economy, China should adhere to the essential requirement of finance serving the real economy, take the weight and status of the virtual economy in the modern social economy seriously, and promote the moderate development of the virtual economy and its integration with the real economy. So far as monetary policy responses are concerned, in the face of the internal and external shocks of the pandemic and U.S. monetary policy adjustments, China needs to introduce a more flexible monetary policy to further stimulate the vitality of different market players. Fourth, China should actively participate in the coordination of international macroeconomic policies and strengthen the linkage of policies and rules between countries or regions, so as to seek advantages and avoid disadvantages, amplify positive spillover effects, reduce negative external effects, and create a favorable external environment for the high-quality development of China's economy in the new era.

References

Caceres C, Carriere-Swallow Y, Demir I, Gruss B. U.S. Monetary Policy Normalization and Global Interest Rates. IMF Working Paper, WP/16/195, 2016.

Chen Q, Filardo A, He D, et al. Financial Crisis, US Unconventional Monetary Policy and International Spillovers. Journal of International Money and Finance, 2016, 67: 62–81.

Chen and Ma. A Study of U.S. Quantitative Easing Policy and Exit Effects and Their Impact on China. World Economy Study, 2016, (6).

Fang, He, and Jing. A Study of the Spillover Effects of China-U.S. Trade Frictions on China's Financial Markets. Finance & Trade Economics, 2019, (6).

Fu. Fed Rate Hikes, RMB Exchange Rate and Price Volatility. Journal of International Trade, 2017, (3).

Guo, Chen, and Chen. A Study of the Declining Effectiveness of China's Monetary Policy and Expectation Management. Economic Research Journal, 2016, 51(01): 28–41.

Góes C, Kamil H, Imus P D, Garcia-Escribano M, Perrelli R, Roache S K, and Zook J. Spillovers from U.S. Monetary Policy Normalization on Brazil and Mexico's Sovereign Bond Yields. IMF Working Paper, WP/17/50, 2017.

Kaketsis A, and Sarantis N. The Effects of Monetary Policy Changes on Market Interest Rates in Greece: An Event Study Approach. International Review of Economics & Finance, 2006, 15(4).

Kalu E, Okoyeuzu C, Ukemenam A, and Ujunwa A. Spillover Effects of the US Monetary Policy Normalization on African Stock Markets. Journal of Economics and Development, 2020, 22(1).

Kolasa M, and Wesołowski G. International Spillovers of Quantitative Easing. Journal of International Economics, 2020, 126.

Li and Gao. A Study of Spillovers from U.S. Monetary Policy Normalization—A Comparison of Emerging and Developed Economies. Shanghai Journal of Economics, 2019, (6).

Liu and Ma. The Impact of U.S. Monetary Policy Adjustments on China's Economy in the Post-Financial Crisis Era, Wuhan University Party Journal (Philosophy and Social Sciences), 2020, (5).

Li and Zhang. Has the U.S. Quantitative Easing Policy Affected China's Inflation?—An Empirical Study based on the SVAR Model. Studies of International Finance, 2013, (8).

Liu and Han. An Analysis of the Spillover Effects of Quantitative Easing Policy on Emerging Markets—A Study Based on the Experience of China and Brazil. Management Review, 2014, (6).

Liu, Xu, and Liu. Will Fed Rate Hike Expectations Cause Asset Price Volatility in China?—Empirical Evidence based on the Exchange Rate Transmission Path. Journal of Xi'an Jiaotong University (Social Sciences), 2016, (4).

Li and Li. A Study of the Impact of Fed Tapering on the Strong Dollar Cycle and Emerging Markets. Forum of World Economics & Politics, 2017, (6).

Lu and Fang. A Study of the Impact of U.S. Quantitative Easing Policy Adjustment on Short-Term Capital Flows in China. Macroeconomics, 2015, (2).

McKinnon R, and Liu Z. Zero Interest Rates in the United States Provoke World Monetary Instability and Constrict the US Economy. Review of International Economics, 2013, 21(1).

Ma and Yu. A Study of the Spillover Effects of U.S. Quantitative Easing Policy on BRICS Countries. Studies of International Finance, 2015, (3): 13–22.

Neely C J. Unconventional Monetary Policy had Large International Effects. Journal of Banking & Finance, 2015, 52.

Nie and Jin. A Study of the Spillover Effects of U.S. Quantitative Easing Policy on the Exports of Chinese Industries. Studies of International Finance, 2015, (3): 3–12.

Pan and Yan. The Macroeconomic Effects of the Fed's Interest Rate Commitment. Studies of International Finance, 2012, (4).

Qi, Cheng, Wang, and Li. The Impact of the Fed's Quantitative Easing Policy on the Chinese Economy and the RMB Exchange Rate. Management Review, 2013, (5).

Sun and Zhang. Time Variance, Fed Rate Hikes and China's Output—An Empirical Analysis Based on the TVP-VAR Model. Studies of International Finance, 2016, (4).

Tillmann P. Unconventional Monetary Policy and the Spillovers to Emerging Markets. Journal of International Money and Finance, 2016, 66.

Wu S, Hu B, and Pan Q. The Impact of the US Interest Rate Hike on Emerging Market Economies and the Belt and Road Initiative. China & World Economy, 2019, 27(3).

Xiao and Lan. The Spillover Effects of the Fed's Monetary Policy Normalization on the Chinese Economy. World Economy Study, 2017(12): 38–49+133.

Yu, Zhang, and Wu. The Impact of the U.S. Exit from QE on the Financial Markets of China and the United States and China's Countermeasures—An Analysis Based on the FAVAR Model. World Economy Study, 2015, (4): 24–32; 127.

CHAPTER 7

Impact of U.S. Interest Rate Cuts and Tariffs on China's Economy

This chapter uses a two-country DSGE model with two types of frictions, namely nominal price stickiness and collateral constraints, to study in depth the impact of the U.S. interest rate cuts and tariffs China's our macroeconomy in the context of the fact that the Fed cut interest rates for the first time since the financial crisis and the trade conflict between China and the United States was escalating in 2019. Through numerical simulation, this study found that U.S. interest rate cuts were mainly due to the negative impact of demand, which had an adverse spillover effect on China's economy, but the overall impact was not significant, and financial frictions would amplify the impact, resulting in a decline of 0.33% and 0.7% in China's output and investment. Relatively speaking, the negative impact of tariffs on China's economy is more pronounced than that of interest rate cuts in that they led to a sharp drop in China's output and investment. The combined effect of the two led to a decline of 1.4% and 2.6% in China's real GDP and investment, and an escalation of the trade dispute would further worsen bilateral economic relations and lengthen the time it takes for the economy to stabilize.

1 Introduction

At present, the United States is the world's most powerful country in terms of overall strength and most economically influential country. Its monetary policy not only plays a very important role in regulating its

L. Weiping, *American Monetary Policy Adjustment and Its Impacts*,
https://doi.org/10.1007/978-981-99-7810-6_7

domestic economy, but also has a decisive impact on the development of countries around the world through various channels such as exchange rate fluctuations, international capital flows and international trade. With the deepening of global value chains, the spillover effects of U.S. interest rate policy on China are becoming all the more noticeable. On July 31, 2019, the Fed announced its first interest rate cut since 2008, followed by successive interest rate cuts on September 19 and October 31. In March 2020, the Fed lowered interest rates directly to the zero lower bound because of the pandemic. Previous studies have focused on quantitative easing and interest rate hikes in the United States, and little research has been done on this round of interest rate cuts. Is this round of rate cuts an active adjustment by the Fed, or a passive response to the development of the economic situation? Is it due to negative shock on the supply side or adverse impact on the demand side? The Fed's monetary policy is a microcosm of global monetary policy adjustments, leading the trend and direction of monetary policy around the world. In order to examine in depth the important impact of this round of monetary policy adjustments on China's macroeconomy, it is necessary to answer the above questions.

With the directional adjustment of U.S. monetary policy, some new developments have emerged in the China-U.S. economic and trade environment. The recent adjustment of U.S. tariff policy has greatly increased the uncertainty of trade policies in many countries, including China and the United States. Judging from U.S. tariff threats against China, Mexico, and European countries, and the increasing trade friction between South Korea and Japan in 2019, uncertainties in global economic development come from multiple regions and fields, and risk factors that pose a threat to economic development directly or indirectly influence the formulation and implementation of U.S. interest rate policy (Bloom 2014), so the new developments in the global economic and trade environment will affect the spillover effects of the Fed's monetary policy. Escalating China-U.S. trade friction dampened the growth of Chinese exports to the United States, which fell from $46.7 billion in September 2018 to $25.2 billion in March 2019, adversely affecting the Chinese economy. In addition, due to the amplifying effect of financial frictions caused by collateral constraints (Davis and Presno 2017), imperfect financial markets may also contribute to further declines in investment and asset prices, thus exacerbating China's economic downturn.

The above facts make us aware that the shift in U.S. interest rate policy adjustments and China-U.S. trade friction will exacerbate uncertainties in the global economic and financial environment, and are also the most important external issues facing China in its efforts to open wider to the outside world on all fronts. In this paper, the U.S. interest rate cuts and tariffs are studied within a theoretical framework, and by comparing the different transmission mechanisms of these two kinds of policy, the relative importance of their impact on China's economy can be quantified and analyzed. In addition, the intrinsic reasons for U.S. interest rate cuts are explored, and the intrinsic motivations and mechanisms for rate cuts are clarified, so that the spillover effects and comprehensive impact of these two kinds of policy combined on China's economy can be measured more accurately. In this paper, by introducing occasionally binding collateral constraints, a two-country DSGE model is established to focus on simulating the transmission mechanisms of the macro impact of U.S. interest rate policy and tariff policy adjustments on China's economy, conduct quantitative research and comparative analysis on the spillover effects of these two kinds of policy, and perform numerical simulation and scenario analysis on whether there are situations such as financial frictions and an escalation of the trade dispute. The research in this paper lays a solid theoretical foundation for discussing and evaluating the impact of the future development of U.S. macro policies on China's economy, and at the same time puts forward targeted policy recommendations for risk prevention, which is of great practical significance.

The possible contributions of this paper are as follows: First, in an asymmetric two-country DSGE model, the relative importance of the spillover effects of U.S. monetary policy and tariff policy on China's economy is comparatively analyzed, and the compound effects of a combination of these two kinds of policy are examined. Second, the Levenberg-Marquardt mixed complementarity problem (LMMCP) algorithm is used to solve the deterministic dynamic simulation results under the tariff policy path to make them more in line with the reality of China-U.S. trade friction. Third, the important role of financial frictions in the impact on China's economy is revealed, and the possible mechanism by which exogenous shocks impacted China's economy is clarified.

2 Literature Review

2.1 Spillover Effects of U.S. Interest Rate Policy

Some studies have focused on the impact of U.S. interest rate policy on exchange rates and international capital flows. A study by Iacoviello and Navarro (2019) showed that in the absence of capital controls, changes in the Fed's interest rate policy would cause changes in the exchange rates of other countries, thereby changing the international competitiveness of the currencies of other economies and further affecting cross-border trade. A study by Jin and Hong (2015) showed that under the conditions of an open economy, the equilibrium state of exchange rates depended on the equilibrium state of both domestic and foreign interest rates. A study by Eichengreen and Gupta (2015) mentioned that U.S. interest rate policy had a direct bearing on the global liquidity of the U.S. dollar, and the tightness of the interest rate policy would affect international capital flows and the stability of global financial markets. A study by Wang et al. (2019) showed that the rise and fall of interest rates in the United States would lead to the tightening and relaxation of collateral constraints in the entrepreneurial sector respectively, and result in asymmetric capital flows in China through the financial friction mechanism.

Some studies have found that U.S. interest rate policy can have a significant impact on other countries' economies. For developed economies, Dedola et al. (2017) found that tight U.S. monetary policy would lead to a decline in industrial production and real GDP, and a rise in unemployment. For emerging market economies, Bernini et al. (2018) found in their research that shocks to U.S. interest rates could explain 14% of the fluctuations in their economic cycles when predictable shocks were considered. In addition, Hanisch (2019) found that tight U.S. monetary policy would lead to an expansion of the output of eurozone countries, but the impact on different countries was heterogeneous. Yang et al. (2018), Xu (2018) and other researchers focused on the spillover effects and impact of U.S. interest rate policy on China's economy, and found that the spillover effects of U.S. interest rate policy had a stronger impact on some of China's economic variables than on its own economy. In addition, the spillover effects of U.S. interest rate policy on China's economy may be heterogeneous across different periods. Ho et al. (2018) found that during the zero lower bound period, a decline in U.S. interest rates would significantly affect China's stock market and property market through the hot money channel, while the impact was not obvious during the non-zero lower bound period.

There are also studies that have focused on the spillover effects of U.S. interest rate policy on interest rate policy in other countries. A study by Bluedorn and Bowdler (2010) showed that the spillover effects of U.S. interest rate policy on interest rates in other countries depended on the driver of changes in U.S. interest rates, that is, whether interest rate adjustments are in line with changes in the fundamentals of the U.S. economy. In addition, a study by Xiao and Lan (2017) also showed that U.S. monetary policy had significant spillover effects on interest rate policy in other economies.

2.2 Economic Impact of Tariff Adjustment

Most of the studies on tariff policy associate it with trade policy uncertainty and suggest that the shock has a significant impact on all aspects of the macroeconomy.

Most of these studies have focused on the economic impact of a decrease in trade policy uncertainty brought about by a reduction in tariffs. As for imports and exports, a study by Imbruno (2019) found that the implementation of WTO-bound tariffs would significantly boost trade. Handley and Limão (2017), after assessing the impact of trade policy uncertainty on heterogeneous firms, argued that reduced trade policy uncertainty increased investment in export entry and technological upgrading, which in turn increased trade flows and consumers' real income. A study by Mao (2020) reached a similar conclusion: tariff cuts can significantly increase export intensity, quality and stability. Regarding output, Yu (2011) studied the impact on firm productivity and found that the reduction or removal of tariffs or tariff barriers had a significant effect on firm productivity growth. With regard to welfare levels, Francois and Martin (2004) found that tariff bindings reduced tariff volatility and increased welfare levels on both sides of the trade. A study by Ossa (2014) came to a similar conclusion after quantifying the welfare effects of eliminating actual tariffs.

A few studies have focused on the economic impact of rising trade policy uncertainty. Studies by Bloom (2009) and Bloom et al. (2018) found that uncertainty shocks could lead to short-term economic downturns, and in a DSGE model with heterogeneous firms, uncertainty shocks would reduce GDP by about 2.5%. In view of rising trade policy uncertainty from trade disputes and tariffs in recent years, a study by Caldara et al. (2020) found that higher expected tariffs and increased uncertainty about future tariffs reduced U.S. investment and output. Ho et al. (2018) found that during the period of quantitative easing at the zero lower bound, U.S. policy uncertainty shocks significantly increased China's property investment through the hot money channel.

2.3 Research on Predictable Shocks

Most studies based on the DSGE model consider unpredictable exogenous shocks, and one of their key features is that residents' expectations about the conditions after future white noise shocks enter the policy function are zero. In recent years, many studies by Chinese and foreign scholars have found that certain predictable shocks can better explain the periodic features in actual economic data. Cao and L'Huillier (2014), for example, examined the impact of predictable shocks to productivity on economic volatility and correlation. Christiano et al. (2014) found that predictable shocks to heterogeneous risks in firms could better explain volatility in the U.S. real economy. Milani and Treadwell (2012) incorporated expected monetary policy shocks into the DSGE model and found that expected shocks had a larger and longer impact on the macroeconomy. A study by Schmitt-Grohé and Uribe (2012) found that expected shocks in the DSGE model could explain about 50% of output volatility.

In addition to the above studies in the field of the conventional business cycle, some scholars have found that predictable exogenous shocks could better explain the dynamic features of credit booms and busts as a crisis event window. Among them, Akinci and Chahrour (2018) studied the ability of predictable shocks to productivity to explain sudden stops in emerging market countries, and Durdu et al. (2013) examined the impact of predictable shocks on sovereign debt crises. Gertler et al. (2020) found that positive predictable shocks to capital quality, while stimulating the real economy in the short run, made the banking sector more vulnerable and eventually led to an increase in the risk of banking crises.

In addition, there are many studies on the policy effects of expected exogenous shocks at home and abroad. Zhuang et al. (2012) found that expected shocks to monetary policy were the most important driver of fluctuations in China's economic cycle after reform and opening-up.

Wang et al. (2016) found that models with expected shocks to monetary policy performed better than models with unexpected shocks. A study by Gomes et al. (2017) on models with expected shocks to monetary policy came to a similar conclusion.

Through literature review, we find that the literature on the spillover effects of U.S. interest rate policy is mostly empirical, and although some of the literature also attempts to explore them with theoretical models, the models are set up in a simpler way and can hardly reflect the overall macroeconomic characteristics of a large emerging market countries like China and the United States accurately. There is limited research on the impact of tariffs, and most of the research focuses on the micro-empirical analysis of the impact of tariff cuts. There is a scarcity of literature that quantitatively analyzes the impact of tariff hikes from the perspective of China-U.S. trade friction, and research on such predictable shocks to tariffs is even more lacking. Therefore, this paper uses a rigorous theoretical model and numerical simulation to quantitatively analyze the overall impact of the U.S. macroeconomic policy mix that combines U.S. interest rate cuts and tariff hikes on China's macroeconomy, and compare the relative effects of the two policies, so as to provide a frame of reference for the Chinese authorities to work out a policy response.

3 Theoretical Models

Suppose there are two types of individuals in the country: a patient household sector and an impatient entrepreneur sector, with a population size of and respectively. The subjective discount rate of the household sector is higher than that of the entrepreneur sector, so the two sectors are the supply side and the demand side of funds respectively. In addition, the entrepreneurial sector owns capital as well as shares in intermediate goods manufacturers. Suppose that the intermediate goods market is a monopolistically competitive market, and all manufacturers produce differentiated products under Calvo contracts. In order to better fit the actual situation in China, we also consider the existence of both local currency pricing (LCP) and producer currency pricing (PCP) for exported goods.

3.1 Patient Household Sector

In order to maximize the effect, a typical household can choose its consumption level C_t and labor supply H_t^h and buy domestic bonds B_t^h

and foreign bonds B_t^f respectively in the domestic and foreign bond markets.

$$\max_{C_t, H_t^h, B_t, B_t^{f*}} E_0 \sum_{t=0}^{\infty} \beta^t \left[\ln(C_t - \upsilon C_{t-1}) - \frac{\left(H_t^h\right)^{1+\sigma_h^{-1}}}{1+\sigma_h^{-1}} \right]$$

The above equation gives the specific form of the utility function, and its budget constraints are as follows:

$$P_t C_t + B_t^h + S_t B_t^f = W_t H_t^h + R_{t-1} B_{t-1}^h + (1 - \tau_t) R_{t-1}^f S_t B_{t-1}^f + T_t \quad (1)$$

The consumer price index and the nominal wage are P_t and W_t respectively, and the nominal yield of domestic bonds and the nominal exchange rate are R_t and S_t respectively. Where β is the subjective discount factor of the household sector, υ reflects the degree of consumption habit, and σ_h is the Frisch elasticity of labor supply. Considering that there is a certain level of capital controls in China, that is, the government taxes international capital flows, assuming a tax rate of τ_t, finally this part of the tax is returned to the household sector through transfer payments T_t. Similar to the analysis by Davis and Presno (2017), this paper introduces the risk premium of foreign bonds in the form $R_t^f = R_t^* e^{-\varsigma \tilde{B}_t^f}$ to ensure the stability of the model. Where R_t^* is the foreign risk-free rate of return, which represents the level of foreign policy rates. Individual portfolio choices in the household sector do not affect the return on total assets. Where $\tilde{B}_t^f = \int_0^{\Psi_h} B_t^f dh$ represents the total holdings of foreign bonds by the domestic household sector.

3.2 *Entrepreneur Sector*

The entrepreneur sector can directly participate in investment activities in the capital market, and is more impatient than the household sector. The utility function of a typical entrepreneur is as follows:

$$\max_{C_t^e, b_t, b_t^f, I_t, , K_t} E_0 \sum_{t=0}^{\infty} (\beta^e)^t \ln\left(C_t^e - \upsilon C_{t-1}^e\right)$$

In addition to budget constraints, the entrepreneur sector also needs to consider the capital accumulation equation and collateral constraints, in the following form:

$$P_t C_t^e + P_t^I \psi_t^{-1} I_t + R_{t-1} b_{t-1} + (1 - \tau_t) R_{t-1}^{ef} S_t b_{t-1}^f$$
$$= P_t^k K_{t-1} + b_t + S_t b_t^f + div_t + T_t^e \quad (2)$$

$$K_t = (1 - \delta) K_{t-1} + \left[1 - \frac{\kappa}{2} \left(\frac{I_t}{I_{t-1}} - 1 \right)^2 \right] I_t \quad (3)$$

$$\theta E_t \left(P_{t+1} P_{t+1}^k \right) K_t \geq R_t b_t + R_t^* E_t (S_{t+1}) b_t^f \quad (4)$$

Under the above constraints, entrepreneurs maximize their expected utility by choosing consumption C_t^e, investment I_t, capital stock K_t and domestic and foreign bonds b_t, b_t^f. Similar to the setting of the household sector, $R_t^{ef} = R_t^* e^{-\zeta \tilde{b}_t^f}$ is the risk premium for entrepreneurs and T_t^e is transfer payments. The budget constraints of the entrepreneur sector are shown in Eq. (2). ψ_t and P_t^k are investment technology shocks and the actual price of capital goods, respectively, and div_t represents dividends on shares held. The capital accumulation equation is Eq. (3).

According to the setting by Liu et al. (2013), creditors can only sell off a certain percentage (θ) of their assets in liquidation, so the debt that entrepreneurs need to repay cannot exceed the expected liquidated assets, that is, $R_t b_t + R_t^* E_t (S_{t+1}) b_t^f$ cannot be greater than $\theta E_t (P_{t+1} P_{t+1}^k) K_t$. The specific form of collateral constraints is given by Eq. (4).

3.3 Final Goods Manufacturer Sector

In this paper, we assume that there exists intermediate goods manufacturer sector with measure 1, which produces and prices in a monopolistically competitive intermediate goods market, and the elasticity of substitution between different intermediate goods is σ. Final goods manufacturers produce in a perfectly competitive market. They buy intermediate goods and use their production technology to convert intermediate goods into final goods. All intermediate goods manufacturers face the same price stickiness. Gopinath (2016) found that Chinese exporters used PCP for no more than 10% of total exports; when exporters chose LCP under sticky prices, the degree to which the prices of their goods in foreign currencies were affected by exchange rate fluctuations was extremely low, that is, price stickiness and the choice of invoicing currency would lead to incomplete pass-through of short-term exchange rates. One of the focuses of this paper is to examine the impact of U.S. tariff policy on China's economy, and the most immediate effect of tariffs is to change the terms of trade between the two countries. The choice of invoicing currency also influences the terms of trade and thus plays an important role in a country's imports and exports. Wang and Qu (2018) conducted an in-depth study on this influencing mechanism. Therefore, in this study, it is necessary to take into account the reality that PCP is used for a small percentage of China's exports.

Suppose there are two types of intermediate goods manufacturers $i_P \in [0, \kappa_P]$ and $i_L \in [\kappa_P, 1]$ in the market, that is, the shares of intermediate goods priced by PCP and LCP are κ_P and $1 - \kappa_P$, respectively. Manufacturers using PCP i_P only set their prices and make settlements in their local currencies and only need to set an optimal price; manufacturers using LCP i_L set their prices based on the market situation, so they need to set two optimal prices, with goods for export priced in foreign currencies. As can be seen from the setting above, final goods produced within the country can be expressed as the sum of the two types of intermediate goods:

$$y_t^d = \left[\kappa_P^{\frac{1}{\sigma}} y_{P,t}^{d\frac{\sigma-1}{\sigma}} + (1 - \kappa_P)^{\frac{1}{\sigma}} y_{L,t}^{d\frac{\sigma-1}{\sigma}} \right]^{\frac{\sigma}{\sigma-1}} \tag{5}$$

The sum of the two types of intermediate goods $y_{P,t}^d$, $y_{L,t}^d$ then satisfies:

$$y_{P,t}^d = \left[\int_0^{\kappa_P} (1/\kappa_P)^{\frac{1}{\sigma}} y_t^d(i_P)^{\frac{\sigma-1}{\sigma}} di_P \right]^{\frac{\sigma}{\sigma-1}},$$

$$y_{L,t}^d = \left[\int_{\kappa_P}^1 (1/1 - \kappa_P)^{\frac{1}{\sigma}} y_t^d(i_L)^{\frac{\sigma-1}{\sigma}} di_L \right]^{\frac{\sigma}{\sigma-1}}$$

The sum of the two types of intermediate goods $y_{P,t}^x$, $y_{L,t}^x$ is defined in a similar form to final exports y_t^x. It can be seen that the elasticity of substitution is the same for intermediate goods produced by intermediate goods manufacturers i_P and i_L, with no difference other than the choice of invoicing currency. Based on the above setting, the demand function of intermediate goods $i \in \{i_P, i_L\}$ can be easily obtained: $y_t^d(i) = \left(P_t(i)/P_t^d\right)^{-\sigma} y_t^d$, $y_t^x(i) = \left(P_t^{x*}(i)/P_t^{x*}\right)^{-\sigma} y_t^x$; from this, the price indexes of goods for domestic sale y_t^d and goods for export y_t^x

can be obtained: $P_t^d = [\kappa_P P_{P,t}^{d\,1-\sigma} + (1-\kappa_P) P_{L,t}^{d\,1-\sigma}]^{1/(1-\sigma)}$, $P_t^{x*} = [\kappa_P P_{P,t}^{x*\,1-\sigma} + (1-\kappa_P) P_{L,t}^{x*\,1-\sigma}]^{1/(1-\sigma)}$.

3.4 *Intermediate Goods Manufacturer Sector*

Assuming that intermediate goods manufacturers $i \in \{i_P, i_L\}$ all have the same form of Cobb–Douglas production function:

$$Y_t(i) = y_t^d(i) + y_t^x(i) = A_t H_t(i)^{1-\alpha} K_t(i)^\alpha \tag{6}$$

Under the given factor price set $\{W_t, R_t^k\}$, the intermediate goods manufacturer's cost is minimized so that $\alpha W_t H_t(i) = (1-\alpha) R_t^k K_t(i)$, so its marginal cost of production satisfies $MC_t = A_t^{-1}(W_t/1-\alpha)^{1-\alpha}(R_t^k/\alpha)^\alpha$.

3.4.1 *Intermediate Goods Manufacturers Using PCP*

Individual manufacturers i_P produce intermediate goods for domestic sale and export $y_t^d(i_P)$, $y_t^x(i_P)$ at the same time. The law of one price holds in the case of PCP, so such manufacturers only need to set an optimal price $\tilde{P}_{P,t}^d$. Assume that manufacturers adjust prices by staggered price setting, that is, the price of goods is adjusted with a probability of $1-\theta_p$ in each period, and the government subsidizes a certain percentage ($\tau_x = \tau_d = 1/\sigma$) of the production costs to eliminate monopoly distortions at steady state. Under the constraints of the demand function, the optimal price $\tilde{P}_{P,t}^d(i_P)$ decision can be obtained by maximizing profits:

$$\tilde{P}_{P,t}^d(i_P) = \frac{E_t \sum_{j=0}^{\infty} (\beta\theta_P)^j v_{t,t+j} \left[y_{t+j}^d(i_P) + y_{t+j}^x(i_P) \right] MC_{t+j}}{E_t \sum_{j-0}^{\infty} (\beta\theta_P)^j v_{t,t+j} \left[y_{t+j}^d(i_P) + y_{t+j}^x(i_P) \right]} \tag{7}$$

Because of symmetry, all intermediate goods manufacturers will set the same optimal price, then $P_{P,t}^{d\,1-\sigma} = (1-\theta_p)\tilde{P}_{P,t}^{d\,1-\sigma} + \theta_p P_{P,t-1}^{d\,1-\sigma}$ can be easily obtained according to the price definition.

3.4.2 *Intermediate Goods Manufacturers Using LCP*

The production function of manufacturers using LCP i_L is exactly the same as that of manufacturers using PCP, but as they use a different pricing method, they need to set two optimal prices: price of goods for domestic sale in local currencies $\tilde{P}_{L,t}^d$ and price of goods for export in foreign currencies $\tilde{P}_{L,t}^{x*}$. At this point, the exchange rate passes through incompletely, and the law of one price no longer holds when the price is sticky. The profit function of such manufacturers is as follows:

$$E_t \sum_{j=0}^{\infty} (\beta\theta_p)^j v_{t,t+j} \Big[y_{t+j}^d(i_L) \Big(P_t^d(i_L) - (1-\tau_d) MC_{t+j} \Big) + y_{t+j}^x(i_L) \big(S_{t+j} P_t^{x*}(i_L) - (1-\tau_x) MC_{t+j} \big) \Big]$$

The price of their goods for domestic sale $\tilde{P}_{L,t}^{d}$ is consistent with the optimal price set by manufacturers using PCP. The specific form of the price of goods for export in foreign currencies $\tilde{P}_{L,t}^{x*}$ is as follows:

$$\tilde{P}_{L,t}^{x*}(i_L) = \frac{E_t \sum_{j=0}^{\infty} (\beta\theta_P)^j v_{t,t+j} \left[y_{t+j}^x(i_L) \right] MC_{t+j}}{E_t \sum_{j=0}^{\infty} (\beta\theta_P)^j v_{t,t+j} \left[y_{t+j}^x(i_L) \right] S_{t+j}} \tag{8}$$

Similarly, using the aggregate price definition, we can get $P_{L,t}^{d/x*\ 1-\sigma} = (1-\theta_p)\tilde{P}_{L,t}^{d/x*\ 1-\sigma} + \theta_p P_{L,t-1}^{d/x*\ 1-\sigma}$.

3.5 Monetary Policy and Capital Control Policy

According to the setting by Wang et al. (2019) and Huang and Guo (2016), on the basis of the standard Taylor rule, the central bank will also peg the exchange rate. In this way the characteristics of a managed floating exchange rate can be reflected to some extent. The specific form of the interest rate rule is as follows:

$$\log(R_t) = (1-\theta_R)\big(\theta_\pi \pi_t + \theta_S \log(S_t/S_{t-1}) + \theta_{\text{gdp}} \log(\text{GDP}_t/\overline{\text{GDP}})\big) + \theta_R \log(R_{t-1}) + \varepsilon_t^R \tag{9}$$

where ε_t^R reflects the exogenous disturbance of monetary policy, which is a white noise shock with a mean of zero, GDP_t is the actual GDP of the country calculated by the expenditure method, and $\overline{GDP}$ is the corresponding steady-state level. Assume that the tax rate on foreign bonds represents the degree of capital control, in the form of $\tau_t = \chi(R_t^* - R_t)$. $\chi > 0$ means the implementation of capital controls, that is, the level of taxation on international capital flows will be affected by the yield spread between domestic and foreign debt instruments; $\chi = 0$ means that the capital account has been fully liberalized.

3.6 Domestic Market Clearing

The total actual domestic investment is $\int_{\Psi_h}^{1} \psi_t^{-1} I_t = (1 - \Psi_h)\psi_t^{-1} I_t$. The investment demand functions of the entrepreneur sector for domestic production and imports are as follows:

$$I_t^d = \Omega_I^d \left(\frac{P_t^d}{P_t}\right)^{-\rho_I} (1 - \Psi_h)\psi_t^{-1} I_t,$$

$$I_t^m = \left(1 - \Omega_I^d\right)\left(\frac{P_t^m}{P_t}\right)^{-\rho_I} (1 - \Psi_h)\psi_t^{-1} I_t \tag{10}$$

where ρ_C, ρ_I represent the elasticity of substitution between domestically produced and foreign-produced consumer goods and investment goods, respectively, and Ω_C, Ω_I represent the share of domestically produced consumer goods and domestically produced investment goods in total consumption and total investment, respectively.

The demand for domestically produced consumer goods and the demand for imported consumer goods are:

$$C_t^d = \Omega_C^d \left(\frac{P_t^d}{P_t}\right)^{-\rho_C} \left(\Psi_h C_t + (1 - \Psi_h) C_t^e\right)$$

$$C_t^m = \left(1 - \Omega_C^d\right)\left(\frac{P_t^m}{P_t}\right)^{-\rho_C} \left(\Psi_h C_t + (1 - \Psi_h) C_t^e\right) \tag{11}$$

Combined with the above definition of investment, the market clearing conditions for domestically produced final goods and imported goods can be expressed as: $y_t^d = C_t^d + I_t^d$, $y_t^m = C_t^m + I_t^m$.

In addition, after achieving market clearing, fixed assets must satisfy $\int_0^1 K_t = \int_{\Psi_h}^1 K_t = (1 - \Psi_h)K_t$; $\int_0^{\Psi_h} B_t^h = \int_{\Psi_h}^1 b_t$ must be satisfied when the debt market cleared, and $\int_0^{\Psi_h} H_t^h = \Psi_h H_t^h = H_t$ must be satisfied when the labor market is cleared.

Finally, the clearing condition for aggregated factors is:

$$A_t[(1 - \Psi_h)K_t]^{\alpha}\left(\Psi_h H_t^h\right)^{1-\alpha}$$

$$= \left(Y^d_{P,t} + Y^x_{P,t}\right)\Xi_{P,t} + Y^d_{L,t}\Xi^d_{L,t} + Y^x_{L,t}\Xi^x_{L,t} \quad (12)$$

where $\Xi_{P,t}$, $\Xi^d_{L,t}$, $\Xi^x_{L,t}$ are price dispersion among manufacturers using PCP and price dispersion among products for domestic sale and export produced by manufacturers using LCP, respectively. Price dispersions is defined as $\Xi^i_{k,t} = \int_0^{\kappa_k} \kappa_k^{-1}\left(p^i_{k,t}(j_k)/P^i_{k,t}\right)^{-\sigma} dj_k$, where $k \in \{L, P\}, i \in \{d, x\}$. Take price dispersion among manufacturers using PCP as an example. We can deduce their price dispersion decision as $\Xi_{P,t} = (1 - \theta)\left(\tilde{P}^d_{P,t} \Big/ P^d_{P,t}\right)^{-\sigma} + \theta\left(\pi_{P,t}\right)^{\sigma}\Xi_{P,t-1}$.

3.7 Foreign Sector

The standard NK-DSGE framework is used to simulate the economic situation of the United States, with the model developed by Faia and Monacelli (2008) serving as a source of reference for the specific setting. In order to examine the impact of U.S. tariffs in the context of trade disputes, this paper will add distortionary taxes to goods imported into the country to indicate the tariffs levied.

The first decision-making issues to consider in the foreign household sector are:

$$\max_{C^*_t, H^*_t, B^*_t, B^{f*}_t} E_0 \sum_{t=0}^{\infty} \beta^t D^*_t \left[\ln\left(C^*_t\right) - \frac{H_t^{*1+\sigma_H}}{1+\sigma_H}\right]$$

$$\text{s.t. } C^*_t + B^*_t + \frac{B^{f*}_t}{S_t} = W^*_t H^*_t + R^*_{t-1}B^*_{t-1} + R^{f*}_{t-1}\frac{B^{f*}_{t-1}}{S_t} + T^*_t \quad (13)$$

In cases where only risk-free bonds are considered, the optimal decision-making conditions for foreign household sector for domestic bonds can be obtained by deforming the three conditions of domestic household sector for foreign bonds, domestic household sector for domestic bonds and foreign household sector for foreign bonds.

The final consumer goods setting of the foreign household sector is consistent with that of the domestic household sector, that is:

$$C^*_t = \left[\Omega_C^{*1/\rho_C} C_t^{d*\frac{\rho_C-1}{\rho_C}} + \left(1 - \Omega^*_C\right)^{1/\rho_C} C_t^{m*\frac{\rho_C-1}{\rho_C}}\right]^{\frac{\rho_C}{\rho_C-1}} \quad (14)$$

In the above setting, foreign residents' demand for consumer goods for domestic sale C_t^{d*} and imported consumer goods C_t^{m*} satisfies:

$$C_t^{d*} = \Omega_C^*\left(\frac{P_t^{d*}}{P_t^*}\right)^{-\rho_C^*} C_t^* = \Omega_C^*\left[\Omega_C^* + (1-\Omega_C^*)T_t^{*1-\rho_C}\right]^{\frac{\rho_C^*}{1-\rho_C^*}} C_t^* \quad (15)$$

$$C_t^{m*} = (1-\Omega_C^*)\left[\Omega_C^* T_t^{*\rho_C - 1} + 1 - \Omega_C^*\right]^{\frac{\rho_C}{1-\rho_C}} C_t^* \quad (16)$$

In the above consumption deduction, the definition of aggregate consumer prices $P_t^* = \left(\Omega_C^* P_t^{d*1-\rho_C^*} + \left(1-\Omega_C^*\right)P_t^{m*1-\rho_C^*}\right)^{\frac{1}{1-\rho_C^*}}$ is used. In addition, if foreign authorities impose distortionary tariffs τ_t^{x*} on goods for export, the relationship between import prices in the foreign sector and prices of goods for export satisfies $P_t^{m*} = P_t^{l*}(1+\tau_t^{x*})$, and the foreign terms of trade are defined as $T_t^* = P_t^{m*}/P_t^{d*}$. According to the above definitions of consumer demand and the sum of consumer goods, the definition of foreign consumer price inflation is:

$$\pi_t^* = \left(\frac{\Omega_C^* + (1-\Omega_C^*)T_t^{*1-\rho_C}}{\Omega_C^* \pi_t^{d*\rho_C - 1} + (1-\Omega_C^*)\pi_t^{d*\rho_C - 1} T_{t-1}^{*1-\rho_C}}\right)^{\frac{1}{1-\rho_C}} \quad (17)$$

Considering that the production function of individual foreign intermediate goods manufacturers is linear, that is, $y_t^*(i^*) = H_t^*(i^*)$, and they produce both goods for export and domestic sale, their production constraint is:

$$y_t^*(i^*) = y_t^{d*}(i^*) + y_t^{x*}(i^*) \quad (18)$$

Assume that foreign intermediate goods manufacturers also have price stickiness, and the relationship between intermediate goods and final goods satisfies:

$$Y_t^* = \left(\int_0^1 \left[y_t^*(i^*)\right]^{\frac{\sigma-1}{\sigma}} di^*\right)^{\frac{\sigma}{\sigma-1}}$$

Foreign manufacturers use PCP and do not set their prices based on the market situation, so their optimal pricing problem is:

$$\max_{P_t^{d*}(i^*)} E_0 \sum_{t=0}^{\infty} (\beta\theta)^t \Lambda_t \left[y_t^*(i^*)\left(P_t^{d*}(i^*) - MC_t\right)\right]$$

$$\text{s.t.} \quad y_t^*(i^*) = \left(\frac{P_t^{d*}(i^*)}{P_t^{d*}}\right)^{-\sigma} Y_t^* \tag{19}$$

According to the sum of prices, their inflation decision satisfies:

$$\left(\frac{\tilde{P}_t^*}{P_t^*}\right)^{1-\sigma} = \frac{1 - \xi_p^* \pi_t^{d*\,\sigma-1}}{1 - \xi_p^*} \tag{20}$$

For foreign manufacturers, the actual marginal cost is:

$$MC_t^* = W_t^* P_t^* / P_t^{d*} = W_t^* \left[\Omega_C^* + (1 - \Omega_C^*) T_t^{*1-\sigma_C}\right]^{\frac{1}{1-\sigma_C}} \tag{21}$$

where $T_t^* = P_t^m / P_t^{d*}$ is the terms of trade of foreign countries relative to their own countries, and $MC_t^* = W_t^*$ when considering that their own countries are small countries. The condition for clearing the foreign labor market is:

$$\int_0^1 H_t^*(i^*) di^* = H_t^*$$

The condition for clearing the product market is:

$$\int_0^1 y_t^*(i^*) di^* = H_t^* = Y_t^* = C_t^{d*} + Y_t^{x*} \tag{22}$$

The condition for clearing the bond market is:

$$\int B_t^* = 0, \int B_t^{*f} = B_t^f \tag{23}$$

After achieving market clearing, imported goods must satisfy:

$$C_t^{m*} = Y_t^x, Y_t^{x*} = Y_t^m \tag{24}$$

According to the definition of terms of trade, the relationship between foreign terms of trade and domestic terms of trade satisfies:

$$T_t^* = \frac{(1 + \tau_t^{x*}) S_t P_t^{x*}}{P_t^m cm_t^m} = (1 + \tau_t^{x*}) \frac{S_t P_t^{x*}}{P_t^d cm_t^m} \frac{P_t^d}{P_t^m}$$

The terms of trade under the actual equilibrium can be obtained by using the definition of the aggregate price of exports in this paper:

$$T_t^* = (1 + \tau_t^{x*}) \frac{\left[\kappa_h + (1 - \kappa_h) cm_t^{1-\sigma}\right]^{\frac{1}{1-\sigma}}}{cm_t^m T_t} \tag{25}$$

Finally, consider that the nominal interest rate rules of foreign central banks satisfy:

$$\log\left(\frac{R_t^*}{\overline{R}^*}\right) = \phi_\pi^* \log\left(\frac{\pi_t^*}{\overline{\pi}^*}\right) + \phi_y^* \log\left(\frac{Y_t^*}{\overline{Y}^*}\right) + \epsilon_t^{R*} \tag{26}$$

4 Parameter Calibration

Considering that the parameters involved in the model are all common parameters, we mainly obtain the relevant parameters through calibration. First, parameter calibration for various sectors in China. By convention, the time discount rates for households and entrepreneurs were set to $\beta = 0.993$ and $\beta^e = 0.98$ respectively, the inertia of consumer preferences was set to $\upsilon = 0.7$, and the capital adjustment cost was set to a common value $\kappa = 2.5$. Drawing on a study by Chang et al. (2015), we set the reciprocal of the Frisch elasticity of labor supply to $\sigma_h = 0.5$. Since the ratio of consumption to GDP is very close to the ratio of investment to GDP, the capital depreciation rate and the share of capital production were set to $\delta = 0.05, \alpha = 0.5$. According to the China Financial Stability Report, the collateral rate of the entrepreneur sector was set to $\theta = 0.6$, and the population size of the household sector was set to $\Psi_h = 0.85$. Drawing on a study by Chen et al. (2018), we set the shares of domestically produced investment goods and consumer goods to $\Omega_C = 0.75$, $\Omega_I = 0.84$ and $\rho_C = \rho_I = 1.5$, respectively. Drawing on a study by Christiano et al. (2011), we set the elasticity of substitution between domestically produced and imported goods to $\sigma_x = 4$. Considering that the share of exports invoiced and settled in RMB is less than 10%, the share of intermediate goods manufacturers using PCP was set to $\kappa_P = 0.1$. The price stickiness of domestic intermediate goods manufacturers was set to a common value $\theta_p = 0.75$. Drawing on a study by Wang et al. (2019), we set the inflation and output peg coefficients to $\theta_\pi = 1.6, \theta_{\text{gdp}} = 0.35$; drawing on a study by Huang and Guo (2016), we set the exchange rate peg coefficient to $\theta_S = 0.8$ and the interest rate lag coefficient to $\theta_R = 0.6$.

Regarding parameter calibration for the foreign sector, drawing on a study by Christian (2010), we set the price stickiness parameter to $\xi_p^* = 0.8$, the elasticity of labor supply to $\sigma_h^* = 1$, and the elasticity of substitution between intermediate goods to $\sigma = 11$. Drawing on a study by Christiano (2011), we set the elasticity of substitution between consumer goods in the foreign sector to $\rho_c^* = 1.5$, the inflation and output peg coefficients in the foreign sector to 1.6 and 0.15, respectively, and the interest rate lag coefficient to 0.6. U.S. imports from China account for about 21% of its total imports, so the foreign import share parameter was set to $\Omega_c^* = 0.95$.

In summary, the parameters in the model were calibrated by drawing on the consistent conclusions of existing studies; in addition, we also performed stability testing by adjusting the relevant coefficients, and the results showed that the basic conclusions of this paper remained unchanged.

5 Numerical Simulation

Through the adjustment and calculation of the theoretical model, we found that shocks to U.S. interest rate cuts were good for both China and the United States, which, while in line with the general economic theory that expansionary monetary policy promotes economic growth, was quite at odds with the reality. U.S. GDP growth in 2019 was 2.3%, down from 2.9% in 2018 and well below the 3% growth target set by the U.S. government. Therefore, it is reasonable to assume that U.S. interest rate cuts were based on Taylor rule-style monetary policy adjustments, and the underlying cause of interest rate adjustments were negative shocks on the demand side. In this way, the decline in U.S. demand directly caused U.S. inflation and output to fall at the same time, and on the other hand, through interest rate rules, prompted the Fed to cut interest rates to mitigate the economic slump. To sum up, here we mainly consider three scenarios: (1) Analysis of the spillover effects of the recession and interest rate decline caused by negative shocks to U.S. demand on China's economy; (2) analysis of the mechanism and extent of the impact of U.S. tariffs on China's economy in the context of trade disputes; (3) analysis of the impact of the above two situations combined on China's economy.

5.1 *Impact of Negative Shocks to U.S. Demand and U.S. Interest Rate Cuts on the Macroeconomy*

Since the Great Recession triggered by the 2008 financial crisis, the U.S. economy had been on a strong recovery path with significant improvements in unemployment, inflation, and economic growth, but by the end of 2018, U.S. economic growth had weakened, a trend that was more pronounced and intensified in 2019. In response, the Fed announced a 25 bp rate cut on July 31, 2019, and cut its benchmark interest rate twice in a row in the following three months. To sum up, here we assume that negative shocks on the demand side led to lower U.S. interest rates, and such shocks had some spillover effects on China. In constructing demand shocks, we mainly referred to the study by Christiano et al. (2014), which assumes that there is a "consumption wedge" in the intertemporal Euler equation of the household sector, and when the wedge rises, residents will prefer safe assets more and reduce consumption and investment, resulting in a decline in real demand. The simulation results of negative demand shocks are shown in Fig. 1.

When there is a negative shock to U.S. demand, the decline in its demand will directly lead to a decline in U.S. real GDP. At the same time, a demand-induced decline in output will lead to insufficient demand for factors of production, which in turn will cause a fall in real marginal costs and inflation in the United States. It should be noted that if a negative shock originates on the supply side, such as productivity, there is usually a fall in the level of output and a rise in real marginal costs, but inflation in this case will rise, which is not consistent with the actual situation. This is the main reason why this paper considers negative demand shocks, which led to interest rate cuts. A negative shock to U.S. demand will also have a weak negative spillover effect on China, as evidenced by China's real GDP and inflation falling at the same time.

The underlying reason is that changes in the level of foreign demand directly affect demand for China's exports, and the impulse response of China's actual exports as shown in Fig. 1 can verify the above logic. A fall in China's actual exports will affect China's actual output and demand for factors of production, and eventually lead to a decrease in the level of output. In addition, a fall in China's exports will cause a fall in the marginal cost of domestic production and negatively affect the prices of domestically produced goods, and U.S. Inflation will also affect the level of final consumer prices in China through imported goods. Through

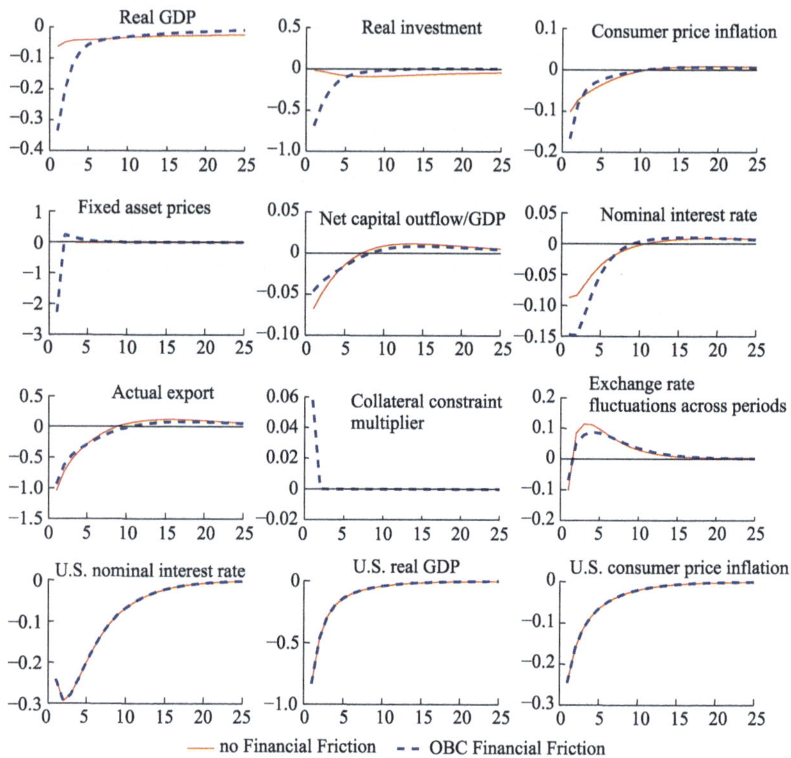

Fig. 1 Impulse responses to negative shocks to U.S. demand (*Note* The units of all variables are percentage deviations from the relative steady state, except for the units of the collateral constraint multipliers, which are horizontal values)

the action of the above two factors, consumer price inflation in China declined to some extent. Overall, the impact of shocks to U.S. demand on China's economy is relatively limited. When a negative shock caused U.S. real GDP and consumer price inflation to fall by 0.6% and 0.2%, respectively, China's real GDP and consumer price inflation only fell by about 0.05% and 0.1%.

Guerrieri and Iacoviello (2017) found that exogenous shocks could produce significant macroeconomic asymmetries when occasionally binding collateral constraints are considered. Wang et al. (2019) also explained the significant asymmetry of international capital flows in China well under the setting of occasionally binding constraints. For this reason, this paper compares and examines two situations: the presence of financial frictions and the absence of financial frictions. The solid line in Fig. 1 represents lax collateral constraints, i.e. the absence of financial frictions we examined earlier. If the presence of financial frictions is considered, as shown by the dotted line in Fig. 1, a negative demand shock will reduce domestic asset prices, and a fall in asset prices in turn will further limit the entrepreneur sector's ability to borrow through collateral constraints, thereby discouraging investment. It can be seen that the financial frictions caused by a tightening of lending constraints have a significant amplifying effect on the economic impact of external shocks, at which point China's real GDP and consumer price inflation will fall as much as about 0.33% and 0.7%, which are six times higher than in the absence of financial frictions.

5.2 *Macroeconomic Impact of U.S. Tariffs*

In recent years, there have been some theoretical studies on changes in tariff uncertainty caused by trade frictions and the impact of such uncertainty on the macroeconomy. Caldara et al. (2020) believed that two types of shocks may occur in the context of the reality of trade frictions: (1) trade policy uncertainty shocks and (2) predictable shocks to future tariffs. The former mainly examines the macro effects of an increase in stochastic volatility in trade policy variables such as tariffs, while the latter emphasizes the macro effects of the expectations that manufacturers and households have about future tariffs. Caldara et al. (2020) found that the latter could better characterize measurements of trade policy uncertainty and that predictable shocks caused larger macroeconomic fluctuations than did volatility shocks. From a dynamic system perspective, the effects of predictable shocks are first-order, while uncertainty shocks such as volatility must enter economic equilibrium through the nonlinear mechanism of economic dynamics to produce real economic effects, and thus their effects are second-order.

When trade friction occurs between two countries, tariff rates usually rise continuously and steadily, while the volatility of tariff policy variables will not rise significantly during the dispute. Under the above circumstances, the time-varying volatility of policy variables may not fluctuate significantly, and therefore uncertainty shocks such as the commonly used volatility cannot be used to explain the macroeconomic impact of an escalation of the trade dispute. The characteristics of U.S.-China trade friction in a real-world context clearly fit the predictable shocks defined by Caldara et al. (2020). This is the key reason why predictable tariff shocks are considered in this paper.

According to a statistical report from China's General Administration of Customs, trade friction will result in a 5% increase in average tariffs on Chinese exports to the United States, and the trend will only last for four quarters. Using the nonlinear LMMCP algorithm, we obtained the deterministic dynamic simulation results under the above tariff policy path, as shown in Fig. 2.

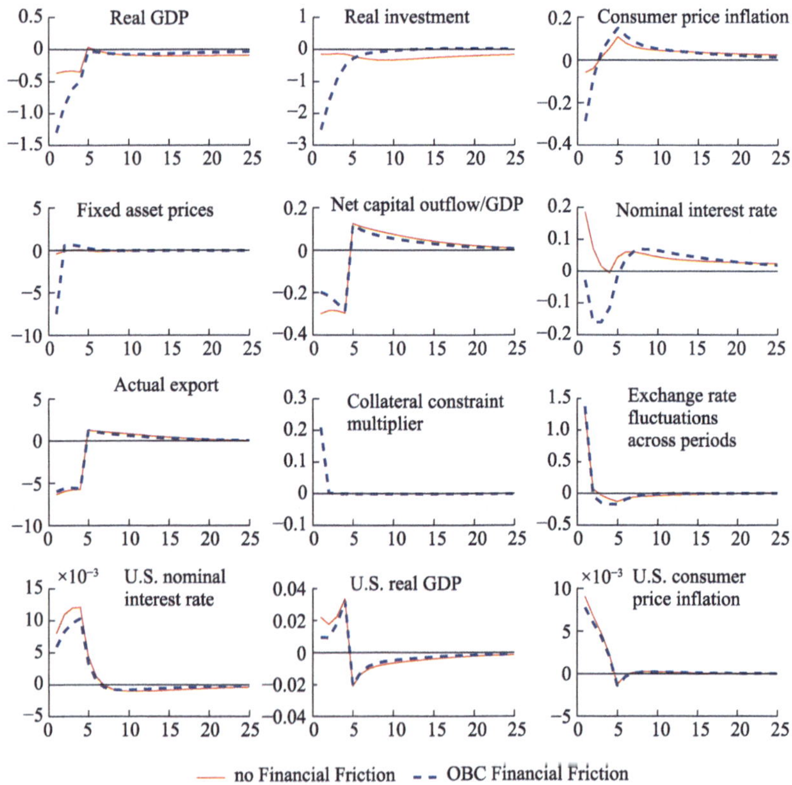

Fig. 2 Dynamic simulation results for U.S. tariffs

In theory, changes in U.S. tariff policy will directly affect the terms of trade for its imports and exports. When tariffs rise, the terms of trade for U.S. imports and exports will deteriorate to a certain extent, leading to a decline in demand for China's exports and China's total exports. A fall in exports will reduce China's output level, and a decline in demand for factors of production will force the marginal cost of production and inflation at home down. In addition, a lack of demand for China's exports will lead to a decline in demand for the RMB, resulting in a depreciation in the exchange rate of the local currency, a decline in net exports, and a sustained net inflow of capital. The simulation results in Fig. 2 are basically consistent with the above theoretical logic. However, it is worth noting that in the short term, U.S. tariff policy has a positive stimulating effect on its real economy. This is because while tariffs will cause an economic downturn in China and a decline in Chinese imports, the deterioration in the terms of trade caused by tariffs will in turn improve demand for goods in the United States, and when these improvements outweigh the negative effects, tariffs can temporarily lift the economy. However, once the United States removes tariffs, as China's economy is still recovering from the downturn, a lack of demand in China's economy will be fed back to U.S. import and export sectors and lead to a deterioration in U.S. economic conditions.

Based on the simulation results of the above theoretical model, this paper holds that U.S. tariffs will have a negative impact on China, but how strong the impact is will depend on the situation of China's financial markets. When U.S. tariff policy restricts financing in China's corporate sector, China's real GDP and investment will fall by about 1.25% and 2.5% respectively; When the financing environment in the corporate sector is normal, real GDP and investment fall by only about 0.4% and 0.1%. In addition, U.S. tariffs can indeed have a small stimulating effect on the U.S. economy in the short term, but in the long run, U.S. tariffs will hurt the real economies of both countries.

Assuming that an escalation of the trade dispute will lead to an increase in the duration of U.S. tariffs from four to eight quarters, next we will examine changes in the impact of an escalation of the trade dispute on the real economies of both China and the United States. In this paper, we find that tariffs have a great impact on the level of investment and leverage in China's corporate sector and can easily lead to financial friction, so we conduct policy comparisons primarily under occasionally binding collateral constraints.

It can be seen from Fig. 3 that China's actual exports did not fall further throughout the four quarters despite an escalation of the trade dispute. On the other hand, short-term improvements in export performance saw a significant further decline in China's real investment. This paper holds that the significant decline in investment at this point stemmed mainly from a serious deterioration in China's domestic financial environment, which was reflected in an increase in the collateral constraint multiplier and credit spreads and a decrease in fixed asset prices. When financial friction intensifies, a significant drop in China's real investment will lead to a further fall in output and a decline in inflation at home. In summary, this paper holds that an escalation of the trade disputes will not worsen China's short-term export performance, but will seriously affect China's financial stability, leading to increased financial friction and further economic decline. Therefore, in the context of China-U.S. trade friction, China should focus on stabilizing domestic financial markets and try to alleviate financing difficulties and liquidity shortages.

5.3 *Macroeconomic Impact of Changes in the Overall External Environment*

Finally, this paper will examine the impact of changes in the overall external environment, such as negative shocks to U.S. demand and tariffs, on the macroeconomies of China and the United States. The specific results are shown in Fig. 4.

A comparative analysis shows that the impact of negative shocks to U.S. demand on China's economy was relatively small, while tariffs were the root cause of China's economic downturn. Second, the imposition of tariffs by the United States throughout the four quarters would positively stimulate its economy to a certain extent, but the stimulating effect was insignificant in the short term, and after the withdrawal of the tariff policy, U.S. real GOP would remain lower than in a tariff-free scenario, that is, the implementation of a tariff policy could improve short-term economic conditions but would have a negative impact on long-term economic fundamentals. As the impact of tariff policy is far greater than the impact of negative shocks to U.S. demand, the decline in demand for the RMB caused by tariffs would dominate fluctuations in the RMB exchange rate and eventually lead to the depreciation of the RMB. This result is completely consistent with the actual data of the past two years.

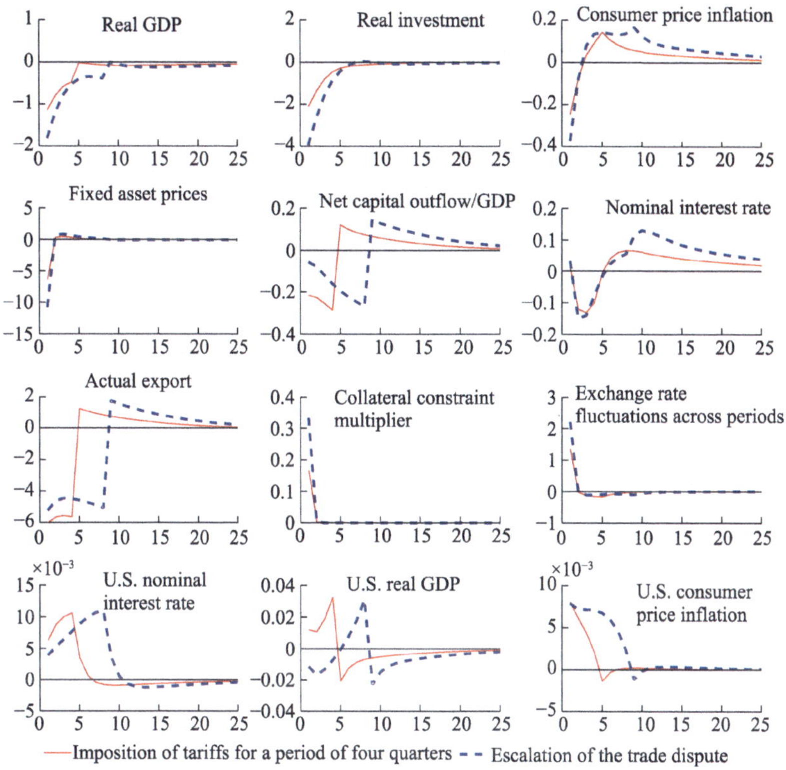

Fig. 3 Dynamic comparison of different tariff policy durations

Judging from the quantitative results, in the absence of any escalation in the trade dispute, the overall changes in the external environment would eventually lead to a decline of more than 5% in China's actual exports and a decline of 1.4% in real GDP and 2.6% in real investment, and a sharp drop in demand for the local currency would lead to a depreciation of about 1.2% in the RMB. Although an exchange rate depreciation would exert upward pressure on China's consumer price inflation, the decline in the prices of goods at home caused by a sharp fall in domestic demand would dominate the movement of China's consumer prices, so China's consumer price inflation eventually fell by 0.4%. All in all, the simulation results in this paper are largely consistent with the actual

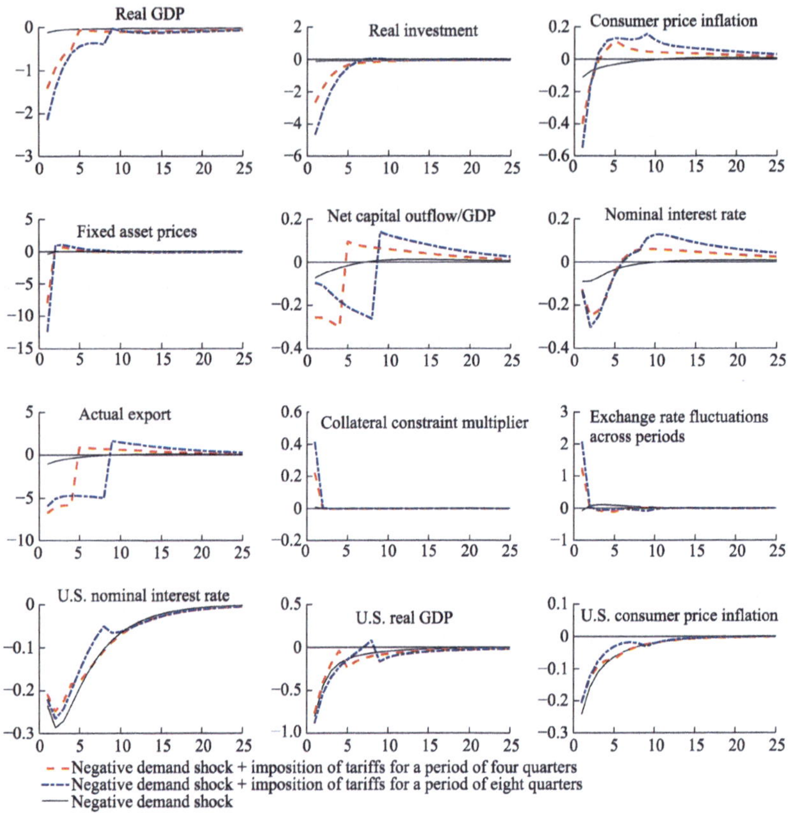

Fig. 4 Dynamic simulation of negative demand shocks and different tariff policy durations

data for China in 2018 and 2019. When the trade dispute intensified, China's actual exports did not decline much and even improved slightly, but other macroeconomic variables deteriorated further, with China's real GDP and real investment falling by 2.1% and 4.6%, respectively, and the RMB depreciating by about 2%, and the time it took for each variable to stabilize lengthened. Meanwhile, we note that rather than providing a short-term boost to the U.S. economy, an escalation of the trade dispute may initially worsen the U.S. economy.

6 Conclusions and Suggestions

This chapter draws on mainstream economic models to explore the underlying causes of U.S. interest rate cuts, and uses them to estimate the quantitative impact of U.S. interest rate cuts and tariff policy adjustments on China's economy. The main conclusions of this paper are as follows:

First, U.S. interest rate cuts mainly originated from negative shocks to U.S. demand, so they had a negative impact on China's economy. Previous theoretical studies have mostly considered Fed rate cuts as expansionary shocks, but the present study finds that falling interest rates herald lower growth, that is, the Fed will reduce interest rates only when it suspects that the economy is weaker than previously thought. Second, tariffs will directly affect the terms of trade for imports and exports, which will lead to a significant decline in China's exports, and thus have a negative impact on China's economy. When financial frictions exist, falling asset prices can severely limit the ability of Chinese firms to raise capital, and have a more significant negative impact. Third, by comparing the economic effects of the above two policies, we can find that the tariff policy has a more significant impact on China's economy. A decline in China's exports due to tariffs will reduce demand for the RMB in international markets, leading to a depreciation of the RMB, which is the main reason why the RMB weakened past seven RMB to one U.S. dollar in 2019.

The research in this chapter has important practical implications for China's policy implementation and monetary regulation in the face of trade disputes. First, the impact of U.S. interest rate cuts on China's economy is relatively limited, and China's monetary authorities do not have to follow the Fed's lead. Especially in the current situation where the United States is implementing zero interest rates and unlimited quantitative easing, China's monetary authorities can implement relatively prudent monetary policy adjustments according to China's own situation, leaving enough room and freedom for future adjustments. Second, the negative impact of the overall external environment on China's economy is greatly enhanced by tightened collateral constraints and restricted financing, so it is necessary to appropriately relax corporate financing constraints and try to alleviate financing difficulties and liquidity shortages to cope with a worsening external environment and prevent further volatility in the economy. Finally, an escalation of the trade dispute will further aggravate the financial frictions and economic deterioration in

China. Although tariffs will benefit the United States in the short term, they will lead to a deterioration of economic conditions on both sides in the long term, so China should actively negotiate with the United States to prevent an escalation of the trade dispute. In addition, China should focus on the stability of domestic financial markets and actively carry out macro-control to stimulate demand and alleviate the economic downturn brought about by changes in the internal and external environment.

References

Akinci Ö, and Chahrour R. Good News is Bad News: Leverage Cycles and Sudden Stops. Journal of International Economics, 2018, 114 (C): 362–375.

Bernini F, González J, Hallak J C, Vicondoa A. The Micro-D Classification: A New Approach to Identifying Differentiated Exports. Economía, 2018, 18(2): 59–85.

Bloom N. The Impact of Uncertainty Shocks. Econometrica, 2009, 77(3): 623–685.

Bloom N. Fluctuations in Uncertainty. Journal of Economic Perspectives, 2014, 28(2): 153–175.

Bloom N, Floetotto M, Jaimovich N, Saporta-Eksten I, and Terry S T. Really Uncertain Business Cycles. Econometrica, 2018, 86(3): 1031–1065.

Bluedorn J C, Bowdler C. The Empirics of International Monetary Transmission: Identification and the Impossible Trinity. Journal of Money, Credit and Banking, 2010, 42(4): 679–713.

Caldara D, Iacoviello M, Molligo P, Prestipino A, and Raffo A. The Economic Effects of Trade Policy Uncertainty. Journal of Monetary Economics, 2020, 109: 38–59.

Cao D, and L'Huillier J P. Technological Revolutions and the Three Great Slumps: A Medium-Run Analysis. Journal of Monetary Economics, 2014, 96: 93–108.

Chang C, Liu Z, and Spiegel M M. Capital Controls and Optimal Chinese Monetary Policy. Journal of Monetary Economics, 2015, 74: 1–15.

Chen, Yang and Zhao. Analysis of the Effects of China's Fiscal and Monetary Policies Under Different Degrees of Capital Account Liberalization. The Journal of Quantitative & Technical Economics, 2018, 35(3): 96–113.

Christiano L J, Motto R, and Rostagno M. Risk Shocks. American Economic Review, 2014, 104(1): 27–65.

Christiano L J, Trabandt M, Walentin K. Introducing Financial Frictions and Unemployment into a Small Open Economy Model. Journal of Economic Dynamics and Control, 2011, 35(12): 1999–2041.

Davis J S, and Presno I. Capital Controls and Monetary Policy Autonomy in a Small Open Economy. Journal of Monetary Economics, 2017, 85: 114–130.

Dedola L, Rivolta G, and Stracca L. If the Fed Sneezes, Who Catches a Cold? Journal of International Economics, 2017, 108(1): 23–41.

Durdu C B, Nunes R, and Sapriza H. News and Sovereign Default Risk in Small Open Economies. Journal of International Economics, 2013, 91(1): 1–17.

Eichengreen B, and Gupta P. Tapering Talk: The Impact of Expectations of Reduced Federal Reserve Security Purchases on Emerging Markets. Emerging Markets Review, 2015, 25: 1–15.

Faia E, and Monacelli T. Optimal Monetary Policy in a Small Open Economy with Home Bias. Journal of Money, Credit and Banking, 2008, 40(4): 721–750.

Francois J F, and Martin W. Commercial Policy Variability, Bindings, and Market Access. European Economic Review, 2004, 48(3): 665–679.

Guerrieri L, and Iacoviello M. Collateral Constraints and Macroeconomic Asymmetries. Journal of Monetary Economics, 2017, 90: 28–49.

Gertler M, Kiyotaki N, and Prestipino A. A Macroeconomic Model with Financial Panics. Review of Economic Studies, 2020, Oxford University Press, 87(1): 240–288.

Gomes S, Iskrev N, and Mendicino C. Monetary Policy Shocks: We Got News. Journal of Economic Dynamics and Control, 2017, 74 (1): 108–128.

Gopinath G. The International Price System. Jackson Hole Symposium Model with Financial Panics, NBER Digest, 2016.

Handley K, and Limão N. Policy Uncertainty, Trade, and Welfare: Theory and Evidence for China and the United States. American Economic Review, 2017, 107(9): 2731–2783.

Hanisch M. US Monetary Policy and the Euro Area. Journal of Banking and Finance, 2019, 100: 77–96.

Ho S W, Zhang J, and Zhou H. Hot Money and Quantitative Easing: The Spillover Effects of U.S. Monetary Policy on the Chinese Economy. Journal of Money, Credit and Banking, 2018, 50(7): 1543–1569.

Huang and Guo. The Impact of the Order in Which Capital Account Liberalization and Interest Rate Liberalization Occur on Macroeconomic Stability. The Journal of World Economy, 2016, 39(9):3–27.

Iacoviello M, and Navarro G. Foreign Effects of Higher U.S. Interest Rates. Journal of International Money and Finance, 2019, 95: 232–250.

Imbruno M. Importing Under Trade Policy Uncertainty: Evidence from China. Journal of Comparative Economics, 2019, 47(42): 806–826.

Jin and Hong. Coordination of Interest Rate Policy and Exchange Rate Policy in the International Monetary Environment. Economic Research Journal, 2015, 50(5): 35–47.

Mao. Has Trade Policy Uncertainty Affected Imports by Chinese Enterprises? Economic Research Journal, 2020, 55(2): 148–164.
Milani F, and Treadwell J. The Effects of Monetary Policy "News" and "Surprises". Journal of Money, Credit and Banking, 2012, 44(8): 1667–1692.
Ossa R. Trade Wars and Trade Talks with Data. American Economic Review, 2014, 104(12): 4104–4146.
Schmitt-Grohé S, and Uribe M. What's News in Business Cycle. Econometrica, 2012, 80(6): 2733–2764.
Xiao and Lan. The Spillover Effects of the Fed's Monetary Policy Normalization on the Chinese Economy. World Economy Study, 2017, (12).
Xu. The Impact of the Effects of the Fed's Monetary Policy on China's Economic Growth: An Interprovincial Study Based on the TVP-VAR-SV model. World Economy Study, 2018 (4): 40–48+135–136.
Wang and Qu. Exchange Rate Pass-through, Currency Mismatch and Optimal Monetary Rules. World Economic Papers, 2018(2): 40–56.
Wang, Wang, and Chen. Monetary Policy Expectations and Inflation Management: A DSGE Analysis Based on News Shocks. Economic Research Journal, 2016, 51(2): 16–29.
Wang, Zhou, and Zhang. Interest Rate Shocks, Capital Flows and Economic Volatility—An Analysis from an Asymmetric Perspective. Economic Research Journal, 2019, 54(6): 106–120.
Yang, Xu, and Wang. A Comparative Study of the Two-way Spillover Effects of the Monetary Policy of China and the United States: Based on A Two-Country DSGE Model. Studies of International Finance, 2018, (11): 14–24.
Yu. Processing Trade, Firm Productivity and Tariff Reductions and Exemptions—Evidence from the Chinese Product Side. China Economic Quarterly, 2011, 10(4): 1251–1280.
Zhuang, Cui, Gong, and Zou. Expectations and Economic Volatility—Are Expectation Shocks the Main Force Driving China's Economic Fluctuations? Economic Research Journal, 2012, 47(6): 46–59.

CHAPTER 8

Dollarization and Monetary Policy Spillovers

At present, international trade is mostly settled in U.S. dollars. The degree of internationalization of the RMB is not high, and Chinese residents need to buy most imported goods with dollars. To this end, this paper explores the spillover effects of U.S. monetary policy in the context of dollarization by constructing an open economy DSGE model with local currency liquidity constraints. Studies have shown that the introduction of RMB liquidity constraints in international financial markets can reflect the common characteristics of the economies of China and other emerging market countries well. Dollarization will significantly strengthen the international spillover effects of external shocks on China's economy and increase volatility in China's macroeconomy. The market-oriented reform of the exchange rate regime can effectively maintain financial and economic stability, improve social welfare, and help mitigate the adverse effects of dollarization. This paper holds that China should continuously improve the Cross Border Interbank Payment System, advance the internationalization of the RMB, deepen the reform of the exchange rate regime and enhance the flexibility of the RMB exchange rate (Wang 2022).

L. Weiping, *American Monetary Policy Adjustment and Its Impacts*,
https://doi.org/10.1007/978-981-99-7810-6_8

1 Introduction

With the development of international trade and the increasing integration of financial markets around the world, different economies are becoming increasingly interconnected. The current complex economic environment poses new challenges to macroeconomic regulation in various countries. As COVID-19 continues to spread around the world, risks in the global economic environment have intensified and destabilizing factors and uncertainties have increased significantly. As a result, China is facing greater difficulties in economic development. The U.S. is the most economically powerful country in the world and China's largest trading partner. Its monetary policy will have significant spillover effects on China, and a dollar-centered international monetary system will further strengthen the impact of such spillover effects on China's financial system and real economy. Therefore, in the context of dollarization, it is of great practical significance to discuss the spillover effects of U.S. monetary policy and analyze China's macro-policy response with a view to avoiding the adverse effects of dollar hegemony.

Since World War II, the U.S. dollar has been the most important international currency in the world. Its functions are mainly reflected in three aspects: invoicing currency, currency of settlement, and international reserve currency. The impact of the degree of dollarization on the spillover effects of U.S. monetary policy is also mainly reflected in these three aspects. In terms of the U.S. dollar's function as an invoicing currency, the degree of dollarization will affect the dollar-denominated share of exporting firms, which in turn will change the expenditure transfer effect of the exchange rate and have a significant impact on a country's economy (Betts and Devereux 2000). In terms of the U.S. dollar's function as a currency of settlement and international reserve currency, the U.S. dollar as a means of payment will affect consumption of imports by a country's residents. Since the vast majority of imports from emerging economies need to be realized through payments in international currencies, when the United States makes monetary policy adjustments, changes in the U.S. dollar payment constraint on consumption of imports are bound to cause adjustments in cross-border capital flows.

Since the 2008 financial crisis, steady progress has been made in the internationalization of the RMB. In 2009, China launched a pilot project to use the RMB in the settlement of cross-border trade, and in 2016, the

RMB was officially added to the SDR basket and became the third-largest currency in the basket. The most important impact of the internationalization of the RMB is to enhance the status of the RMB in international settlement. In the past ten years, the global market share of the RMB in international payment has increased significantly. However, as of now the U.S. dollar is still the most dominant trade settlement currency. According to SWIFT statistics, in March 2020, the U.S. dollar accounted for 44.1% of the international settlement system, while the RMB accounted for only 1.85%; if only the settlement share in international trade is considered, the share of the U.S. dollar is more than 80%. In international financial markets, the currencies of major emerging market countries are subject to strong liquidity constraints, i.e., in the context of dollarization, periphery countries must hold large amounts of dollar-denominated assets to sustain import demand and are thus more vulnerable to U.S. economic volatility and monetary policy.

The Fed began its monetary policy cycle of rate hikes in 2015, raising the federal funds rate nine times in four years, bringing the rate range to 2.25–2.50%. Since then the downward pressure on the U.S. economy has increased, and the Fed cut its benchmark interest rate three times in the second half of 2019; when the COVID-19 pandemic broke out in March 2020, the Fed cut interest rates even more sharply twice in quick succession, bringing interest rates back to the zero lower bound range, and launched an unlimited quantitative easing program at the same time. According to traditional theory, a Fed rate hike will lead to an increase in foreign yields, capital outflows from emerging economies, and currency devaluation; a Fed rate cut will send a flood of capital into emerging economies and drive down the dollar. However, in the first and second quarters of 2020, despite the Fed cutting interest rates and China keeping its interest rate policy relatively stable, the RMB still depreciated modestly against the U.S. dollar; at the same time, the U.S. dollar index rose strongly and did not depreciate as expected.

China, Colombia, India and Brazil are typical emerging economies with a high degree of dollarization. Kim et al. (2013) found that almost 100% of U.S. goods exported to China were priced in U.S. dollars; it wasn't until 2009 that U.S. exports to China were priced in euros and yuan, but the share was quite small. According to Gopinath (2015) statistics, only 7.2% of China's imports were settled in yuan; up to 98.9% of Colombia's imports were settled in U.S. dollars; India and Brazil also settled up to 85.5% and 84.4% of their imports in U.S. dollars. After the

Fed began to cut interest rates in 2019, the currencies of these emerging market countries depreciated to varying degrees, as shown in Fig. 1 (in order to present the values in the figure on the same order of magnitude, the exchange rate of the dollar against the peso in Fig. 1 was divided by 1000, and the exchange rate of the dollar against the rupee was divided by 10). In addition, as most of the currencies of emerging market countries are not freely convertible, they can only pay for foreign purchases in hard currencies such as the U.S. dollar and thus face liquidity constraints on their currencies. According to IMF statistics, there was a massive capital flight from emerging economies in the first quarter of 2020, with investors pulling $83 billion out of developing country markets, more than during the 2008 financial crisis. Foreign investors took $11.8 billion from Brazil's stock market from February to May, 2020 and $18.7 billion from its bond market between February and April, 2020. China's non-reserve financial account swung from a surplus of $15.783 billion to a deficit of $13.87 billion in the first quarter of 2020, with capital flowing out of the private sector.

It is easy to find that U.S. interest rate hikes and cuts have asymmetric effects on emerging market countries. When the United States cuts interest rates, emerging markets also generally experience capital outflows and currency devaluations, which is inconsistent with traditional economic theory. This paper will explain the economic causes and mechanisms of

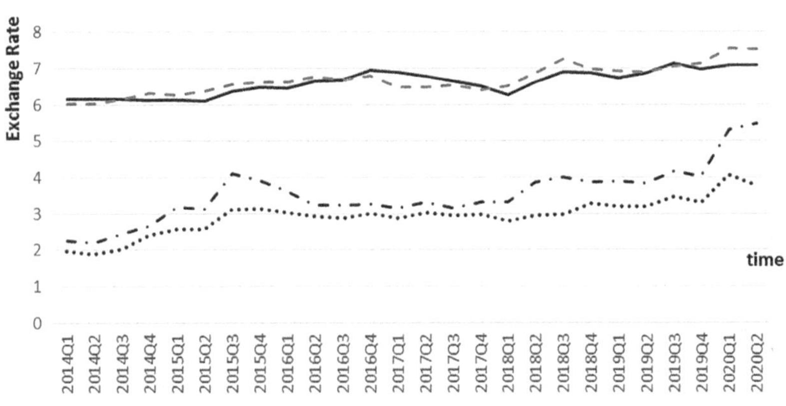

Fig. 1 Exchange rates in emerging market countries (U.S. dollar against local currencies) (*Source* Wind)

action of the above phenomenon from the perspective of dollarization. As the U.S. dollar is a currency for international payments, Fed rate cuts will lead to tighter constraints on consumption of imports by residents of emerging economies, who must hold more dollar-denominated assets in order to smooth out consumption of imports, which in turn may lead to increased capital outflows and downward pressure on local currencies. When the Fed raises interest rates, consumption of imports is no longer subject to the U.S. dollar payment constraint. High foreign yields lead residents to increase their holdings of foreign assets, which in turn increases capital outflows and forces down local currencies. Thus, Fed rate hikes and rate cuts may have asymmetric spillover effects on emerging markets.

In summary, this paper introduces the dollarization feature into an open economy DSGE framework in two ways and examines the spillover effects of U.S. interest rate policy shocks on other economies at different degrees of dollarization. Compared with the existing literature, the marginal contribution of this paper is mainly reflected in the following three points: First, drawing on the method developed by Benigno and Nistico (2017), this paper introduces the different liquidity characteristics of a variety of assets under an open economy DSGE framework to better characterize dollarization as measured by the function of the U.S. dollar as a means of payment. Second, this paper introduces an examination of dollarization starting from the function of the U.S. dollar as a means of payment and invoicing currency, and comparatively analyzes the mechanisms of action and effects of the two degrees of dollarization on monetary policy spillovers. Third, on the basis of analyzing the spillover effects of U.S. monetary policy, this paper systematically examines the mechanism of action and effects of China's market-oriented exchange rate reform and explores policy responses to avoid the downside of dollarization.

The rest of this paper is structured as follows: Sect. 2 is literature review, Sect. 3 is the theoretical model, Sect. 4 is parameter calibration, Sect. 5 discusses the impact of U.S. interest rate cut shocks on China's macroeconomy, Sect. 6 gives the effects of different policies, and Sect. 7 is conclusions and policy recommendations.

2 Literature Review

To discuss the impact of U.S. monetary policy on China's macroeconomy in the context of dollarization, this paper mainly draws on two strands of literature, one about monetary policy spillovers and the other about exporting firms' choice of invoicing currency and currency liquidity constraints in the context of dollarization.

2.1 Spillover Effects of Monetary Policy

In the context of globalization, the U.S. dollar is the most important international currency, and the Fed's monetary policy will not only affect the U.S. economy, but also have an impact on emerging markets through cross-border capital flows and cross-border trade. Some studies suggest that after the implementation of unconventional monetary policy in the United States, emerging economies will suffer huge capital flow shocks and face greater adverse effects (Chen et al. 2016).

When discussing the spillover effects of monetary policy in an open economy, most of the literature takes the trilemma as the theoretical basis, and selects different measurement methods and data to empirically analyze the spillover effects of monetary policy. One strand of the literature argues that a floating exchange rate regime can work well in providing a country with an independent monetary policy. Aizenman et al. (2016) examined how the monetary policies of central economies were transmitted to periphery countries and how they affected the financial environment of other developing countries, and found that a policy mix in the trilemma triangle still had great explanatory power for the economic policies of developing countries. Obstfeld (2015) explored how emerging economies could attenuate the impact of external shocks on their macroeconomies through their own monetary policies in the face of adverse financial shocks. The study confirmed the results of the trilemma, arguing that economic globalization had an adverse impact on domestic macroeconomic regulation, and that choosing a floating exchange rate regime would be more conducive to insulating emerging economies from the negative impact of shocks. Another strand of the literature argues that a floating exchange rate regime cannot guarantee a country's monetary policy independence, but capital controls can mitigate monetary policy shocks from core countries. Rey (2015) believed that the global financial cycle had transformed the trilemma into a dilemma. The study found that monetary policy was independent when and only when capital controls were adopted, regardless of the country's choice of exchange rate regime. Bianchi (2011) and Bianchi and Mendoza (2018) pointed out that monetary externalities arose when capital flowed freely in incomplete financial markets. At this point, the optimal monetary policy of the central bank responds to external interest rates, which means the loss of monetary policy independence. A study by Davis and Presno (2017) found that the results of the dilemma were very significant empirically, and verified the extent to which capital controls affect the central bank's response to external interest rates by building a DSGE model. There is also a view that the reality lies somewhere between the trilemma and the dilemma. Han and Wei (2018) discussed the mechanism of monetary policy transmission from developed to emerging countries. The study found that when the monetary policies of core countries were tightened, the floating exchange rate regime could provide some monetary policy independence for periphery countries even without capital controls; however, when core countries lowered interest rates, periphery countries would not be able to maintain monetary policy independence.

2.2 *Economic Impact of Dollarization on Developing Countries*

Regarding exporting firms' choice of invoicing currency, Engel (2011) constructed an open-economy two-country DSGE model with sticky prices. The analysis showed that optimal monetary policy should target not only inflation and the output gap, but also exchange rate fluctuations. The study distinguished firms using producer currency pricing (PCP) from firms using local currency pricing (LCP), and emphasized the important role of exchange rate pass-through in the international transmission mechanism of monetary policy. Wang and Zou (2015) and Wang and Guo (2016) used an asymmetric invoicing currency setting to introduce the dollarization feature in a two-country model to examine optimal monetary policy under a dollar standard. Zhang (2022) analyzed the impact of U.S. monetary policy on the domestic economy under different invoicing currency choices, and found that the more often a country's exports were settled in foreign currencies, the less effective domestic monetary policy was. Some scholars have put forward the concept of dominant currency pricing (DCP) (Gopinath et al. 2016; Boz et al. 2017), i.e., for any export destination, exporting firms set their prices in dominant currencies (like the U.S. dollar) The study found that DCP fit actual data better than PCP and LCP. Actual data and empirical analysis show that the U.S. dollar is a dominant currency in international financial markets and that U.S. monetary policy affects not only global financial conditions but also, to a large extent, global trade, import prices in various countries and global inflation. Georgiadis and Schumann (2021) developed a three-country DSGE model to comparatively analyze the spillover effects of U.S. monetary policy when exporting firms adopt the three pricing options of PCP, LCP, and DCP. The results showed that the spillover effects of U.S. monetary policy could be reduced by reducing the share of settlements made in U.S. dollars when exporting firms mostly use DCP.

On the issue of the global price system and monetary liquidity constraints, some scholars believe that extensive holdings of foreign assets in U.S. dollars can be seen as a constraint on domestic monetary policy and may pose a threat to financial stability in emerging markets (Ongena et al., 2015). Gopinath (2015) explored the international price system and analyzed the spillover effects of U.S. monetary policy on other countries. The study concluded that there was asymmetry in the international monetary system, with the U.S. dollar used as an invoicing currency in most international trade and most currencies facing liquidity constraints in international financial markets; thus the sensitivity of a country's imported inflation to exchange rate shocks was influenced by the degree of dollarization, and U.S. monetary policy had a large spillover effect on inflation in other countries. Zhang (2022) built an open-economy NK model based on the model developed by Engel (2011). The study concluded that the extent of the spillover effects of U.S. monetary policy can be explained by the dominant position of the U.S. dollar in international trade; the higher the U.S. dollar's share of consumer payments, the stronger the spillover effects of U.S. monetary policy. Considering the actual situation in China, Fan and Chen (2015) believed that international liquidity shortage was the norm of the modern international monetary system, and the breakthrough point for the internationalization of the RMB lied in enhancing the liquidity of the RMB. China should promote pricing and settlement in the RMB, develop RMB offshore financial markets, and enhance the liquidity of the RMB in international trade and international finance.

Most of the existing studies have postulated that Chinese exporting firms set prices in the producer's currency, but this setting is not applicable to the current economic situation in China. In addition, the vast majority of the existing studies have postulated that RMB-denominated assets are fully liquid in international financial markets and can be used for payment and settlement in international trade, which is also clearly inconsistent with the facts. Therefore, literature that considers constraints on consumption of imports by residents and incomplete exchange rate pass-through to Chinese exports in the context of dollarization is scarce. The spillover effects of U.S. monetary policy depend to a large extent on the degree of dollarization in various countries. The internationalization of the RMB is a kind of reverse dollarization process. At present, it is an important task to examine the impact of dollarization on spillover effects and explore how to mitigate the negative impact of spillover effects through regulation, maintain domestic economic and financial stability and improve social welfare.

3 Theoretical Model

Based on the basic theoretical framework developed by Liu et al. (2013) and Davis and Presno (2017), this paper introduces a dollarization setting to discuss the impact of external policy shocks on China's macroeconomy and social welfare under different exchange rate regimes. This paper introduces the dollarization feature starting from the function of the U.S. dollar as an invoicing currency and trading instrument: First, dollarization has an important impact on exporting firms' choice of invoicing currency. This paper reflects the degree of dollarization by adjusting the shares of exporting firms using PCP and LCP, which reflects the U.S. dollar's function as an invoicing currency. Second, drawing on Benigno and Nistico (2017)'s idea of introducing different liquid assets, this paper postulates that the RMB is subject to liquidity constraints in international payments, and households and firms need to pay for imports in U.S. dollars, which reflects the U.S. dollar's function as a currency of settlement and international reserve currency.

In this paper, a DSGE model is constructed under an open-economy framework, in which the residents of the country are divided into two sectors, namely the patient household sector and the impatient entrepreneur sector. The population size of the patient household sector is Ψ_h, and the population size of the impatient entrepreneur sector is $1 - \Psi_h$. The entrepreneur sector has a lower subjective discount rate, while the patient household sector has a higher subjective discount rate and can provide loanable funds to the entrepreneur sector. The household sector provides labor to intermediate goods manufacturers for production and consumes final goods but does not own productive capital; the entrepreneur sector does not provide labor but owns productive capital and produces through wage labor. In addition, both the household and entrepreneur sectors can engage in cross-border financing activities in international capital markets.

3.1 Patient Household Sector

Consider the optimal decision of a typical household. Assume that a typical patient household, which does not own productive capital, provides credit funds to the entrepreneurial sector by purchasing domestic bond B_t^h, and at the same time smoothes its intertemporal consumption by buying and selling foreign bond B_t^f in the international lending market. The utility function of the typical patient household is:

$$E_0 \sum_{t=0}^{\infty} \beta^t \left(\log(C_t - \upsilon C_{t-1}) - \Psi \frac{\left(H_t^h\right)^{1+1/\sigma_h}}{1+1/\sigma_h} \right) \tag{1}$$

where β is the discount factor, C_t and H_t^h are the consumption and labor supply of the patient household respectively, υ is the parameter for measuring consumption habits (Justiniano et al. 2010), $\Psi > 0$ is the utility weight of leisure, and $\sigma_H > 0$ is the Frisch elasticity of labor supply.

The actual budget constraint that the patient household faces in order to maximize utility is as follows:

$$C_t + B_t^h + B_t^f = w_t H_t^h + \frac{P_{t-1} R_{t-1}}{P_t} B_{t-1}^h + R_{t-1}^f \frac{P_{t-1} S_t}{P_t S_{t-1}} B_{t-1}^f + T_t + \Xi_t \tag{2}$$

where w_t is the real wages of patient residents of the country, R_t and R_t^f represent the nominal yields of domestic and international bonds respectively, P_t is the price of final consumer goods, S_t is the nominal exchange rate, and T_t is the actual lump-sum transfer payment from the government to households. Ξ_t is the additional profits generated by intermediate goods manufacturers due to nominal price rigidity. Since intermediate goods manufacturers belong to the household sector, their excess profits are assumed to belong to the two types of residents.

In addition, the RMB is subject to liquidity constraints in international markets. Drawing on the method developed. by Benigno and Nistico (2017), we assume that households' consumption of imports needs to be paid for in U.S. dollars.

$$R_{t-1}^{f}\frac{P_{t-1}S_{t}}{P_{t}S_{t-1}}B_{t-1}^{f}\geq \text{degree}^{*}(1-\Omega_{C})C_{t} \tag{3}$$

where Ω_C represents domestic consumption as a percentage of total household consumption and degree denotes the proportion of consumption of imports that needs to be paid for in U.S. dollars. This liquidity constraint reflects the impact of the dollar as a trading instrument on residents' consumption of imports. The higher the degree of dollarization, the more foreign assets residents must hold to meet their needs for imports.

In order to ensure the stability of the model, this paper draws on the method developed by Davis and Presno (2017) to introduce a risk premium factor for foreign bond yields, specifically $R_t^f = R_t^{*}\exp\left(-\varsigma\overline{B}_t^f/\overline{B}_{ss}^f\right)$. Where $\overline{B}_t^f = \int_0^{\Psi_h} B_t^f\,dh$ is the total holdings of foreign bonds by the domestic household sector, and $\overline{B}_{ss}^f$ is the steady-state value of the total holdings of foreign bonds, which means that the household sector ignores the impact of its own portfolio on asset returns. R_t^{*} is the foreign risk-free rate of return, which represents the level of foreign policy rates.

3.2 Entrepreneur Sector

This paper postulates that the entrepreneur sector does not provide labor and its utility depends only on its level of consumption. The specific utility function is:

$$E_0\sum_{t=0}^{\infty}(\beta^e)^t\left[\log\left(C_t^e-\upsilon^e C_{t-1}^e\right)\right] \tag{4}$$

where C_t^e is consumption by the entrepreneur sector, and υ^e is the parameter for measuring the consumption habits of the entrepreneur sector. The entrepreneur sector is less patient, more focused on current consumption, and has a smaller subjective discount factor than the patient household sector, which ensures that the entrepreneur sector is a borrower of funds at steady state. The entrepreneur sector owns productive capital and participates in investment activities in capital markets, so it will get capital gains and part of the corporate profits. In addition, the entrepreneur sector is also involved in lending activities in international markets. Like the patient household sector, the entrepreneur sector faces a budget constraint:

$$C_t^e + P_t^I I_t + \frac{P_{t-1}R_{t-1}}{P_t}b_{t-1} + b_t^f$$
$$= R_t^k K_{t-1} + b_t + R_{t-1}^f \frac{P_{t-1}S_t}{P_t S_{t-1}} b_{t-1}^f + \text{div}_t \tag{5}$$

where I_t is real investment by entrepreneurs, K_t. is the capital stock, R_t^k. is the real rate of return on capital, b_t. is the actual scale of domestic financing for firms, b_t^f . is foreign bonds purchased, and div_t is the actual profit obtained by the entrepreneur sector from holding corporate shares.

Like the patient household sector, the entrepreneur sector faces a liquidity constraint on its consumption of imports, which needs to be paid for in U.S. dollars.

$$R_{t-1}^f \frac{P_{t-1}S_t}{P_t S_{t-1}} b_{t-1}^f \geq \text{degree}^*(1 - \Omega_C)C_t^e \tag{6}$$

Assuming that there are investment adjustment costs, the capital accumulation equation of the entrepreneur sector is:

$$K_t = (1-\delta)K_{t-1} + \psi_t \left[1 - \frac{\kappa}{2}\left(\frac{I_t}{I_{t-1}} - 1\right)^2\right] I_t \tag{7}$$

The entrepreneur sector has a limited ability to collateralize loans. According to the setting developed by Kiyotaki and Morre (1997), considering that the total amount of the principal and interest on their borrowings does not exceed the expected value of capital in the next period multiplied by the collateral rate θ_t, the collateral constraint is:

$$\theta E_t\left(P_{t+1}^k \pi_{t+1} K_t\right) \geq R_t b_t \tag{8}$$

where P_t^k is the market price of capital goods, which has a direct bearing on the value of entrepreneurs' collateral.

3.3 Final Goods Manufacturers

Assume that the country's final goods sector obtains final goods by summing up differentiated intermediate goods, and that the final goods production sector is perfectly competitive. Suppose there are two types of intermediate goods manufacturers j_p and j_l in the market, whose measures are κ_h and $1-\kappa_h$ respectively. Both types of intermediate goods manufacturers produce intermediate goods for domestic sale and export, and type j_p. manufacturers use PCP and type j_l manufacturers use LCP. The shares of manufacturers using the two pricing methods can reflect the impact of U.S. dollar as the valuation currency on exporters in the country. The shares of manufacturers using these two pricing methods reflect the impact of the U.S. dollar as an invoicing currency on the country's exporters. The higher the degree of dollarization, the greater the share of manufacturers using LCP.

Assuming that there is a manufacturer of final goods for domestic sale in the country, the intermediate goods for domestic sale of the two types of intermediate goods manufacturers a summed to obtain the final goods, i.e.:

$$y_t^d = \left[\kappa_h^{\frac{1}{\sigma}}(y_{p,t}^d)^{\frac{\sigma-1}{\sigma}} + (1-\kappa_h)^{\frac{1}{\sigma}}(y_{l,t}^d)^{\frac{\sigma-1}{\sigma}}\right]^{\frac{\sigma}{\sigma-1}} \tag{9}$$

where $y_{p,t}^d$ is the total demand for goods for domestic sale produced by intermediate goods manufacturers using PCP, $y_{l,t}^d$ is the total demand for goods for domestic sale produced by intermediate goods manufac turers using LCP, σ denotes the elasticity of substitution between different intermediate goods, and the sum of the two types of intermediate goods $y_{p,t}^d$, $y_{l,t}^d$ satisfies:

$$y_{p,t}^d = \left[\int_0^{\kappa_h}\left(\frac{1}{\kappa_h}\right)^{\frac{1}{\sigma}} y_t^d(j_p)^{\frac{\sigma-1}{\sigma}}\,dj_p\right]^{\frac{\sigma}{\sigma-1}} \tag{10}$$

$$y_{l,t}^d = \left[\int_{\kappa_h}^{1}\left(\frac{1}{1-\kappa_h}\right)^{\frac{1}{\sigma}} y_t^d(j_l)^{\frac{\sigma-1}{\sigma}}\,dj_l\right]^{\frac{\sigma}{\sigma-1}} \tag{11}$$

where $y_t^d(j_p)$ is the demand for goods for domestic sale produced by intermediate goods manufacturers using PCP j_p, and $y_t^d(j_l)$ is the demand for goods for domestic sale produced by intermediate goods manufacturers using LCP j_l.

Similarly, the sum of the two types of intermediate goods for export $y^x_{p,t}, y^x_{l,t}$ as well as final goods for export y^x_t can be defined. Solving the cost minimization problem easily yields the demand function for intermediate goods $i \in \{i_p, i_l\}$ satisfying $y^d_t(i) = \frac{1}{\kappa_h}\left(\frac{p^d_t(i)}{P^d_{P,t}}\right)^{-\sigma} y^d_{p,t}$. and $y^x_t(i) = \frac{1}{\kappa_h}\left(\frac{p^{x*}_t(i)}{P^{x*}_{P,t}}\right)^{-\sigma} y^x_{p,t}$. Based on the above demand function we get the price index of goods for domestic sale y^d_t as $P^d_t = \left[\kappa_h P^{d\,1-\sigma}_{P,t} + (1-\kappa_h) P^{d\,1-\sigma}_{L,t}\right]^{\frac{1}{1-\sigma}}$ and the price index of goods for export y^x_t as $P^{x*}_t = \left[\kappa_h P^{x*\,1-\sigma}_{P,t} + (1-\kappa_h) P^{x*\,1-\sigma}_{L,t}\right]^{\frac{1}{1-\sigma}}$.

The demand function of exporting firms is:

$$y^x_t = \left(\frac{P^x_t}{S_t P^*_t}\right)^{-\sigma_x} y^*_t. \tag{12}$$

where σ_x denotes the elasticity of substitution between goods for export, P^*_t is the price of foreign goods denominated in a foreign currency, and y^*_t is the total demand for imports.

Assume that there is also a third type of final goods manufacturers in the open economy, namely, imported goods manufacturers. Such manufacturers obtain final goods through the aggregation of imported intermediate retail goods $y^m_t(j_m)$, and the production function also satisfies the CES form, namely:

$$y^m_t = \left[\int_0^1 y^m_t(j_m)^{\frac{\sigma-1}{\sigma}} dj_m\right]^{\frac{\sigma}{\sigma-1}} \tag{13}$$

If the market where final goods manufacturers sell their products is perfectly competitive, then

$$y^m_t P^m_t = \int_0^1 y^m_t(j_m) p^m_t(j_m) dj_m \tag{14}$$

By solving the cost minimization problem, the demand function of final imported goods manufacturers for various retail goods can be obtained as:

$$y_t^m(j_m) = \left(\frac{p_t^m(j_m)}{P_t^m}\right)^{-\sigma} y_t^m \tag{15}$$

3.4 Intermediate Goods Manufacturer

Assume that the products of intermediate goods manufacturers are differentiated, and they price optimally in a monopolistically competitive market. On the other hand, in order to introduce nominal stickiness, it is assumed that all intermediate goods manufacturers are faced with stickiness arising from standard Calvo-type staggering, that is, in each period, there is a certain probability that manufacturers will not be able to adjust prices.

Assume that any intermediate goods manufacturer i has the same production function with constant returns to scale:

$$y_t(i) = y_t^d(i) + y_t^x(i) = A_t(H_t(i))^{1-\alpha}(K_{t-1}(i))^{\alpha} \tag{16}$$

where α is the share of capital in the production process and A_t. is the level of production technology. For a given wage and rate of return on capital, by solving the cost minimization problem, the equations for the demand for inputs can be obtained as follows:

$$w_t H_t(i) = (1-\alpha)\left(y_t^d + y_t^x\right) MC_t \tag{17}$$

$$R_t^k K_{t-1}(i) = \alpha\left(y_t^d + y_t^x\right) MC_t \tag{18}$$

where $MC_t = A_t^{-1}\left(\frac{w_t}{1-\alpha}\right)^{1-\alpha}\left(\frac{R_t^k}{\alpha}\right)^{\alpha}$ the marginal cost of output.

3.4.1 Intermediate Goods Manufacturers Using PCP

Manufacturers using the PCP strategy j_p produce both intermediate goods for domestic sale y_t^d and intermediate goods for export y_t^x, but only need to set an optimal price $P_{P,t}^d$ in local currency. The export price of the good satisfies the law of one price $S_t P_{P,t}^{x^*} = P_{P,t}^d$, at which point the exchange rate pass-through is complete. Assume that there is an independent probability θ_p that they will not be able to adjust prices in each period. The maximized profit function of manufacturers using PCP is as follows:

$$E_t \sum_{j=0}^{\infty} (\beta\theta_p)^j v_{t,t+j} \Big[y^d_{t+j}(j_P)\Big(P^d_t(j_P) - (1-\tau_d)MC_{t+j}\Big) + y^x_{t+j}(j_P)\Big(P^d_t(j_P) - (1-\tau_x)MC_{t+j}\Big)\Big] \tag{19}$$

where $v_{t,t+j}$ is the random discount factor. In order to eliminate monopoly distortions at steady state, it is assumed that the government subsidizes $\tau_x = \tau_d = 1/\sigma$ percent of manufacturers' production costs. By solving the first-order condition and using the definition of price aggregation, we can write the relationship between optimal pricing and the corresponding inflation as follows:

$$(\hat{p}_{p,t})^{1-\sigma} = \frac{1 - \theta_p \pi_{p,t}^{(\sigma-1)}}{1-\theta_p} \tag{20}$$

3.4.2 *Intermediate Goods Manufacturers Using LCP*

Intermediate goods manufacturers using LCP j_l have the same production function as manufacturers j_p., but such manufacturers need to set two optimal prices, one is the domestic sales price in local currency $P_{L,t}(j_l)$ and the other is the export price in foreign currency $P^*_{L,t}(j_l)$. Assuming that there is an independent probability θ_p that such manufacturers will not be able to adjust prices in each period, the maximized profit function of such manufacturers is as follows:

$$\mathbb{E}_t \sum_{j=0}^{+\infty} (\beta\theta_p)^j v_{t,t+j} \Big[P^d_t(j_l) y^d_{t+j}(j_l) + S_{t+j} P^{x*}_t(j_l) y^x_{t+j}(j_l) - \Big[y^d_{t+j}(j_l) + y^x_{t+j}(j_l)\Big](1-\tau_x)MC_{t+j}\Big] \tag{21}$$

Similarly, we can write the relationship between the optimal pricing of manufacturers using LCP and the corresponding inflation as follows:

$$(\hat{p}^d_{l,t})^{1-\sigma} = \frac{1 - \theta_p \pi_{l,t}^{d(\sigma-1)}}{1-\theta_p} \tag{22}$$

$$(\hat{p}_{l,t}^{x*})^{1-\sigma} = \frac{1 - \theta_p \pi_{l,t}^{x*(\sigma-1)}}{1 - \theta_p} \tag{23}$$

3.5 *Central Bank Policy*

With regard to domestic monetary policy, drawing on the practice of Huang and Guo (2016), this paper holds that the interest rate rule adopted by the central bank should consumer price inflation, exchange rate movements, and the output gap at the same time. The specific interest rate rule is set as follows:

$$\begin{aligned}\log R_t = (1 - \theta_R)\left(\theta_\pi \pi_t + \theta_S\left(\frac{S_t}{S_{t-1}}\right) + \theta_{\text{gdp}} \log\left(\frac{\text{GDP}_t}{\text{GDP}_{ss}}\right)\right) \\ + \theta_R \log(R_{t-1}) + \varepsilon_t^R\end{aligned} \tag{24}$$

where ε_t^R is the white noise rate shock with a mean of zero. $\text{GDP}_t = y_t^d + y_t^x$ represents the country's aggregate output and GDP_{ss} corresponds to its static equilibrium level. According to the method developed by Chen Shi et al. (2015), A is used to reflect the adjustment of interest rates in response to exchange rate movements, meaning that the country has a managed floating exchange rate regime. $\theta_S = 0$ means that the exchange rate is completely free floating and the interest rate will not respond to any exchange rate changes. A larger θ_S reflects a higher degree of exchange rate control in the country.

3.6 *Foreign Sector*

Most studies of emerging markets under the open economy framework use the small country open model framework, which assumes that the domestic economy does not have an impact on foreign countries, but this assumption is not entirely consistent with China's current economic context. In order to make the model more realistic and analyze the interaction and feedback mechanisms between economies, the foreign sector is introduced in this paper.

The vector autoregressive (VAR) model regresses endogenous variables with their lags by constructing multiple regression equations to estimate the dynamic relationship between endogenous variables and to analyze the impact of exogenous shocks on endogenous variables. In order to better fit the interaction between the Chinese and U.S. economies and to take into account the simplicity of the model, this paper draws on the VAR model to describe the interaction between foreign inflation, import demand, and interest rates, and includes domestic output as an exogenous variable in the model. The specific setting is as follows:

$$\begin{pmatrix} \Pi_t^* \\ Y_t^* \\ R_t^* \end{pmatrix} \begin{pmatrix} a_{11} & a_{12} & a_{13} \\ a_{21} & a_{22} & a_{23} \\ a_{31} & a_{32} & a_{33} \end{pmatrix} \begin{pmatrix} \Pi_{t-1}^* \\ Y_{t-1}^* \\ R_{t-1}^* \end{pmatrix} + \begin{pmatrix} b_1 \\ b_2 \\ b_3 \end{pmatrix} y_{t-1} + \varepsilon_t$$

where Π_t^* is foreign inflation, Y_t^*. is foreign import demand, R_t^* is the foreign interest rate, y_{t-1} is one-period lagged domestic output, and ε_t is the stochastic disturbance term.

This paper uses the monthly data of relevant variables from January 2011 to December 2019 as samples for parameter estimation. Foreign inflation is calculated using the U.S. consumer price index; the value of U.S. imports from China is used as a proxy variable for foreign import demand and is converted using the import price index (January 2011 = 100) as the fixed-base price index; the federal funds rate is selected as the foreign interest rate indicator; and the fixed-base index of China's industrial value-added (January 2011 = 100) is selected as a proxy variable for domestic output and is converted using the Producer Price Index (PPI) for all industrial products (January 2011 = 100) as the fixed-base price index. The U.S. data are from FRED and the Chinese data are from Wind.

The above raw data were seasonally adjusted and the VAR regression was performed by taking the logarithm and subtracting the mean. The estimates of the parameters are as follows: $a_{11} = 0.9078, a_{13} = -0.0591, a_{21} = 0.5194, a_{22} = 0.1890$, $a_{23} = 0.0917, a_{33} = 0.9714, b_3 = -0.0503$, and all other parameters are not significantly different from zero.

In order to ensure the robustness of the results, other Chinese macro variables (e.g., inflation and interest rates) and different lags are also selected as exogenous variables for estimation in this paper. The results show that the empirical findings are largely consistent, i.e., only domestic output has a significant effect on the U.S. macro variables. Since this paper mainly considers the spillover effects of foreign interest rate cut shocks on the domestic economy in the context of dollarization, only negative foreign interest rate shocks are considered in the analysis.

3.7 Market Clearing

The demand for domestically produced and imported consumer goods by households and entrepreneurs in the country is respectively:

$$C_t^d = (1 - \Omega_c)\left(\frac{P_t^d}{P_t}\right)^{-\sigma_C} (\Psi_h C_t + (1 - \Psi_h)C_t^e) \tag{25}$$

$$C_t^m = \Omega_c\left(\frac{P_t^m}{P_t}\right)^{-\sigma_C} (\Psi_h C_t + (1 - \Psi_h)C_t^e) \tag{26}$$

If the total real investment by domestic entrepreneurs is I_t, then the demand for domestically produced and imported investment goods by the entrepreneur sector will respectively satisfy:

$$I_t^d = \Omega_I\left(\frac{P_t^d}{P_t}\right)^{-\sigma_I} (1 - \Psi_h)I_t \tag{27}$$

$$I_t^m = (1 - \Omega_I)\left(\frac{P_t^m}{P_t}\right)^{-\sigma_I} (1 - \Psi_h)I_t \tag{28}$$

where Ω_c denotes the share of imported consumer goods in total consumption, Ω_I denotes the share of domestically produced investment goods in total investment, σ_C denotes the elasticity of substitution between domestically produced and foreign-produced consumer goods, and σ_I denotes the elasticity of substitution between domestically produced and foreign-produced investment goods.

For the given market clearing condition for consumer goods and investment goods and demand for consumer goods and investment goods for domestic sale, the market clearing for final goods for domestic sale is:

$$y_t^d = \left[\kappa_h^{\frac{1}{\sigma}} y_{p,t}^{d\,\frac{\sigma-1}{\sigma}} + (1 - \kappa_h)^{\frac{1}{\sigma}} y_{I,t}^{d\,\frac{\sigma-1}{\sigma}}\right]^{\frac{\sigma}{\sigma-1}} = C_t^d + I_t^d \tag{29}$$

The market clearing for imported final goods is:

$$y_t^m = \left[\kappa_h^{\frac{1}{\sigma}} y_{p,t}^{m\,\frac{\sigma-1}{\sigma}} + (1 - \kappa_h)^{\frac{1}{\sigma}} y_{I,t}^{m\,\frac{\sigma-1}{\sigma}}\right]^{\frac{\sigma}{\sigma-1}} = C_t^m + I_t^m \tag{30}$$

The following condition must be satisfied when the capital market is cleared:

$$\int_0^1 K_t(j)dj = (1 - \Psi_h)K_t \tag{31}$$

The following condition must be satisfied when the labor market is cleared:

$$\int_0^1 l_t(j)dj = \Psi_h H_t^h = H_t \tag{32}$$

The following condition must be satisfied when the domestic lending market is cleared:

$$\Psi_h B_t^h = (1 - \Psi_h)b_t \tag{33}$$

The following condition must be satisfied when the aggregated factor market is cleared:

$$A_t[(1 - \Psi_h)K_t]^\alpha H_t^{1-\alpha} = \left(Y_{P,t}^d + Y_{P,t}^x\right)\Xi_{P,t} + Y_{L,t}^d \Xi_{L,t}^d + Y_{L,t}^x \Xi_{L,t}^x \tag{34}$$

where $\Xi_{P,t}, \Xi_{L,t}^d and \Xi_{L,t}^x$ are price dispersion among goods for domestic sale produced by manufacturers using PCP and manufacturers using LCP and among goods for export produced by manufacturers using LCP, respectively. Price dispersion is defined as $\Xi_{k,t}^i = \int_0^{\kappa_k} \kappa_k^{-1}\left(p_{k,t}^i(j_k)/P_{k,t}^i\right)^{-\sigma} dj_k$, where $k \in \{L, P\}, i \in \{d, x\}$.

4 Parameter Calibration

The calibration of the parameters involved in various sectors in the country is considered first. Drawing on a study by Xi Wang et al. (2017), we calibrated the time discount factor of the patient household sector to $\beta = 0.993$, i.e., the steady-state quarterly risk-free rate is 1.007; drawing on a study by Davis and Presno (2017), we set the time discount factor of the entrepreneur sector to $\beta^e = 0.98$. Drawing on a study by Chang et al. (2015), we set the inverse of the Frisch elasticity of labor supply to 2, corresponding to $\sigma_h = 0.5$ in this paper. Considering that the ratio of consumption to GDP is very close to the ratio of investment to GDP, the capital depreciation rate and the share of capital production were set to $\delta = 0.05$ and $\alpha = 0.5$. The share of imported consumer goods was set to $\Omega_C = 0.3$, and the share of domestically produced investment goods was set to $\Omega_I = 0.7$. The price elasticity of imported consumer goods and the price elasticity of imported investment goods were calibrated to $\rho_C = \rho_I = 1.2$. According to the financial stability report, the collateral rate of the entrepreneur sector was set to $\theta = 0.6$ and the population size of the patient household sector was set to $\Psi_h = 0.85$. Drawing on a study by Christiano et al. (2010), we set the elasticity of substitution between domestically produced and imported goods to $\sigma_x = 3.2$. In addition, considering the current low share of exports settled in RMB, we set the share of manufacturers using PCP κ_h to 0.35. We set the price stickiness of domestic intermediate goods manufacturers θ_p to a common value $\theta_p = 0.75$. Drawing on a study by Guo et al. (2016), we set the inertia of consumer preferences to $v = 0.7$. and the capital adjustment cost to a common value $\kappa = 2.5$. We set the inflation and output peg coefficients to $\theta_\pi = 2.5$ and $\theta_{gdp} = 0.35$; we calibrated the exchange rate peg coefficient to $\theta_S = 0.23$ and the interest rate lag coefficient to $\theta_R = 0.6$.

For the foreign sector, the corresponding parameters were set by referring to the results derived from the VAR model. Based on actual data, we calibrated the risk premium factor for foreign bond yields to 0.995. According to Gopinath (2015), only 7% of the consumption of imports in China was paid for in the RMB, so in the benchmark model, we set degree, the share of payments made in U.S. dollars, to 0.93.

In summary, the parameters in the model were calibrated by drawing on the consistent conclusions of existing studies; in addition, we also performed stability testing by adjusting the relevant coefficients, and the results showed that the basic conclusions remained unchanged. The values of the above parameters are summarized in Table 1.

5 Impact of Dollarization on the Spillover Effects of Interest Rate Cuts

This section first analyzes the spillover effects of U.S. interest rate cut shocks on China's macroeconomy, and then discusses the steady state of macroeconomic variables at different degrees of dollarization and the response to adverse external shocks. As mentioned earlier, we analyze the impact of dollarization on the spillover effects of monetary policy,

Table 1 Calibration of benchmark model parameters

Parameter	*Description*	*Value*
β	Household sector discount factor	0.993
β^e	Entrepreneur sector discount factor	0.98
υ	Consumption inertia	0.7
σ_h	Frisch elasticity of labor supply	0.5
δ	Capital depreciation rate	0.05
α	Share of capital production	0.5
Ω_I	Share of domestically produced investment goods	0.7
Ω_C	Share of imported consumer goods	0.3
θ	Collateral rate	0.6
Ψ_h	Population size of the patient household sector	0.85
σ_x	Elasticity of substitution between domestically produced and imported goods	3.2
κ_h	Share of settlements made in local currency	0.35
θ_p	Price stickiness of domestic intermediate goods manufacturers	0.75
κ	Capital adjustment cost	2.5
θ_π	Inflation peg coefficient	2.5
θ_{gdp}	GDP peg coefficient	0.35
θ_S	Exchange rate change peg factor	0.23
θ_R	Interest rate rule lag coefficient	0.6
Degree	Share of residents' consumption of imports paid for in U.S. dollars	0.93

starting mainly from the function of the U.S. dollar as a means of payment and an invoicing currency, and taking constraints on consumption of imports by households and exporting firms' choice of invoicing currency as manifestations of dollarization.

5.1 *Impact of Foreign Interest Rate Cut Shocks on the Domestic Macroeconomy*

Figure 2 shows the impulse response of the domestic macroeconomy to foreign interest rate cut shocks. The solid line represents the situation where assets denominated in local currency are subject to liquidity constraints (i.e., constraints on consumption of imports) and exporting firms use LCP, the dash-dotted line represents the situation where the local currency is subject to liquidity constraints and exporting firms use PCP, the dashed line represents the situation where residents are not subject to consumption constraints and exporting firms use LCP, and

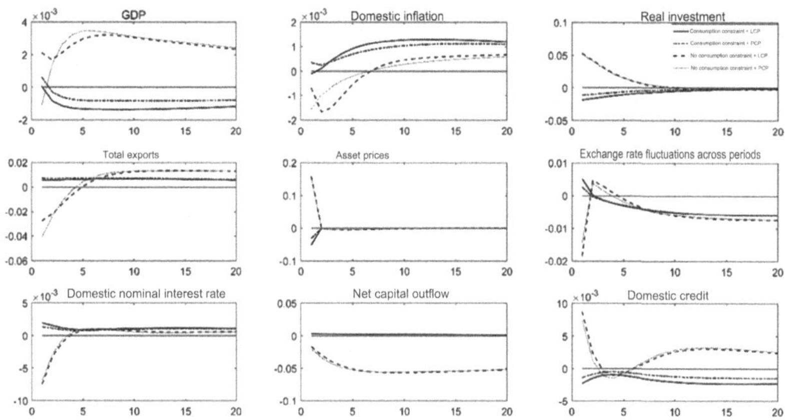

Fig. 2 Impulse response of the domestic macroeconomy to foreign interest rate cuts at different degrees of dollarization

the dotted line represents the situation where residents are not subject to consumption constraints and exporting firms use PCP.

When the liquidity constraints on the local currency in international financial markets are not considered, i.e., when households do not need to hold dollars to sustain consumption of imports, foreign interest rate cuts will lead to relatively high domestic yields, large capital inflows into the country, and an appreciation of the local currency, which will have a dampening effect on exports. Capital inflows will lead to an increase in financing and investment by domestic firms. With rising capital prices, there may be a temporary decline in aggregate output due to a fall in exports, a situation that is particularly pronounced when exporting firms use PCP. The situation of foreign interest rate hikes is exactly the opposite of the above transmission mechanism, and foreign interest rate hikes and cuts will produce completely different impulse responses. The above analysis is consistent with basic economic theory, but not with the reality of emerging economies such as China: The United States entered a phase of sustained interest rate cuts starting in the second half of 2019, but while China kept its interest rate policy relatively stable, the RMB basically depreciated against the U.S. dollar, resulting in capital outflows.

This paper attempts to give a new explanation from the perspective of currency liquidity constraints. Considering the function of the U.S.

dollar as an international trading instrument, when the local currency is not freely convertible, foreign purchases must be paid for in U.S. dollars, and the household sector will face liquidity constraints on its consumption of imports. Fed rate cuts will lead to tighter constraints on consumption of imports in China, forcing residents to hold more dollar-denominated assets in order to sustain consumption of imports. Consequently, capital outflows from China will increase. Meanwhile, domestic firms will scale back financing and investment, leading to a fall in capital prices. In addition, capital outflows weaken the yuan, which is a boost to exports. In the short run, the boost to exports offsets the decline in investment, and aggregate output rises to a certain extent, but in the long run, the stimulating effect of currency depreciation on exports is limited, the negative impact of falling investment is greater, and aggregate output declines. At this point, the higher the proportion of exporting firms using the U.S. dollar as the invoicing currency, i.e., the larger the share of exporting firms using LCP, the stronger the above adverse effects will be. This is mainly because when the proportion of exporting firms using the U.S. dollar for settlement increases, incomplete exchange rate pass-through will lead to a larger depreciation of the RMB exchange rate, and corporate financing and investment will decline even more, eventually leading to a more serious long-term decline in aggregate output. It should be noted that at this point, foreign interest rate hikes and cuts have an asymmetric impact: Foreign interest rate hikes will loosen constraints on consumption of imports, and higher foreign yields will increase the pressure of capital outflows, so at this point, interest rate hikes have the same effect as when there are no liquidity constraints.

The above transmission mechanism is closer to the actual situation in China. Considering the function of the U.S. dollar as a means of payment, RMB liquidity constraints can be introduced into the model to better describe the macroeconomic situation in China. The RMB has been weakening since the Fed started cutting interest rates in 2019. The RMB still depreciated in March 2020 when the U.S. began to implement a zero interest rate policy and launched a massive quantitative easing program of $700 billion. In May, the RMB fell to 7.0986 against the dollar. China's non-reserve financial account posted a surplus of $15.783 billion in the fourth quarter of 2019, compared with a deficit of $13.87 billion in the first quarter of 2020, indicating large capital outflows during the pandemic. The above facts can be better presented by introducing liquidity constraints on residents' consumption of imports in the model: When the Fed cuts interest rates, residents must hold more foreign assets in order to sustain consumption of imports. Consequently, capital outflows increase and the RMB depreciates. Similar phenomena are observed in other emerging markets. Since the currencies of most emerging economies are not freely convertible, emerging markets need to hold U.S. dollars to maintain ample liquidity. As a result, emerging economies suffered $83 billion in capital outflows and saw their currencies depreciate during the Fed rate cut cycle.

It is easy to see from Fig. 2 that both types of dollarization affect the spillover effects of monetary policy, but the impact of the choice of invoicing currency is relatively limited. If the function of the U.S. dollar as a trading instrument is considered, whether RMB-denominated assets face liquidity constraints has a bearing on whether the spillover effects of monetary policy are positive or negative. This is because the presence of constraints on residents' consumption of imports will directly change the direction of cross-border capital flows, thereby affecting exchange rate fluctuations, which in turn will have a big impact on the macroeconomy.

5.2 *Comparison of the Development of the Domestic Real Economy at Different Degrees of RMB Liquidity Constraint*

As mentioned earlier, considering the function of the U.S. dollar as a means of payment, RMB liquidity constraints can be introduced into the model to provide a good description of the current macroeconomic phenomenon in China. Due to the existence of RMB liquidity constraints, residents must change their foreign asset holdings in order to maintain the relative stability of consumption, so the direction of cross-country capital flows has a significant impact on the development of the real economy. That's different from what traditional theory suggests. The benchmark model assumes degree- = 0.93, i.e. the vast majority of residents' consumption of imports needs to be paid for in U.S. dollars. Different degrees of constraint on consumption of imports will lead the domestic real economy to converge to different steady states. This section compares the steady state of the real economy at different degrees of dollarization by setting different shares of consumption of imports paid for in U.S. dollars. The share of payments made in U.S. dollars (degree) reflects the degree of dollarization as a means of payment. Table 2 gives the steady-state ratios of major macroeconomic variables at different degrees of dollarization relative to the benchmark model.

Table 2 Comparison of steady states at different degrees of constraint on consumption of imports

Degree	*0.65*	*0.3*
GDP	1.000246	1.000492
Real investment	1.000242	1.000484
Domestic exports	1.000565	1.001129
Capital outflows	0.933297	0.871068
Domestic credit	1.000245	1.000494
Total consumption	1.000033	1.000070
Consumption by households	1.000036	1.000072
Consumption by entrepreneurs	1.000034	1.000071

When the degree of RMB liquidity constraint is reduced, residents only need to hold fewer foreign bonds to maintain their original consumption of imports, so there are fewer steady-state capital outflows and relatively more consumption by households and entrepreneurs when dollarization is reduced. Meanwhile, less capital outflows will be accompanied by more household savings, more capital flows into the domestic real economy, more aggressive investment and financing by firms, and eventually a steady-state rise in real aggregate output. In terms of the steady-state magnitude of changes in real economic variables, as the degree of constraint on consumption of imports decreases, the household and entrepreneur sectors smooth consumption through domestic and foreign borrowings, leading to a lower steady-state magnitude of changes in consumption. The intertemporal decisions of residents have a large impact on domestic credit, a decline in the degree of consumption constraint substantially raises real investment at steady state, and the final output also increases significantly. In summary, advancing the internationalization of the RMB and reducing dependence on the U.S. dollar for payments can increase social consumption and output at steady state, which will greatly boost the development of the real economy.

In order to compare the short-term impact of foreign interest rate cuts on the domestic real economy at different levels of dollarization, Fig. 3 gives the impulse responses of the domestic macroeconomy to external interest rate cuts at different shares of payments made in U.S. dollars. The solid line indicates that all consumption of imports needs to be paid for in U.S. dollars, the dashed line indicates that the share of consumption of imports paid for in U.S. dollars is 0.65, and the dotted line indicates that the share of consumption of imports paid for in U.S. dollars is 0.3. It is easy to see that a decline in the level of dollarization loosens constraints on households' consumption of imports, allowing households to sustain their consumption of imports with relatively few holdings of foreign assets. The lower the level of dollarization in the face of a foreign interest rate cut shock, the lower the degree of constraint on residents' consumption and the less deviation of capital outflows from steady state. At this point, the adverse impact of U.S. interest rate cuts on corporate financing and investment is reduced, the fall in capital prices slows, the decline in aggregate output from steady state is minimal, and the economy returns to steady state more quickly. Therefore, the relaxation of liquidity constraints on RMB-denominated assets can mitigate the adverse impact of the U.S. interest rate cut shocks.

In summary, in the process of de-dollarization, the relaxation of international liquidity constraints has an important impact on cross-border capital flows and boosts consumption by domestic residents and aggregate output at steady state. In addition, enhanced RMB liquidity can mitigate the impact of adverse external shocks on the macroeconomy and enable the economy to return to steady state more quickly. Therefore, advancing the internationalization of RMB and enhancing the liquidity

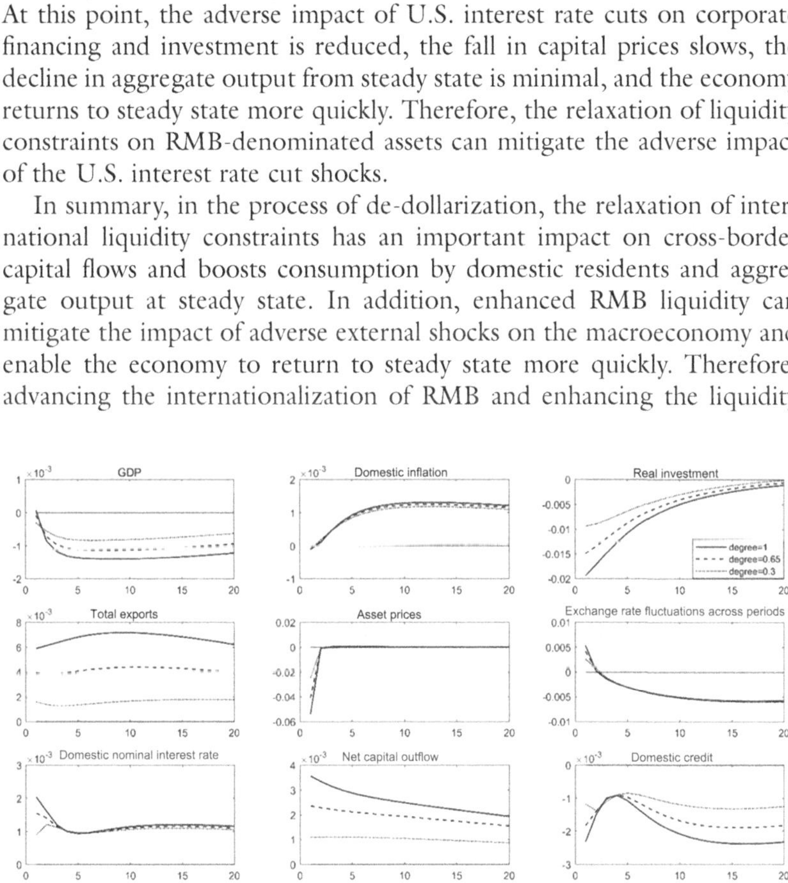

Fig. 3 Impulse response of the domestic macroeconomy to foreign interest rate cut shocks at different degrees of constraint on consumption of imports

of RMB-denominated assets in international financial markets are of great significance to the development of the real economy.

6 Policy Simulation Analysis

6.1 *Impact of Exchange Rate Reform on Domestic Economic and Financial Stability*

This section mainly examines the impact of China's choice of exchange rate regime on the domestic macroeconomy in the process of de-dollarization. First, the standard deviations of major macro variables in different scenarios are compared. In view of the specific implementation of China's exchange rate regime reform, this paper mainly examines two scenarios: a managed floating exchange rate regime (benchmark model) and a free floating exchange rate regime ($\theta_s = 0$). RMB liquidity constraints in international financial markets have a significant impact on cross-border capital flows, but most of the existing studies have not examined the effects of different policies on the macroeconomy from the perspective of the function of the U.S. dollar as a trading instrument. In addition, most of the existing studies have assumed that exporting firms all use PCP and ignored the impact of exporting firms' choice of invoicing currency on the economy. In order to compare the results with the existing literature, this paper gives the standard deviations of macro variables in two situations, namely a benchmark model (degree $= 0.93$, $\kappa_h = 35\%$) and a low level of dollarization (degree $= 0.5$, $\kappa_h = 50\%$), by setting the degree of dollarization (including the share of payments made in U.S. dollars and the share of exporting firms using PCP).

Table 3 shows the standard deviations of macro variables in the face of foreign interest rate cut shocks under different exchange rate regimes.

The following conclusions can be easily drawn from a comparative analysis of the results in Table 3.

First, de-dollarization is very good for domestic economic and financial stability. A decrease in the degree of dollarization causes the standard deviation of asset prices to fall from 0.0519 to 0.0295 and also significantly reduces the volatility of other macro variables such as aggregate output, inflation, investment, and exports. A decrease in the degree of dollarization loosens liquidity constraints on households' consumption of imports and increases the share of exporting firms using PCP. The relaxation of RMB liquidity constraints allows residents to sustain their

Table 3 Standard Deviations of Macro Variables Under Different Policies

	Benchmark model	*Low dollarization*	*Floating exchange rate*	*Low dollarization and floating exchange rate*
GDP	0.0073	0.0044	0.0072	0.0043
Domestic inflation	0.0115	0.0113	0.0021	0.0013
Real investment	0.0364	0.0224	0.0380	0.0234
Domestic exports	0.0364	0.0201	0.0369	0.0205
Asset prices	0.0519	0.0295	0.0517	0.0293
Exchange rate fluctuations	0.0294	0.0307	0.0393	0.0410
Domestic nominal interest rates	0.0117	0.0114	0.0026	0.0015
Capital outflows	0.0133	0.0089	0.0135	0.0090
Domestic credit	0.0128	0.0077	0.0130	0.0078
Total consumption	0.0369	0.0206	0.0367	0.0202

consumption of imports with fewer holdings of foreign assets, which reduces capital outflows and thus mitigates shocks to corporate financing and investment, so the relaxation of RMB liquidity constraints reduces the adverse impact of external shocks on fluctuations in the domestic economy; an increase in exports settled in RMB enables the exchange rate to play a regulatory role to buffer negative external shocks to the macroeconomy. Therefore, de-dollarization reduces the dependence of the domestic economy on the outside world, and makes macro variables less responsive to adverse shocks, which is conducive to domestic economic and financial stability.

Second, reform of the exchange rate regime fosters financial stability, but has a negative impact on economic stability. Exchange rate liberalization reform helps reduce financial volatility, with the standard deviations of domestic nominal interest rates and asset prices falling to varying degrees. In the face of external interest rate cut shocks, exchange rate liberalization reform will further push down the value of the RMB and provide an even bigger boost to exports, thus better regulating the relationship between domestic and foreign supply and demand, and contributing to the stability of domestic asset prices. However, when the degree of dollarization is high, the standard deviations of most macro variables in the benchmark model are smaller than in the case of a free floating regime, but numerically, exchange rate liberalization only slightly increases macroeconomic volatility. Exchange rate liberalization reform reduces control of the exchange rate and increases exchange rate volatility, so in the face of external shocks, the volatility of macro variables such as capital outflows and exports increases.

Third, domestic economic and financial stability can be effectively maintained by simultaneously advancing the internationalization of the RMB and exchange rate liberalization reform. When the degree of dollarization is low, the differences between the standard deviations of macroeconomic variables under the managed floating exchange rate regime and those under the free floating regime are small, that is, the adverse effect of exchange rate reform on economic stability is not significant. However, de-dollarization can have a more significant stabilizing effect on domestic macroeconomic and financial indicators, so the simultaneous advancement of the internationalization of the RMB and exchange rate liberalization reform is more conducive to maintaining financial stability, and reducing dependence on the U.S. dollar will mitigate the impact of adverse external shocks on the domestic economy.

6.2 Impact of Different Exchange Rate Regime Choices on Social Welfare

In order to compare the regulatory effects of different macroeconomic policies, this section assesses the impact of different policy mixes on the domestic macroeconomy from the perspective of social welfare. This section compares social welfare in three scenarios: high degree of exchange rate control ($\theta_s = 0.5$), benchmark model ($\theta_s = 0.23$) and floating exchange rate regime ($\theta_s = 0$).

Drawing on a study by Wang Xi et al. (2017), the welfare analysis method adopted in this paper considers only the measure of the deviation of consumption from steady state at the first-order level of approximation, as follows.

$$U\left((1+\omega_t)\overline{C}, \overline{H}\right) = U(C_t, H_t) \tag{35}$$

where ω_t represents the equivalent welfare measure of steady-state consumption. $\omega_t > 0$ means that the immediate utility of representative individuals increases relative to steady-state consumption level $\overline{C}$. In calculating the conditional welfare measure, we used impulse response simulation to obtain the conditional expectation $E_0(\omega_t)$ of the welfare measure variable ω_t over 20 periods for a given shock, and calculated the present discounted value:

$$W_0 = \sum_{t=0}^{20} \beta^t E_0(\omega_t) \tag{36}$$

The welfare effects under foreign interest rate cut shocks are examined. Total social welfare is the sum of the household sector and the entrepreneur sector by population size. The specific results are shown in Table 4.

By analyzing the results in Table 4, the following conclusions can be easily drawn:

First, the differences in social welfare in the face of a U.S. interest rate cut shock are evident at different degrees of dollarization. Liquidity constraints on residents' consumption of imports require households and firms to hold dollar-denominated assets for international settlements. When there are external shocks, residents must maintain a certain amount of holdings of foreign bonds in order to sustain their consumption of imports. Cross-border capital flows will affect households' domestic savings, resulting in a greater deviation of domestic firms' investment and financing behavior from steady state, which in turn affects aggregate

Table 4 Social welfare levels under different exchange rate regimes

	High dollarization			*Low dollarization*		
	High degree of exchange rate control	*Benchmark model*	*Floating exchange rate*	*High degree of exchange rate control*	*Benchmark model*	*Floating exchange rate*
Households	−0.0895	−0.0813	−0.0733	−0.0561	−0.0492	−0.0429
Entrepreneurs	0.2289	0.2021	0.1711	0.1524	0.1247	0.0929
Total welfare	−0.0418	−0.0388	−0.0367	−0.0248	−0.0231	−0.0225

domestic output, so foreign monetary policy has large spillover effects. When the degree of dollarization decreases, i.e., a smaller proportion of residents' consumption of imports needs to be paid for in U.S. dollars, the above spillover effects will be significantly reduced. In addition, when the degree of dollarization is high, there will be a larger negative deviation in household consumption from steady state, and social welfare will decline even more. Figure 4 shows the impulse responses of domestic macro variables under foreign interest rate cut shocks. It is easy to find that U.S. interest rate cut shocks have a greater impact on the entrepreneur sector and a relatively small impact on the household sector. Since firms are partly dependent on the savings of the patient household sector for financing, and the patient household sector hopes to maintain the relative stability of consumption, external shocks will affect the foreign asset holdings of the patient household sector and thus change domestic savings, the financing and investment activities of firms will be more affected, and their consumption will fluctuate more significantly.

Second, exchange rate liberalization reform has a significant effect on the improvement of social welfare. Regardless of the degree of dollarization, there will be a significant increase in social welfare as the degree of exchange rate control decreases. In order to compare the differences under different exchange rate systems, Fig. 4 shows the impulse responses

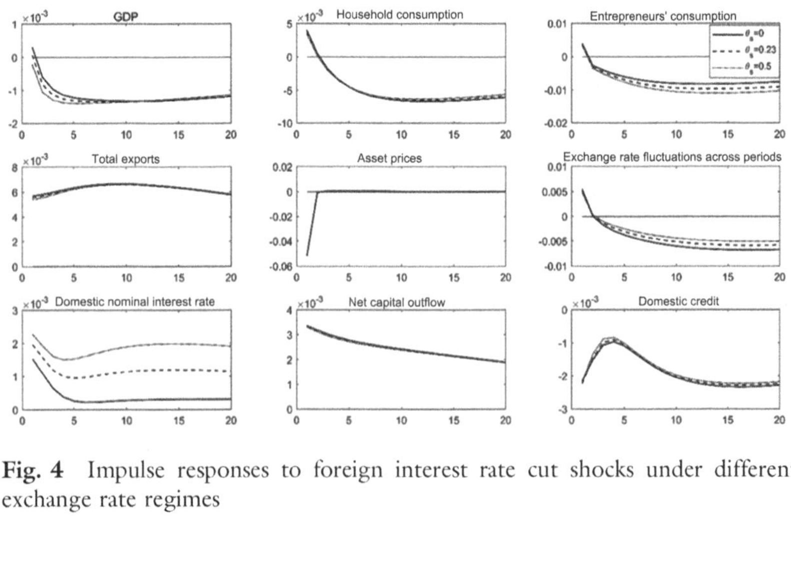

Fig. 4 Impulse responses to foreign interest rate cut shocks under different exchange rate regimes

of domestic macro variables to foreign interest rate cut shocks under the three exchange rate regimes. The solid line represents the floating exchange rate regime, the dashed line represents the benchmark model, and the dotted line represents a high degree of exchange rate control. As exchange rate controls are relaxed, foreign interest rate cut shocks will lead to a further depreciation of the local currency, which will induce increased exports and output, and by monetary policy rules will bring lower domestic interest rates. In the face of adverse shocks, both households and firms will achieve higher levels of consumption than they would when exchange rate controls are in place. Therefore, exchange rate liberalization reform can significantly improve social welfare.

7 Conclusions

In the past decade, China's economy has grown rapidly, its share of global trade has continued to rise, and its financial markets have been opened up further. However, in the international monetary system, the U.S. dollar is still the world's main invoicing, settlement currency and reserve currency, RMB-denominated assets are subject to strong international liquidity constraints, and most domestic imports and exports need to be paid for in U.S. dollars. Under the impact of COVID-19, the external environment faced by China and other emerging economies has significantly worsened. The current monetary policy adjustments by the Fed have also brought more instability and uncertainty to the world economy, and dollarization has further increased the spillover effects of its monetary policy. The complex international financial and economic environment has posed new challenges to China's macroeconomic regulation and control.

With an open-economy DSGE model as the analytical framework, this chapter considers the function of the U.S. dollar as a means of payment and an invoicing currency, examines the transmission channels and the mechanism of action of U.S. interest rate cut shocks in the context of dollarization starting from liquidity constraints on consumption of imports and the function of the U.S. dollar as an invoicing currency for exports, and comparatively analyzes the macroeconomic volatility and welfare effects under different exchange rate regimes. After introducing the U.S. dollar payment constraint on consumption of imports, the model can provide a good description of the current economic situation of China and other emerging market countries. The main conclusions of this chapter are as follows: First, the degree of dollarization has an important impact on China's macroeconomic volatility in the face of foreign interest rate cut shocks; the impact of RMB liquidity constraints on macroeconomic volatility and social welfare is very large, while the impact of the currency's share as an invoicing currency for exports is relatively limited. Second, a decrease in the share of payments made in U.S. dollars is conducive to the development of the real economy, and can reduce the impact of adverse external shocks on the domestic macroeconomy and promote economic recovery. Finally, exchange rate liberalization is conducive to the stability of asset prices, but there are certain costs to the real economy; as the degree of dollarization decreases, exchange rate reform is conducive to economic and financial stability, and can significantly improve social welfare.

With the development of economic globalization, economic dependence and mutual influence between countries are becoming more and more important. Especially for economies with a high degree of dollarization, the domestic economic environment is more vulnerable to foreign policy shocks, and China's monetary authorities should pay attention to the impact of external shocks on the domestic economy in the process of monetary regulation. The policy recommendations in this chapter are as follows: First, continuously advance the internationalization of the RMB, improve the cross-border RMB payment mechanism and system on a larger scale, reduce dependence on the U.S. dollar for consumption of imports, and mitigate the adverse impact of international spillover effects on the domestic economy. Second, deepen exchange rate liberalization reform, enhance the flexibility of the RMB exchange rate, and carry out international macro policy coordination with China as the main focus, so as to achieve macroeconomic and financial stability and improve social welfare.

References

Aizenman J, Chinn M D, and Ito H. Monetary Policy Spillovers and the Trilemma in the New Normal: Periphery Country Sensitivity to Core Country Conditions. Journal of International Money and Finance, 2016, 68: 298–330.

Benigno P, and Nistico S. Safe Assets, Liquidity and Monetary Policy. American Economic Journal. Macroeconomics, 2017, 9(2): 182–227.

Betts C, and Devereux M. Exchange Rate Dynamics in a Model of Pricing-to-Market. Journal of International Economics, 2000, 50(1): 215–244.

Bianchi J. Over Borrowing and Systemic Externalities in the Business Cycle. American Economic Review, 2011, 101 (7): 3400–3426.

Bianchi J, and Mendoza E G. Optimal Time-Consistent Macroprudential Policy. Journal of Political Economy, 2018, 126: 588–634.

Boz E, Gopinath G, and Plagborg-Moller M. Global Trade and the Dollar. NBER Working Papers, No. 23988, 2017.

Chang C, Liu Z, and Spiegel M M. Capital Controls and Optimal Chinese Monetary Policy. Journal of Monetary Economics, 2015, 74: 1–15.

Chen Q, Filardo A, He D, et al. Financial Crisis, US Unconventional Monetary Policy and International Spillovers. Journal of International Money and Finance, 2016, 67: 62–81.

Christiano L, Ilut C L, Motto R, et al. Monetary Policy and Stock Market Booms. National Bureau of Economic Research, 2010.

Davis J S, and Presno I. Capital Controls and Monetary Policy Autonomy in a Small Open Economy. Journal of Monetary Economics, 2017, 85: 114–130.

Engel C. Currency Misalignments and Optimal Monetary Policy: A Reexamination. The American Economic Review, 2011, 101(6): 2796–2822.

Fan and Chen. International Liquidity Arrangements and RMB Internationalization. Nankai Journal (Philosophy and Social Science Edition), 2015, (5): 131–139

Georgiadis G, and Schumann B. Dominant-Currency Pricing and the Global Output Spillovers from U.S. Dollar Appreciation. Journal of International Economics, 2021, 133, 103537.

Gopinath G. The International Price System. NBER Working Papers, 2015, No. 21646.

Gopinath G, Boz E, Casas C, Dies F J, Gourinchas P O, and Plagborg M M. Dominant Currency Paradigm. NBER Working Papers, No. 22943, 2016.

Guo, Chen, and Chen. A Study of the Declining Effectiveness of China's Monetary Policy and Expectation Management. Economic Research Journal, 2016a, 51(01): 28–41.

Guo, Xu, and Tong. A Study of the Characteristics of Japanese Quantitative Easing Policy and Its Short-term Impact on the Stock Market—Based on An Event Study Methodology. Studies of International Finance, 2016b, (5).

Huang and Guo. The Impact of the Order in Which Capital Account Liberalization and Interest Rate Liberalization Occur on Macroeconomic Stability. The Journal of World Economy, 2016, 39(9):3–27.

Justiniano A, Primiceri G E, and Tambalotti A. Investment Shocks and Business Cycles. Journal of Monetary Economics, 2010, 57(2): 132–145.

Kim M, Nam D, Wang J, and Wu J. International Trade Price Stickiness and Exchange Rate and Pass-Through in Micro Data: A Case Study on US-China Trade. Working Papers, No. 202013, 2013.

Kiyotaki N, Moore J. Credit Cycles. Journal of Political Economy, 1997, 105: 211–248.

Liu Z, Wang P, and Zha T. Land-Price Dynamics and Macroeconomic Fluctuations. Econometrica, 2013, 81(3): 1147–1184.

Obstfeld M. Trilemmas and Tradeoffs: Living with Financial Globalization. BIS Working Papers, No. 480, 2015.

Ongena S, Schindele I, and Vonnak D. In Lands of Foreign Currency Credit, Bank Lending Channels Run Through? CFS Working Papers, No. 474, 2015.

Rey H. Dilemma Not Trilemma: The Global Financial Cycle and Monetary Policy Independence. NBER Working Papers, No. 21162, 2015.

Wang C, and Zou H F. Optimal Monetary Policy Under a Global Dollar Standard: The Effect of Vertical Trade and Production. Open Economies Review, 2015, 26: 121–137

Wang S, and Guo R F. Asymmetric Exchange Rate Pass-through and Monetary Policy in Open Economy. Annals of Economics and Finance, 2016, 17(1): 33–53.

Wang, Xiao, Liu, and Wu: Dollarization and Monetary Policy Spillovers, World Economy Studies, No. 6, 2022.

Zhang T. Monetary Policy Spillovers Through Invoicing Currencies. Journal of Finance, 2022, 77: 129–161.

CHAPTER 9

Impact of Continued U.S. Interest Rate Hikes on the RMB Exchange Rate and China's Countermeasures

On November 2, 2022, the Fed announced a 75 basis point hike, bringing the federal funds rate to a target range of 3.75%–4.00%. This was the fourth consecutive 75 basis point rate hike by the Fed in the current monetary policy tightening cycle, and the cumulative rate hike during the year has reached 375 basis points. It was the Fed's biggest and most intensive rate hike since Paul Volcker, the former Fed chairman, raised rates aggressively to fight inflation in 1981.

As the U.S. dollar is a world currency, U.S. monetary policy has strong spillover effects. Therefore, as the world's most important central bank, the Fed has every its move closely watched. Interest rate adjustment is the most fundamental monetary policy of the Fed and the bellwether for global interest rate markets. What are the possible trends in U.S. interest rate policy adjustments against the backdrop of persistently high U.S. inflation and growing pressure from the global energy crisis? Given recurrent COVID-19 outbreaks and an increasingly tense international

Liu and Wang: The Impact of U.S. Interest Rate Hikes on the RMB Exchange Rate and China's Response Strategy, Economic Daily—Special Report on Information, 2022.

L. Weiping, *American Monetary Policy Adjustment and Its Impacts*,
https://doi.org/10.1007/978-981-99-7810-6_9

financial environment, what impact will the Fed's interest rate adjustments have on the RMB exchange rate and the Chinese economy? What countermeasures should China take? These are all issues that deserve our attention and research.

1 Future Trends in U.S. Interest Rate Policy Adjustment

1.1 *Under Inflationary Pressure, the United States Is Very Likely to Continue to Raise Interest Rates*

The Fed's recent policy of continuing to raise interest rates is mainly due to the situation of three major economic variables: domestic economic growth, unemployment and inflation. First, the U.S. economy is growing strongly, with unemployment falling, so the United States has largely shrugged off the negative impact of COVID-19 on its economy. Under the new statistical rules, U.S. economic growth in 2021 was revised up by 0.3 percentage points to 5.9% from the previously reported 5.6%, further consolidating its global dominance. In the third quarter of 2022, the U.S. economy grew at an annualized rate of 2.6%, a relatively good level. The U.S. unemployment rate continued to fall–to a 50-year low of 3.5% in September 2022, matching the level before the COVID pandemic. Second, inflation has been high in the United States, and controlling inflation has become the primary goal of the Fed's interest rate policy. On October 13, 2022, the U.S. Department of Labor released data showing that the U.S. Consumer Price Index (CPI) rose 0.4% in September and was up 8.2% from a year earlier. The month-over-month increase exceeded expectations, and the year-over-year increase remained at a record high. The core CPI (excluding volatile energy and food prices) rose 6.6% from a year earlier, the biggest increase since August 1982. Food price inflation reached a high of 11.2% in the fifth consecutive month in which it exceeded 10%.

With CPI growth remaining close to a 40-year peak, both practical needs and statements from Fed officials suggest that the pace of U.S. interest rate hikes will continue. The Fed's post-meeting statement showed that the Fed remained unwaveringly committed to returning inflation to the 2% target; it also said that in line with the commitment, the federal funds rate was expected to be raised further in the short term.

1.2 There is Limited Room for More Rate Hikes By the Fed

First, from the long-term perspective of economic development, with the advancement of science and technology and the reduction of transaction costs, there will be a gradual decline in interest rates in the long run. The current range of the Federal funds rate is 3.75% to 4.00%, lower than before the 2008 financial crisis but the highest since January 2008. In addition, a number of agencies expect the Fed to raise rates by another 50 bp in December 2022 to as high as 4.5%, leaving the Fed with limited room for further hikes in 2023.

Second, high interest rates need to be supported by strong economic growth. In October 2022, the U.S. manufacturing PMI compiled by Markit initially came in at just 49.9, a record low since June 2020 after two straight years of decline and falling below the threshold that separates contraction from expansion for the first time; the services PMI initially came in at 46.6, lower than expected and the previous reading, after contracting for four consecutive months. The PMI survey underscored the growing risk that the U.S. economy will contract in the fourth quarter. In addition, the impact of various emergencies, such as the escalation of the Russia-Ukraine conflict, anti-globalization trends and COVID-19 resurgences, makes the current world economic development fraught with considerable uncertainties. Various international economic organizations such as the International Monetary Fund and the World Bank have lowered their economic growth forecasts for next year. In October 2022, the IMF forecasted in its latest World Economic Outlook that U.S. economic growth would be only 1.6% in 2022, the lowest among major developed countries, and would decline to 1% by 2023. Thus, the expected weak growth of the U.S. economy will weaken the basis for future Fed rate hikes.

2 Possible Impact of U.S. Interest Rate Adjustment

Successive sharp interest rate hikes by the Fed have also put a lot of external pressure on the decision-making of other countries. Meanwhile, the United Kingdom, Norway, Switzerland, Sweden and other countries have also announced sharp interest rate hikes, setting off a new round of interest rate hikes around the world. The Fed's monetary policy not only exacerbates the risk of a hard landing for the U.S. economy, but also puts downward pressure on the RMB exchange rate, which will have many negative effects on the Chinese economy.

First, with aggressive interest rate hikes by the Fed, expectations for depreciation of the RMB exchange rate continue to grow, making it easy for the market to lose confidence in the RMB. Confidence is particularly important for international capital markets, and once confidence in the RMB is lost, the internationalization of the RMB will be greatly jeopardized. Expectations for RMB depreciation will cause a significant decline in the willingness to use the RMB in international settlement, and encourage Chinese importers and exporters to use the U.S. dollar for settlement, which will cause offshore RMB to flow back to China. Depreciation expectations will also reduce the liquidity of offshore RMB and increase the backflow of offshore RMB, which will put further downward pressure on the RMB, thus forming a vicious circle of self-fulfilling depreciation expectations.

Second, the divergence of monetary policy between China and the United States has further deepened, the U.S. dollar has continued to strengthen, and China's imported inflationary pressure has increased, leaving limited room for monetary policy adjustment. Since the beginning of 2022, the U.S. dollar index has risen from 95 to over 110, up more than 15% in less than a year. At the same time, the RMB has depreciated by more than 15%. China is a large manufacturing exporter and needs to import large amounts of raw materials and fuel, and the U.S. dollar is the mainstream currency for international settlement. The continued depreciation of the RMB will cause a rapid rise in the cost of China's imports, which will make it even more difficult for Chinese import enterprises to survive on the one hand, and transmit inflation from abroad to China to create inflationary pressure at home on the other hand. In the face of COVID-19 resurgences, China's economic development is under the triple pressure of demand contraction, supply shocks and weakening expectations, and the domestic economy is in dire need of support from loose monetary policy, so the central bank's policy is faced with a difficult choice between coping with imported inflation and stimulating the domestic economy.

In addition, the boost to Chinese exports as a whole from RMB depreciation should not be overestimated. First, the United States is only our third largest trading partner, accounting for about 12.3%, so its overall impact is relatively limited; second, exchange rate pass-through to Chinese exports is low, and the expenditure transfer effect of RMB depreciation is not significant; third, given that there is little room for further depreciation of the RMB, the boost to exports is likely to be modest.

Once again, with the Fed continuing to aggressively raise interest rates, the yield spread between Chinese and U.S. bonds has inverted further, leading to massive capital outflows from developing countries. From March to July 2022, total capital outflows from emerging economies reached $39.3 billion. Emerging Asian economies bore the brunt of capital outflows, with net portfolio outflows from them reaching $48.2 billion. Foreign institutions have begun to reduce their holdings of Chinese government bonds since March 2022, and the trend is accelerating. As of July, net capital outflows from China were $54.8 billion, including $5.9 billion in equities and $48.8 billion in bonds. This has a lot to do with the continued interest rate hikes in the United States. The yield spread between Chinese and U.S. bonds became inverted in April this year. The 10-year Treasury yield is now above 4.0% and peaked at 4.24%, its highest level since 2009. As China will continue its loose monetary policy to ensure stable economic development, the inversion of the yield spread between Chinese and U.S. bonds is likely to get worse, which will put considerable pressure on China's capital markets.

Finally, tighter monetary policy has dampened global demand, leading to slower growth in emerging markets as a whole. Against the background of Fed rate hikes, a tightening of global financial conditions will, on the one hand, cause the cost of production and consumption in China to rise rapidly, severely dampening demand; on the other hand, the deterioration of the international financing environment will inhibit various investment activities, resulting in sluggish economic growth in China.

3 Policy Recommendations for Coping with U.S. Interest Rate Adjustment

At the present stage, China's monetary authorities have taken a series of measures to deal with the depreciation of the RMB, and have achieved certain results. However, with the Fed continuing to tighten, the RMB remains under considerable pressure, so we recommend the following:

3.1 *Convey the Central Bank's Attitude to Stabilize RMB expectations*

The first task in reversing the recent weakness of the RMB exchange rate is to dispel expectations of a sustained depreciation of the RMB against the U.S. dollar and re-establish confidence in the strength of the RMB. First, central bank officials can speak or publish articles through different channels to convey the central bank's attitude towards the RMB exchange rate to the market, and strengthen the confidence of investors and the general public by guiding market expectations. Second, the central bank can restart the counter-cyclical factor. The central parity rate of the RMB against the U.S. dollar is mainly composed of "closing price + changes in the exchange rate against a basket of currencies+ counter-cyclical factor", of which the first two parts mainly reflect the market supply and demand and changes in the exchange rate against a basket of currencies, and the "counter-cyclical factor" plays a role in stabilizing exchange rate fluctuations. The "counter-cyclical factor" was first introduced in May 2017 and is often used when there is great downward pressure on the RMB exchange rate, but the specific implementation time is not transparent. Currently, there is speculation in the market that the central bank has restarted the counter-cyclical factor, although the central bank has not yet made an official announcement. Therefore, the central bank's formal restart of the counter-cyclical factor in due course will greatly help restore market confidence and stabilize expectations for the RMB.

3.2 *The central bank prudently implements monetary policy and strengthens the management of foreign exchange liquidity*

China is currently facing the double pressure of recurrent COVID-19 outbreaks and the depreciation of the RMB exchange rate. The benchmark interest rate is already at a low level. In order to prevent capital outflows from increasing the downward pressure on the RMB, the central bank should be cautious about further interest rate cuts. Monetary policy should focus on maintaining an appropriate amount of liquidity and improving the structure, with various measures coordinated with each other. Excessive release of liquidity is inadvisable. First, interest rate policy, as a benchmark for asset market prices, should be prudently operated and can be fine-tuned several times to boost confidence in domestic economic development. Meanwhile, structural monetary policy can be implemented to effectively reduce the financing costs of small and medium-sized enterprises and stimulate economic recovery. Second, a variety of measures should be adopted to increase the supply of foreign exchange and ease the downward pressure on the RMB. On May 15, 2022, the central bank lowered the reserve requirement ratio for foreign currency deposits from 9 to 8%; on September 15, the central bank further lowered the reserve requirement ratio for foreign currency deposits to 6% to increase the supply of foreign exchange in the foreign exchange market. In response to the U.S. interest rate hike policy in 2015, the central bank adjusted the reserve requirement ratio for foreign currency deposits to 3%, so judging from the historical operation, there is still much room for lowering the reserve requirement ratio for foreign currency deposits. 3. Strengthen macro-prudential management to avoid excessive fluctuations in exchange rates caused by exchange rate speculation. On September 28, the central bank raised the foreign exchange risk reserve ratio for forward foreign exchange sales from 0 to 20%. This is the central bank's attempt to curb excessive volatility in the foreign exchange market by incorporating banks' forward foreign exchange sales into the macro-prudential policy framework and collecting foreign exchange risk reserves from financial institutions that carry out forward foreign exchange sales on behalf of customers. The foreign exchange risk reserve ratio has repeatedly played a role as a "regulator" of foreign exchange purchases amid volatility in the foreign exchange market. 4. Scale up the issuance of central bank bills in China Hong Kong market to tighten offshore RMB liquidity. Since late October, the difference between the onshore and offshore RMB exchange rates has been close to 600 basis points, leading to heightened expectations of a fall in the RMB exchange rate. Cross-border exchange rate arbitrage transactions will put considerable downward pressure on the RMB, so offshore RMB can be tightened by appropriately issuing additional central bank bills in China Hong Kong market, thereby alleviating the downward pressure on the RMB.

3.3 Strengthen macro-prudential management to guide healthy cross-border capital flows

Under the current situation, China needs to take into account both the stability of the exchange rate and the independence of monetary policy, so at the present stage, the principle of prudence should be adopted for capital account liberalization and the management of capital inflows and outflows should be strengthened. International capital flows will directly affect the supply and demand in the foreign exchange market, so strengthening macro-prudential management to guide healthy cross-border capital flows and prevent China's economy from being shocked by international speculative capital undoubtedly helps stabilize the supply of U.S. dollars in China and ensure the healthy and orderly operation of the foreign exchange market and the stability of the RMB exchange rate. First, the macro-prudential adjustment parameters of cross-border financing for enterprises and financial institutions can be appropriately adjusted upward to increase the sources of cross-border funds for enterprises and financial institutions and guide them to optimize their asset-liability structures, which will help attract capital inflows, increase domestic U.S. dollar liquidity and stabilize market expectations. Second, through prudent management of capital outflows, the cross-border behavior of financial institutions and entities is regulated, thus indirectly affecting the supply and demand of liquidity in the foreign exchange market and subsequently the pricing of exchange rates. For example, the macro-prudential adjustment coefficient for overseas lending by enterprises can be adjusted downward, thus reducing the supply of RMB in the international market and easing the downward pressure on the RMB. Considering that the business caters to a niche market and most enterprises have not fully utilized their overseas lending quota, a cut in quotas serves more as a signal that the central bank hopes to better guide healthy fund flows and realize the two-way balance of cross-border capital flows.

3.4 *Implement reasonable supporting policies to promote domestic economic development*

Whether the RMB can regain strength depends not only on the Fed's future interest rate policy, but also to a large extent on whether the Chinese economy can achieve reasonable growth and maintain a global leading edge in economic recovery. The fundamental reason for the recent depreciation of the RMB is the ongoing downward pressure on the Chinese economy. Therefore, various supporting policies should be actively adopted to strengthen the core drivers of domestic economic growth. First, we should implement a reasonable fiscal policy. With the growth of fiscal revenue slowing down, the corresponding spending pressure will grow. In the future, fiscal policy should be more focused on exerting its structural influence in the fields of socio-economic restructuring and income distribution, and the accuracy of fiscal policy in structural regulation should be improved. Second, we should strengthen financial infrastructure development and promote opening-up at a high level. We will study and promote the promulgation of laws, regulations and supporting industrial policies related to the digital RMB, strengthen the legal and regulatory foundation for the development of the digital RMB, leverage the role of financial infrastructure, steadily expand the scope of trials of the digital RMB, and push forward the internationalization of the RMB. Third, we should advance supply-side structural reform, speed up the phasing-out of excess production capacity, encourage entrepreneurship and innovation, foster new economic growth points, promote industrial upgrading, and maintain our competitive edge in international trade.

PART III

China's Strategic Choices

CHAPTER 10

China's Strategic Choices for Monetary Policy and Economic Adjustment

In the post-financial crisis era, China's strategy in the future reform of the international monetary policy and financial system, while dealing with uncertainties arising from the transition of the international monetary system from a dollar-dominated system to a multipolar system, should proceed from the needs of China's reform and opening-up and pursue the three major foreign financial strategies of participating in the governance of international financial institutions, expanding regional monetary cooperation in East Asia, and internationalizing the RMB in parallel.

Along with the great achievements that China has made in more than 40 years of reform and opening-up, the changes taking place in China are changing the rules of the world. How to cleverly follow and adapt to these changes and achieve rebalancing challenges the wisdom of China and other major countries in the world The 14th Five-Year Plan period is an important period of strategic opportunities for China's development. An in-depth and thorough analysis of the important and rare period of strategic opportunities for further development combined with the current global situation will help us comprehensively and accurately judge the current economic situation, and is of great significance for developing correct policy responses.

The financial system is an important part of the socialist market economy system. Since the launch of reform and opening-up, China has gradually established and improved its socialist market economy system, basically established a financial system that meets the requirements of the

L. Weiping, *American Monetary Policy Adjustment and Its Impacts*,
https://doi.org/10.1007/978-981-99-7810-6_10

market economy, and continuously improved its financial macro-control and financial regulatory systems. Financial resources are core resources in a modern economy, and the market should play a decisive role in the allocation of resources. We should improve the financial institution system in which there is a reasonable division of labor and complementarity between commercial finance, development finance, policy-based finance, and cooperative finance. We should build a multi-layered, extensive and differentiated banking institution system. We should promote the rapid and steady growth of a number of Chinese financial institutions that are internationally competitive and have the power to allocate financial resources across borders. We should rely on cooperative economic organizations to guide the healthy development of cooperative finance and form an extensive, sustainable and complementary organizational system. We should improve the quality of services provided by financial institutions and reduce financing costs for enterprises. We should improve the system for managing state-owned financial capital and increase the vitality, control and influence of state-owned financial assets (Zhou 2015).

1. **The current situation in China in the aftermath of the economic crisis**

The international financial crisis has slowed down China's real economy, greatly reduced foreign demand and made exporting difficult. The adjustment period may be quite long. Nevertheless, the fundamentals of the Chinese economy remain sound and the trend of growth has not changed. Moreover, liquidity in China is now very abundant compared with other markets, including developed countries. These are all signs of China's economic recovery. China is facing export pressure, but because China's economy is large and in the stage of development, it is entirely possible to maintain a relatively stable growth of the Chinese economy through consumption stimulation, proactive fiscal policy, and moderately accommodative monetary policy.

2. **Direction of economic reform**

China's potential is more geared towards increasing domestic demand than increasing exports. In the next 40–50 years, China will need to invest in many areas to expand the pace of urbanization, and it will also move more towards an urban economy that is more environmentally friendly and efficient. In addition to the 4 trillion yuan investment plan in 2008, China needs a longer-term, higher-level public investment. Therefore, China needs a better strategy for financing public spending.

In the context of the economic crisis, the ability to use the SOE dividend system to build the social security system, to further increase social security efforts, to reform the price formation mechanism of resource factors and to further improve capital markets is the key to the sustainable development of China's economy. However, we need to realize that any adjustment at the institutional level must be based on China's national conditions and basic realities. This predestines the transformation of China's economy to be a gradual process.

3. **Impact on trade imbalances**

From a financial point of view, China actually carried out reforms from the very beginning. At the very beginning, China needed foreign exchange reserves, and the United States was the only country that could print dollars, so at the very beginning there was a convergence of interests that brought the two countries together.

Developing countries, including China, are still keen to use the dollar as the main currency in their foreign exchange reserves, which is why they now hope that the dollar's value will not fall so fast. In China and other developing countries, it is difficult to de-peg from the U.S. dollar, because some countries have been pursuing such a policy from the beginning, and China's financial markets are not particularly mature.

China can contribute to the world on issues such as exchange rates and reserves, but there are a few points to note. First, with regard to China's financial opening-up, it suggests that markets can fail, and that coordinated bailouts between the United States and China mean more intervention and control by the government, which could slow down China's deregulation and financialization. Second, China's monetary policy is also a stabilizing force.

From the Asian financial crisis, we can see that China's policy and Asia's policy have a very big external impact. China and Japan are working together to help troubled financial institutions, and China's contribution is very important to the United States. Now is the best time to raise the issue of the internationalization of the RMB. To internationalize, we need to diversify, which is the best choice. As long as China continues to grow, the market will continue to work for China. The convertibility of the RMB will increase and the RMB is likely to become one of the world's major currencies in the future (Liu 2010).

1 Evolution of China's Monetary Policy and Economic Strategy

After World War II (also known as the Anti-Fascist War, which lasted from September 1, 1939 through September 2, 1945), many countries summed up their experience of industrialization and put forward different economic development models, such as the "import substitution development strategy" and the "export substitution development strategy". The United Nations also formulated international development strategies for the three decades of the 1960s, 1970s and 1980s, making "development strategy" a widely used concept in the world. The so-called economic development strategy refers to general ideas about the development of the national economy that are overarching, long-term and fundamental in nature, and overall plans, guidelines and policies implemented in connection therewith. It is the overall plan and strategy of the state for economic development, generally including the main objectives to be achieved by the economic system over a long period of time, as well as major policies and measures taken to achieve these objectives, or an overarching and long-term guideline for economic development (Li 2009). In 1958, Albert O. Hirschman, an American development economist, published the book the Strategy of Economic Development, which first put forward the important concept of "economic development strategy". Due to the popularity of the system of modern theories after the war, the economic development strategy gradually evolved from a reference to the strategy of economic growth in all countries to a reference to a strategy for developing countries' transition from a backward economy to a modern economy. For this reason, in China, in the late 1970s, some scholars began to invoke the concept of "development strategy" and conducted special studies on it. After the launch of reform and opening-up, with China's transition from a planned economy to a market economy, not only an economic development strategy was clearly put forward, but it also became the focus of the Party and the government's efforts to govern the country and manage state affairs.

Since the founding of New China, China's economic development strategy has undergone several major adjustments and changes. Especially since the establishment of the socialist market economy system, the economic development strategy has promoted China's economic and social development and transformation alongside fiscal, monetary and financial policies.

The economic strategy of the People's Republic of China can be roughly divided into two stages: before and after the launch of reform and opening-up in 1978. The two stages are distinctly different from each other, as one is the planned economy stage and the other is the market economy stage. Although the transition between these two stages was a long process, from the point of view of the way in which the economy is organized, the economic strategy before 1978 (1949–1978) generally negated the role of the market and adopted a planned and centralized resource allocation method, and the position of the market gradually strengthened after 1978. However, it must be made clear that one thing remained unchanged throughout process, that is, the basic socialist economy system had not changed in any fundamental way. In other words, the state-owned economy's hold on the lifeline of social and economic development, and the core and dominant position of socialist public ownership remained unchanged. The evolution of China's economic strategy is highly consistent with the pace of China's economic development, reflecting the interplay between economic development and economic strategy. Of course, the two stages before and after 1978 can be subdivided into different stages (Zhi 2002).

As far as the specific evolution process of China's economic strategy is concerned, because during different periods, China faced different domestic and foreign environments and was influenced by various historical factors, China's economic development strategy took on different characteristics (Zhi 2002). After the founding of the People's Republic of China, the economic strategy was first aligned with the overall development goal of transitioning from New Democracy to socialism, so the basic thinking behind the economic development strategy in this period was to fully realize a publicly-owned economy, vigorously develop industry, especially heavy industry, and lay the groundwork for a socialist economy. After 1956, with the establishment of the basic socialist economy system, developing the socialist economy in an all-round way became the core of the economic strategy of this period. But this period was in a process of continuous exploration, during which the development strategy experienced two major setbacks, and major social and economic problems were surfacing. During this period, the economic strategy was characterized by an emphasis on the development of industry and the strengthening of economic planning and concentration. Under the guidance of this strategy, on the one hand, the level of industrialization in China continuously improved; on the other hand, the highly centralized planned or command economy led to a gradual decline in the capacity and efficiency of social and economic organizations. During this period, the whole society was relatively poor, but social distribution was relatively reasonable. In addition, the adoption of a socialist planned economy system similar to that of the Soviet Union made it difficult to integrate into the world economic system, so the external development of the economy was basically at a standstill. After 1978, the reform and opening-up strategy was not only a national development strategy, but also an economic strategy in a narrow sense. This transformation was of epoch-making significance in the history of China's economic development and overall social development. Reform and opening-up, first of all, is economic reform and opening-up. Since then, economic development has become the center of social development. This process can be roughly divided into three stages: 1978–1992, 1992–2001, and 2001–present. Among them, 1978–1992 was the specific exploration stage of the economic strategy under the reform and opening-up strategy. The basic thinking behind the economic strategy at this stage was to surrender part of the profits and delegate powers, and comprehensively enhance the enthusiasm of various social and economic factors. However, due to the lack of development experience, the economic development strategy of this period had the shortcomings of both a planned economy and a market economy. The concept of overall public ownership in a planned economy was combined with the distribution problems of a market economy, spelling trouble for economic development. Then, after Deng Xiaoping's Southern Tour of 1992, the general thinking behind the economic development strategy was to further emancipate the mind, integrate the advantages of a market economy and a planned economy, and creatively put forward the concept of a socialist market economy—that is to say, to maintain the basic socialist economy system and give full play to the role of the market, but carry out strong macro-control. By 2001 or so, a socialist market economy had taken shape after two big strides: the reform of the fiscal dual-track system and the reform of state-owned enterprises. After 2001, China's economic development strategy was based on reform and opening-up. In the face the situation at home and abroad, driving the economy by consumption, investment and exports became the basic development thinking. China's economy rapidly grew into the second largest in the world. However, there were various problems with this economic development strategy, such as the wasting of resources, environmental problems and distribution problems, which were becoming increasingly serious. Although overall social development strategies related to the economic development strategy such as sustainable development and the scientific outlook on development were put forward in this period or earlier, problems such as an unsound legal system increasingly affected economic development. After the 18th CPC National Congress, the economic development strategy was further improved. On the one hand, comprehensively deepening reform became a basic task; in terms of ruling the country by law, economic development was required to be subject to the rule of law in all aspects. On the other hand, opening-up gradually "went out" and the "Belt and Road" strategy was put forward. Meanwhile, comprehensive innovation became the source of driving force for economic development. After decades of exploration, the economic development strategy has been improved in an all-round way.

1.1 Evolution of China's Monetary Policy

In a narrow sense, China's monetary policy is part of China's economic development strategy, so its evolution is consistent with China's economic development strategy. However, due to the particularity and independence of monetary policy itself, especially its unique significance to the contemporary market economy system, the evolution of China's monetary policy has different characteristics.

China's monetary policy can also be roughly divided into two stages: Before 1978, China's monetary policy was monetary policy for a planned economy. Because money was ideologically associated with the comprehensive criticism and negation of capital, monetary policy was suppressed in an all-round way during this period and the whole social credit system was undiversified and inelastic. The monetary strategy of this period did not exist in the strict sense. The state had absolute control over money, and money virtually had little market function. After 1978, China's economy changed from a highly centralized planned economy to a market-oriented economy, the role of money began to become increasingly important, the social credit system became market-oriented, and the state gradually switched from controlling to regulating the social credit system. After 1979, the People's Bank of China first transformed itself from a national bank to a central bank. Before the socialist market economy was established, China's monetary policy was still focused on the creation of a national basic credit system. Meanwhile, in order to adapt to the opening-up strategy, attempts to reform national monetary policy were mainly directed at the outside world principally for the purpose of creating a favorable credit environment for opening-up. This way of thinking was also conducive to exploring the experience of building a monetary system, and gradually applying the experience to domestic monetary policy, so as to avoid the risks brought about by drastic reforms at home. After 1993, with the establishment of the socialist market economy system, China's monetary policy became an important tool for the state to regulate the market. During this period, the central bank system was gradually established and perfected, and the People's Bank of China truly became a vehicle for implementing monetary policy. Meanwhile, market-oriented reform of state-owned banks was carried out, a number of policy banks were established, regulation was improved, and the CBRC was founded. It could be seen that a social credit system with the market economy as its core had been basically established. At this stage, monetary policy became a key tool to stimulate and regulate economic development. Through interest rate regulation, inflation and deflation were comprehensively monitored and regulated to stabilize monetary circulation.

Unlike China's economic development strategy, China's monetary policy reform has lagged behind overall economic development. The change of the thinking behind monetary policy also tends to lag behind the economic development strategy. This is because, on the one hand, the use of monetary policy not only requires specialized team practice, but also, on the other hand, the use of monetary policy is a double-edged sword, and its improper use often leads to serious economic crises, so monetary policy must be adopted with caution—especially for a country like China that lacks experience in the use of monetary policy!

In the era of the planned economy, it could be said that there was fiscal policy but no monetary policy and financial policy. After the launch of reform and opening-up, with the gradual establishment of the socialist market economy system, in addition to financial policy, monetary and financial policy increasingly became an important support for the economic development strategy. Deng Xiaoping once pointed out: "Finance is very important, because it is the core of the modern economy. Handling financial affairs well is the key to success in this sphere" (General Office of the People's Bank of China 2008). This statement succinctly clarifies the core position and importance of finance in the construction of a modern economic development strategy. The process from the economic development model dominated by an inflexible fiscal policy under the planned economy system to the building of a modern financial system in which fiscal policy and monetary and financial policy complement each other under the market economy system with Chinese characteristics marks the gradual maturation of China's modern financial policy. In the future economic transformation and upgrading strategy oriented towards global competition, innovation in the financial system and the systematic construction of financial policy will become an important support for the implementation of the economic development strategy, and even have a direct bearing on the success or failure of the economic development strategy.

1.1.1 Fiscal Policy and Its Operation under the Planned Economy System (1953–1980)

Under the catch-up economic development strategy in the era of the planned economy, in order to concentrate financial and material resources to do great things, the state directly regulated and comprehensively intervened in the national economy mainly through the fiscal policy of "unified collection and allocation of funds by the state" and "state monopoly over purchase and marketing".

The period from the founding of the People's Republic of China to 1953 was a recovery period for China's national economy. The Chinese economy was facing serious difficulties. On the one hand, the Kuomintang had left behind a mess with production paralyzed, workers unemployed and inflation running out of control. On the other hand, there were few sources of revenue and it was difficult to centralize them, while the expenditure was huge, resulting in imbalances in the national budget. Under such circumstances, in order to heal the wounds of war, resume production, develop the economy and stabilize society as soon as possible, the central government had to concentrate financial and material resources, so it implemented a highly centralized fiscal system where the collection and allocation of funds was under the unified control of the state. The core essence of this system was that the power to manage the national budget and the power to decide on institutions were concentrated in the central government, and all revenue and expenditure items, revenue- and expenditure-related measures, the scope of revenues and expenditures, and revenue- and expenditure-related standards were formulated by the central government in a unified manner; financial resources were concentrated in the central government, and budgetary revenues and expenditures were subject to unified control and distribution by the central government, that is, local revenues were concentrated in the central government, local expenditures must be examined and approved by the central government, funds required to cover local expenditures were allocated level by level, and there was basically no relationship between fiscal revenue and expenditure.

After "industrialization and three transformations", China established a catch-up economic development strategy centered on heavy industry. In order to implement this strategy smoothly, China gradually established a system of state monopoly over purchase and marketing for the allocation of materials. The system of state monopoly over purchase and marketing was initially designed to solve the problem of food shortage. According to the National Bureau of Statistics, the total urban population increased from 57.65 million in 1949 to 82.49 million in 1954, an increase of 43% in five years (China Statistical Yearbook 1984). With the development of industrial construction, the urban population continued to increase substantially, worsening the food supply situation. The food panel at the National Conference on Finance and Economics in June 1953 pointed out that the problem was very big, there were not many solutions, and the situation was really unsustainable (Bo 1993). In the face of the acute contradiction of food shortage, Mao Zedong asked the Central Financial and Economic Affairs Commission to come up with a solution. Chen Yun, the then head of the Central Financial and Economic Affairs Commission, worked out eight solutions, of which the solution of state monopoly over purchase and marketing was finally chosen. On the evening of October 2, 1953, Mao Zedong chaired the enlarged meeting of the Political Bureau of the CPC Central Committee, at which he listened to Chen Yun's report and adopted Chen Yun's suggestions. On October 16, the Political Bureau of the CPC Central Committee discussed and passed the Resolution of the CPC Central Committee on the Planned Purchase and Planned Supply of Grain. After that, the Government Administration Council issued relevant orders and implementation measures. From then on, "all purchase and supply quantities, purchase and supply standards, purchase and supply prices, etc. must be uniformly set by the central government or approved by the central government" (Editorial Committee on Party Literature of the CPC Central Committee 1995). At that time, state monopoly over purchase and marketing was not only a means to solve the problem of food shortage in cities, but also laid a solid foundation for the establishment of a planned economy system and the carrying out of the industrialization strategy.

1.1.2 The Gradual Establishment of A Modern Financial System After the Launch of Reform and Opening-Up (1980–2008)

After the launch of reform and opening-up, with the transition of the economic system, a modern financial system marked by the establishment of the central bank system, the reform of the commercial bank system and the establishment and development of a securities market was gradually established.

In 1984, the People's Bank of China started to exclusively exercise the functions of a central bank, and China formally established a modern central bank system, marking the beginning of the practice of monetary policy in the real sense of the term in China. Generally speaking, in these nearly 30 years, China's monetary policy before 1997 was primarily focused on combating inflation and therefore curbed demand; monetary policy after 1997 aimed primarily at combating deflation and promoting economic growth and therefore expanded demand.

After the establishment of the central bank, the focus of the reform of the financial system was to speed up the reform of China's commercial bank system. According to Professor Liu Hongru, in order to establish a socialist market economy system, there must be a new financial system that is compatible with it, and central to the new financial system is the reform of commercial banks. Without the reform of the commercial bank system, it will be difficult to deepen the reform of the financial system (Jin 1998). Since the beginning of reform and opening-up, great achievements have been made in the reform and development of China's banking sector. China's banking system has formed a multi-level and multi-form landscape where five state-controlled banks, 12 joint-stock banks, 147 local commercial banks, a number of village and town banks, and some foreign banks coexist and compete with each other. A banking landscape characterized by gradually opening-up and all-round competition has gradually taken shape (Hu and Chen 2008).

In addition, the establishment and development of a securities market had been an important task in the building of a modern financial system since the launch of reform and opening-up. China has long managed its economy under a highly centralized planning system, forming a pattern of "big budgetary allocations and small banks", that is, investments are mostly made with budgetary allocations. With the establishment of a modern banking system, China had gradually strengthened the functions of banks, and credit funds had come to dominate the landscape. But economic development at different levels requires the diversification of forms of finance and the introduction of the market mechanism into the financial market to achieve financial securitization. A securities market should be established and developed, so as to make enterprises fundraisers, financial institutions intermediaries, and financing market-oriented. This model will revolutionize China's fiscal, planning and financial systems. Therefore, the securities market is an important part of the financial markets, occupies an important position in the financial market system, and plays a tremendous role in promoting the reform of China's economic system as a whole. For more than 20 years since the early 1990s, China's securities market has gradually matured, with regulation gradually improved and the market size growing significantly. The securities industry has become an important industry in China's national economy, and has made significant contributions to promoting national economic growth.

1.1.3 Financial Development Strategy Oriented Towards a New Global Financial Order (2009–Present)

This paper discusses the current financial reform measures and the construction of future financial strategies in terms of the current situation and drawbacks of the existing areas of finance such as finance, banking, securities and insurance, and their incompatibility with the economic strategy oriented towards global competition.

For example, since the Shanghai Stock Exchange and the Shenzhen Stock Exchange officially started operations more than 30 years ago, China's securities market has grown from nothing into the world's second largest securities market with a market capitalization of more than 50 trillion yuan. The number of listed companies in China is now approaching 3,500, with 1,400 listed companies in Shanghai and 2,095 listed companies in Shenzhen. The number of listed companies in China is still on the rise. But there is still a long way to go before the strategic objective of building an international financial center is achieved. This is mainly reflected by the fact that the degree of marketization is low, administrative or non-market forces play a significant role in allocating resources, the level of internationalization is low, information disclosure and market transparency are yet to be improved, there is a lot of speculation, and the investment function is inadequate. The underlying causes of these problems are mainly cognitive errors, design deviations, unclear policies and imperfect laws. Wu Xiaoqiu believes that in order to build big power finance that matches China's status as a big power, we need to correctly understand the function of the securities market, deeply appreciate the strategic significance of developing the securities market, and push ahead with the market-oriented reform and the strategy for the internationalization of the securities market. We should amend the contents of relevant laws and regulations concerning the approval of stock issuance; focus on pushing for the reform of the issuance system, the adjustment of rules governing mergers, acquisitions and restructuring, and the strict implementation of the delisting mechanism; clarify the order of capital market opening; clarify the sequence in which capital markets are opened up (National People's Congress 2014).

1.2 Evolution of China's Economic Development Strategy

1.2.1 Strategy for Building A Planned Economy System (1949–1978)

In fact, for a long time after the founding of the People's Republic of China, China did not explicitly and specifically mention any national economic development strategy. But the general lines, general tasks, general guidelines and general policies put forward in different periods actually implied an economic development strategy.

China's first economic development strategy after the founding of the People's Republic of China could basically be called a "strategy for building a planned economy system", with "industrialization and three transformations" as the path to practicing the economic development strategy. After the founding of the People's Republic of China in October 1949, the Party led the people of all ethnic groups in quickly restoring the national economy that was severely damaged in the old China and embarking on the great journey of transforming from New Democracy to socialism. At the end of 1952, the CPC Central Committee, in accordance with comrade Mao Zedong's proposal, put forward the Party's general line during the transition period, pointing out the tasks, ways and steps during the transition from New Democracy to socialism in China. Its essence was to change the relations of production, solve issues surrounding ownership of the means of production and create conditions for the further liberation and development of productive forces. On June 15, 1953, at the enlarged meeting of the Political Bureau of the CPC Central Committee, Mao Zedong made a relatively complete statement on the Party's general line and tasks during the transition period for the first time: to basically realize the industrialization of the country and the socialist transformation of agriculture, handicrafts and capitalist industry and commerce over a fairly long historical period.

The "general line for the transition period" was the first national economic development strategy after the founding of New China. Its most remarkable feature was that socialist industrialization and socialist transformation were carried out simultaneously, with industrialization as the main body and the three transformations as the two wings, and the two adapting to each other, promoting each other and developing in a coordinated manner. The general line aimed to solve the ownership issue by changing capitalist private ownership of means of production to socialist public ownership of means of production. The great significance of this economic development strategy lies in the fact that, first, it expanded the socialist public sector of the economy, and second, it basically established a planned economy system, which lasted until the early stage of reform and opening-up. As one study has pointed out, "From the founding of the People's Republic of China until the beginning of reform and opening-up, China basically adopted a catch-up development strategy that prioritized the development of heavy industry as its economic development strategy." This strategy and the traditional planned economic system serving it were not suitable for China's resource endowment structure, resulting in the distortion of resource allocation and the general inefficiency of the economy. China had not achieved the expected goal of catching up with Western developed countries (Lu 2003).

1.2.2 Strategy for Building a Market Economy with Chinese Characteristics (1979–2008)

The 10-year Cultural Revolution brought China's economy and society to the brink of collapse. In 1978, the Third Plenary Session of the 11th CPC Central Committee decided to shift the focus of the Party's work to socialist modernization, and made the great historical choice of reform and opening-up, ushering in a new historical period of China's economic and social development.

On the economic development strategy, the Third Plenary Session of the 11th CPC Central Committee initiated a new process of rural reform. When discussing the national economic plan for 1979 and 1980, the plenary session put forward the requirement that attention should be paid to solving major imbalances in the national economy and maintaining an overall balance. The plenary session also discussed agriculture, believing that agriculture as the foundation of the national economy was still very weak overall, and only by vigorously restoring and accelerating the development of agricultural production could the living standards of the Chinese people be improved. The plenary session put forward a series of policies and measures for the development of agriculture, and agreed to send documents such as the Decision of the CPC Central Committee on A Number of Issues Concerning Accelerating Agricultural Development (Draft) to provinces, municipalities and autonomous regions for discussion and trial implementation. This document was revised and enriched before it was officially released, followed by the formulation, issuance and implementation of some important agricultural documents, which gave a strong impetus to the process of rural economic and social reform (Xinhua News Agency 1978).

On January 1, 1982, the CPC Central Committee approved and forwarded the Minutes of the National Conference on Rural Work, pointing out that the various responsibility systems in practice in rural areas at that time, including contracting out a certain farming job or work at a certain stage of farming and paying remuneration on the basis of work quotas, contracting production tasks out to laborers according to their skills and paying remuneration according to their output, contracting land out to laborers and letting them take responsibility for output, fixing farm output quotas for each household or group, and contracting work out to households or groups, etc. were all systems of responsibility for production in the socialist collective economy. In 1983, the Central Committee issued a document stating that the household responsibility system was a great creation of Chinese peasants under the leadership of the Party, and a new development of Marxist agricultural cooperation theory in China's practice. The Eighth Plenary Session of the 13th CPC Central Committee, held from November 25 to 29, 1991, adopted the Decision of the CPC Central Committee on Further Strengthening Agriculture and Rural Work. The Decision proposed to stabilize the two-tier management system that integrated unified with separate management on the basis of household contract management as a basic system of China's rural collective economic organizations for a long time, and to continuously enrich and improve it. As the first step in the reform of China's rural economic system, the household responsibility system marked a departure from the old system where people's communes were large in size and publicly owned and everyone was rewarded equally regardless of merit. Moreover, with the implementation of the contract system, contributions by individuals were linked to their income, so that peasants were much more motivated to engage in production, greatly liberating the rural productive forces.

The success of the rural economic system reform centered on the "household responsibility system" provided important experience for the state's reform of the urban planned economy system. After 1984, the reform of the urban economic system kicked into full gear. The focus of the reform of the urban economic system was the reform of state-owned enterprises, which proceeded mainly along three lines: first, develop the economy in which the only form of ownership is public ownership into an economy in which public ownership is dominant and multiple forms of ownership coexist; second, implement the separation of government functions from enterprise management for state-owned enterprises, gradually expand enterprises' autonomy in production and management, and implement the management responsibility system; third, implement a system in which distribution according to work done is dominant and multiple modes of distribution coexist.

On the basis of exploration during a decade of reform, the 14th CPC National Congress held in 1992 put forward the great strategy of establishing a socialist market economy system, pointing out that the reform of state-owned enterprises should move from the delegation of powers, the surrender of part of the profits and policy adjustment to the stage of mechanism transformation and institutional innovation pursuant to the requirements for establishing a socialist market economy system. In an useful exploratory effort to establish a modern enterprise system, pilot programs on the establishment of a modern enterprise system were carried out at a large number of state-owned enterprises, with them undergoing reform aimed at introducing the corporate system and shareholding system in state-owned enterprises (Fu and Yu 2009).

Generally speaking, we can call China's economic development strategy over the past 30 years of reform and opening-up, which has gone from the delegation of powers, the surrender of part of the profits and the fiscal responsibility system to the development of a planned commodity economy to the development of a socialist market economy with Chinese characteristics, a "strategy for building a socialist market economy system". Under this strategy, the household responsibility system, township enterprises and rural industrialization, small-town development models, and regional economic development models (represented by the Wenzhou model, the southern Jiangsu model and the Pearl River model) became the main implementation paths for the strategy for building a rural market economy system; the delegation of powers, the surrender of part of the profits, the restructuring of state-owned enterprises, the separation of government functions from enterprise management, and the creation of a modern enterprise system became important operational paths for the strategy for building an urban market economy system.

The reform of the economic and social systems initiated by the Third Plenary Session of the 11th CPC Central Committee was carried out under the principle of progressive reform that was described as "crossing the river by feeling the stones", and took place in the favorable circumstance of international specialization in the fields of economy and industry brought about by a new round of globalization. By relying on its unique resource and labor endowment, building a market economic system and joining the WTO, China quickly found its niche in the new global division of labor—the creation of an export-oriented economic system. The "three plus one trading mix" became the core business model of companies in coastal areas. This model took full advantage of the large amount of cheap labor released by China's rural reform, catapulting China into being the "factory of the world" and the world's second-largest economy. For this reason, Justin Yifu Lin and Cai Fang among others referred to China's economic development strategy during this period as a "comparative advantage strategy" (Justin Yifu Lin et al. 1994).

1.2.3 Economic Transformation and Upgrading Strategy Oriented Towards Global Competition (2009–Present)

The global financial crisis of 2008 was a wake-up call for the export-oriented Chinese economy. Global trade disputes are intensifying and escalating, the WTO has achieved little, and the profit model of the

Chinese economic system is facing the major challenge of deep transformation. The factor dividend, demographic dividend and globalization dividend which had sustained China's rapid economic growth for a long time were losing momentum. The ultra-high-speed growth of exports driven mainly by low costs was gradually returning to normal growth. The extensive mode of growth maintained by substantially increasing the input of resources and capital had come to an end. The Chinese economy still had a long way to go before it could achieve high-quality and cost-effective growth in the face of many variables in the external environment, increased resource and environmental constraints and higher costs of factors of production.

Against this background, during the 13th Five-Year Plan period, the state set 24 major targets in the 13th Five-Year Plan for national economic development, including 12 anticipated targets and 12 binding targets, to help adjust the economic structure and change the mode of economic development. These targets mainly focused on economic structure, science and technology education, resources and the environment, fostering domestic demand and improving people's livelihood (Central Government Portal).[1]

In May 2014, during his inspection tour to Henan Province, General Secretary Xi pointed out that "China's development is still in a period of important strategic opportunities. We should strengthen our confidence, adapt to the new normal based on the characteristics of China's economic development in the current phase, and maintain a strategically normal state of mind." The biggest feature of the new normal of the economy is that speed is "down" and efficiency is "up"; the new normal of the economy is distinctively characterized by a shift in growth drivers and a rebalancing of the economic structure. The specific characteristics are as follows: ① The stage of imitative and wave-style consumption is basically over, and personalized and diversified consumption is becoming mainstream; ② There has been an explosion of investment opportunities for infrastructure connectivity and new technologies, products, formats and business models; ③ China's comparative advantage of low cost has been transformed. Bringing in at a high level and going out on a large scale are happening simultaneously; ④ New industries, service industries,

[1] *Source* Central Government Portal, Outline of the Twelfth Five-Year Plan for National Economic and Social Development, http://www.gov.cn/2011lh/content_1825838_2.htm.

and small and micro enterprises are playing a more prominent role, and the miniaturization, intellectualization and specialization of production are becoming the new features of industrial organization; ⑤ The population is aging, the surplus population in agriculture is decreasing, the driving force provided by the large-scale input of factors is weakening, and economic growth will rely more on the quality of human capital and technological progress; ⑥ Market competition is gradually shifting to quality-oriented and differentiation-based competition; ⑦ The carrying capacity of the environment has reached or is close to the limit, and a new way of green, low-carbon and circular development must be promoted; ⑧ Economic risks are generally controllable, but it will take some time before risks characterized by high leverage and bubbles are resolved; ⑨ We must not only completely phase out excess production capacity, but also explore the direction of future industrial development by leveraging market mechanisms.[2]

In order to cope with the various crises and challenges brought about by the new economic normal, the new generation of leadership is working on a global strategy for economic transformation and upgrading. From the perspective of Western industrial and capital powers, particularly the United States, the establishment of various multilateral strategic cooperation platforms, the founding of the New Development Bank and the Asian Infrastructure Investment Bank, the Belt and Road Initiative, and planning for a Free Trade Area of the Asia–Pacific (FTAAP) all boil down to an attempt to challenge the U.S.-led institutionalized financial and trade system. The international hype surrounding the "China's Marshall Plan" is actually an attempt to push China to the forefront of strategic competition with the United States early.

In fact, as an important part of the strategic transformation of economic development, China's move to build itself into a global industrial and capital power by devising various constructive strategic measures is an inevitable trend of China's economic development strategy. The rise of high-end manufacturing represented by high-speed rail in the global value chain is changing the stereotype that Chinese manufacturing is characterized by OEM. The continuous improvement of the competitiveness of innovative Chinese companies such as Huawei, Alibaba and

[2] *Source* Sohu News, Central Economic Work Conference Closes The Nine Features of the New Economic Normal Mentioned For the First Time. http://news.sohu.com/20141211/n406872393.shtml.

Tencent in international markets is an important indicator that Chinese companies have won international respect. The acceptance of Alibaba by American investors shows that Chinese companies can make a difference in international capital markets. With the acceleration of the liberalization of cross-border RMB flows, the New Development Bank and the BRICS Contingent Reserve Fund may create a basket of reserve currencies including the RMB in the future. If the RMB becomes the monetary capital of the New Development Bank, combined with the China Development Bank, the Export–Import Bank of China and the Asian Infrastructure Investment Bank, it will significantly promote the economic development of developing countries (Zhang 2014). All this, of course, also shows that China's future economic development strategy must go beyond the framework of the U.S.-dominated international economic and financial order to actively build a new global economic and financial order.

If we follow the thinking of economists such as Justin Yifu Lin, we can call the economic transformation and upgrading strategy oriented towards global competition a "competitive advantage strategy". In today's increasingly globalized international economic landscape, the construction of such a competitive advantage-based economic development strategy goes far beyond the horizon of labor and resource endowment in traditional economic development, and is increasingly dependent on the close support and cooperation of industrial strategy, geopolitics, diplomatic strategy, as well as supporting systems such as modern fiscal, monetary and financial systems.

2 Strategic Choices for China's Monetary Policy

The RMB has successfully joined the International Monetary Fund (IMF)'s Special Drawing Rights (SDR) basket. Just as this paper was being completed, good news came at 1:00 a.m. Beijing time on December 1, 2015, when Christine Lagarde, IMF Managing Director said at a press conference, "The Executive Board's decision to include the RMB in SDR basket is an important milestone in the integration of the Chinese economy into the global financial system. It is also a recognition of the progress that the Chinese authorities have made in the past years in reforming China's monetary and financial systems." The IMF finally approved the RMB's inclusion in the SDR basket exactly five years after the last IMF review of the RMB.[3]

The reform of international financial rules in the post-financial crisis era will certainly focus on diversifying international reserve currencies, increasing the voice of emerging markets in rule-making, and building a global financial safety net aimed at maintaining global financial stability. Although the RMB went through a relatively long journey before becoming an international reserve currency, the diversification of international reserve currencies has become an irreversible process in the post-financial crisis era.

Although the RMB still has a long way to go to become a global reserve currency in the true sense of the phrase, joining the SDR basket is undoubtedly a new starting point for the RMB and China's financial markets to move towards the international stage. Analysis suggests that the main functions of reserve currencies are to maintain sufficient foreign exchange reserves to cope with external financing difficulties in the event of external shocks or crises, to repay foreign debt and back up the domestic currency with external assets, and to provide the government with the means to deal with foreign debt and respond to domestic natural disasters. Proper management of foreign exchange reserves is crucial for ensuring the proper implementation of these functions. Proper management of foreign exchange reserves is, first, to ensure an appropriate size of foreign exchange reserves; second, to ensure the liquidity of foreign exchange reserves and control the exposure of foreign exchange reserves to market and credit risks; and third, to provide a certain level of profitability in the medium-to long-term while ensuring liquidity and effective risk control. However, the financial crisis has posed significant challenges to the reserve management of foreign exchange reserve holders. Since the U.S. dollar has been the main currency in the foreign exchange reserves of various countries, the long-term depreciation of the U.S. dollar has made the preservation of foreign exchange reserves an significant challenge for various countries. It is expected that the reform of the international monetary system will be characterized by the weakening of the hegemony of the U.S. dollar and the diversification of international currencies in the next 5–10 years.

[3] *Source* RMB Successfully Joins SDR Basket and Will Not Depreciate Significantly in the Future, china.com.cn, December 01, 2015.

2.1 Strategic Choices for the Reform of the International Monetary System and the Internationalization of the RMB

The international financial crisis that swept the world has exposed the flaws in the international monetary system with the U.S. dollar as the main currency. It is essential that the reform of the international monetary system be advanced and a new international financial order built. The internationalization of the RMB faces unprecedented opportunities and is also an important part of the reform of the international monetary system. The internationalization of RMB has both benefits and costs, but the benefits as a whole far outweigh the costs. Therefore, we should actively create favorable conditions for internationalization and gradually and steadily advance the internationalization of the RMB.

2.1.1 The Flaws Inherent in the International Monetary System and the Diversification of International Currencies

The international financial crisis has exposed the flaws inherent in the international monetary system. In 2008, the outbreak of the international financial crisis caused by the U.S. subprime mortgage crisis shattered the facade of prosperity in international financial markets. Former Federal Reserve Chairman Alan Greenspan said publicly that this financial crisis was a once-in-a-century event and its possibility of it triggering a recession was increasing. Regarding the causes of the financial crisis, different scholars have given different judgments from different perspectives, and opinions are widely divided. To sum up, there are the theory of excessive financial innovation, the theory of weak financial regulation, the theory of promotion by rating agencies, and the theory of the ineffectiveness of international accounting standards. Generally speaking, these analyses of the causes of the financial crisis are generally one-sided, and abstractly summarize the causes of the financial crisis based on the reality of the outbreak of the financial crisis. Dialectically, there is some truth to all these theories, but in the absence of comprehensive and in-depth research, they fail to reveal the essence of the crisis. It can be said that the flaws in the current international monetary system are one of the major causes of the crisis. The most fundamental problem revealed by the international financial crisis is that the current international monetary system is inherently flawed. So, how to understand the current international monetary system? What are the flaws inherent in the current international monetary system? Why are the flaws inherent in the current international monetary system one of the major causes of the international financial crisis? The exploration of these issues requires us to have a deep understanding of the basis for the emergence and operation of the current international monetary system.

The current international monetary system was formed on the basis of two major international agreements. One is the Bretton Woods system of 1944. The establishment of the system was essentially based on the international position of the United States as the only superpower of the world. Such absolute dominance made the U.S. dollar the only standard currency in the world and saw the creation of a gold exchange standard centered on the U.S. dollar, namely the "double peg", under which the U.S. dollar was pegged to gold and currencies around the globe were pegged to the U.S. dollar. Meanwhile, the system also established the U.S. dollar as a super reserve currency. The other is the Jamaica Accords of 1976. The agreement made the long-standing gold standard and free-floating exchange rate regime legally recognized. The core of the agreement can be summarized in two parts, one is multiple standard currencies, and the other is a floating exchange rate mechanism. In theory, the Jamaica Accords aimed to break the international monetary system with the U.S. dollar as a single standard currency, and establish an international monetary system with multiple standard currencies plus floating exchange rates. However, the reality often went beyond the imagination of the designers of the agreement. The Jamaica Accords came against an international political and economic background in which the United States still had a strong international financial position and political voice. Consequently, instead of weakening U.S. hegemony, the newly established international monetary system legitimized the United States' unilateral abandonment of the international obligations incumbent on the U.S. dollar as a standard currency.

However, an analysis from the perspective of private versus public goods shows that there is a profound contradiction between sovereign currencies and international currencies. It is undeniable that the U.S. dollar, as a sovereign currency, alone assuming the function of an international currency is a historical choice in the political and economic game among the world's major powers. This result reflects the national interests of the United States and is also accepted by countries around the world for a certain period of time and to a certain extent. It can be said that the internationalization of the U.S. dollar has facilitated international trade and investment to a certain extent, and promoted economic globalization and the prosperity and growth of the world economy. However, it must be emphasized that such an arrangement as the internationalization of a single sovereign currency essentially reflects the contradiction between sovereign and international currencies. This contradiction can be analyzed from multiple angles. In essence, it can be analyzed by drawing on the basic framework of the private versus public goods theory. For all countries in the world, a country's sovereign currency and the monetary system derived from it evidently possess the attributes of a private good. The sovereign currency functions as a measure of value, a means of circulation, a means of payment and a store of value within the country. The central bank's monetary policy serves the country's economic growth, price stability, full employment, and balance of payments. Different monetary policy instruments produce different policy effects, and such effects only act on (or serve) the population within the country. Other countries have no right to interfere with the implementation of the country's monetary policy regardless of their policy demands. The fact that a sovereign currency and the monetary system derived from it possess the attributes of a private good suggests that a government's monetary supply is the result of a trade-off between the marginal cost and marginal benefit of its own policy. In theory, monetary equilibrium should be satisfied with the marginal benefit of policy being equal to the marginal cost. However, the international currency that acts as the standard currency and the international monetary system derived from it evidently possess the attributes of a public good. An international currency is a currency that acts as a measure of value, a means of circulation, a means of payment, a store of value and a world currency in the world. We can think of the international monetary system as a global public good, and the reform of the international monetary system or the provision of a new international monetary system is equivalent to the provision of a global public good.

There is a clear contradiction between the two. Specifically, as far as the U.S. dollar and international currencies are concerned, it is an irreconcilable contradiction in two respects. On the one hand, the policy cost of sovereign states is not equal to the cost of international economic operation. From the perspective of policy costs of sovereign states: First, the U.S. deficit costs little and can even bring some benefits. For the United States, a deficit-driven increase in debt is not scary. The current international monetary system actually gives the U.S. dollar the status of a "credit" standard currency. The United States can dump its currency into the world almost unconstrained in the form of a balance of payments deficit, and this process is often accompanied by the Federal Reserve printing money, issuing dollars to pay off debts, and obtaining a considerable amount of international seigniorage revenue. Second, thanks to the reserve status of the U.S. dollar, the United States does not need to arrange any economic policy to increase foreign exchange reserves, nor does it have the problem of insufficient foreign exchange reserves, but other countries are forced to coordinate their domestic policy arrangements in order to gain a comparative price advantage on their exports and thus increase their foreign exchange reserves. Basic international trade theory has proved that the consequence is that the welfare of U.S. consumers increases at the expense of the welfare of other countries' residents. Third, the United States does not need to worry about the increase in money supply causing domestic inflation, because the dollar can always flow around the world in an open economic environment, forming Eurodollars, Asian dollars, etc. The factor behind this currency flow mechanism is that countries have no other international currencies to choose from and are forced to hold large amounts of U.S. dollars in the hope of hedging against potential currency risks and allow funds to flow back to the United States. In this process, the direct manifestation of the cost of U.S. monetary policy is the devaluation of the U.S. dollar, but the United States obtains considerable policy benefits on the basis of bearing the cost of currency devaluation; other countries can only bear the high cost of dollar devaluation, and their policies are held hostage to the economic risk of dollar devaluation. In the final analysis, the United States can borrow from the world without restrictions, but its repayments are skewed by the devaluation of the U.S. dollar, leaving the international economy operating on a platform fraught with risk.

On the other hand, policy rationality promotes a vicious cycle of "free-rider" behavior, which eventually leads to global economic imbalances amid a flood of liquidity. It is undeniable that the economic policy of any sovereign state under this institutional arrangement is rational. In order to seize the economic benefits of the "dollar standard", the rational policy of the United States has prompted it to repeatedly take a free ride on the "overissuance of U.S. dollars" and to stimulate the rejuvenation of its real economy through the successive launch of QE1, QE2 and QE3 to shift the high cost of dollar debt. Other countries, in order to prosper their own capital markets and obtain the excess benefits of cheap funds, are also prompted by rational policies to take a free ride on the "overissuance of U.S. dollars" without thinking and to replenish funds in their virtual economies and open up channels of international capital flows through the opening of domestic capital markets. This vicious circle of "free-rider" behavior, as well as immediate "free-rider" benefits, have enabled the United States and other sovereign states to reach a high degree of tacit understanding on short-term interests. Over time, this vicious cycle of "free-rider" behavior became solidified, forming the basic pattern of world economic operation. The net result is a global flood of liquidity; capital-exporting countries have a large current account deficit, while capital-importing countries have a large current account surplus and capital financial account surplus, accompanied by excess foreign exchange reserves; international hot money is flooding the markets of the world's major economies, constantly feeding and inflating capital market bubbles, resulting in serious global economic imbalances.

Throughout the history of international currencies, we can see that whether it is with the gold standard centered on the British pound, the Bretton Woods system centered on the U.S. dollar, or the current Jamaican system, there is a fundamental problem, that is, the instability of international currencies, and this is because there is an insurmountable internal contradiction in the international monetary system, that is, the Triffin dilemma. Whenever international currencies change places, there will be severe economic turmoil, and the cyclical occurrence of this situation frustrates efforts to meet the world economy's need for a stable monetary system. This is illustrated by the transformation of the international monetary system from the Bretton Woods system with the U.S. dollar as the single world currency to the current diversified international monetary system with the U.S. dollar as the main currency. The diversification of the international monetary system can alleviate the Triffin dilemma to a large extent. The diversification of reserve currencies can reduce excessive dependence on the U.S. dollar and gradually end the U.S. economy's tight monopolistic grip on the world economy; meanwhile, the diversification of international reserve currencies also reduces exchange rate risk for periphery countries' foreign exchange reserves. The outbreak and spread of the U.S. subprime mortgage crisis and the global financial crisis show that the new Triffin dilemma of a country's currency being an international currency is still an unsolvable institutional problem in the international monetary system. The international monetary system with the U.S. dollar as the only core is unstable and uncoordinated, and no longer meets the needs of global economic and financial development. The international monetary system must be diversified in the future. There have been growing calls in the international community for reform of the current monetary system. In addition, the risk of loss to a large amount of dollar-denominated foreign exchange assets held by China arising from U.S. quantitative easing in recent years demonstrates the benefits of reserve currency diversification for emerging economies.

2.1.2 Currency Internationalization as a National Competitive Strategy: World Experience and Its Implications

The financial crisis has exposed many flaws in the current dollar-dominated international monetary system, which has triggered a profound rethinking in the international community. Increasing calls for reform of the international monetary system also provide a good opportunity for the internationalization of the RMB. This chapter objectively analyzes and evaluates the internationalization process of major international currencies such as the U.S. dollar, the Japanese yen, the euro and the British pound, summarizes their experience and lessons, and sorts out their commonalities and characteristics with a view to providing a frame of reference for advancing the internationalization of the RMB.

1. **The U.S. dollar: The largest economy and the most developed financial markets have made it a super international currency**

As the most deeply internationalized and widely used currency in the world, the U.S. dollar underwent three stages of internationalization: the accumulation stage before the two world wars, the stage of the "double peg" exchange rate system established by the Bretton Woods system from 1944 to 1971, and the international dollar standard stage since 1973. The U.S. economy began to grow rapidly in the late eighteenth century and had become the world's most powerful economy by the time World War I broke out. The United States profited hugely from the two world wars by supplying goods to the Allies (John Gordon 2007). The U.S. dollar, with its stable value, quickly became the most preferred foreign exchange reserve of all countries, and its international status rose dramatically. After World War II, the Bretton Woods system centered on the U.S. dollar was formed. But due to the Triffin dilemma and the flaws of the gold standard itself, the system eventually collapsed. The Bretton Woods era ended in 1973 with the collapse of the fixed exchange rate system. After the collapse of the Bretton Woods system, due to factors such as strong economic strength, the "incumbent advantage" of the U.S. dollar and developed financial markets, the U.S. dollar inherited the status of the main international currency. So far, no international currency has been able to compete with the U.S. dollar.

2. **Euro: a classic case of currency internationalization**

The euro is a typical product of regional monetary integration. The euro came into being after decades of economic and political cooperation among European countries, inherited the advantages of the Deutsche Mark as an international currency, and internationalized rapidly backed by the economic strength of the Eurozone (Tong and Cheng 2001). Leading up to the birth of the euro was a preparation period of about thirty years from initial conception to legal preparation. The idea of a European monetary union was first mooted at the 1969 Hague Summit, and the Werner Plan was later adopted, but never put into practice. In 1989, the Delors Report revived the idea of the "Werner Plan". In December 1991, the European Community adopted the draft Maastricht Treaty, which aimed at the creation of a single currency, a single exchange rate system and the European System of Central Banks. After that, the Stability and Growth Pact, the Legal Status of the Euro and the New Exchange Rate Mechanism were signed, laying the legal groundwork for the birth of the euro. The euro was officially launched on 1 January 1999 and went into circulation on 1 January 2002. So far, 17 countries have adopted the euro as legal tender. In 2011, the International Monetary Fund adjusted the weighting of the euro in the SDR basket to 37.4% from 34% in 2006.[4] In 2001, the euro's share of global foreign exchange reserves was only 19.2%, but in the first quarter of 2008 this share rose to 26.7%,[5] reflecting the euro's enhanced status as an international reserve currency. The eurozone also has institutional flaws and deficiencies. The European debt crisis which began in 2009 has exposed some serious problems within the eurozone. First, the rigid "convergence" criterion of the Maastricht Treaty ignores the different economic circumstances of member states. Second,

[4] *Source* IMF, World Economic Outlook Database.

[5] *Source* IMF, Currency Composition of Official Foreign Exchange Reserves.

the unified monetary policy and coordinated fiscal policy in the eurozone not only have difficulty working together, but also make it harder for the central bank to develop monetary policy (Eijffinger 2003). Third, in the absence of fiscal and political union, the expansion of the euro as an international currency is always limited, and the possibility of further expanding the euro's share in the international monetary system is very small.

3. **The British pound: the historical legacy of a great power and the world's financial hub complement each other**

The internationalization of the British pound is divided into three stages: developing rapidly from the late seventeenth century until the end of the eighteenth century, functioned as a major international currency from the early nineteenth century until World War I, and declining after the two world wars. In the mid-to-late seventeenth century, Britain established a modern financial system through the Financial Revolution, and in the second half of the eighteenth century, London became the world's largest financial hub. At the same time, Britain became a hegemonic power through the Industrial Revolution, and the British pound was continuously exported along with overseas trade, foreign investment and colonial activities. The formation of the international gold standard in the 1870s allowed Britain to dominate the world financial system, and the British pound has been the most important international currency ever since. After World War I, with the rise of emerging capitalist countries such as the United States, Britain's economic and other advantages gradually weakened. With gold reserves were depleted by the war, in 1931, the Bank of England announced the abandonment of the gold standard, marking the end of the "British pound era". Looking back at the internationalization of the British pound, we can see that the internationalization of the British pound unfolded along with Britain's growing economic strength and control over the international financial industry. The rise of the British pound, the first currency in the modern world to complete internationalization, was a historical inevitability, a choice that maximized British interests and also a natural choice for the development of the international economy at that time.

The internationalization of the yen was a tortuous process, which can be divided into three stages: the start-up stage from 1960s to early 1980s, the active advancement stage from mid-late 1980s to mid-1990s, and the transition from internationalization to regionalization in the late 1990s. Since the 1960s, the yen had successfully survived the two dollar crises and become an internationally recognized "hard currency" (Xu 2010). The Japanese government gradually relaxed currency controls. In 1980, Japan achieved capital account convertibility, and the internationalization of yen entered the stage of comprehensive advancement. Throughout the 1970s, the yen internationalized rapidly, with the shares of exports and imports settled in yen in foreign trade increasing from 0.9% and 0.3% to 29.4% and 24%, respectively (Xia 2012). In 1985, the United States and Japan signed the Plaza Accord, which appreciated the yen. Although the agreement caused serious damage to Japan's economic development, it provided a good opportunity for the internationalization of the yen. Japan's overseas investment grew rapidly on the back of a stronger yen. The Tokyo offshore market was established in December 1986. In the late 1980s, the yen became the third largest reserve currency after the dollar and the mark. As Japan entered its "lost decade" in the early 1990s, the internationalization of the yen went into reverse. In 1996, the Japanese government put forward the "Tokyo Financial Big Bang" reform plan, but the reform was hit by the Asian financial crisis at the very beginning. The Japanese government took the opportunity to adjust the yen's internationalization strategy to promote the return of the yen to Asia. The internationalization of the yen was not successful for the following reasons: First, the Japanese government had been cautious or even passive in the early days of the yen's internationalization, and had not formed a consistent policy and guideline. Second, Japan's domestic financial markets are limited in size. Third, squeezed by the "incumbent" dollar, the internationalization of the yen can hardly reach a high level. The yen's return to Asia through the Asian financial crisis was actually a step backwards.

3 Trends in the Evolution and Direction of the Reform of the International Monetary System, and Historical Opportunity for the RMB

In recent years, due to changes in the international economic situation and flaws in the dollar standard, the reform of the international monetary system has become a consensus of the international community.

3.1 New Challenges for the U.S. Dollar

The Triffin dilemma remains unsolved, and the "double deficit" is unsustainable. The Triffin dilemma points out that any country whose currency serves as an international currency will find itself in a dilemma: On the one hand, in order to meet the needs of international trade, payments and reserves, the country must maintain a balance of payments deficit for a long period of time; on the other hand, in order to maintain currency stability, the country must run a surplus for a long period of time. Under the current international monetary system centered on the U.S. dollar, the Triffin dilemma remains unresolved. After the outbreak of the financial crisis, large amounts of capital moved into Asian and European financial markets, making the U.S. double deficit unsustainable (Yin and Cui 2009). No balance could be struck between an expanding flow of dollars out and a relatively shrinking flow of dollars back, and the downward pressure on the dollar was increasing.

The United States enjoys many economic, political, cultural and other benefits brought by the dollar standard, but lacks a corresponding constraint mechanism in terms of responsibility. According to the "core-periphery" theory, various countries export raw materials, oil and all kinds of low-priced industrial products to the "core country", the United States, in exchange for the international currency - the U.S. dollar, while the United States, with its well-developed and sound financial markets, "exports" bonds and other financial products to various countries, thus causing dollars to flow back. The result of the combination of these two aspects is the rapid development of the U.S. financial industry, a highly developed U.S. virtual economy, and the "deindustrialization" of the U.S. real economy, which puts the United States in an absolutely dominant position in the international division of labor (Zhang 1998). Because of this serious inequality, other countries are not willing to maintain the status quo for a long time, but are committed to exploring and building a new international monetary system.

Due to the unbalanced development of the world economy, U.S. economic supremacy has been gradually shaken in recent years. European countries and Asian countries, in particular Japan and China are catching up by taking advantage of being latecomers. The currencies of these countries have also embarked on the road to internationalization, and the U.S. dollar's position as the leading international currency is being increasingly impacted by other international currencies such as the euro, the yen and emerging Asian currencies.

Countries around the world are questioning the status of the U.S. dollar. First, although the United States still ranks first in the world in terms of economic aggregates, its high debt and deteriorating fiscal and balance of payments deficits have shaken the international community's confidence in the dollar, and concerns about the ability of the United States to service its debt have also affected the international community's long-term expectations for the dollar. Second, in the absence of regulation and restrictions, the United States has long relied on printing money to maintain its high consumption and high deficit development model, and neglected the obligations incumbent on international currencies, which has raised many questions. The instability of the monetary system dominated by a single sovereign currency has become increasingly prominent, making the international community hope to break the system as soon as possible and establish a more stable and reasonable international monetary system.

3.2 Direction of Reform of the International Monetary System

At present, there are mainly two types of views: One direction is to seek a super-sovereign currency to replace the status of the U.S. dollar in the current international monetary system, so as to completely solve the Triffin dilemma. Its ultimate form is to establish SDRs as a global reserve currency and promote the full application of SDRs (Wu 2010a). Another direction is to establish a diversified international monetary system and accept more sovereign currencies, including the euro and future Asian currencies, into the global mainstream.

The possibility of SDRs, a super-sovereign currency, replacing the dollar as the international reserve currency. The SDRs have advantages and disadvantages as an international currency. The SDRs as an international currency have the following advantages: First, using SDRs as an international reserve currency completely avoids the "Triffin dilemma" that sovereign currencies must face when acting as international currencies. Second, using SDRs as an international reserve currency is conducive to avoiding exchange rate risks. Third, using SDRs as the main international currency leads to greater fairness. After SDRs are used as an international currency, the seigniorage and other income obtained by IMF from SDR issuance can be shared by all countries around the world, which is conducive to the common development and progress of the world economy. Nevertheless, there are still some problems with the SDR that limit its function as an international currency: first, the SDR quota is a very small and its use is very limited. Second, the allocation range of SDRs is small and unreasonable. At present, most of the SDR quota is allocated to developed countries led by the United States, and developing countries receive a small share. Third, the basket of currencies on which the value of SDRs is based is narrow. At present, there are only four currencies on which the value of SDRs is based: the U.S. dollar, the euro, the British pound and the Japanese yen, which are very limited in scope and not very representative. Fourth, in order for SDRs to become an international reserve currency, the issuer of SDRs must be strong in its ability to exercise control and make decisions, completely independent, impartial and non-sovereign, and free from interference and influence by any sovereign state. The IMF is clearly not doing enough in this regard.

In view of the existing problems of SDRs, the academic community has explored a series of reform options covering various areas. In summary, there are mainly the following three suggestions: First, expand the scope of SDR use and increase the issuance quota. Second, reform the composition of the SDR basket to include the currencies of emerging market countries such as the BRICS countries. Third, set up a substitution account (Wu 2010b). This is done by allowing central banks to convert part of their countries' foreign exchange reserves into SDRs, deposit the SDRs in the IMF's "substitution account", and convert the SDRs back into foreign exchange reserves whenever they want.

The above analysis shows that the reform of the international monetary system that involves replacing the current dollar standard with a super-sovereign currency is fraught with difficulties, and even if it can be achieved eventually, it will take a very long time.

Compared with the creation of a super-sovereign currency based on SDRs, the reform idea of diversifying international currencies is more down-to-earth and easier to realize. The international monetary system will be further diversified in the future. First, the U.S. dollar will remain the dominant player in the international monetary system for a long time, but its position will gradually decline. Second, the international influence of the euro will continue to expand. Although the long-term development potential of the euro is not as great as people think, the eurozone has been taking a down-to-earth and steady path of development (Xu and Wang 2009), and its status as an international currency will rise steadily in the long run. Third, the status of major Asian currencies will steadily improve. Among them, the RMB, as the currency with the greatest development potential, has been favored by the international community. We should seize the opportunity of reform of the international monetary system in the post-crisis era to make steady progress. Of course, to build a diversified international monetary system, we need to solve the following issues: First, we need to create an independent, impartial and professional international regulatory body. Second, we need to establish a more reasonable and orderly exchange rate constraint mechanism. Third, we need to promote the internationalization of the key Asian currency, the RMB, as soon as possible. In the future scenario where major international currencies—the U.S. dollar, the euro and Asian currencies stand like the three legs of a tripod, the RMB is undoubtedly the key currency that will play a pivotal role among Asian currencies. In the process of building a new diversified international monetary system, we must promote the internationalization of the RMB in a stable and orderly manner, so that it will have the ability and status to compete with the other two "legs" as soon as possible.

In the light of the above discussion, we believe that of the two reform options of creating a super-sovereign currency and diversifying the international monetary system, the latter is more feasible. The diversification of the international monetary system is a more realistic reformist way of change, which is conducive to balancing the interests of all parties and alleviating these contradictions and conflicts. In the long run, a diversified international monetary system can be regarded as a transitional stage before the ideal state of creating a supra-sovereign currency is realized.

3.3 Historical Opportunity for the RMB

The financial crisis is a good opportunity for the RMB to step onto the international stage as it has weakened the U.S. dollar's position as the leading international currency and created a more open international environment for the internationalization of the RMB. China should seize the opportunity and proactively advance the internationalization of the RMB.

4 Analysis of the Benefits and Costs of RMB Internationalization

In recent years, there have been growing calls for the internationalization of the RMB. It has become a common aspiration both at home and abroad to realize the internationalization of the RMB as soon as possible and make it an international currency matching China's economic strength. In the face of these calls, we should take a prudent and comprehensive view of the issue. We must not only see the huge benefits that the internationalization of the RMB may bring, but also analyze its possible costs.

4.1 Analysis of the Benefits of RMB Internationalization

First, the acquisition of seigniorage will bring the most direct benefits to China. It is estimated that by the end of 1992, the gross amount of U.S. paper currency exported by the United States had exceeded $700.9 billion, and at present, U.S. currency in circulation outside the United States amounts to $250–300 billion, while the cost of printing and issuing a one-dollar bill is negligible. It goes without saying that as a developing country, China is dependent on actual resources for its economic growth, so once the RMB is internationalized, it will not only reduce China's wealth loss caused by the use of foreign currency, but will also open up a new channel for China to utilize capital. Second, the internationalization of the RMB will help China expand foreign trade and reduce risks. The internationalization of the RMB will also promote China's foreign trade and economic activities and international exchanges, and will especially promote China's economic and offshore investments in neighboring countries and regions. As an international currency, especially as the pivot currency in Asia, the RMB can play a key role in trade invoicing. A considerable portion of trade can be invoiced and settled in RMB, or partially in RMB, which will greatly reduce settlement risks and expand international trade. Third, the internationalization of the RMB will help China control the size of its foreign debt and optimize its debt structure. At present, most of China's external debt is denominated in U.S. dollars and Japanese yen. The sharp fluctuations of the U.S. dollar and the Japanese yen will increase China's external debt burden or lead to higher volatility, so the denomination of external debt in U.S. dollars and Japanese yen is not conducive to external debt management.

As an international currency, the RMB will improve our ability to pay off debt. We can stabilize international financial markets through the stability of the RMB, and defuse foreign debt risk through the conversion of transactions between the RMB and the U.S. dollar, the Japanese yen and the euro. Third, the internationalization of the RMB will help promote the internationalization of China's financial industry. After the RMB becomes an international currency, more international trade and international capital transactions will be invoiced in RMB. In these transactions, China's banking and other financial service sectors are endowed with significant advantages, which is conducive to enhancing the comprehensive competitiveness of China's financial industry and promoting its internationalization. The internationalization of the RMB will effectively promote the modernization and internationalization of China's financial system. Fifth, the internationalization of the RMB will reduce the demand for international reserves and provide multiple means for achieving balance-of-payments equilibrium. At present, China holds large international reserves and has to pay a high cost for them. On the one hand, international reserves put pressure on the injection of base money and lead to a large amount of funds outstanding for foreign exchange; on the other hand, a large amount of U.S. dollar reserves are deposited in the form of U.S. government bonds, which actually contributes to the U.S. economy and reduces the holding and control of foreign exchange resources by Chinese commercial banks and enterprises. After the RMB is internationalized, China's ability to pay off its debt can be realized in RMB. Foreign exchange reserves will be significantly reduced, allowing a diversion of the current large amount of foreign exchange reserves for investment and use. Meanwhile, the current account deficit is compensated by the inflow of funds from abroad, making the exchange rate of the RMB less correlated with the current account position, which is conducive to the implementation of China's internal economic policies and internal and external economic equilibrium. Sixth, the internationalization of the RMB expands China's international influence and enhances China's ability to participate in global resource allocation and policy coordination. After the RMB becomes a major international currency, China can have a greater say in international affairs. For the domestic economy, the internationalization of the RMB helps adjust industrial structure, enables domestic enterprises to further integrate into the world market, and promotes technological progress and improves production efficiency through international competition. Meanwhile, it enables domestic enterprises to enjoy both domestic and international resource factor markets and product sales markets, and promotes the rational allocation and full utilization of factors of production.

4.2 Analysis of the Costs of RMB Internationalization

An international currency is an intermediary through which the world economy operates. Once a country's currency becomes an international currency, it means that the currency has gone beyond national boundaries and needs to assume the role of a world credit intermediary. Therefore, after a country's currency becomes an international currency, what it gets is not only the benefits, but also the corresponding costs. First, the weakening of monetary policy autonomy. After the RMB becomes an international currency, the Chinese government no longer has direct control over the exchange and use of the RMB, and the adjustment and implementation of monetary policy will be severely constrained by international factors. The formulation of monetary policy should not only consider the development of the domestic economy, but also take into account the development cycle of the world economy. The RMB also has to face the "Triffin dilemma" that the dollar once faced under the Bretton Woods system, and any fluctuations in the international market will be amplified and affect the security and stability of China's domestic economic operation. Second, the scale of capital flows will have a big impact on the domestic market. As the current capacity of China's domestic capital market is small, the financial opening required by the free convertibility of the RMB will cause a large amount of capital to flow into the domestic stock market and real estate market, which will lead to "irrational exuberance" in the stock market and a rise in real estate prices. Once the bubble bursts, it will cause great damage to the domestic economy and finance. In addition, the internationalization of a currency will increase the average demand for the currency, and a large inflow of foreign capital will lead to a significant appreciation of the nominal exchange rate, which will weaken the external competitiveness of domestic products and lead to domestic economic turmoil. Third, the large-scale circulation of RMB abroad makes it more difficult to stabilize the RMB exchange rate. The internationalization of the RMB enables a large amount of RMB to circulate abroad, which should theoretically be aided by a mature offshore RMB market. When an offshore RMB market is formed, the price formed by the market according to actual supply and demand will be an important frame of reference for the domestic RMB exchange rate, making the formation mechanism of the RMB exchange rate more complicated, increasing the difficulty of accurately assessing the equilibrium exchange rate level of the RMB and the long-term factors affecting the RMB exchange rate, and consequently making it more difficult for the central bank to intervene in the RMB exchange rate. Fourth, China's international responsibility will increase the burden on its domestic economy to some extent. After the RMB becomes an international currency, China will have to assume part of the responsibility for stabilizing international financial markets. When a liquidity crisis appears in the relevant countries, China must use its foreign exchange reserves or issue RMB credit to provide liquidity support to those countries in crisis. In addition, the internationalization of the RMB will make it more difficult for China's monetary authorities to manage and monitor RMB cash.

All in all, the internationalization of the RMB will bring huge benefits to China and at the same time bring many new problems to the domestic macroeconomy and government macro-control. By then, the demand for RMB and the level of the RMB exchange rate will not only depend on the economic situation at home, but will also be influenced by the economic situation abroad. Monetary policy needs to take into account both internal and external equilibrium, and make the necessary choices in the event of a conflict. The international flow of funds through the internationalized RMB will directly affect interest rates, exchange rates and prices in China.

5 Path Selection and Strategic Design for RMB Internationalization

As the international status of China's economy continues to rise, the internationalization of the RMB will become an important way for China to develop its economy and elevate its international status. China's growing economic strength has laid a solid economic foundation for the internationalization of the RMB.

5.1 Conditions for the Internationalization of the RMB

What supports the international status of a country's currency is the country's comprehensive strength, including its economic and trade strength, the credibility and inertia of its currency, the level of development of its financial markets, its political status, etc. More than three decades of reform and opening-up have created favorable conditions for the internationalization of the RMB. ① The economy is growing steadily. China's economy has grown rapidly since the launch of reform and opening-up, becoming the world's second largest economy after the United States. China is still expected to grow at an average annual rate of about 7% over the next decade. Inflation is low compared to other developing countries. All these have laid a solid foundation for the RMB to go abroad and go global. ② There is no huge depreciation or appreciation pressure. Over the years, the market's ability to adapt to changes in the RMB exchange rate and to control risks has gradually strengthened. Since 2012, there has been a consensus that the RMB exchange rate is close to the average rate and will only appreciate slightly in the future; fluctuations in the RMB exchange rate are "bilateral". ③ Both the Chinese government and the Chinese public hold a positive attitude. As early as the 1990s, China started to settle border trade with many of its neighbors using the RMB, and the RMB began to go out of the country. ④ The RMB is generally accepted outside China. In recent years, with the further expansion and deepening of trade and economic exchanges between China and neighboring countries and regions, more and more countries and regions have begun to accept the RMB. In Southeast Asia, the RMB has become a hard currency after the U.S. dollar, the euro and the Japanese yen; in the southwestern border region, the RMB is also known as the "small dollar".

To sum up, the conditions for the internationalization of the RMB are increasingly ripe. The RMB has been accepted as a payment and settlement currency by more and more countries, and many central banks have included it among their foreign exchange reserve currencies, so the RMB is gradually taking on the role of an international reserve currency. In addition to Belarus, Malaysia, Thailand, Cambodia, Russia and the Philippines, the central banks of Nigeria and Tanzania also subscribed for RMB bonds worth a total of RMB 500 million in 2012. Japan was allowed to purchase up to RMB 65 billion ($10.3 billion) of Chinese government bonds in 2012, making the RMB a foreign exchange reserve for developed countries for the first time. On November 30, 2015, the IMF Executive Board decided to include the RMB in the Special Drawing Rights (SDR) currency basket. Since then, the RMB has taken a landmark step on the road to internationalization, becoming the fifth currency in the SDR basket after the U.S. dollar, euro, British pound and Japanese yen. In May 2022, the IMF announced that it would raise the weighting of the RMB in the SDR basket from 10.92% to 12.28%. This reflects greater freedom to use the RMB, which will help further elevate the status of the RMB as an international reserve currency and increase the international appeal of RMB-denominated assets.

5.2 *Assessment and Prevention of Potential Risks Associated with the Internationalization of the RMB*

Currency internationalization is a double-edged sword, and with benefits come risks. With the deepening of the internationalization of the RMB, the issue of risk will become increasingly prominent (Shi 2012). ① Threaten domestic economic and financial stability. An internationalized currency will easily become a transmission tool. The internationalization of the RMB will make the domestic economy closely related to the world economy, which will expose the domestic economy to external shocks in the event of an economic or financial crisis in other countries. After a country's currency is internationalized, differences between interest rates at home and abroad will stimulate short-term speculative capital flows, triggering arbitrage behavior involving huge amounts of hot money and threatening domestic economic and financial stability. ② Face the "Triffin dilemma". For a currency to become an international currency, its liquidity must be guaranteed throughout the world. As other countries need to increase RMB holdings in their reserves, China's imports may increase faster than exports, resulting in a balance of payments deficit. China's chronic balance of payments deficit, in turn, will affect RMB-holding countries' confidence in the RMB. Therefore, after the RMB is internationalized, we must find the right balance between the RMB as an international payment currency, an international reserve currency and an international investment currency. ③ Make it more difficult to judge and make decisions about the macroeconomic situation. According to the "trilemma", the free flow of capital across countries, the stability of the exchange rate and the effectiveness of monetary policy cannot be guaranteed at the same time. The internationalization of the

RMB is preconditioned on the stability of the exchange rate and the free flow of capital across countries, which will undermine the independence of the formulation and implementation of China's monetary policy. The large amount of RMB flowing in international financial markets will inevitably disrupt domestic monetary policy and make it more difficult to judge and make decisions about the macroeconomic situation. ④The risk of illicit outflows of RMB. If RMB that have flowed out of China cannot return to China through normal channels, then most of them are likely to return to the mainland through illicit channels, resulting in active underground banking and currency smuggling, which not only greatly threatens China's financial security, but also makes it difficult for China's neighboring countries and regions to use the RMB as a major regional reserve currency. Drug trafficking has been growing exponentially and casinos in China's neighboring countries have been exploding in both number and size, which coupled with the complexity and secrecy of transnational "money laundering" activities has led to a dramatic increase in the outflow of RMB through illicit channels. In the context of economic globalization and the internationalization of the RMB, these activities will become more and more rampant, which will do great harm to the security of the international financial system and the international political and economic order.

Risks associated with the internationalization of the RMB should be guarded against as early as possible. ① Adjust macroeconomic policies according to progress in the internationalization of the RMB. The formulation of macroeconomic policies should be adjusted appropriately, taking into account not only the impact of domestic economic variables, but also interference by external factors such as the supply of and demand for the RMB outside China and speculation on the RMB by international hot money. ② Internationalize monetary policy. First, we should control total liquidity with monetary policy. If increases in liquidity cannot be effectively regulated at the aggregate level, they will affect the sustained and stable growth of the economy. Meanwhile, we also need to optimize and adjust structure by starting with policies on finance, revenue, industry, and foreign trade. Second, in the formulation of internationalized monetary policy, we should strive to increase the flexibility of the RMB exchange rate and further liberalize the RMB interest rates, and should guide the orderly cross-border flow of RMB through market mechanisms, appropriately control the level of international reserves and the current account surplus, and create conditions for capital account liberalization as soon as possible. Finally, efforts should be made to strengthen international monetary policy coordination. At present, it is particularly important to strengthen international monetary policy coordination, especially between China and the United States. The United States should be made to realize that the rise of the RMB will only help the dollar play a better role as an international currency, and the RMB will not exclude or even replace the dollar. We hope that the United States will bear in mind the big picture and get a clear understanding of the situation, and both sides will jointly adopt a forward-looking monetary policy and pay active attention to the impact of monetary policy on the global economy, so as to jointly create a good atmosphere for the international monetary system. ③ Actively promote the development of offshore RMB markets. As an offshore RMB market, China Hong Kong should expand the scale of RMB deposits in the future, and in the process, encourage foreign-funded enterprises to replace foreign currency FDI with RMB FDI, encourage trade settlements in RMB, and promote the use of RMB in China Hong Kong and third countries, especially the borrowing of RMB in Hong Kong for use abroad by foreign-funded enterprises. Meanwhile, we should appropriately control financing and repatriation by Chinese-funded enterprises in the China Hong Kong RMB market. ④ Guard against financial risks. First, we should actively expand the scale and scope of cross-border trade settlements in RMB. Second, we should accelerate the creation of a RMB backflow mechanism to enhance the confidence of overseas residents and institutions in holding RMB. Finally, we should accelerate the pace of reform of the domestic financial system and establish an internationalized financial regulatory service system.

5.3 Strategic Objectives and Path Selection for RMB Internationalization

In the long run, whether China should act alone in the world as the United States does, or whether it should adopt the German model to fully integrate itself into Asia is a strategic issue that China must consider when formulating policy on the internationalization or regionalization of the RMB (Gao and Yu 2010). In other words, will the RMB be or become an independent international currency parallel to the U.S. dollar and the euro, or will it be or become fully integrated with other Asian currencies as part of a new Asian dollar?

The U.S. dollar and the euro are two of the most successful cases of currency internationalization since the end of World War II. However, the internationalization paths of these two currencies are quite different, and we can roughly classify them under two models: the German model and the U.S. model. The German model is a two-step process: Germany first joined a regional monetary arrangement, that is, the well-known European currency unit (ECU), and then created a new single regional currency to replace the currencies of all member states. Since this model would eliminate all participating currencies, with this model, China should first join a fully guaranteed Asian monetary union and the Yuan would become self-extinguishing and eventually be replaced by a new Asian single currency. Since this model will eliminate the currencies of all participating countries, with this model, China should first join a fully guaranteed Asian monetary union, and the RMB will die out on its own, and eventually be replaced by a new single Asian currency. The German model is to give up sovereign currencies as a compromise and rely on a high degree of regional integration to gain a place in the global financial order in the form of a monetary union.

The U.S. model, on the other hand, is a model of currency internationalization in which the U.S. dollar seeks to play a leading role alone in the world. This model requires the currency-issuing country to have sufficient economic, political and military power on a global scale. Adopting the U.S. model could make the RMB a completely independent international currency parallel to the U.S. dollar, euro or Japanese yen.

It is too early to decide which model is more suitable for China. But the current financial crisis has forced China to assume greater financial responsibility in Asia and the world, and it is more urgent than ever for China to do so. Due to concerns about potential losses on China's foreign exchange assets and in order to avoid exchange rate risks, China's monetary authorities are now taking a more positive attitude towards the internationalization of the RMB. In this context, the internationalization of the RMB, the reform of the international financial system, and regional financial cooperation are being put on China's policy agenda.

The current international monetary system is characterized by the dominance of the U.S. dollar as an international reserve currency and the de facto U.S. dollar standard. This system allows the United States to run a current account deficit. The United States is now the world's largest debtor. Because U.S. debt is denominated in U.S. dollars, foreign countries have no way to punish the U.S. monetary authorities. If the U.S.

government wishes to dilute its debt, it can easily do so by creating inflation, which would mean capital losses for holders of dollar-denominated assets worldwide. In this context, China proposed to reform the international monetary and financial system. Zhou Xiaochuan, former governor of the People's Bank of China, has called for the creation of a super-sovereign currency, but reform of the international monetary system is easier said than done. The United States will never relinquish the dollar's prerogative as an unassailable reserve currency. One thing that is clear: China's fortunes would be much better if the RMB were to become an international currency and if the majority of China's holdings of U.S. debt were denominated in RMB.

The goal of the internationalization of the RMB is to solve the problem of mismatch and incongruity between the RMB's status in the international monetary system and the status of China's economy in the world economy by establishing a sound mechanism for circulating the RMB in international payment, investment and financing, and capital markets, and to create an international currency that is commensurate with China's economic strength, so that the RMB can have a place in the international monetary arena. Taking into account the lessons learned from the internationalization of other currencies, China's macroeconomic situation and the development of financial markets, we believe that the internationalization of the RMB should be carried out in 10–15 years, i.e. from 2025 to 2030, under the principle of controlled risk and gradual advancement, so that the RMB can become the dominant currency in the Asia and the third largest reserve currency in the world after the U.S. dollar and the euro.

In a situation where the RMB is still not fully convertible and China is still running a trade surplus, in order to smoothly advance the internationalization of the RMB, we should continue to steadily expand the RMB's trade settlement function, prioritize the development of the Asian market, and strive to make the RMB an invoicing currency for commodities. Subject to limited capital account liberalization, we should expand outbound investment, deepen the development of offshore RMB centers, actively carry out international cooperation, and expand cooperation with relevant countries and international organizations such as the IMF in currency swaps and special drawing rights (SDRs).

In addition, given that the international community cannot find a currency that can replace the U.S. dollar for the time being in the reform of the international monetary system, supporting the expanded role of

SDRs and actively pursuing the inclusion of the RMB as an SDR basket currency is conducive not only to breaking the monopoly of the U.S. dollar in the international monetary system, but also to enhancing the status of the RMB in international financial markets, which is in line with China's interests. With the rapid development of China's economy in recent years, the RMB officially joined the SDR (Special Drawing Rights) basket on October 1, 2016. On August 1, 2022, the International Monetary Fund (IMF) officially raised the weighting of the RMB in the SDR currency basket from 10.92% to 12.28%. Considering the political and economic influence of China, the RMB's share in the SDR basket should be further raised, so as to deepen the internationalization of the RMB.

References

Bo. Review of Several Major Decisions and Events (Part I), Beijing: Central Party School Press, 1993, pp. 255– 256.

China Statistical Yearbook 1984, China Statistics Press, 1984, p. 81.

Editorial Committee on Party Literature of the CPC Central Committee, Selected Works of Chen Yun, Vol. 2, Beijing, People's Publishing House, 1995, p. 208.

Eijffinger Sylvester C W. European Monetary and Fiscal Policy (translated by Xiang Yu), Beijing, China Renmin University Press, 2003.

Fu and Yu. 30 Years of Urban Economic Development and Institutional Reform in China. China Urban Economy, 2009, (1).

Gao and Yu. The Implications and Conditions of RMB Internationalization. International Economic Review, 2010, (1).

General Office of the People's Bank of China, Selected Documents on Financial Policies and Regulations, Beijing, China Financial Publishing House, 2008.

Hu and Chen. The Development and Changes of China's Banking Industry Over the Past Thirty Years of Reform and Opening-Up, China Finance No. 17, 2008.

Jin. The Thinking Behind and Focus of China's Commercial Banking System Reform—An Interview with Professor Liu Hongru, Zhejiang Finance, No. 01, 1998.

John Gordon. An Empire of Wealth (translated by Dong Yikun), Beijing, CITIC Press, 2007 edition, pp. 208–211.

Justin Yifu Lin, Cai Fang, and Li Zhou. China's Miracle: Development Strategy and Economic Reform, Shanghai, Shanghai Sanlian Bookstore and Shanghai People's Publishing House, 1994.

Li. Economic Development Strategy, Beijing, Intellectual Property Publishing House, 2009.

Liu. Strategies and Measures for China's "Strategic Opportunity Period". Study Times, Central Party School, December 31, 2010, Page 4: Economist Column.

Lu. Learning, Path Dependence and Latecomer Disadvantages: The Adjustment of China's Economic Development Strategy, Economic Review, No. 01, 2003.

National People's Congress, A Securities Market That Matches China's Status as a Great Power Must be Established, Caijing.com.cn, December 30, 2014. http://www.ctjin.com/ziben/caijing/pinglun/2014-12-30/57347.html.

Shi. On the Benefits of and Risk Prevention for RMB Internationalization, China Economic & Trade Herald, December 2012.

Tong and Cheng. Research on the Regionalization and Internationalization of the Euro, Nankai Economic Studies, No. 6, 2001.

Wu. A Study on Special Drawing Rights as a Super-sovereign Reserve Currency, Financial Development Review, No. 4, 2010a.

Wu. Reform of the International Reserve System and SDR Substitution Account: Literature Review, Financial Development Review, No. 6, 2010b.

Xia. The Experience of Currency Internationalization in the United States, Japan and Germany, China Entrepreneur, No. 8, 2012.

Xinhua News Agency, The Third Plenary Session of the Eleventh Central Committee of the Communist Party of China (1978), http://news.xinhuanet.com/ziliao/2003-01/20/content_697755.htm.

Xu and Wang. The Development of and Challenges to the Influence of the Euro in the Past Decade. Financial Perspectives Journal, No. 1, 2009.

Xu. The Experience of the Internationalization of the Japanese Yen and Its Implications for the RMB, Financial Review, No. 4, 2010.

Yin and Cui. Dollar Hegemony: Survival Foundation, Survival Influence and Survival Conflict, Studies of International Finance, No. 12, 2009.

Zhang. Examining the Growing "Center-Periphery" Pattern of Modern Capitalism from a Global Perspective, People's Forum, No. 3, 1998.

Zhang. Seek a Fundamental Breakthrough in the Strategic Transformation of the Economy, xinhuanet.com, November 10, 2014, http://news.xinhuanet.com/fortune/2014-11/10/c_127195384.htm.

Zhi K. New Advances in Research on Modern Chinese Economic History. Contemporary China History Studies, 2002, (2): 96–102.

Zhou. Innovative Monetary Tools—Enhance Fiscal and Monetary Policy Coordination, People's Daily, November 25, 2015.

CHAPTER 11

China's Economic Adjustment and Rebalancing: Challenges and Strategies

Over the past 40-plus years of reform and opening up, while China has made great achievements, the changes that have taken place are also changing the rules of the world. How to skillfully follow and adapt to such changes and achieve a new balance challenges not only the wisdom of China, but also the wisdom of major countries in the world. The new era of socialism with Chinese characteristics and the 14th Five-Year Plan period are an important period of strategic opportunity for the development of China's open economy. How to grasp this rare period of strategic opportunity? An in-depth and thorough analysis in the light of the current global situation will help us make a comprehensive and accurate judgment of the current economic situation, and is also of great significance for formulating the right response measures.

The current situation in China in the aftermath of the economic crisis. The international financial crisis has slowed down China's real economy, greatly reduced foreign demand and made exporting difficult. The adjustment period may be quite long. Nevertheless, the fundamentals of the Chinese economy remain sound and the trend of growth has not changed. Moreover, liquidity in China is now very abundant compared with other markets, including developed countries. These are all signs of China's economic recovery. China is facing export pressure, but because China's economy is large and in the stage of development, it is entirely possible to maintain a relatively stable growth of the Chinese economy

L. Weiping, *American Monetary Policy Adjustment and Its Impacts*,
https://doi.org/10.1007/978-981-99-7810-6_11

through consumption stimulation, proactive fiscal policy, and moderately accommodative monetary policy (Liu 2018).

The direction of economic reform. China's potential is more geared towards increasing domestic demand than increasing exports. In the next 40–50 years, China will need to invest in many areas to expand the pace of urbanization, and it will also move more towards an urban economy that is more environmentally friendly and efficient. In addition to the 4 trillion yuan investment plan in 2008, China needs a longer-term, higher-level public investment. Therefore, China needs a better strategy for financing public spending.

Improve capital markets. In the context of the economic crisis, the ability to use the SOE dividend system to build the social security system, to further increase social security efforts, to reform the price formation mechanism of resource factors and to further improve capital markets is the key to the sustainable development of China's economy. However, we need to realize that any adjustment at the institutional level must be based on China's national conditions and basic realities. This predestines the transformation of China's economy to be a gradual process.

1 Insights from China's Economic Adjustment and Rebalancing Strategy

The general thinking behind China's strategy for participating in global economic rebalancing. The global economy has been operating in a state of continuous imbalance for more than 40 years. The East Asian financial crisis, the U.S. subprime mortgage crisis, and the global financial tsunami caused by them during this period were all the results of asymmetric shocks to the unbalanced world economy. Global economic imbalances are manifested principally as the buildup of a massive U.S. current-account deficit and the continued growth of current-account surpluses in emerging East Asian economies such as China and oil-producing countries. External current-account imbalances are caused by imbalances in the internal economic structure on both sides of the imbalance and formed under the influence of the inherent international economic system. In the cyclical mechanism of global economic imbalances, the United States and others provide consumer demand, while East Asian countries and oil-producing countries are responsible for production and supply. This mechanism is highly unstable. Once developed countries such as the United States encounter a crisis and fail to provide sufficient consumer demand, the entire world economy will be struggling, and countries with a trade surplus such as China, being in a completely passive position, will not enjoy the growth dividends corresponding to the amount of their reserve assets, but will be on the receiving end of the consequences of the crisis.

Therefore, global economic rebalancing is on the surface to achieve an external balance of payments on current account, but in essence to optimize, adjust and balance the internal consumption, saving and investment structures of developed and emerging economies.

New trends in global economic rebalancing in the post-financial crisis era. Under the influence of the international financial crisis, global economic imbalances have been temporarily adjusted. While there has been no fundamental change in the cyclical mechanism that creates imbalances, there have been some new trends in global economic rebalancing.

The goal of economic rebalancing has been expanded from mere trade rebalancing to balanced development among countries. The spread of the international financial crisis across the globe shows that global economic imbalances are not only trade imbalances, but also global imbalances in finance, investment and other areas. At the Paris summit after the outbreak of the crisis, the G20 put forward imbalance assessment indicators including public debt, fiscal deficits, personal saving rates and trade accounts, extending the adjustment indicators of global economic rebalancing from trade to multiple areas.

The G20 has become the most prominent imbalance governance mechanism in the world, and emerging economies have gained a greater say in global economic governance. The G20 not only enables more equal dialogue between developed and emerging economies, but also provides a better platform for coordination and dialogue on differences and discrepancies among the 11 emerging economies within the G20, and provides more opportunities for G20 members to engage with institutions such as the IMF and World Bank under the Bretton Woods system. Through the G20, emerging economies, China in particular, have successfully achieved reform of IMF voting shares.

International economic and trade conflicts in the name of global economic rebalancing will increase. Developed countries such as the United States, which are deeply affected by the financial crisis, will ask emerging economies, the BRICS countries in particular, to take up more global economic governance obligations, thus implementing new trade protection in the name of global economic rebalancing. As a result, global trade protectionism may rise again and international economic and trade conflicts will continue to increase. In addition, the "re-industrialization" of developed countries may also have further impacts on the international economic and trade landscape and rebalancing.

China's overall strategy for participating in global economic rebalancing. After more than 40 years of reform and opening-up, China has become a major economic power in the world, deeply integrated into the global economic system, and its influence and radiation on the world economy have been growing. Meanwhile, as one of the countries with the highest trade surplus, China is an important force in global economic rebalancing, both in terms of its own economic development and in terms of its image as a responsible power. Due to the impact of the financial crisis, the U.S. economic recovery is weak, so the United States will exert great pressure on China in various aspects, bringing new challenges and tests to China-U.S. economic and trade relations.

Therefore, when devising a strategy for participating in global economic rebalancing, China must follow the principles of taking China as the main player, giving consideration to both internal and external issues, actively participating, and achieving mutual benefit and win-win results. China, as a large developing country, one of the countries with the highest trade surplus, and a country which is faring well economically, is under a lot of pressure from the international community when participating in global economic rebalancing. However, as a developing country, China still faces many problems in its own economic development. Global economic imbalances are neither primarily caused by China, nor can they be resolved solely through China's adjustments. Therefore, we must remain self-centered, grasp the direction, speed and extent of rebalancing, shoulder our responsibilities to the best of our ability, and safeguard national economic security and interests.

The strategic goal of China's participation in global economic rebalancing should not stop at achieving a relative balance of payments, but should focus on the following aspects. First, by adjusting the unbalanced internal and external economic structure, we will transform the economy driven by investment and exports into one driven by consumption and the economy driven by resource input into one driven by innovation, so as to provide new impetus for China's sustainable economic growth. Second, by taking an active part in the G20-led global economic rebalancing, we will leverage the unique role of China as a large developing country, safeguard the interests of China and other developing countries, enhance China's voice and participation in global economic governance, and improve China's international standing. Third, by creating consumer demand, we will gradually achieve a balance between imports and exports, achieve mutual benefit and win-win results for economic and trade partners, and create a more favorable external environment for China's economic development.

The internal and external paths of China's participation in global economic rebalancing. China's participation in global economic rebalancing must be both internal and external. The internal path focuses on restructuring, while the external path focuses on coordinating relations. Only by pursuing development in the context of a closer relationship with the rest of the world can China truly solve the structural problems plaguing its sustainable economic development in a relatively relaxed external environment, so as to achieve true rebalancing.

In terms of the internal path, first, stimulate domestic private consumption and balance savings and investment through equalization of opportunities and income. Constrained by preventive motives arising from uncertainties concerning elderly care, health care, housing, and children's education and traditional ideas about consumption, private consumption remains weak in China. Existing policies promote the equalization of income distribution mainly through the government's secondary distribution of income and the building of a social safety net, but ignore the impact of equalization of opportunities on the primary distribution of income. Therefore, on the basis of policies such as continuing to improve the social safety net and increasing farmers' real income, we should strengthen the equalization of opportunities in education, employment, entrepreneurship and public services, steadily push forward the collection of inheritance tax and gift tax, and appropriately reduce the actual tax burden of the people in due course.

Second, strengthen the market competition mechanism, speed up the building of an innovative country, upgrade the value chain, and reduce the level of "pass-through" surpluses. A considerable portion of China's current account surplus is attributable to the "pass-through" export of final processed and assembled goods brought about by other countries' direct investment in China. This reflects the position of China's current resource endowment and comparative advantage in the international division of labor. Under the current international division of labor system, China should pay more attention to the upgrading of the value chain, so as to truly improve the quality of economic growth. The key to achieving this goal remains the improvement of innovation capacity and technology. Only by further strengthening the market competition mechanism can we create the soil necessary for innovation as a commercial activity, which is more important than increasing government investment in R&D.

Third, improve the efficiency of the virtual economy and optimize the structure of the real and virtual economies. As finance is the core of resource allocation in a modern economy, China should move faster to deepen reform of the banking market, strengthen the building of capital market institutions and supervision, and improve the efficiency of finance in allocating resources for the real economy. The development of the virtual economy is conducive to keeping the current account surplus for domestic use, promoting enterprises' innovation activities, and stimulating internal private consumption, and is one of the keys to rebalancing China's economy.

In terms of the external path, first, promote the institutionalization of the G20 international coordination mechanism. The G20 is more broadly representative than the G8, as the recovery in Europe, the U.S. and Japan falters, the more dynamic emerging economies are set to have a bigger say than ever in rebalancing the global economy. China needs to join hands with the BRICS and other emerging economies to promote the institutionalization of the G20 mechanism, strengthen the coordination of domestic and international policies with developed economies, and promote global economic rebalancing.

Second, strengthen bilateral coordination with the United States, Japan and Europe, and develop economic and trade relations with developing countries in Asia, Africa and Latin America. The coordination of China-U.S. economic and trade relations is the most important part. If China and the United States, as the most important surplus and deficit sides of the imbalance, can truly rebalance their economic structures, then global rebalancing will come naturally. This requires the two major powers to coordinate their domestic and international policies while pursuing their domestic economic goals. In addition, in order to enhance the stability of economic operation and reduce the concentration of imbalances, China should gradually change its high dependence on European and U.S. markets and diversify its export markets. Meanwhile, we should continue to expand imports, provide new export markets for other countries, strengthen their adhesion to the Chinese economy, share the fruits of China's economic growth, diminish the "China threat" theory, and achieve mutual benefit and win-win results.

Third, actively participate in the reform of the international monetary system and steadily advance the internationalization of the RMB. The dollar-dominated international monetary system established by the strong economic and financial power of the United States is one of the major causes of global economic imbalances. Therefore, reforming the dollar-dominated international monetary system is an important condition for multiple parties to actively participate in global economic rebalancing. The internationalization of the RMB is a prerequisite for enhancing China's position in the future international monetary system, but the internationalization of the RMB should be a gradual, steady and controllable process. As the process towards a freely convertible RMB accelerates, there is an urgent need for the Chinese government and Chinese enterprises to improve their risk management capabilities under a floating exchange rate regime.

2 Challenges to China's Economic Adjustment and Rebalancing Strategy

After the international financial crisis, the global financial landscape has not changed fundamentally on the whole, but shocked by the crisis, the financial sectors of various countries have made corresponding adjustments in reflection, which has caused some new changes in the global financial landscape. How to further develop China's financial sector in this evolving financial environment and how to avoid the occurrence of crisis as much as possible in its development so as to better serve the real economy are important issues that must be faced after the crisis. The timely response measures taken by the Chinese government enabled the economy to achieve a V-shaped reversal and maintain a relatively high growth rate, which helped support the two-speed recovery of the global economy. Nevertheless, the sovereign debt crisis in some European countries and developed countries may lead the global economy to a second recession. At the same time, fundamental problems that constrain China's economic development, such as insufficient consumer demand and unreasonable economic structure, can hardly be solved in a short period of time. The Chinese economy is facing multiple challenges at home and abroad.

Rising inflation and declining economic growth are increasing the risk of "economic stagflation". After the outbreak of the global financial crisis, faced with plummeting foreign demand, the Chinese government decisively implemented expansionary policies to stimulate domestic demand. At the end of 2008, the central government decided to invest 4 trillion yuan to stimulate domestic investment. In 2009, the total money supply reached 13.5 trillion yuan, an increase of 28.42%. Thanks to the strong stimulus from expansionary fiscal and monetary policies, the task of "maintaining an 8 percent" economic growth in 2008 was accomplished and the GDP growth rate reached 8.7% in 2009. However, in an international environment where interest rates are generally low worldwide and two rounds of quantitative easing have been completed in the United States, China's expansionary macroeconomic policies have led to rising inflation levels.

On the one hand, economic recession and trade protection in Europe and the United States have worsened China's export environment. China's GDP growth is strongly dependent on the trade surplus, and Europe and the United States are China's most important export markets, so changes in the external economic environment have greatly constrained the development of the domestic economy. On the other hand, the unreasonable economic structure weakens the effect of policies, and at the same time, the effect of economic stimulus policies is getting weaker and weaker, the space for further stimulus measures is getting smaller and smaller, private investment has not been fully mobilized, small and medium-sized enterprises have difficulty getting financing, and the tightening of monetary policy to reduce inflation has further increased the burden on enterprises, and economic growth is likely to slow down. In addition, China's economy is overly dependent on exports, and exports are mainly labor-intensive and low value-added products. With rising labor costs and the opening up of countries such as Vietnam, relying on export dominance to promote economic growth will not be sustainable.

Many economists believe that the phenomenon of "stagflation" that appeared in developed Western countries in the 1970s was mostly the result of the implementation of demand management policies. According to Keynes' theory, a combination of proactive fiscal policy and expansionary monetary policy in response to the crisis can increase effective demand in the national economy and thus promote the growth of the national economy. However, inflation occurs when too much money is chasing too few goods. In order to reduce inflation, the authorities often pursue a tight policy. The tightening of monetary policy raises interest rates, thereby increasing the cost of production for enterprises and thus the cost of running the economy as a whole, resulting in a decline in economic growth and "stagflation". The United States experienced "stagflation" from 1970 to 1983, when economic growth was high but inflation was also high, resulting in zero or negative real growth.

At present, if China cannot effectively manage inflation expectations, curb rising inflation and remove adverse factors leading to slowing economic growth, it may see "stagflation". The Chinese economy is at a critical stage of development, and we must be vigilant against the risk of "stagflation" that may arise from rising inflation and declining economic growth.

Changes in the international division of labor system and rising corporate costs have brought the pressure of rebuilding competitive advantages in industries. The re-industrialization of developed countries, the rising costs of Chinese enterprises, and the advantages of low costs and a young population that are becoming increasingly apparent in India and other countries make it necessary to upgrade China's industrial technology in order to maintain its advantages.

China is in a relatively low position in the international division of labor system, and its technological innovation capacity is insufficient. Changes in the international division of labor system and their interactions with each other will have a great impact on China's existing export-oriented mode of economic development. Not only that, Chinese enterprises are also facing the challenge of rising costs. Corporate costs rose sharply after the financial crisis. First, the rise in commodity prices has raised costs for enterprises. U.S. quantitative easing policy has led to a continuous depreciation of the U.S. dollar, resulting in a rapid rise in global commodity prices in U.S. dollar terms. Coupled with the continuous appreciation of the RMB against the U.S. dollar, the prices of these commodities, when converted to RMB, have risen even more, which has a greater impact on exporters. Secondly, developed countries' design for carbon emissions has put China under huge pressure to reduce emissions, and energy conservation and emission reduction by enterprises have also fueled the rise in corporate costs.

In the face of changes in the international division of labor system and the trend of rising costs, Chinese enterprises are facing unprecedented challenges to their competitiveness and need to build new competitive advantages.

The Chinese economy is facing new tests in coping with climate change and pursuing low-carbon development. In order to cope with climate change, the development of a low-carbon economy has become a global consensus, which poses great challenges to China's existing development mode. China's coal-based energy consumption structure is difficult to adjust, and more technology and capital inputs will be needed in the transition to a low-carbon development mode. China's industrialization, new-type urbanization and modernization are still in a stage of rapid development, a period of rapid growth in demand for conventional energy, which will inevitably lead to high greenhouse gas emissions. International pressure to cut emissions on the one hand, and the inherent requirements of domestic development on the other, put China in a dilemma. Therefore, China will face great challenges in developing low-carbon economy.

For a developing country like China, the development of a low-carbon economy will have a great impact on the existing production structure, consumption structure and foreign trade structure, and directly affect the smooth transformation of the economy in the post-crisis period. First, according to developed countries' current design for "carbon tariffs", China's previous advantages of cheap labor and low prices will no longer exist, while the prices of industrial products in developed countries will decline relatively, and their technological lead will be even more pronounced. Second, the power to set standards for advanced technologies has always been in the hands of developed countries, and in the general trend of low-carbon economic development, developed countries will undoubtedly use their technological advantages to set standards that serve their own interests. Third, the burden of emission reduction is heavy. Due to China's limited overall technology research and development capacity and technological backwardness, the equipment and technology needed to develop a low-carbon economy need to be imported, which is an economic burden for China. Fourth, China is constrained by emission reduction responsibility. Emission reduction is a global consensus, and for China, it is both a commitment and a responsibility. While China is transforming its mode of economic growth and restructuring its economy, the limited global budget space for carbon emissions will make China take on too many international obligations such as emission reduction at a time when it is under enormous pressure to develop at home. Developed countries have also put forward unrealistic carbon emission requirements for China, which is bound to put a lot of pressure on China.

The intensification of the global sovereign debt crisis will also have a negative impact on the Chinese economy. Since the outbreak of the Greek crisis, Belgium, Portugal and Spain have been running deficits, resulting in a full-blown European sovereign debt crisis. In fact, globally, developed countries, including the United States, are generally facing high levels of sovereign debt. The problems with China's monetary policy platform cannot be ignored, and if not properly handled, they are likely to develop into a global public debt crisis.

It is conceivable that the intensifying European debt crisis will eventually affect the entire European economy, and the Chinese economy will certainly also be affected. This shock is mainly reflected in two aspects: exports and hot money inflows. From an export perspective, the first to be affected are companies that rely heavily on exports to the euro area. With the deepening of the global financial crisis, European demand for imports is bound to decline, and trade protectionism against China will rise again in the euro area. In addition, as the dollar continues to move higher against the euro, there will be a rebound in the effective exchange rate of the RMB on the basis of the RMB keeping appropriating against the dollar, which will eventually be detrimental to exports.

The scale of foreign exchange reserves has grown tremendously, and the management system is in urgent need of reform and innovation. In the 17 years from the reform of the foreign exchange system in 1994 to 2001, China's foreign exchange reserves rose from $51.62 billion to $3,044.674 billion, an increase of nearly 58 times, with an average growth rate of 35.98%. Especially in recent years, with expectations of a stronger RMB running high, the balance of payments has shifted from a traditional current account surplus to a "double surplus" in the current account and the capital and financial account, and the inflow of hot money has further contributed to the expansion of reserves. Such huge foreign exchange reserves make management even more difficult in the post-financial crisis period. The current state of investment of China's reserve assets poses a huge challenge to the management of stock assets.

Commodity prices fluctuate sharply, increasing uncertainty in economic development. After the international financial crisis, commodity prices fell by nearly 40% from their all-time highs in April 2008, but by September 2010, they had roughly recovered to their 2008 levels. Since then, commodity prices have been on an upward trend. China is the processing center in the global industrial structure. Processing trade in which China relies on international markets for raw materials and sales accounts for a relatively large share of the overall trade structure, making China one of the world's top importers of energy and primary products. Fluctuations in international commodity markets will have a more obvious and significant impact on China's economy. At present, there is still an excess of international liquidity. Meanwhile, amid the sustained recovery of the world economy and a short supply of commodities, prices of international commodities have been high, bringing enormous pressure on China's economic development.

First, imported inflationary pressure in China will intensify. As energy expenditures such as oil and food expenditures account for a larger share of China's economic operation, fluctuations in international commodity markets have a more pronounced impact on China. Prices in international markets are transmitted to the domestic market through international trade, raising the domestic price level and leading to increased imported inflationary pressure. Moreover, as China's economic prospects are good in the long run, its demand for commodities will be stronger, and it will inevitably face imported inflation.

Second, there is the risk of "second-round effects". Higher prices of commodities such as food and energy will push up the consumer price index, adding to inflation expectations. In theory, as long as commodity prices fall, rising inflation will return to rational levels. However, due to increased inflation expectations, employees will demand higher wages to maintain their purchasing power, and enterprises will have to raise the prices of their products and services due to rising costs. Therefore, as long as expectations about inflation take hold, enterprises and employees will be caught in a vicious cycle of price increases, and even if commodity prices fall, it will be of no help. This is known as the "second-round effects" and is also the potential danger that China now faces.

Third, the export trade situation is grim. Due to a chronic shortage of domestic demand in China, economic development is highly dependent on export trade, and passing on production costs by hiking prices is not an option. As a result, the profit margin for enterprises is squeezed and the export trade is greatly affected, which to a certain extent will cause fluctuations in the Chinese economy.

A large amount of hot money flows in and out, affecting the smooth operation of the market. In the aftermath of the financial crisis, as hot money flows can easily cause economic bubbles, financial risks have increased. As a result, China's current real estate bubble has emerged, making government regulation more difficult. Once the international environment changes, the sudden withdrawal of hot money will make the bubble burst quickly, causing serious market turmoil, and the blow to China's economy will be fatal. The more hot money flows into China, the more foreign exchange reserves there are, forcing the central bank to passively increase the supply of money. If hot money keeps pouring in, the demand for RMB will rise, which will eventually increase the upward pressure on RMB, and the continued strengthening of the RMB will attract international hot money, thus causing a vicious circle and dampening the effect of macro-control. Hot money flows disrupt the financial order and impact economic development. After the financial crisis, China's economy took the lead in recovery, and its good development prospects attracted an influx of hot money. In recent years, hot money has entered China in various ways, speculating around for high profits, mainly in areas such as the domestic real estate market and stock market, posing a threat to the healthy development of the economy. Moreover, hot money can be seen everywhere in commodity markets, which further fuels a strong rise in commodity prices, increasing production costs for Chinese companies and hurting China's economy.

3 China's Economic Adjustment and Rebalancing Strategy

Challenges: resources, environment, and coordinated social and economic development. At present, three issues need to be resolved urgently for China's economic development: first, coordinate urban-rural and regional development and change the urban-rural dual system; second, change the mode of economic development and upgrade and transform economic structure; third, address the three major challenges of "resources", "environment" and "coordinated social and economic development" in the process of internationalization. Meanwhile, China also faces three major challenges in its economic development: uneven economic development, energy and environmental bottlenecks, and the widening gap between the rich and the poor. Without a large net transfer of capital from rich to poor regions, there will be huge disparities in the distribution of financial resources between regions. The imbalance between economic and social development, and structural imbalances within society and within the economy have become the unique background of China's reform and development.

Although China has entered the mid-term stage of industrialization, it is still a developing country with half of its labor force engaged in agricultural production. The task of industrialization is far from complete. On the one hand, according to national development strategies and macroeconomic policies, there are still a large number of key areas and weak links that need financing; on the other hand, at the important stage of transforming the mode of economic development and restructuring the economy, a prominent issue that we need to solve is how to transform low value-added products that require a lot of energy to produce into high value-added products that require little energy to produce.

In 2020, China's urbanization rate just exceeded 60%, which is still far behind the average level of around 80% in developed countries. It is this gap and pressure that determines the huge space for China's urbanization development, and also determines the needs of China's urbanization and industrial upgrading, transformation and development in the coming decades or even centuries, and will be a driving force for stable economic growth in China and beyond. At the international level, China has entered a new stage of development and is facing new development opportunities in implementing the Go Out policy. Meanwhile, China also needs to participate in international cooperation through various channels, and in the process become familiar with international rules and seek and control its development space. On the one hand, we need to go to international markets to "tap" resources for the country's development; on the other hand, while promoting global GDP growth, as a responsible major country, China needs to effect a paradigm shift from the concept of "tap" to the concept of "develop", and export the whole set of sustainable development plans to the countries it invests in, so as to promote the transformation of the mode of economic development and the balanced and coordinated development of society.

Specifically, as long as China continues to grow, the market will continue to work for China. When China becomes a major power integrating energy, resources, population, capital, and technology around the world, these factors of production will inevitably begin to be highly mobile. This will change the rankings of countries that are associated with China economically and politically in the world economy, and changes in the rankings of countries will eventually lead to a change in the entire international political and economic order. At the macro institution level, China's drive for globalization will be a process of significant change in the international financial and trade order, and as convertibility gradually increases globally, the RMB will certainly develop into one of the major currencies of the world in the future. At the micro market supply and demand level, China's basic industries such as energy, raw materials and transportation will be the next breakthrough point of reform. But the pace of reform of basic industries has been slow, and monopolistic practices are rampant, leading to inefficient operation of the economy. The reform of basic industries will unleash the potential for future economic growth.

Act fast: shift to comprehensive planning for economic and social development. As early as the end of the twentieth century, China put forward the slogan of boosting domestic demand, but why domestic demand is shrinking? A high level of income polarization and the excessive marketization of education, social security and housing are no doubt two of the main reasons, but people have not noticed that the export-oriented model of economic development and foreign direct investment, which are closely related to the international circular economy development strategy, are another main reason, and the international circular economy development strategy is one of the important factors that cause a high level of income polarization. In the era of globalization, China's mode of economic development is marked by its status as the world's factory. China participates in the global division of production based on its comparative advantage of cheap labor, and expands its exports through the vigorous absorption of efficiency-driven foreign direct investment, as well as trade between multinational corporations. China imports and exports energy, resources and products on a large scale, and drives domestic economic growth through exports. China has been relying on processing trade to develop its economy and on the division of labor at the lower end of the global production chain to participate in the entire globalization process. In fact, more than 70% of China's current GDP is related to trade, and multinational corporations account for nearly 60% of China's foreign trade, both in imports and exports.

From a domestic point of view, in order to speed up the transformation of the mode of economic development, China should make strategic planning as soon as possible, learn from the historical experience of the United Kingdom and the United States, and gradually realize the strategic transition from "international circulation" to "domestic circulation". We must be soberly aware that contrary to the original intention of the international circular economy development strategy, "importing and exporting on a large scale", instead of resolving the contradiction between the coastal and inland areas, has led to the siphoning of capital, resources and labor to the export-oriented sectors of the coastal areas, creating a distorted "dual economy" divided between external and domestic demand, which is the main reason why domestic demand has not been able to start for a long time, the investment opportunities of national enterprises have been crowded out by foreign capital, and serious economic bubbles have occurred. Instead of bridging the circular relationship between agriculture and heavy industry, this strategy has created a situation where there is an overcapacity of low-end products and high-end technologies are still monopolized by multinational companies in heavy industry, and has become the main cause of the lack of a way out for higher education, a serious delay in urbanization development, an impasse on the "three rural issues", and worsening unemployment. In the author's opinion, China should make a strategic shift from "comparative advantage" to "competitive advantage" and from "science" to "ideology" in its future development philosophy for the world economy and global governance, and with this end in view, develop strategies and methods that are in line with China's national conditions and the needs of participating in global governance. This is a major issue for the development of medium- and long-term investment and financing brought forward by the current social system crisis.

However, from an international perspective, the transnational planning of Chinese investment in Africa may need to go further, from development finance to comprehensive economic and social development planning. The recent political turmoil in the Middle East and North Africa, especially China's investment experience in Libya and Sudan, shows that only helping capital-importing countries achieve economic growth does not solve a series of political and social problems arising from economic growth in these countries. These development plans must also incorporate indicators for social development. Only if economic growth is accompanied by a solution to the distribution problem, ensuring that the fruits of growth are shared by all social groups, can we expect political stability in these countries and thus reduce the risks of Chinese investment. But this problem is precisely the problem that China has not been able to solve well at home. The need for future Chinese investment in Africa in turn requires that China must first address its own social problems in the development process.

Set a reform agenda that goes beyond the economy: investment and aid. An analysis of the international economic situation shows that the goal of economic rebalancing has been expanded from mere trade rebalancing to balanced development among countries. As developing countries have similar starting conditions and world political status, China's economic and social development is inherently complementary to and consistent with that of Asian, African and Latin American countries. Because the future long-term growth of the Chinese economy inherently contains elements of development of Asian, African and Latin American countries, the ability of Asian, African and Latin American countries to achieve their own development is closely related to the development of the Chinese economy, and even must rely on the development of the Chinese economy.

Aid to and investment in Asia, Africa and Latin America can be divided into two categories: "social infrastructure development" and "economic infrastructure development". EU countries focus on "social infrastructure development", while the main direction of forward planning for China's development finance is to invest in "economic infrastructure development" in Africa. "Social infrastructure development", which does not have the "blood-making" function, is "non-quantifiable and non-material", "project oriented", and "unplannable". Therefore, EU aid to African countries cannot be planned in a country-specific and transnational sense; whereas "economic infrastructure development", which has the "blood-making" function, is "quantifiable and material", "structured overall", and "plannable". In this process, the EU is just an international NGO. It is impossible for the EU to act like a national development bank and use national financial behavior to encourage enterprises to "go out" and make investment in a forward country-specific and transnational planning manner based on the needs of national development strategies. This win-win model of "forward planning", which "teaches people how to fish", is increasingly welcomed by many African countries and Chinese enterprises that are "going out".

Meanwhile, China's development finance institutions will carry out large-scale investment and aid in Asia, Africa and Latin America, i.e. "economic infrastructure development" and "social infrastructure development" together. However, the crux of the matter is how development finance institutions that are backed by state credit such as the China Development Bank compare with international organizations that are not backed by state credit such as the World Bank and the European Union, and how will we integrate "investment" with "aid". These two questions need to be answered simultaneously. Therefore, we should set a reform agenda that goes beyond the economy and includes important elements of investment and aid in national development strategies. Meanwhile, China should continue to expand imports, provide new export markets for other countries, strengthen their adhesion to the Chinese economy, share the fruits of China's economic growth, diminish the "China threat" theory, and achieve mutual benefit and win-win results, so as to gradually change the dual political and economic structure that appeared in international economic and trade cooperation, especially in the process of investing in Asia, Africa and Latin America.

Demonstrate confidence and determination in reform: promote westward opening-up under the Belt and Road Initiative and advance the Eurasian strategy. The Chinese economy is in a critical period of shifting to a new growth phase and seeking a new balance. The shift to a new growth phase is essentially the shift to new growth drivers, a process in which the original competitive advantages are gradually weakened and new competitive advantages are gradually formed, as well as a process in which the original balance is broken and a new balance needs to be found and established. The economy as a whole is fragile. In this strategic context, the development goal of "accelerating the transformation of the mode of economic development and promoting long-term stable and rapid economic development, with restructuring the economy as the major goal and expanding domestic demand as the strategic focus" put forward by the central government will surely become an important strategy for transitioning from the traditional development mode to a comprehensive plan for economic and social development in an effort to seek economic growth drivers and rebalancing, and is also a demonstration of China's confidence and determination in reform and development to the world.

In the next decade, few decades or even longer, in the important strategic process of economic transformation and development and expansion of domestic demand, to develop industrialization, urbanization, modernization and internationalization, we must harness complementarity between the blue ocean strategy, the land power strategy, the Eurasian economic integration strategy, and opening up westward. In particular, the development of the western region and the use of high-speed rail as a basic means of transport connectivity to promote the economic integration of Eurasia will bring about an era of land power that will enable the country to establish a hedging posture that matches the blue ocean strategy. We should adapt to the new situation, and while continuing to open up the coastal areas and open up eastward, speed up the opening up of border areas and westward opening-up to expand the space for open development and cooperative development. The new round of aid to Xinjiang should also be planned and promoted in this context.

The construction of high-speed railway lines from China to Central Asia, South Asia, the Middle East, Eastern Europe, Russia and finally Western Europe will strongly drive the building of the Silk Road Economic Belt and Eurasian economic integration. Transport arteries that run through Eurasia will recombine factors of production in countries along the routes, creating new demand and attracting new investments in various countries. This will lay a foundation for regional economic integration. In the process of Eurasian economic integration, China can become the driving force in the east, the European Union the driving force in the west, Russia the driving force in the north, and India the driving force in the south, with progress in all directions converging in the Middle East.

Developing the west under the grand strategy of promoting Eurasian economic integration under the Belt and Road Initiative and making it a pole of China's economic development will inevitably lead to migration to the west. Such migration would ease pressure on land use in the east and create conditions for strict control of commercial development of arable land. This will bring the development of the west to a new level of significance: The development of the western regions will no longer be a natural extension of the economic development of the coastal areas, nor will it be a social policy that simply solves imbalance in regional development, still less will it be a necessary measure to maintain stability, it will become an important pillar of China's grand international strategy; the development of the west will promote a transition from the traditional development mode to a comprehensive plan for economic and social development, and will also become an important driving force for the balanced development of China's economy. This land power strategy will fundamentally reverse a series of economic structural imbalances and uneven social development brought about by relying solely on the blue ocean strategy over the past 40 years, as well as the resulting political and social problems.

To sum up, the construction of high-speed rail to promote Eurasian economic integration under the Belt and Road Initiative will bring about rapid development of western China. The economic development and opening up of the west will put a second engine in the long-term balanced development of the Chinese economy. Not only that, it will also help China address the serious development imbalance caused by the blue ocean strategy over the past 30–40 years. This is a grand strategy that deserves China's serious consideration in the twenty-first century.

4 Five Supporting Points for the Chinese Economy to Address Current Challenges (Liu and Chen 2020)

The sudden outbreak of COVID-19 has had a major impact on China's politics and economy. The real challenge facing China today lies in the unsustainability of its economic growth rate, which is due to insufficient demand. To address the issue of expanding demand and sustaining growth, reforms need to be pursued on multiple fronts. First, the current fiscal system has played an important role in promoting economic growth, but there are problems with the revenue and expenditure structure, central and local fiscal arrangements, and information-gathering capabilities, and reform of the fiscal system is an effective way to solve these problems. Second, China's economy will experience its weakest quarter since 2009, slowing in a soft slump. Therefore, the principle of competitive neutrality should be implemented to break up monopolies and enable private enterprises to play a greater role. Third, we should actively yet prudently proceed with urbanization and improve the quality of urbanization. Fourth, China has entered a decisive stage of building a moderately prosperous society in all respects, and profound changes are taking place in the internal and external economic environment, with opportunities and challenges coexisting. Therefore, while increasing internal demand, China must upgrade the export-oriented economy in all respects. Fifth, we should promote the high-quality development of China's economy in the new era, with scientific and technological innovation as the primary driving force for development. The 14th Five-Year Plan period is the first five-year period when our country moves from high-speed development to high-quality development. Therefore, the development mode and development pattern required for high-quality development and the institutional basis for development need to be further reformed and upgraded during the 14th Five-Year Plan period.

China's economic growth is facing a shift in gears, some long-accumulated social problems are becoming more and more prominent, and the original social structure and system are facing challenges.

Promoting structural adjustment and achieving industrial upgrading and transformation through institutional changes so as to complete economic and social transformation is the basic thinking behind China's efforts to get out of the middle-income trap. However, when it comes to advancing economic and social transformation, there are two conflicting trends that deserve great attention.

First, institutional problems are becoming more and more prominent, but the impetus for institutional change is getting weaker. China's reform has entered the deep-water zone and a critical stage. The remaining hot spots and difficulties in reform are inextricably linked to current institutions at the root, and China's institutional reform is far from complete. With China entering the middle-income stage, the extensive mode of growth adopted at the time of economic take-off is no longer effective, so there is an urgent to reform the social structure and the interest pattern at the institutional level. However, as institutional reform becomes more and more urgent, the impetus for reform from within the system is getting weaker.

Second, the problems that were not solved in the early days of reform became more and more difficult to solve later. China pursues progressive rather than radical reform, and the determination of what to put on the reform agenda often follows the principle of big returns and little resistance. For example, rural areas where the cost of reform was smaller rather than cities where the cost of reform was bigger were chosen as the starting point of reform. One problem with progressive reform is that it puts off "hard bones" that are difficult to gnaw. In the end, the most difficult areas of reform come together to form a complex situation where any slight change will trigger a huge reaction, making it difficult to start reform. For problems not solved in the early stages of reform, the cost of reform will not decrease, but may increase, and eventually the situation will become unmanageable.

In view of these two conflicting trends in the process of promoting economic and social transformation, as well as the decline in aggregate demand caused by the combined effects of factors such as COVID-19, China-U.S. trade, economic downturn, and employment, the following four aspects need to be taken as the supporting points for reform.

4.1 *Improving the Fiscal System to Compensate for Slowing Economic Growth and Weakening Exports*

While socialist economies are characterized by the ability to own and control critical resources and dominate major strategic activities, China's total budget is only 28% of GNP, which is small compared to other similar countries or economies (35% in upper-middle-income countries and 40–45% in most OECD economies). According to the World Banks China 2030 report, China's budget provides the third lowest percentage of GDP for social services and other consumption needs compared with other similar countries or economies. This explains why China's overall consumption as a share of GDP (household and government) is 10–15% lower than that of other similar countries or economies. A budget reform that increases government spending on social services and other consumption needs (4–5% of GDP) would ensure that China has enough demand to sustain an average annual growth rate of about 6%. Specifically, this should be done in the following three ways.

(1) Control the scale of public finance and optimize the tax structure. First, we should adjust the VAT rate. According to the announcement on matters related to VAT reform in 2019, "for general VAT payers who engage in sales or import goods that are subject to VAT, the tax rate will be adjusted to 13% if the 16% tax rate was originally applied; and the tax rate will be adjusted to 9% if the 10% tax rate was originally applied." Second, we should improve the system for collecting enterprise income tax and individual income tax and increase the share of these two types of tax in government revenue. Third, we should improve income distribution and introduce inheritance tax and gift tax.

(2) Improve the fiscal expenditure structure and increase spending on unemployment insurance as a share of GDP. Spending on unemployment insurance as a share of GDP should be increased from 0.07% during the 11th Five-Year Plan period to 0.5% during the 13th Five-Year Plan period. During the 14th Five-Year Plan period, we should further improve the mechanism for adjusting unemployment insurance benefits as a percentage of wages and moderately raise the level of unemployment insurance benefits. In addition, subsidies for urban and rural "subsistence allowances" should be increased. In order to improve income distribution and promote economic growth, a subsidy program for children from poor families should be established to solve the problem of intergenerational transmission of poverty. Meanwhile, in order to better solve the

social security problems brought about by the COVID-19 pandemic, the government also needs to establish a unified social security number and citizen information system covering the whole country to serve macro-control and income distribution adjustment.

(3) Adjust the functions of the central government and build a new type of relationship between the central government and local governments. We should focus on government transformation, adjust the relationship between the central and local governments, and clarify their respective functions. The central government should take on more functions in regulating economic fluctuations, improving income distribution, responding to major emergencies, and managing the ecological environment. Local governments could focus more on things like local education and fire protection. "Enterprise income tax and individual income tax must be the responsibility of the central government; unemployment insurance, pension insurance, medical insurance, and social assistance should be the responsibility of the central government, and a regular and emergency system covering all people in the country should be established."

4.2 *Implementing the Principle of Competitive Neutrality to Break Up Monopolies and Enable Private Enterprises to Play a Greater Role*

Implementing the principle of competitive neutrality to break up monopolies and enable private enterprises to play a greater role will help China's economy grow more. The essence and soul of a market economy is competitive neutrality, i.e., treating all economic agents equally.

Given that the private sector now accounts for about three-quarters of total economic output and employment, it makes sense for China to pursue an anti-monopoly agenda that would open up more sectors of the economy. But the real question is whether China is really willing to let its economy move in that direction. For now, the answer is no. But as the economy continues to grow at a lower rate, the Chinese government should reconsider this question. If the right choice is made, there is still a lot of room for China's economic growth.

While we are aware of the need for reform, stronger than expected resistance from state-owned enterprises remains a major obstacle to the implementation of reform. Overinvestment is a structural problem rooted in China's mode of economic growth. Solving this problem requires analyzing and understanding the overall framework of China's economic imbalances.

First, the economic adjustment process. Economic growth will lead to economic imbalances to some extent, and economic imbalances will eventually cause recession. The measure of a developing country's economic capacity is not its performance in terms of economic growth, but its ability to adjust the economy. The cost of economic adjustment is much higher than expected. Therefore, economists and policy makers should think more about how to deal with economic adjustment and minimize the cost of adjustment than how to make the economy grow.

Second, debt and balance sheet. In a nutshell, the aggregate and maturity structure of debt is the "largest" part of the cost of economic adjustment, which is basically measured by the ratio of long-term debt to total debt, namely the balance sheet method. For this reason, economists must understand national balance sheets and sovereign financial crises at the same level that corporate finance experts understand corporate balance sheets and corporate financial crises.

Third, savings imbalance. Capital markets provide a direct channel for converting savings into productive investment, and despite the abundance of opportunities for productive investment, institutional constraints in individual countries have greatly reduced the ability to invest productively. Income inequality and mechanisms that constrain the level of median household income (which is closely related to GNP growth) often lead to excess savings. The results of excess savings include speculative asset booms, trade imbalances, unemployment, and unsustainable growth in debt.

Fourth, globalization. Globalization has enabled all national economies to interact with each other. If there is an economic imbalance in one country or region, there is bound to be a corresponding imbalance in another country or region. The more open a country's economy is, the more likely it is to be affected by economic imbalances elsewhere.

4.3 *Actively Yet Prudently Proceeding with Urbanization and Improving the Quality of Urbanization*

Urbanization is an inevitable trend in economic and social development, and also an important symbol of industrialization and modernization. Under the circumstances of an open economy in the new era, actively yet prudently proceeding with urbanization and improving the quality of urbanization is the basic way and main strategy for building a moderately prosperous society in all respects and developing the cause of socialism with Chinese characteristics. The core of China's urbanization development is how to modernize traditional economic and social structure in rural areas in a relatively short period of time. This requires a high degree of correlation of human, material and financial resources between large, medium-sized and small cities, small towns and rural areas. While continuously strengthening the structural mutualistic effect of urbanization, we should form a system of cities and towns led by central cities, dominated by medium-sized cities and based on small cities and central towns, and continuously improve the agglomeration effect of urbanization.

Improving the agglomeration effect of urbanization has two meanings. First, industrial agglomeration to form leading cities and central towns. Urbanization should be based on industrial development. Without industry and employment, leading cities and central towns cannot be developed. Without the development of leading cities and central towns in a region, it is impossible to form a driving force and radiating power that can drive urban and rural economic and social development in the region. Second, the combination of the agglomeration of cities and the agglomeration of towns. The agglomeration of cities and towns is the guarantee and foundation of urbanization. Only by achieving the agglomeration of large and medium-sized cities, central towns and small towns in a certain region, can industries be highly integrated and then economic and social structure in the vast rural areas be modernized.

To this end, we should prioritize the development of central cities and central towns. We should vigorously develop medium-sized cities in an effort to build a county-centric urban growth core led by central cities, prosper county economies, develop counties into small cities with a population of 100,000 to 200,000, form an urban network based on central towns, with medium-sized cities and small county-level cities as the satellite cities of regional central cities, and continuously increase the radiation and diffusion of the system of cities and towns towards rural areas, so as to modernize rural economic and social structure.

Urbanization is not simply an increase in the size of cities and towns, but involves improvement in the quality of urbanization. If there is only a simple expansion of cities and towns, without the improvement of the quality of urban industries and the strengthening of the influence of cities and towns on rural areas, then such urbanization is not real urbanization. A "make a big pie"-style extensive increase in the size of cities and towns is contrary to the inherent requirements for urbanization. In order to achieve the short-term, medium-term and long-term goals of urbanization, we should attach great importance to technological innovation and environment protection for urban and rural industries on the basis of increasing the structural mutualistic effect, opening-up effect and agglomeration effect of urbanization, and increase the structural upgrading effect of urbanization.

Improvement in the quality of urbanization is mainly reflected in the following aspects: First, the capacity for technological innovation of urban industries is enhanced, and technological upgrading is accelerated; second, the transformation and integration of rural industries by technologically advanced urban industries is accelerated, the level of technology of rural industries is improved, and cooperation between rural and urban industries in technological innovation is continuously strengthened; third, with the integration of urban and rural industries, institutional barriers in education, employment, social security, and household registration between urban and rural areas are gradually eliminated, allowing resources to be shared between urban and rural areas; fourth, urban and rural lifestyles are gradually integrated; with the integration of urban and rural economy and culture, farmers are becoming increasingly "de-ruralized"; traditional farmers are transformed into modern farmers, and farmers truly become part of the industrial workforce; fifth, the environment in urban and rural areas is improving, and people and nature are developing harmoniously.

At present, there are about 200–300 million semi-urbanized residents (migrant workers) in China, which is a resource with great potential in terms of consumption. Accelerating the transformation of migrant workers into urban residents will also greatly promote growth in consumer demand. To speed up the process of transforming farmers into urban residents, we should do the following: First, promote the rationalization of urban housing prices. There will be no urbanization if housing prices are high. The current housing price level in China is significantly higher than normal compared with the income level. Reducing housing prices will unleash huge demand for housing, and correspondingly speed up the urbanization process. Second, implement large-scale housing projects for migrant workers, which mainly involve the use of government power to build indemnificatory housing for migrant workers. Third, encourage the transfer of coastal labor-intensive industries to the central and western regions, and promote the urbanization of the central and western regions.

Maintaining the stability of farmers' land contracting management rights to enable farmers to move in both directions between urban and rural areas is crucial to the healthy development of urbanization. Lessons from India and Brazil remind us that the healthy development of urbanization has much to do with the rural land system. China's basic national conditions dictate that for a long time to come, land will still be the most basic livelihood security for farmers. For migrant workers, most of whom are in a state of instability, land in their hometown is the last line of defense for their livelihoods. Before farmers settle down in cities or towns and obtain stable employment and social security, keeping their land contracting management rights to enable them to move in both directions between urban and rural areas will help prevent a large number of farmers from concentrating in cities, leading to the formation of slums. In the process of expanding the scale of agricultural land and promoting agricultural industrialization, we must not "pull up seedlings to help them grow", deprive farmers of their land contracting management rights, and create landless farmers.

We should adjust the thinking behind urban construction, and consider the needs of migrant workers in urban planning, housing construction, public services and community management. The cases of India and Brazil show that in addition to employment, another major issue for rural migrants is housing. By comparison, the situation is very different for Chinese farmers in that some of them can return to the countryside when they are out of work. But a considerable number of them will work and live with their families in cities and towns for a long time. Cities should treat them as permanent residents, and incorporate their needs for housing, education, medical care and other amenities into urban construction planning.

4.4 *Upgrading the Export-Oriented Economy in All Respects and Improving the Level, Standard and Benefits of Opening-Up*

China has completed an important stage of building a moderately prosperous society in all respects, and profound changes are taking place in the internal and external economic environment, with opportunities and challenges coexisting. To achieve the grand goal of building a moderately prosperous society in all respects and successfully overcoming the middle-income trap, we need to further expand opening-up, constantly improve the open economic system, and give full play to the powerful driving force of opening-up.

Internationally, for some time to come, the world economy could face a prolonged slump, weak external demand could become the norm, various forms of protectionism will be on the rise, and economic and trade frictions will peak. Competition among countries in market, resources, talents, technology, rules and standards is becoming more intense. China is increasingly competing with developing countries in traditional advantageous industries, and with developed countries in medium—and high-end industries. The external environment for development is becoming more complex.

Domestically, since China's accession to the World Trade Organization more than a decade ago, China has seen great improvement in social productivity, comprehensive national strength and people's living standards, formed a relatively complete industrial system, and has become more capable of participating in international competition and cooperation, so the foundation and conditions for further expanding and upgrading opening-up are already in place. The international community also has higher expectations of China's role in assuming international responsibility. But China's existing mode of economic development is relatively extensive, resource and environment constraints have intensified, traditional advantages have been weakened, new advantages have not yet been established, the task of changing the development mode and optimizing economic structure is arduous, there are still many structural and institutional obstacles to the development of an open economy, opening-up is facing increasing risks, and the level, standard and efficiency of opening-up need to be improved.

In order to comprehensively improve the standard of China's opening-up in the future, we need to make breakthroughs in the following three areas.(1) We should work hard to change the mode of foreign trade growth. First, we should change the mode of export that mainly depends on low cost and quantity, change the extensive and quantity-oriented mode of economic growth, and diversify the forms of exporters and trade; work hard to create exports of goods and services with our own intellectual property rights and brands, control the production and export of resource-intensive, energy-intensive and highly polluting products, and expand exports of new technologies, new products and high value-added products; improve the level of processing trade, change the current situation where the volume of product trade is increasing but the value added of trade is low, accelerate the upgrading of products, and shift export trade from quantitative expansion to quality improvement. Second, we should adjust the product and market structures of imports, prioritize imports of high-tech products, high-tech equipment, high and new technologies, and strategic resources that are necessary for domestic development, important and in short supply, diversify sources of imports of strategic materials and ways to import strategic materials, and stabilize channels for importing strategic materials. Third, we should develop trade in green products and strictly control trade in energy-intensive and highly polluting products, so as to form a trade structure conducive to resource conservation and environmental protection.

(2) We should work hard to improve the quality and level of foreign capital utilization. First, we should combine the introduction of foreign capital with the upgrading of the domestic industrial structure and technological level, with the promotion of coordinated regional development and the enhancement of enterprises' independent innovation capability, reform and improve existing enterprises through the introduction of foreign capital, achieve economies of scale through the optimization and upgrading of technology, and strive to increase the benefits of structural optimization, economies of scale and the regional division of labor; switch from relying mainly on increasing the amount of capital input to relying mainly on improving the quality of factors of production, and increase the contribution of total factor productivity to economic growth. Second, we should make rational use of foreign capital, develop an open economy, change the situation of unreasonable structure, poor product quality and low value-added, accelerate the optimization and upgrading of industrial structure by introducing a batch of high value-added and high-tech products, and do a good job of transforming, assimilating and innovating imported technologies. Third, we should strengthen efforts to steer foreign capital into specific industries and regions, seize the opportunity of international industrial transfer to expand the scale of foreign direct investment, and get foreign investors to participate in capital construction projects encouraged by the State, including comprehensive agricultural development and construction projects involving energy, transportation and important raw materials, technological upgrading projects that possess advanced technology and can improve product performance, save energy, reduce consumption, and improve the economic efficiency of

enterprises, technology projects that can prevent environmental pollution through the comprehensive use of energy, etc.

(3) We should work hard to implement the Go Out policy for Chinese enterprises. The implementation of the Go Out policy is an important measure for opening-up in the new stage and a necessary requirement for implementing a sustainable development strategy. The report to the 16th CPC National Congress clearly stated that "we should encourage and support foreign investment by enterprises under various forms of ownership that have comparative advantages, promote the export of goods and services, and form a group of powerful multinational enterprises and famous brands". To this end, first, we should better optimize the allocation of resources around the world, make full use of foreign natural resources, scientific and technological resources and human resources, implement strategic overseas investment, and create our own world-class brand-name products; second, we should take our technologies, equipment and products out of China, increase their share in the international market, give full play to our comparative advantages, promote the development of the national economy in a mutually beneficial and win-win manner; third, we should actively participate in international economic competition and cooperation, carry out transnational operations and investment, cultivate transnational companies, and make investment abroad mainly through enterprises, guided by the market and with a view to improving economic efficiency and enhancing international competitiveness. Investment should be focused on energy, raw materials and high technology.

4.5 *Promoting the High-Quality Development of China's Economy in the New Era, with Scientific and Technological Innovation As the Primary Driving Force for Development*

According to the report on the 14th Five-Year Plan, as the Chinese economy is still in the historical stage of industrialization, IT application, urbanization and agricultural modernization, the development of the real economy is still the main part of economic growth. Therefore, China's manpower and talent resources are vast in scale and abundant in supply. In terms of technology supply, on the one hand, market-led applied technology research and development is becoming increasingly active and is becoming an important source of technology; On the other hand, state-led efforts to achieve breakthroughs in core technologies in important areas are speeding up, becoming an important potential source of technology. China's economic modernization is also a process from catching up to surpassing in terms of core technologies, and technological innovation will always remain active.

Therefore, we must be soberly aware that the development path that China has been pursuing for 40 years is still fraught with troubles and challenges, China's development path is not yet a complete development model, and some social, economic, and political issues have not been fundamentally resolved because of rapid economic development. The 14th Five-Year Plan proposes to systematically strengthen scientific and technological innovation and institutional innovation. The core of high-quality development is to improve efficiency and enhance innovation capacity. Scientific and technological innovation is the primary driving force for development, the strategic support for promoting high-quality development and building a modern economy, and the core task during the 14th Five-Year Plan period. Institutional innovation is an inexhaustible driving force for development, a source of creativity and innovation in the whole society, and an institutional guarantee and source of power for scientific and technological innovation. Therefore, "science and technology" is the driving force behind innovation, and "talent" is the guarantee for stimulating greater vitality. This is a profound understanding of the 14th Five Year Plan. The shift to "improving innovation capability" as the core growth engine of the economy requires major adjustments to the existing distribution structure and incentive mechanism, the establishment of a new distribution structure and incentive mechanism, and the acceleration of the reform of important economic systems that restrict the upgrading of industries and the expansion of domestic demand.

First, we should encourage scientific and technological innovation, improve industrial competitiveness, and pursue innovation-driven development. The 14th Five-Year Plan period is the first five-year period when our country moves from high-speed development to high-quality development. Therefore, the development mode and development pattern required for high-quality development and the institutional basis for development need to be further reformed and upgraded during the 14th Five-Year Plan period.

After China enters the middle-income stage, the low-cost advantage of the economy will be gradually lost. We must improve R&D capabilities, attach importance to human capital, carry out industrial upgrading and foster new competitive advantages. The gap between South Korea and Brazil in the 1980s was not that big. The 1978 energy crisis had a great impact on South Korea, depriving the country of its comparative advantage in labor-intensive industries. But South Korea actively sought change. It promoted industrial upgrading by implementing the strategy of "founding the nation on science and technology", and finally completed the transition from light industry to technology-intensive heavy industry and from "technological imitation" to independent innovation. Its spending on scientific research continued to grow at a high rate, accounting for 3.47% of GDP in 2007, surpassing the United States and Japan. Today, technological innovation contributes up to more than 70% to South Korea's economic growth.

To change the mode of economic development by relying on technological advances and improving capacity for technological innovation, we need to start from the following two aspects: First, increase investment in education and scientific research, improve the quality of education, cultivate excellent technological innovation talents and teams, and accumulate a solid foundation for scientific research and innovation; second, reform the education and scientific management system, and innovate new ways and methods to encourage scientific research. On the one hand, provide a good and relaxed research environment for researchers; on the other hand, shift from the government-led scientific research management system into a market-driven enterprise spontaneous innovation mechanism, vigorously develop higher vocational and technical education based on market demand, strengthen communication and interaction between institutions of higher learning, scientific research institutes and enterprises in R & D, and improve the efficiency of the popularization of research findings.

To encourage independent technological innovation is mainly to reduce excessive incentives for areas other than independent innovation. As long as there are more incentives than those for independent innovation (e.g., excessive incentives for foreign investment and real estate), investment in independent innovation will not increase, but instead will decrease. Therefore, the government should improve the incentive environment or direction. First, reduce the proportion of state-owned capital in strategic competitive industries, and give full play to the important role of private capital in industrial upgrading. Second, use capital markets to promote independent innovation. Funnel surplus social funds into the real economy, so that they are combined with industrial upgrading to promote industrial competitiveness.

Second, promote the high-quality development of China's economy in the new era. Strategic competition between major powers has replaced counter-terrorism, the world has entered the era of coopetition, and where China-U.S. relations are going has a bearing on policies and positions in global geopolitical competition. China and the United States account for 41% of global GDP, 50% of global economic growth, and 35% of global trade in goods. China and the U.S. should recognize that there are some uncertainties in China-U.S. economic relations at the present stage, such as trade deficits, differences in trade rules and disputes over intellectual property rights, which are inevitable in the era of coopetition.

Therefore, we must be soberly aware that the development path that China has been pursuing for 40 years is still fraught with troubles and challenges, China's economic development is not yet a complete development model, and some social, economic, and political issues have not been fundamentally resolved because of rapid economic development. The report to the 19th CPC National Congress stated, "As socialism with Chinese characteristics has entered a new era, the principal contradiction facing Chinese society has evolved. What we now face is the contradiction between unbalanced and inadequate development and the people's ever-growing needs for a better life." The key to the high-quality development of China's economy in the new era of socialism with Chinese characteristics lies in emancipating the mind and achieving sustainable development. The basic idea is to shift from "two overdependence's" to "two reliance's", that is, we should rely mainly on the expansion of domestic demand for economic growth, expand and upgrade domestic demand mainly by expanding consumer demand, and rely mainly on independent innovation capability rather than an excessive input of resources and capital. This shift in growth dynamics requires major adjustments to the existing distribution structure and incentive mechanism, the establishment of a new distribution structure and incentive mechanism, and the acceleration of the reform of important economic systems that restrict the upgrading of industries, the expansion of domestic demand, and dual circulation.

A century of ups and downs in the world economy shows that benefiting all citizens is the key to effectively expanding demand and promoting healthy economic development. For economically developed countries such as the United States, which are consumer economies that have completed the "infrastructure construction" and "industrialized economy" stages, the so-called effective expansion of domestic demand is to let money flow as little as possible into the pockets of high-income groups who save money and as much as possible into the hands of low-income groups who need to spend money, so as to solve the social problems caused by the gap between rich and poor. Achieving this goal requires policymakers to carefully design fiscal policy, monetary policy, tax policy and public service policy under the dual principles of efficiency and equity. For developing countries such as China, which are "rigid" economies in the "infrastructure construction" and "industrialized economy" stages, the so-called expansion of domestic demand is to improve weak links, to allow as much capital as possible to be invested in non-redundant infrastructure construction, to expedite the process of industrialization, to allow more citizens to benefit from the country's economic development, and to solve the social problems brought about by uneven economic development. To achieve this goal, it is necessary for the policymakers of major economies such as China and the United States to follow market principles while allowing planning and the market to play a regulatory role, give play to the role of national macro-control, develop more effective social mechanisms, further observe the economic revitalization plans of various countries and economies, ensure "self-rescue" when global supply and demand is bound to change fundamentally, and keep reviewing changes in the global economy with great wisdom and new perspectives.

Third, the high-quality development of China's economy requires deepening reform. First, we need to deepen economic restructuring and transform government functions. The Communiqué of the Third Plenary Session of the 18th CPC Central Committee and the report to the 19th CPC National Congress clearly pointed out that deepening the reform of the economic system is the key to accelerating the transformation of the mode of economic development. The issue at the heart of the reform of the economic system is to properly handle the relationship between the government and the market. We must show more respect for the law of the market and give better play to the role of the government. The role of the government in a well-regulated and mature market economy is mainly reflected in the following aspects: adjusting income distribution; correcting market failures; safeguarding justice; restricting monopoly and encouraging competition; providing public goods and services; and carrying out macro-control. The government's failure to perform its functions adequately is mainly manifested in: the adjustment of income distribution is inadequate; the monitoring of market failures needs to be strengthened and made more efficient; the provision of public goods and services needs to be strengthened; a service-oriented government culture has yet to be established; fair market norms and rules need to be better maintained; a judicial system independent of administrative intervention has yet to be established. The government's overstepping of its functions is mainly manifested in: interfering too much in industries and resources that have no natural monopolistic attributes and do not involve national security.

Therefore, the first priority is to clarify the relationship between businesses and the government and the boundaries of its rights. The government needs to change its role from a mutitasker to a provider of social services who maintains the smooth operation of the rules of fair play. The role of the government is mainly reflected in the following aspects: **First,** in areas not related to the national economy and people's livelihood, lower the threshold for market access and bring in diverse investors. **Second,** provide public goods and services more effectively, reduce market failures and lower the cost of trial and error. **Third,** build community services and social governance with Chinese characteristics, and further improve the public management capability and model for mobilizing resources and organize emergency responses in times of crisis. **Fourth,** guide the formation of a healthy culture and social atmosphere on the basis of respecting democracy. **Fifth,** establish a sound legal and regulatory system and a more efficient and fair judicial system.

Second, we need to narrow the income gap, urban-rural gap and inter-regional gap. Since the start of reform and opening-up, although rapid economic growth has covered up the huge negative impact of the three gaps on social development to some extent, but we believe that as China's gear of growth shifts from high speed to medium-to-high speed, these gaps will become a major obstacle to sustained economic growth. When the economy reaches a certain stage of development, the main growth momentum will come from technological progress and household consumption. Narrowing the gap can deliver a significant Pareto improvement, and narrowing the gap by one point has a greater growth-boosting effect than increasing investment by many points. If the income gap, urban-rural gap and inter-regional gap remain unimproved for a long time, they will constitute a significant constraint on the expansion of consumption.

Third, we need to encourage scientific and technological innovation, improve industrial competitiveness, and pursue innovation-driven development. After China enters the middle-income stage, the low-cost advantage of the economy will be gradually lost. We must improve R&D capabilities, attach importance to human capital, carry out industrial upgrading and foster new competitive advantages. To change the mode of economic development by relying on technological advances and improving capacity for technological innovation, we need to start from the following two aspects: First, increase investment in education and scientific research, improve the quality of education, cultivate excellent technological innovation talents and teams, and accumulate a solid foundation for scientific research and innovation; second, reform the education and scientific management system, and innovate new ways and methods to encourage scientific research. On the one hand, provide a good and relaxed research environment for researchers; on the other hand, shift from the government-led scientific research management system into a market-driven enterprise spontaneous innovation mechanism, vigorously develop higher vocational and technical education based on market demand, strengthen communication and interaction between institutions of higher learning, scientific research institutes and enterprises in R & D, and improve the efficiency of the popularization of research findings.

Fourth, we need to upgrade the export-oriented economy in all respects. The practice of China's reform and opening-up has proved that reform and opening-up, as the two fundamental means of China's development, promote each other and are inseparable. At present, China's reform has entered a critical stage and the deep-water zone. Faced with deep-seated contradictions and development bottlenecks, we need to further promote the reform of domestic systems through a higher level of opening-up, so as to create another opening-up dividend period for the sustainable development of China's economy.

References

1 Liu, China's Economic Adjustment and Rebalancing. Revelations, Challenges and Strategies, People's Forum - Academic Frontier, late January 2018.
2 Liu and Chen, Four Supporting Points for the Chinese Economy to Address Current Challenges, People's Daily—People's Forum, May 11, 2020.

CHAPTER 12

Global Financial Changes and China's Monetary Policy in the New Era

The financial system is an important part of the socialist market economy system. Since the launch of reform and opening-up, China has gradually established and improved its socialist market economy system, basically established a financial system that meets the requirements of the market economy, and continuously improved its financial macro-control and financial regulatory systems. Financial resources are core resources in a modern economy, and the market should play a decisive role in the allocation of resources. We should improve the financial institution system in which there is a reasonable division of labor and complementarity between commercial finance, development finance, policy-based finance, and cooperative finance. We should build a multi-layered, extensive and differentiated banking institution system. We should promote the rapid and steady growth of a number of Chinese financial institutions that are internationally competitive and have the power to allocate financial resources across borders. We should rely on cooperative economic organizations to guide the healthy development of cooperative finance and form an extensive, sustainable and complementary organizational system. We should improve the quality of services provided by financial institutions and reduce financing costs for enterprises. We should improve the system for managing state-owned financial capital and increase the vitality, control and influence of state-owned financial assets (Liu 2018).

In the post-financial crisis era, China should, in the future reform of its international monetary policy and financial system, while dealing with

L. Weiping, *American Monetary Policy Adjustment and Its Impacts*,
https://doi.org/10.1007/978-981-99-7810-6_12

uncertainties arising from the transition of the international monetary system from a dollar-dominated system to a multipolar system, should proceed from the needs of China's reform and opening-up and pursue the three major foreign financial strategies of participating in the governance of international financial institutions, expanding regional monetary cooperation in East Asia, and internationalizing the RMB in parallel. From a financial point of view, China needed foreign exchange reserves at the beginning of reform, and the United States was the only country that could print dollars, so at the very beginning there was a convergence of interests that brought the two countries together. Developing countries, including China, are still keen to use the dollar as the main currency in their foreign exchange reserves, which is why they now hope that the dollar will not depreciate so fast. For China and other developing countries, it is difficult to de-peg from the U.S. dollar, because these countries have been pursuing such a policy from the beginning, and China's financial markets are not particularly mature.

China can contribute to the world on issues such as exchange rates and reserves, but there are a few points to note. First, with regard to China's financial opening-up, it suggests that markets can fail, and that coordinated bailouts between the United States and China mean more intervention and control by the government, which could slow down China's deregulation and financialization. Second, China's monetary policy is also a stabilizing force.

From the Asian financial crisis, we can see that China's policy and Asia's policy have a very big external impact. China's contribution is very important to the United States. Now is the best time to raise the issue of the internationalization of the RMB. As long as China continues to grow, the market will continue to work for China. The convertibility of the RMB will increase and the RMB is likely to become one of the world's major currencies in the future.

1 Global Financial Changes and Insights from China's Financial Positioning

Since the international financial crisis, certain changes have taken place in the financial landscape. China needs to reposition itself in the process of continuous adjustment of the global financial industry.

The global financial landscape before the crisis. After World War II, the political, economic, and military strength of countries around the world underwent major adjustments. The Bretton Woods system, which was created on this basis in the 1870s, was actually a distinctly hierarchical global financial structure centered on the U.S. dollar. It was characterized by the fact that the U.S. dollar acted as the international currency and was pegged to gold, while the currencies of other countries were pegged to the U.S. dollar. Through the coordination of international organizations such as the International Monetary Fund, the World Bank, the Bank for International Settlements, and the General Agreement on Tariffs and Trade, the Bretton Woods System had to some extent ensured the temporary stability of the world financial and economic order. During this period, the United States also acted as an engine of capital accumulation, offering vast markets and investment opportunities that attracted large amounts of commodity and monetary capital. But that period ended around 1970 because of the Triffin dilemma, international competition, racism, the Cold War and many other factors.

It was replaced by the Jamaica Agreement of 1976. Although the supremacy of the United States was already declining with the revival of Europe and Japan and the rise of emerging countries, the Jamaican system largely retained the monopoly of the U.S. dollar established by the Bretton Woods system. More importantly, after the U.S. dollar ceased to be convertible into gold, the international monetary system lost its solid material foundation and slipped into the stage where the U.S. dollar, a credit currency, was the main reserve currency, thus getting rid of the hard constraints on the issuance of international reserve currencies under the gold standard and Bretton Woods system. Through the dollar-centered floating exchange rate mechanism, the United States also gained the power to impose minting and inflation tax on other countries, further exacerbating the contradiction between the United States and the diversified development of the world economy.

The birth of the euro in the late 20th and early twenty-first centuries was the result of the aspiration of European countries to continuously improve their political and economic status, and was the most important adjustment of the international financial system since the collapse of the Bretton Woods system in the 1870s. It replaced the declining Japanese yen, greatly challenged the dominance of the U.S. dollar, changed the currency composition of central banks' reserve holdings and the direction of private investment, and prompted a large amount of dollar-denominated assets inside and outside the EU to be converted into euro-denominated assets, thus having a profound impact on global financial markets, especially currency markets.

In addition, the globalization and liberalization of finance and the financialization of the economy are constantly reshaping the global financial landscape. The technological revolution in the fields of micro-electronics, information technology and modern informatics over the past 40-plus years has helped to establish extensive and complex connections within and between banks, reducing the cost of transactions, settlements and other operations and making them faster while enabling information sharing; non-bank financial institutions of various types, such as investment banks, insurance companies, mutual funds and pension funds, have proliferated and become important participants in global financial markets. In their pursuit of profit maximization, they have stimulated innovation in financial products and financial markets. According to incomplete statistics, securitized bonds account for almost 140% of world GDP, and financial derivatives account for over 800% of world GDP. Meanwhile, the rapid development of the Eurodollar market and the gradual opening up of emerging markets have facilitated global capital flows, but also objectively caused the accumulation and spread of financial and economic risks in the world. Under such circumstances, how to establish an effective supervision and inspection mechanism around the world, as well as a linkage mechanism for crisis prevention, has become an indispensable and important part of the international financial system.

In short, before the outbreak of the 2008 international financial crisis, so far the global financial landscape from the perspective of international currencies is concerned, the euro became the main competitor of the U.S. dollar in international markets, and if we include the "lost" yen, there actually existed a situation in which "two big currencies (U.S. dollar and euro) and one small currency (Japanese yen)" were playing against each other as international currencies; from the perspective of economic location, financial institutions and markets in Europe and the United States, especially in the United States, still dominated, and the progress of science and technology, as well as the development of financial liberalization and globalization had linked the financial sectors of countries around the world into a whole, and promoted the accumulation logic of the latter to the whole society as a universal value, so that capital could transcend time, space, physical forms and its own limitations to achieve profit maximization. But behind this pattern, there had always been contradictions between the declining status of the U.S. economy and the monopoly of the U.S. dollar, between developed and developing countries, and between the real economy and the virtual economy, and the long-term accumulation of these contradictions had created the conditions for the outbreak of the crisis and the readjustment of the global financial landscape.

Global financial changes after the crisis. We must reflect deeply on our performance in the crisis in terms of global financial concepts, models and patterns. In the long run, further changes are needed to provide a solid foundation for sustainable economic development.

The scale and operating mode of global finance will change dramatically. As a consequence of the financial crisis, the nominal value of these financial assets has shrunk sharply, and the scale of bank assets will also shrink rapidly. Financial derivatives trading, bond trading, leverage financing and other off-balance-sheet activities will gradually decrease. With the separation of Citigroup into Citicorp and Citi Holdings, the universal banking model aggressively pursued by traditional banks has also been called into question.

The global financial market will undergo structural changes, and the trend towards diversification of international finance is inevitable. The United States United States was hit hard by the financial crisis, with a large number of enterprises going bankrupt, unemployment rising and its economic strength declining significantly. In response to the crisis, the eurozone adopted expansionary fiscal and monetary policies, which to some extent contributed to the overall recovery of the region's economy. But the rise of the euro has yet to be further tested by time, as weak economic growth and rising fiscal deficits have pushed eurozone countries such as Iceland and Greece into sovereign debt crisis. After years of efforts, Asia is emerging as the world's center of economic growth, in sharp contrast to declining growth rates in the United States, Europe and Japan. Meanwhile, Asia's position in the international financial market is gradually rising. Its huge amount of official foreign exchange reserves plays a pivotal role in the global financial market, and the responsible attitude of major countries such as China in several crises has been fully recognized and praised by the international community. Therefore, as the world redefines the structure of financial markets, Asia will receive more attention. Major cities such as Tokyo, Hong Kong and Shanghai will usher in new development opportunities, and diversification of the global financial landscape has become an inevitable trend.

Sovereign funds are emerging as a new force in the international financial market. For a long time, the international financial market has been the stage for Western private financial capital. As a consequence of the financial crisis, the strength of these private financial institutions has been greatly weakened in the process of deleveraging and nationalization. After the outbreak of the 2007 financial crisis, major financial institutions in Western developed countries sought capital injections from sovereign funds. Non-Western sovereign wealth funds, including the Abu Dhabi Investment Council, the Kuwait Investment Board, China Investment Corporation, and Government of Singapore Investment Corporation successively acquired stakes in financial giants such as Citigroup and Goldman Sachs, with investments amounting to tens of billions of dollars, greatly stabilizing the international financial market.

The global financial regulatory framework urgently needs to be rebuilt. The crisis has fully exposed the weaknesses and loopholes of the original Basel Accords, making all countries realize the importance of consolidated regulation, unified regulation and global regulation. At present, almost all financial stock institutions, financial markets and financial instruments will be properly regulated, a thought that has been reflected and implemented in the financial regulatory reform programs issued by the United States and the European Union. In addition, in response to the rapid and large-scale flow of capital, international consultation and coordination on regulation will be unprecedentedly close, and bilateral and multilateral financial cooperation will become an important form of international finance.

Of course, the development of the global financial landscape in the above four dimensions will be a complex process of competition, cooperation and dynamic game among various economic, financial, political and military forces, involving core and sensitive issues such as the world's standard currency, international reserves and balance of payments. This requires countries to constantly seek cooperation amid competition, seek common ground while shelving differences, and work together to prevent another global financial crisis and promote the sustainable development of the world economy, and also requires major developed and developing countries to assume their responsibilities and fulfill their obligations in relation to promoting consultation and establishing a new international financial order.

The positioning of China's financial sector in the world after the crisis. Affected by the international financial crisis and many domestic factors, China still faces major challenges in terms of its overall macroeconomic situation, mode of economic growth, outward direct investment, and export trade. However, the steady improvement in the overall scale and development of China's economy and financial sector over the past decades is an indisputable fact, and the decline in the relative status of the United States and the U.S. dollar has opened a "window of opportunity" for the accelerated development of China's financial sector. In the next 10 to 20 years, the global economic and financial landscape will undergo tremendous changes. As the world's largest developing country, China must plan ahead, plan early, strive to establish a voice in international discourse that is commensurate with its status as a major power, actively promote the formation of a new international financial order, and demonstrate the responsibility and leadership qualities expected of a rising power. To this end, China's financial sector should find its position in the ever-changing new global financial landscape and achieve leapfrog development.

China should strive to become one of the global financial centers. Already the world's second largest economy and top exporter, and with $3 trillion in foreign exchange reserves, China needs to establish an international financial center that is commensurate with its level of economic development and serves its own development needs. To this end, we need to actively regulate the daily operation of domestic financial institutions in accordance with the basic principles of international financial management, accelerate the construction of financial infrastructure and supporting facilities, promote the development of financial products, improve the efficiency and level of financial services, strive to ensure the stability of the financial system, and actively push for the development of Hong Kong and Shanghai into regional and even global financial centers.

The RMB should become one of the world's major currencies. It is an inevitable trend of history for the currencies of major countries to become world currencies, as illustrated by everything from the British pound to the U.S. dollar and the euro. Since the resumption of the RMB exchange rate reform, the RMB has appreciated by 5.5% against the U.S. dollar, indicating the confidence of international markets and major institutions in the future development of the RMB and China's economy and financial sector. A World Bank forecast published on June 15, 2011 also declared that the RMB is expected to join the U.S. dollar and the euro as a major international currency in the next 10 to 15 years. However, considering the long-term development of China's economy, we should try to ensure the balance of payments while promoting the economic development of neighboring regions in the process of RMB internationalization, so the process is bound to be gradual and depends largely on the development status of and trends in the new international financial landscape. The RMB has achieved convertibility under current account and partial convertibility under capital account. In the next stage, we can, in due course, explore ways and paths to realize RMB convertibility under capital account.

China should have a number of strong financial institutions that rank among the world's leading financial institutions. The consolidation of China's financial position cannot be achieved without the support of a number of financial institutions with certain influence worldwide. At the end of June 2009, with a market capitalization of $257 billion, Industrial and Commercial Bank of China (ICBC) became the world's largest bank, followed by China Construction Bank and Bank of China, at a time when U.S. banks were reeling from the crisis and European and Japanese banks were recovering. However, China should also be fully aware that its financial competitiveness depends more on soft power such as talent, technology, management and culture, and even the comprehensive improvement of the government's regulatory capabilities, and there is still a considerable gap between China and developed countries in these aspects. Therefore, while expanding their global business and network and seizing the opportunity to "go out" as soon as possible, Chinese financial enterprises should focus on cultivating and improving their own management and innovation capabilities.

China should be a positive factor in maintaining global financial stability. Over the years, China's economy has maintained a momentum of rapid growth, playing a pivotal role in terms of economic aggregate, growth potential and contribution to the world. With this strong economic backing, China's financial sector has contributed to the stability of the regional and world financial system. During the 1998 Asian financial crisis, the Chinese government, proceeding from the overall interests of maintaining stability and development in the region, made a commitment not to devalue the RMB, effectively curbing the further spread of the crisis and showing the demeanor of a financial power. In the face of the severe test of the 2008 global financial crisis, China's economy and financial sector continued to run smoothly, which strengthened the confidence of countries around the world in getting out of the trough and crisis.

China should become a leading player in regional financial cooperation and a driving force for the establishment of a new global financial order. Developing countries in general have played and will continue to play an increasing role in the global economy, and China should rely on the rising emerging markets and play a leading role in the "10+1", "10+3", Shanghai Cooperation Organization, "BRICS" and other cooperation frameworks and mechanisms. China should further promote inter-regional financial cooperation within such cooperation frameworks and mechanisms as "10+1", "10+3", the Shanghai Cooperation Organization and BRICS, relying on rising emerging markets, to achieve mutual benefit and win–win results for all parties. Meanwhile, China should also take an active part in the joint actions of countries around the world in response to crises, enhance interaction with developed countries in the financial sector, strengthen negotiations, consultations, coordination and cooperation on the establishment of a new international financial order, and strive to gain more voice for developing countries, which is not only the trend of international financial competition, but also a necessary requirement for enhancing China's international status and promoting the sustainable development of the world economy.

2 Challenges Facing China's Financial Sector in Achieving Global Strategic Positioning

In the changing global financial landscape, China's financial sector must have a clear understanding of the main difficulties and challenges it faces in order to achieve global strategic positioning.

The degree of financial marketization needs to be increased. McKinnon and Shaw's research in the 1960s and 1970s already pointed out that financial development and economic growth reinforce and restrict each other. They believed that developing countries should implement financial marketization and liberalization reforms to lift financial repression, promote financial deepening, and boost economic growth. On the other hand, inappropriate financial marketization and liberalization can threaten the stability of the financial system, which in turn can cause economic recession and social unrest, as this international financial crisis has amply demonstrated. Nevertheless, judging from the evolution of the international financial system and the historical experience of developed countries, a free and open macro financial environment is essential if a country, especially a large developing country like China, which is transforming from a planned economy to a market economy, wants to take its place in the global financial landscape and achieve strategic positioning and leapfrog development for the financial sector in the post-crisis era. Therefore, for some time to come, China should continue to deepen financial reform, increase the degree of financial marketization, and strive to overcome the following three kinds of obstacles:

First, obstacles to interest rate liberalization. Interest rate is the basic price of financial products and services, and is a benchmark for the pricing of many other financial innovations and derivatives, so it plays an extremely important role in the allocation of resources by the market. Through interest rate liberalization, financial institutions can independently provide a diverse range of financial products and services, and realize the survival of the fittest in the free choice of consumers, so as to balance the supply of and demand for different financial products and services, help enterprises make correct judgments about risks and set the right price, and promote the optimal allocation of funds. In addition, liberalized interest rates are also a basic guarantee for establishing a smooth and effective monetary policy transmission mechanism and reflect the needs of macro-control. Interest rate liberalization in China is a process that connects the preceding and the following. It has gone through stages such as liberalizing the interest rates paid on deposits and loans in domestic and foreign currency, expanding the range within which interest rates on bank loans and deposits are allowed to float, applying market-based pricing to corporate bonds, financial bonds, commercial paper and money market transactions, and expanding the range within which interest rates on commercial individual housing loans are allowed to float, but this is far from meeting the inherent requirements of the socialist market economy for the liberalization of capital prices, so we must continue to unswervingly push forward interest rate liberalization in a planned and step-by-step manner.

Second, obstacles to capital flows. With the steady advancement of China's economic reform and the gradual expansion of economic space, capital markets have seen considerable development and are becoming increasingly important. At present, China is playing an increasing role in the international economy, but its influence in international capital markets is minimal. One of the important reasons is that capital markets are not open enough, which hinders the inflow of international capital. Although controls on capital flows can effectively prevent risks arising from rapid capital flows, they also lose the benefits of optimizing resource allocation on a global scale. In the future, if China wants to strike a balance between economic development and resource utilization and expand its role in international financial markets, it must appropriately remove obstacles to capital flows and ensure fair competition under the conditions of a market economy.

Third, exchange rate obstacles. According to Krugman's "impossible trinity" model, a country cannot have free capital movement, an independent monetary policy, and a stable exchange rate all at the same time. In the future, if China wants to achieve global capital allocation while having an independent monetary policy, it must pursue market-based exchange rate reform. More importantly, the reform of the exchange rate system can also create a favorable monetary environment for the internationalization of the RMB. In the future, it is still necessary to further push forward the reform of the RMB exchange rate formation mechanism, enhance the flexibility of the RMB exchange rate, and improve the ability to resist risks in the process of capital account opening, so as to lay the foundation for the strategic goal of the RMB becoming one of the world's major currencies.

The financial structure is not entirely reasonable. At present, China's financial structure system is still dominated by banks, which is mainly reflected in the following aspects: bank assets make up for the bulk of all financial assets; although the development of capital markets has increased the proportion of direct financing, the dominant position of indirect finance has not been fundamentally changed; the development of insurance, trust and financial leasing is slow; social financing risks are highly concentrated in the banking industry. An excess supply of monetary assets will undoubtedly squeeze the paths and space for social finance, reduce the ability and motivation to innovate in finance, and contribute to high levels of corporate debt, which is not conducive to the optimization of the financial structure and the development of the real economy. Resources are allocated largely to state-owned enterprises and large enterprises, thus excluding most SMEs and private enterprises from organized financial markets. This has objectively spawned various forms of private financial markets, and increased the difficulty of financial regulation while exacerbating the instability of the financial system.

China's urban–rural dual financial structure is obvious, and the gap between the east and the west is large. On the one hand, due to a low degree of industrialization, insignificant economic returns, high information costs and a lack of sufficient collateral and alternative means to prevent risks, financial institutions are often reluctant to conduct business in these rural and underdeveloped areas, resulting in "market failure"; on the other hand, due to reasons such as adverse selection and moral hazard, funds injected through government subsidies and donations from non-profit organizations are used inefficiently in practice, and defaults occur from time to time, which affects the recycling of funds and lowers the overall credit status of rural and underdeveloped areas, resulting in "government failure". These two "failures", in turn, will produce a significant siphon effect, causing the reverse flow of funds from rural areas to cities and from the west to the east, and further hindering local economic development and the formation of a reasonable and balanced financial structure.

Therefore, if China's finance is to achieve its strategic rise after the international financial crisis, it must first focus on solving its own structural problems, constantly optimize the internal structure of the financial sector, establish a unified national financial market, and promote the healthy development of the financial system.

The core competitiveness of the financial sector has not yet been formed. Through more than 20 years of financial reform, China's banking, securities and insurance industries have made great progress, but the international competitiveness of the financial sector is still low. In the Banker/Brand Finance's Top 500 Banking Brands 2010, ICBC, the largest bank in China, ranked 12th, down seven places from the beginning of 2009. This change fully illustrates that the brand value and core competitiveness of financial institutions do not depend entirely on market capitalization and assets, but rather on a comprehensive competition over hard and soft power, involving product development, market influence, human resources, information technology, risk control, corporate governance, etc. It is precisely in these dimensions that China's financial sector lags considerably behind those of developed countries.

This is mainly because the quality of commercial bank assets is not high. The Statement of Non-performing Loans of Commercial Banks disclosed by the CBRC on a quarterly basis shows that although the balance of non-performing loans of Chinese commercial banks has been on a downward trend in recent years, and the non-performing loan ratio has also dropped from more than 10% to about 1%, this is mainly attributable to the divestment of non-performing assets and overall restructuring initiated in 2005 and the new economic cycle, rather than substantial improvements in operating capacity, and their asset structure and quality need to be further optimized and improved.

Financial innovation is relatively backward. The starting point of financial innovation and financial product development is to activate financial market transactions and effectively improve the service level and efficiency of the financial sector. In the wake of the international financial crisis, western countries have begun to re-examine financial innovation and the slowdown in derivatives trading. Therefore, financial innovation is a double-edged sword. However, as far as China's current situation is concerned, financial innovation is still in the "initial stage", and many innovations that improve the operation and management of financial institutions, promote capital markets and improve the efficiency of the financial system have not yet appeared or taken place on a large scale. At the present stage, vigorously promoting financial innovation and diversifying financial products will help enhance the core competitiveness of China's financial sector.

The risk management capability is weak. With the development of financial liberalization and economic globalization, as well as breakthroughs in information technology, the scale and speed of capital flows are increasing, financial innovations and derivatives trading are expanding, and financial risks have become more complex and diverse. Therefore, it is particularly important to identify, measure and control financial risks. Most Chinese financial institutions do not have independent risk management departments, and their internal organizational and governance structures are not yet perfected. This, coupled with a lack of effective information disclosure mechanisms and risk-diversifying innovative financial products, objectively increases the difficulty of risk management. On the other hand, Chinese financial institutions have little awareness of the importance of risk prevention and do not have a deep enough understanding and knowledge of financial products and financial risks in trading in international financial markets, which often results in the accumulation of financial risks within them and huge investment losses.

In order to continue to develop and grow in international coopetition, China's financial sector needs to focus on at least the above three aspects of its own development, strive to cultivate and form its own core competitiveness, refer to international standards, learn from international experience, and continue to learn, improve and innovate, with a view to occupying a place in the transformation of the post-crisis global financial landscape.

3 Reform of the International Monetary System and RMB Internationalization Strategy

The RMB has successfully joined the International Monetary Fund (IMF)'s Special Drawing Rights (SDR) basket. Christine Lagarde, IMF Managing Director said at a press conference, "The Executive Board's decision to include the RMB in SDR basket is an important milestone in the integration of the Chinese economy into the global financial system. It is also a recognition of the progress that the Chinese authorities have made in the past years in reforming China's monetary and financial systems." The IMF finally approved the RMB's inclusion in the SDR basket exactly five years after the last IMF review of the RMB.

The reform of international financial rules in the post-financial crisis era will certainly focus on diversifying international reserve currencies, increasing the voice of emerging markets in rule-making, and building a global financial safety net aimed at maintaining global financial stability. Although the RMB went through a relatively long journey before becoming an international reserve currency, the diversification of international reserve currencies has become an irreversible process in the post-financial crisis era.

Although the RMB still has a long way to go to become a global reserve currency in the true sense of the phrase, joining the SDR basket is undoubtedly a new starting point for the RMB and China's financial markets to move towards the international stage. Analysis suggests that the main functions of reserve currencies are to maintain sufficient foreign exchange reserves to cope with external financing difficulties in the event of external shocks or crises, to repay foreign debt and back up the domestic currency with external assets, and to provide the government with the means to deal with foreign debt and respond to domestic natural disasters. Proper management of foreign exchange reserves is crucial for ensuring the proper implementation of these functions. Proper management of foreign exchange reserves is, first, to ensure an appropriate size of foreign exchange reserves; second, to ensure the liquidity of foreign exchange reserves and control the exposure of foreign exchange reserves to market and credit risks; and third, to provide a certain level of profitability in the medium-to long-term while ensuring liquidity and effective risk control. However, the financial crisis has posed significant challenges to the reserve management of foreign exchange reserve holders. Since the U.S. dollar has been the main currency in the foreign exchange reserves of various countries, the long-term depreciation of the U.S. dollar has made the preservation of foreign exchange reserves a significant challenge for various countries. It is expected that the reform of the international monetary system will be characterized by the weakening of the hegemony of the U.S. dollar and the diversification of international currencies in the next 5–10 years.

Take advantage of the withdrawal of quantitative easing in the United States to continue to promote the internationalization of the RMB. The internationalization of the RMB itself is facing unprecedented opportunities. Meanwhile, the RMB is bound to become an important part of the reform of the international monetary system in the post-financial crisis era. The internationalization of the RMB has both benefits and costs, but the benefits as a whole far outweigh the costs. Therefore, we should take advantage of the withdrawal of quantitative easing in the United States to actively create favorable conditions for internationalization and gradually and steadily promote the internationalization of the RMB.

Meanwhile, we should step up the acquisition of commodities and strategic resources from emerging economies. With falling commodity prices and the continued appreciation of the RMB, China's foreign trade in goods and strategic resource conditions have improved significantly. From a demand perspective, although China is in a critical period in which demand is declining due to economic restructuring, there is still room for greater demand for China's urbanization and infrastructure resources as economic reforms deepen. Therefore, now is a good time to acquire commodities and strategic resources from emerging economies.

The global financial market will undergo structural changes, and the trend towards diversification of international finance is inevitable. The United States United States was hit hard by the financial crisis, with a large number of enterprises going bankrupt, unemployment rising and its economic strength declining significantly. The large amounts of bonds and dollars issued to stabilize the market and stimulate the economy will affect the monopoly of the U.S. dollar, which will inevitably lead to the devaluation of the U.S. dollar in the long run and put enormous pressure on the existing floating exchange rate system which is mainly pegged to the U.S. dollar. In response to the crisis, the eurozone adopted expansionary fiscal and monetary policies, which to some extent contributed to the overall recovery of the region's economy. But the rise of the euro has yet to be further tested by time, as weak economic growth and rising fiscal deficits have pushed eurozone countries such as Iceland and Greece into sovereign debt crisis. After years of efforts, Asia is emerging as the world's center of economic growth, in sharp contrast to declining growth rates in the United States, Europe and Japan. Meanwhile, Asia's position in the international financial market is gradually rising. Its huge amount of official foreign exchange reserves plays a pivotal role in the global financial market, and the responsible attitude of major countries such as China in several crises has been fully recognized and praised by the international community. Therefore, as the world redefines the structure of financial markets, Asia will receive more attention. Major cities such as Tokyo, Hong Kong, China and Shanghai will usher in new development opportunities, and diversification of the global financial landscape has become an inevitable trend. The large amounts of bonds and dollars issued to stabilize the market and stimulate the economy will affect the monopoly of the U.S. dollar, which will inevitably lead to the devaluation of the U.S. dollar in the long run and put enormous pressure on the existing floating exchange rate system which is mainly pegged to the U.S. dollar.

New challenges for the U.S. dollar. The Triffin dilemma remains unsolved, and the "double deficit" is unsustainable. The Triffin dilemma points out that any country whose currency serves as an international currency will find itself in a dilemma: On the one hand, in order to meet the needs of international trade, payments and reserves, the country must maintain a balance of payments deficit for a long period of time; on the other hand, in order to maintain currency stability, the country must run a surplus for a long period of time. Under the current international monetary system centered on the U.S. dollar, the Triffin dilemma remains unresolved. After the outbreak of the financial crisis, large amounts of capital moved into Asian and European financial markets, making the U.S. double deficit unsustainable. No balance could be struck between an expanding flow of dollars out and a relatively shrinking flow of dollars back, and the downward pressure on the dollar was increasing.

The United States enjoys many economic, political, cultural and other benefits brought by the dollar standard, but lacks a corresponding constraint mechanism in terms of responsibility. According to the "core-periphery" theory, various countries export raw materials, oil and all kinds of low-priced industrial products to the "core country", the United States, in exchange for the international currency—the U.S. dollar, while the United States, with its well-developed and sound financial markets, "exports" bonds and other financial products to various countries, thus causing dollars to flow back. The result of the combination of these two aspects is the rapid development of the U.S. financial industry, a highly developed U.S. virtual economy, and the "deindustrialization" of the U.S. real economy, which puts the United States in an absolutely dominant position in the international division of labor. Because of this serious inequality, other countries are not willing to maintain the status quo for a long time, but are committed to exploring and building a new international monetary system.

Due to the unbalanced development of the world economy, U.S. economic supremacy has been gradually shaken in recent years. European countries, Japan and other Asian countries, China in particular, are catching up by taking advantage of being latecomers. The currencies of these countries have also embarked on the road to internationalization, and the U.S. dollar's position as the leading international currency is being increasingly impacted by other international currencies such as the euro, the yen and emerging Asian currencies.

After the financial crisis, countries around the world questioned the hegemony of the U.S. dollar. First, although the United States still ranks first in the world in terms of economic aggregates, its high debt and deteriorating fiscal and balance of payments deficits have shaken the international community's confidence in the dollar, and concerns about the ability of the United States to service its debt have also affected the international community's long-term expectations for the dollar. Second, in the absence of regulation and restrictions, the United States has long relied on printing money to maintain its high consumption and high deficit development model, and neglected the obligations incumbent on international currencies, which has raised many questions. The instability of the monetary system dominated by a single sovereign currency has become increasingly prominent, making the international community hope to break the system as soon as possible and establish a more stable and reasonable international monetary system.

The direction of reform of the international monetary system. At present, there are mainly two types of views: One direction is to seek a super-sovereign currency to replace the status of the U.S. dollar in the current international monetary system, so as to completely solve the Triffin dilemma. Its ultimate form is to establish (special drawing rights) SDRs as a global reserve currency and promote the full application of

SDRs. Another direction is to establish a diversified international monetary system and accept more sovereign currencies, including the euro and future Asian currencies, into the global mainstream.

The possibility of SDRs, a super-sovereign currency, replacing the dollar as the international reserve currency. The SDRs have advantages and disadvantages as an international currency. The SDRs as an international currency have the following advantages: First, using SDRs as an international reserve currency completely avoids the "Triffin dilemma" that sovereign currencies must face when acting as international currencies. Second, using SDRs as an international reserve currency is conducive to avoiding exchange rate risks. Third, using SDRs as the main international currency leads to greater fairness. After SDRs are used as an international currency, the seigniorage and other income obtained by IMF from SDR issuance can be shared by all countries around the world, which is conducive to the common development and progress of the world economy. Nevertheless, there are still some problems with the SDR that limit its function as an international currency: first, the SDR quota is a very small and its use is very limited. Second, the allocation range of SDRs is small and unreasonable. At present, most of the SDR quota is allocated to developed countries led by the United States, and developing countries receive a small share. Third, the basket of currencies on which the value of SDRs is based is narrow. At present, there are only four currencies on which the value of SDRs is based: the U.S. dollar, the euro, the British pound and the Japanese yen, which are very limited in scope and not very representative. Fourth, in order for SDRs to become an international reserve currency, the issuer of SDRs must be strong in its ability to exercise control and make decisions, completely independent, impartial and non-sovereign, and free from interference and influence by any sovereign state. The IMF is clearly not doing enough in this regard.

In view of the existing problems of SDRs, the academic community has explored a series of reform options covering various areas. In summary, there are mainly the following three suggestions: First, expand the scope of SDR use and increase the issuance quota; second, reform the composition of the SDR basket to include the currencies of emerging market countries such as the BRICS countries; third, set up a substitution account. This is done by allowing central banks to convert part of their countries' foreign exchange reserves into SDRs, deposit the SDRs in the IMF's "substitution account", and convert the SDRs back into foreign exchange reserves whenever they want.

The above analysis shows that the reform of the international monetary system that involves replacing the current dollar standard with a super-sovereign currency is fraught with difficulties, and even if it can be achieved eventually, it will take a very long time.

Compared with the creation of a super-sovereign currency based on SDRs, the reform idea of diversifying international currencies is more down-to-earth and easier to realize. The international monetary system will be further diversified in the future. First, the U.S. dollar will remain the dominant player in the international monetary system for a long time, but its position will gradually decline. Second, the international influence of the euro will continue to expand. Although the long-term development potential of the euro is not as great as people think, the eurozone has been taking a down-to-earth and steady path of development, and its status as an international currency will rise steadily in the long run. Third, the RMB, as the currency with the greatest development potential, will see its status gradually rise as a key Asian currency. We should seize the great opportunity of reforming the international monetary system in the post-financial crisis era to make steady progress. Of course, to build a diversified international monetary system, we need to solve the following issues: First, we need to create an independent, impartial and professional international regulatory body. Second, we need to establish a more reasonable and orderly exchange rate constraint mechanism. Third, we need to promote the internationalization of the key Asian currency, the RMB, as soon as possible. In the future scenario where major international currencies—the U.S. dollar, the euro and Asian currencies stand like the three legs of a tripod, the RMB will be a key currency, playing a pivotal role among Asian currencies. In the process of building a new diversified international monetary system, we must promote the internationalization of the RMB in a stable and orderly manner, so that it will have the ability and status to compete with the other two "legs" as soon as possible.

In the light of the above discussion, we believe that of the two reform options of creating a super-sovereign currency and diversifying the international monetary system, the latter is more feasible. The diversification of the international monetary system is a more realistic reformist way of change, which is conducive to balancing the interests of all parties and alleviating these contradictions and conflicts. In the long run, a diversified international monetary system can be regarded as a transitional stage before the ideal state of creating a supra-sovereign currency is realized.

The historical opportunity for the RMB. The financial crisis is a good opportunity for the RMB to step onto the international stage as it has weakened the U.S. dollar's position as the leading international currency and created a more open international environment for the internationalization of the RMB. China should seize the opportunity and proactively advance the internationalization of the RMB.

Strategic opportunity for the reform of the international monetary system and the internationalization of the RMB. While the global financial crisis has had a profound impact on financial markets and economies, it has also exposed the shortcomings of the U.S. dollar-centered international monetary system. This is an unprecedented opportunity for China, as the world's second largest economy, to internationalize the RMB, which is an important part of the reform of the international monetary system.

The global financial crisis has exposed the flaws inherent in the international monetary system. In 2008, the outbreak of the global financial crisis caused by the U.S. subprime mortgage crisis shattered the facade of prosperity in international financial markets. Former Federal Reserve Chairman Alan Greenspan said publicly that this financial crisis was a once-in-a-century event and its possibility of it triggering a recession was increasing. Regarding the causes of the financial crisis, different scholars have given different judgments from different perspectives, and opinions are widely divided. To sum up, there are the theory of excessive financial innovation, the theory of promotion by rating agencies, the theory of weak financial regulation, and the theory of the ineffectiveness of international accounting standards. Generally speaking, these analyses of the causes of the financial crisis are generally one-sided, and abstractly summarize the causes of the financial crisis based on the reality of the outbreak of the financial crisis. Dialectically, there is some truth to all these theories, but in the absence of comprehensive and in-depth research, they fail to reveal the essence of the crisis. It can be said that the flaws in the current international monetary system are one of the major causes of the crisis. The most fundamental problem revealed by the global financial crisis is that the current international monetary system is inherently flawed. So, how to understand the current international monetary system? What are the flaws inherent in the current international monetary system? Why are the flaws inherent in the current international monetary system one of the major causes of the international financial crisis?

One of the current international monetary systems is the Bretton Woods international monetary system (1944). The system established the international status of the U.S. dollar as the dominant currency, making it the only standard currency in the world, and saw the creation of a "double peg" gold exchange standard centered on the U.S. dollar, under which the U.S. dollar was pegged to gold around the globe. This move established the U.S. dollar as a super reserve currency. The other is the Jamaica Accords. In 1976, the agreement made the long-standing gold standard and free-floating exchange rate regime legally recognized. The core of the agreement can be summarized in two parts, one is multiple standard currencies, and the other is a floating exchange rate mechanism. In theory, the Jamaica Accords aimed to break the international monetary system with the U.S. dollar as a single standard currency, and establish an international monetary system with multiple standard currencies plus floating exchange rates. However, the reality often went beyond the imagination of the designers of the agreement.

An analysis from the perspective of private versus public goods shows that there is a profound contradiction between international currencies and sovereign currencies. The U.S. dollar, as a sovereign currency, alone assumes the function of an international currency, which is also a historical choice in the political and economic game among the world's major powers. This result reflects the national interests of the United States and is also accepted by countries around the world for a certain period of time and to a certain extent. It can be said that the internationalization of the U.S. dollar has facilitated international trade and investment to a certain extent, and promoted economic globalization and the prosperity and growth of the world economy. However, it must be emphasized that such an arrangement as the internationalization of a single sovereign currency essentially reflects the contradiction between sovereign and international currencies. This contradiction can be analyzed from multiple angles. In essence, it can be analyzed by drawing on the basic framework of the private versus public goods theory. For all countries in the world, a country's sovereign currency and the monetary system derived from it evidently possess the attributes of a private good. The sovereign currency functions as a means of circulation, a measure of value, a means of storage and a means of payment within the country. The central bank's monetary policy serves the country's economic growth, full employment, price stability, and balance of payments. Different monetary policy instruments produce different policy effects, and such effects only act on the population within the country. Other countries have no right to interfere with the implementation of the country's monetary policy regardless of their policy demands. The fact that a sovereign currency and the monetary system derived from it possess the attributes of a private good suggests that a government's monetary supply is the result of a trade-off between the marginal cost and marginal benefit of its own policy. In theory, monetary equilibrium should be satisfied with the marginal benefit of policy being equal to the marginal cost. However, the international currency that acts as the standard currency and the international monetary system derived from it evidently possess the attributes of a public good. An international currency is a currency that acts as a measure of value, a means of payment, a means of circulation, a store of value and a world currency in the world.

There is a clear contradiction between the two. Specifically, as far as the U.S. dollar and international currencies are concerned, it is an irreconcilable contradiction in two respects. On the one hand, the policy cost of sovereign states is not equal to the cost of international economic operation. On the other hand, policy rationality promotes a vicious cycle of "free-rider" behavior, which eventually leads to global economic imbalances amid a flood of liquidity. It is undeniable that the economic policy of any sovereign state under this institutional arrangement is rational. In order to seize the economic benefits of the "dollar standard", the rational policy of the United States has prompted it to repeatedly take a free ride on the "overissuance of U.S. dollars" and to stimulate the rejuvenation of its real economy through the successive launch of QE1, QE2 and QE3 to shift the high cost of dollar debt. Other countries, in order to prosper their own capital markets and obtain the excess benefits of cheap funds, also take a free ride on the "overissuance of U.S. dollars" without thinking and replenish funds in their virtual economies and open up channels of international capital flows through the opening of domestic capital markets. This vicious circle of "free-rider" behavior, as well as immediate "free-rider" benefits, have enabled the United States and other sovereign states to reach a high degree of tacit understanding on short-term interests. Over time, this vicious cycle of "free-rider" behavior became solidified, forming the basic pattern of world economic operation. The net result is a global flood of liquidity; capital-exporting countries have a large current account deficit, while capital-importing countries have a large current account surplus and capital financial account surplus, accompanied by excess foreign exchange reserves; international hot money is flooding the markets of the world's major economies, constantly feeding and inflating capital market bubbles, resulting in serious global economic imbalances.

In recent years, due to changes in the international economic situation and flaws in the dollar standard, the reform of the international monetary system has become a consensus of the international community.

Measures and suggestions for the internationalization of the RMB. We should strengthen the regulation of cross-border capital flows and promote RMB convertibility under capital account. The turmoil in emerging markets was mainly due to capital outflows triggered by the Fed's exit from quantitative easing. China's capital account, which is not yet fully open, has been affected by limited shocks, but China cannot postpone the process of capital account convertibility in isolation. Regulators should strengthen monitoring of the integrity of international short-term capital flows, change hot money, improve the statistical analysis of hot money flowing into the market mechanism of Chinese assets, and form a complete monitoring system for cross cross-border capital flows to effectively prevent financial risks. Cooperation among customs, foreign exchange, industry and commerce, and the central bank should be strengthened to avoid the trap of forex arbitrage.

Prudently advance reform of the RMB exchange rate formation mechanism. The current RMB exchange rate is close to its equilibrium level. In the short term, the increased volatility of emerging market currencies can bring about certain expectations of RMB exchange rate depreciation, as well as two-way fluctuations. We should seize this favorable opportunity to promote the realization of interest rate liberalization determined by market supply and demand and an exchange rate formation mechanism determined by demand. We should continue to pursue market-based exchange rate reform in an effort to boost the international status and influence of the RMB. China should closely monitor the ability of the RMB exchange rate to fluctuate, continue to expand the range of RMB exchange rate fluctuations, and further improve the flexibility of the RMB exchange rate; the improved RMB central parity formation mechanism truly reflects market supply and demand; we should expand the range of participants and transactions in the forex market.

Take advantage of the withdrawal of quantitative easing in the United States to promote the internationalization of the RMB. In the context of emerging economies, the U.S. quantitative easing policy is under liquidity pressure, thus creating tensions. At this time, China can conditionally start currency swaps between signatory countries. For example, we can take advantage of the fact that the BRICS countries have established a $10 billion foreign exchange stabilization fund and launched a range of RMB-denominated financial products and credits to strengthen the widespread use of the RMB for cross-border settlement, investment financing, and force governments to recognize the important role of the RMB as one of the reserve currencies for some Southeast Asian countries, Eastern Europe and Africa. We can take advantage of the withdrawal of quantitative easing and the process of balance sheet reduction to fully advance the internationalization of the three elements of the RMB: settlement, reserve and investment.

Adjust the investment strategy for foreign exchange reserves appropriately. China should proactively adjust its investment strategy for foreign exchange reserves and steadily diversify its foreign exchange reserve assets. In the long run, growing foreign exchange reserves should be curbed in order to reduce the proportion of reserve assets held in foreign currencies and "hide" the direction of change. Meanwhile, we should make innovative use of foreign exchange reserves and strongly support Chinese enterprises in "going out". It is recommended that a sovereign wealth fund be set up in the elderly care and energy sector to invest in alternative assets globally in order to improve the return on investment of foreign exchange reserves.

Step up the acquisition of commodities and strategic resources from emerging economies. With falling commodity prices and the continued appreciation of the RMB, China's foreign trade in goods and strategic resource conditions have improved significantly. From a demand perspective, despite the decline in demand due to China's economic restructuring, there is still room for greater demand for China's urbanization and infrastructure resources as economic reforms deepen. Therefore, now is still a good time to acquire commodities and strategic resources from emerging economies.

4 Advancing Medium- and Long-term Financing and the Building of the Legislative System in China

In 2010, Shanghai, as the first pilot city to issue local bonds, successfully issued 7.1 billion yuan worth of local construction bonds. Zhejiang, Guangdong and Shenzhen will follow suit. At a time when China's economy and society are at an important stage of urbanization, industrialization and internationalization, the lack of capital for investment projects and the inability to convert huge amounts of "savings funds" and "social funds" into centralized, large-sum and long-term construction funds have become the basic contradiction in China's investment and financing pattern. In the important period when the state is promoting the financial reform of interest rate liberalization, how to speed up the development of China's medium- and long-term financing system with innovative thinking and creative working methods, and vigorously develop policy-based and development finance has a crucial bearing on whether China's economy can develop steadily and rapidly (Liu 2011).

4.1 Moving Forward with the Development of China's Medium- and Long-Term Financing System

4.1.1 The Inherent Demand for Medium- and Long-Term Financing in National Development Strategies

Over the years, in the process of international business development, working closely around China's Go Out policy, development finance institutions have actively leveraged their role as financial levers, and made positive contributions to easing China's energy and resources constraints and serving national development and security strategies. At the same time, China also needs to participate in international cooperation through various channels, familiarize itself with international rules and seek and control its development space. While actively participating in international cooperation, development finance institutions can not only bring opportunities for China's Go Out policy, but also bring development finance concepts and platforms to Asian, African and Latin American countries. This model not only challenges the traditional concept of international assistance, but also greatly influences the pattern of South-South exchanges and will increasingly become a new theoretical basis for exchanges between Asian, African and Latin American countries.

Urbanization creates demand, industrialization creates supply, and internationalization expands space—all of which are impossible without intensive, large-scale and long-term investments from policy-based and development finance. It has become inevitable that we speed up the development of a medium—and long-term financing system.

4.1.2 *Development Finance Needs to Speed Up the Development of A Medium- and Long-Term Financing System*

Throughout the course of global economic development, policy-based and development finance institutions have been important policy tools to compensate for market failure. No matter in developing or developed countries, and no matter in the stage of stable economic development or in the stage of coping with financial crisis, policy-based and development banks, as the mainstay of medium- and long-term investment and financing, are an indispensable part of the financial system and play an important role in moving the market. In line with this, the task of policy-based and development finance is to solve the maturity mismatch risk that is common for development loans by issuing medium- and long-term bonds for direct finance, and provide long-term stable, sustained and rapid financing support for infrastructure construction and other areas. These prescriptive and developmental factors determine that in the building of China's medium- and long-term financing system, national financial policymakers and development finance institutions must, in accordance with the requirements of national development strategic planning, drive "savings funds" and "private funds" to the building of medium- and long-term financing systems while making fiscal or bond-type development finance inputs into medium - and long-term projects, so as to effectively coordinate domestic and international overall situations and markets.

4.1.3 *Medium- and Long-term Financing is a Key Way to Balance Total Social Financing*

Since 2011, the central government has required that monetary policy should employ a combination of tools, maintain a reasonable scale and pace of social financing, and replace the credit index with the total social financing as the intermediate variable in line with changes in China's financing structure. Social financing other than RMB loans is expected to overtake RMB loans in 2011, which is an inevitable trend stemming from changes in China's financing structure and the rapid development of direct financing.

Whether in the period when total RMB loans were used as the intermediate variable of monetary policy or in the period when total social financing was used as the intermediate variable of monetary policy, through a financing mechanism dominated by the issuance of financial bonds, supplemented by corporate deposits and other sources, policy-based and development finance institutions mobilized and absorbed large amounts of long-term and relatively low-cost social funds for the construction of key national projects, thus lending strong support to the implementation of national macroeconomic policies and the growth of the national economy, and ensuring the sustainable development of development finance. A medium- and long-term investment and financing system has become a key way to smooth out cyclical fluctuations in the national economy and balance total social financing, as well as an important lever to balance overall steady upward progress in national economic and social advancement and development.

4.1.4 Challenges and Opportunities for the Development of A Medium- and Long-Term Financing System

In the context of the implementation of a separate operation and management system in China's financial sector, it has become a significant financial phenomenon that those with surplus funds (savers), social funds and those who are short of funds (investors) directly conduct financial transactions without going through banks' indirect financing intermediaries. The impact of the change of "financial disintermediation" on China's financial operation and macro-control is multifaceted. On the micro side, it shrinks banks' traditional sources of income, and on the macro side, it makes regulators' policy intention to curb high investment by controlling the "credit gate" lose its basis for implementation. What we need to realize is that in the context of a comprehensive shift to a market-oriented economic system, the development of direct financing has become an important part of China's financial reform and development. The lessons learned from other economies dictate that interest rate liberalization in China will be a consistent gradual process, and that it will take a long time to fully liberalize interest rates.

In view of this change in the financial landscape, for China's policy-based and development finance institutions, which mainly focus on "direct bond financing", how to make the most of the opportunities and meet the challenges brought by the process of financial reform and development which is seeing a shift from "indirect financing" to "direct financing" and "interest rate liberalization" will be a very important historical issue.

4.1.5 *Drawing on Foreign Experience in "Opening Up" and Innovating A New Bond Financing System*

The practice of strict separate operation and management in the financial sector by the U.S. monetary authorities before the mid-1980s showed that such practice was not only futile, but also jeopardized the process of financial modernization, causing the U.S. economy to lag behind Germany and Japan for a long time. After the mid-1980s, the U.S. monetary authorities changed their mindset and, in a departure from the tradition of "strict separation" in the financial sector, gradually committed themselves to "opening up" the connection between banks and markets, increasingly blurring the boundary between direct financing and indirect financing. Only then did the United States finally break free from the problem of "separate operation". With this new financial system, the United States regained its position as a world leader in the financial sector. The U.S. experience tells us that the modernization of a country's financial system usually goes through the process from "separate operation" to "mixed operation", and only by finally breaking the boundary between direct and indirect financing and implementing mixed financial operation can the financial system be modernized.

Currently, China is pursuing a strategy of developing direct financing, which in fact allows mixed financial operation to take place. This makes it possible for China to avoid the problems that come with other countries pushing for direct financing in the context of strict separation. In this light, China is now facing a rare strategic opportunity to modernize its financial sector.

At a time when the hidden debt of local governments has become commonplace in China, reducing the proportion of commercial bank credit and developing more transparent policy-based and development finance and bond financing on local government platforms will not only help make local debt more transparent and reduce the information asymmetry between the central government and local governments, but also effectively reduce the scale of local governments' hidden debt, promote the diversification of financing channels, and relieve the huge pressure brought by the current financing structure to the commercial banking system. At the same time, local government ratings should be introduced into the issuance of urban investment bonds to more accurately reflect the economic development level and fiscal revenue and expenditure of the region where the issuing enterprises are located, so as to form a multi-level credit rating framework and provide a reference system for the accurate pricing of urban investment bonds.

4.1.6 Policy Recommendations

There is no existing experience and model to follow in China's development, and the development of a medium- and long-term financing system depends on the soundness of the financial system. We must speed up the development of China's medium—and long-term financing system with innovative thinking and creative working methods in order to formulate policies and methods that suit China's national conditions and development needs.

First, formulate policies that are conducive to the development of bond banks. In the current bank financing-denominated financial landscape with high savings rates and abundant liquidity, in order to solve the problem of converting huge amounts of savings and social capital into medium- and long-term construction funds, financial policy-making and regulatory authorities need to formulate development policies that strengthen the important role of bond banks in conversion, manage and control medium- and long-term risks, and guard against systemic risks caused by a mismatch between the maturities of short deposits and long loans. Internationally, policy and development banks that use bonds as their main financing method are a long-term objective existence. The development of China Development Bank, the Export–Import Bank of China and the Agricultural Development Bank of China shows that the operation of bond banks is successful and effective. Bond banks not only play a role in raising large-sum, centralized and long-term construction funds for the country, but also promote the development of the bond financial market.

Bond banks, which mainly issue bonds to raise funds, have very different business characteristics from savings banks, so it is difficult to apply the regulatory and performance evaluation standards of savings retail banks. In order to better promote the development of bond banks, financial policy-making and regulatory authorities should draw on the international practice of specialized classification, statistics, management and legislation for bond banks, and put in place systematic institutional arrangements compatible with such practice, including regulatory and performance evaluation standards, to create the basic conditions necessary for the survival and development, business operation and risk control of bond banks.

Second, promote the conversion of savings and social funds into medium—and long-term funds. In the current situation where the separated operation and management pattern of Chinese banks cannot be completely changed, in the process of financial reform and market development which is seeing a shift from indirect financing from banks to direct financing from society, a "buffer zone" of bond investment and financing can be established to promote the conversion of savings and social funds into centralized, large-sum and long-term funds, so as to increase financing support for key areas and weak links.

In the process of implementing interest rate liberalization, it is recommended that financial policy-making and regulatory authorities should allow interest rates on large and long-term deposits to float within a larger range, and design a reform plan for converting savings and social funds into centralized, large-sum and long-term construction funds that are urgently needed at China's development stage of urbanization, industrialization and internationalization, so as to alleviate the basic contradiction of lack of capital for investment projects.

Third, strengthen international cooperation and expand overseas financial markets. In the context of economic globalization, financial markets basically dominate the risk of all economic activities. Government entities are the main issuers in China's bond market, and China's state-owned banks are the main investors. The government should build a stronger bond market. As the issuance of RMB bonds to overseas investors develops, it is recommended that the state's fiscal and monetary authorities and development finance institutions consider issuing Chinese medium- and long-term financing bonds overseas to attract funds from all over the world to China.

The Chinese Ministry of Finance issued RMB 20 billion worth of bonds in Hong Kong in August 2011. Although the move attracted demand for RMB, what it took in were Hong Kong dollars, which were directly pegged to the U.S. dollar, so it could not lead to the conversion of U.S. dollars into RMB. If China chooses to issue additional government bonds at home, its dollar-denominated trade surplus stranded abroad will still be hindered by liquidity and foreign exchange controls, and the result will be to recycle RMB at home. Only by issuing RMB-denominated special government bonds in dollar-rich capital markets can China resist the expansion of dollar-denominated assets.

Since the RMB market is highly bullish on the investment value of special government bonds, concerns about issuance and distribution costs can be overcome. In the European and U.S. markets, special government bonds can recover part of the dollar-denominated trade surplus, and in countries or regions where China is actively promoting trade settlement in RMB, they can also be used by foreign importers to store the long-term RMB funds they need, which essentially boosts cross-border settlement in RMB. RMB-denominated overseas special government bonds can lure RMB out of China, and with a currency-carrying instrument, the internationalization of the RMB will not just be empty talk. The RMB obtained from the issuance of government bonds overseas can be used for trade settlement and financing, and can also satisfy investors' demand for RMB accounts. China should actively promote medium- and long-term bonds to its major trading partners, and help them store the potentially high-value RMB in addition to U.S. and European bonds, to the benefit of both sides.

4.2 Building A Policy-Based Financial System and Developing A Legislative System

At present, China's economy and society are at an important development stage of new-type urbanization, industrialization, informationization and agricultural modernization. On the one hand, the task of infrastructure construction is arduous, the industrial foundation is weak, and consumption has not yet become the main driving force; on the other hand, there is a lack of capital for investment projects, and huge amounts of "savings funds" and "social funds" cannot be converted into centralized, large-sum and long-term construction funds. This has become the basic contradiction in China's investment and financing pattern. As a bridge between the government and the market, policy-based finance plays a pioneering and dominant role in medium—and long-term financing for China's economic development, providing stable and efficient financing support for the strategic planning of new-type urbanization and industrialization. It is a powerful strategic tool for implementing the country's macro strategic intentions and promoting national economic and social development. Therefore, building a reasonable and effective policy-based financial system, developing a legislative system, and giving full play to the advantages and functions of policy banks will play a very key role in supporting the realization of national development strategic goals (Guo and Liu 2015).[1]

4.2.1 Objective Necessity and Importance of Policy-Based Finance Under the New Situation

Different from general commercial finance, policy-based finance means the government's participation in the allocation of funds and resources in response to "market failure", effectively serves China's implementation of the national modernization catch-up strategy, and has the characteristics of "policy purpose, market-oriented operation, and specialized management". Its main functions include: filling financing gaps or deficiencies in bottleneck areas, and playing a pioneering role in forward-looking and strategic investment; building and improving financing markets and institutions and acting as an institutional builder in areas where markets are insufficient and institutions are lacking; attracting and driving social funds into areas where funds are scarce, and leveraging the guiding role of private capital; serving certain specific development goals of the government, promoting social equity, assisting in the resolution of financial risks, and acting as a supporter of public interest and social stability.

The policy-based financial system can effectively reduce the social cost of achieving national policy objectives, promote social equity and implement specific strategic intentions. From the perspective of the history of economic development and the internal logic of economic growth, the development of a policy-based financial system is necessary in the long term. According to international experience, policy financial institutions not only exist widely in developing countries, but also exist in developed countries with sound financial systems, becoming a useful and necessary supplement to market mechanisms, and there are large-scale policy-based financial institutions in Britain, Germany, France, Japan, Brazil and even the United States. For developing countries that implement the modernization catch-up strategy, the necessity and strategic significance of developing policy-based finance are even more prominent.

[1] Chen Yuan, vice chairman of the National Committee of the Chinese People's Political Consultative Conference and ex-chairman of the China Development Bank, instructed that: development finance should be legislated as soon as possible, and its relationship with money, public finance, government, and market should be clarified. July 4, 2015.

In view of China's situation, policy-based finance should not be weakened in the short term, but should be further developed, improved and innovated.

On the whole, the framework of China's policy-based finance is not yet sound and complete. There are a number of problems, such as lack of legal norms, an overlap between the business of policy banks and commercial banks, unsound risk compensation and subsidy mechanisms, lack of evaluation criteria for policy banks, weakened policy objectives, vaguely defined functions, an unsound supervisory framework, and limited fundraising options. The process of resolving the contradictions between policy-based and commercial business and reforming the policy finance system is far from over, and the institutional guarantee for the sustainable operation of the policy-based financial system has not yet been effectively established. In addition, there are still some problems in such areas as policy-based secured financing, urban investment bond financing and infrastructure construction franchise financing.

To build a reasonable and effective policy-based financial system, we need to adopt the following basic line of thinking: First, we should strive to clarify the policy objectives of policy-based finance and its boundary with commercial finance; second, we should actively address issues related to the operating mechanism of policy-based financial institutions with market-oriented goals; third, we should make great efforts to build a risk-sharing mechanism and improve the benefit compensation mechanism to support the realization of market-oriented goals; in addition, we should reasonably build a performance evaluation system to ensure the realization of policy goals. Therefore, the main contents of the overall framework should include: first, to determine the business scope of China's policy-based finance; second, the way to realize the various services included in China's policy-based finance; third, in order to realize the services included in policy-based finance, what kind of governance structure does China need to build for policy-based financial institutions; fourth, to reasonably set up a regulatory body for policy-based finance.

Effective supervision is a necessary condition for the healthy development of policy-based finance, and different countries and regions need to make corresponding regulatory arrangements for the development of policy-oriented financial institutions. As far as China is concerned, first, we need to gradually establish a legal framework for policy-based finance; second, we need to establish and improve the regulatory committee system for policy-based finance. It is recommended that a stakeholder-based corporate governance structure that incorporates the advantages of the German, American and Japanese models and takes into consideration China's practice be established, and a market-oriented operation model featuring specialized division of labor and cooperation between policy-based financial institutions and commercial financial institutions be implemented for business development.

4.2.2 The Reform of China's Policy-Based Finance Should be Viewed From A Strategic and Long-Term Perspective

Policy-based financial institutions all over the world are generally developing in different directions, with some moving away from policy-based finance towards commercialization and some continuing to adhere to the operating guidelines and strictly prohibiting competition with commercial financial institutions. The commercialization of policy-based financial institutions is constantly being tested around the world. Its theoretical basis is not yet mature, and the final results are even more unpredictable. We should try to draw lessons from this trend which is fraught with uncertainties and use them to guide the practice of reforming policy-based finance in China.

Judging from the development of policy-based finance, China has not had a clear understanding of it from the very beginning, and has clearly positioned it incorrectly, only treating policy banks as a "by-product" of the commercialization of specialized banks, serving only to bear the burdens of certain policy-based financing business left by specialized banks. Basically, the long-term development of policy finance has not been planned from the perspective of the national economic development strategy, and the scope of policy-based business undertaken by the three policy banks, namely China Development Bank, the Export–Import Bank of China and the Agricultural Development Bank of China, has not been clearly defined. This has a great impact on the development of policy-based finance in China, not only affecting the integrity of the policy-based financial system, but also affecting decision makers' judgment on the necessity of policy-based finance.

For this reason, designing a reform approach for China's policy-based financial system requires strategic thinking and a long-term perspective on this issue. From the perspective of the strategic development of the policy-based financial system, according to the stage of China's economic development and the actual demand for policy-based finance, the policy-based financial system should cover a very wide range of fields far beyond the existing scope of business. Therefore, we should understand the significance of policy-based finance from the strategic height of economic development, consider the design of China's policy-based financial system from a long-term perspective, pay more attention to the role of policy-based finance, reasonably plan for the areas of business of policy-based finance, continuously improve the policy-based financial system, and strengthen the role of policy-based financial institutions. We must not think only of the present. We cannot one-sidedly emphasize the negative effects caused by policy-based financial institutions such as unfair competition and insufficient profit orientation, still less take them as the main factor and basis for determining the path to reform of policy-based finance. China's policy-based financial system needs to be actively built, developed in a reasonable manner, and maintained for a long time.

In the policy banking reform that China has begun since 2007, a noteworthy tendency is to gradually transform policy banking into an operation mode dominated by commercial banking and supplemented by policy-based business. Between the lines there is a message that policy-based financing has become obsolete and that commercial financing channels are expected to basically cover all financing needs. This kind of thinking, when applied in practice, will have a negative impact on the development of China's financial system.

For China, which is in the process of "comprehensive deepening reform" and "economic transformation and industrial restructuring", we must base ourselves on the greatest reality that China will remain in the primary stage of socialism for a long time to come. The existence of policy-based finance must first meet the traditional demand for policy-based finance in the areas of import and export, agriculture, and SMEs. This is because China's economic dependence on the outside world is increasing, the financing difficulties of SMEs have been difficult to solve, the development of agriculture, rural areas and farmers has been lagging behind for a long time, and the gap between urban and rural areas is widening. The problems in these fields are more serious than those in other countries, and it is difficult to obtain commercial funds to meet the huge demand for funds in the process of development, which points to an apparent failure of the market and urgently requires the intervention of government policy funds. Second, while focusing on the strategic goals of "new-type urbanization" and "going out", China needs to make great efforts to upgrade its economic structure and transform its development mode with the help of policy-based finance. The high-tech industries, new energy industries, green industries and the building of reasonable industrial chains in the circular economy that China will focus on in the next stage all require huge investments. These industries are risky and commercial banks are reluctant to get involved. Therefore, the government needs to continuously support them through policy-based financial institutions.

4.2.3 *Drawing on Successful International Experience to Promote Legislation for Policy-Based Finance*

Unlike policy banks in most developed countries, China's policy banks have been developing in the absence of a complete legal and regulatory system, and no clear legal positioning of policy banks has been formed so far, putting China's policy banks in an embarrassing situation where there are no laws to go by for operation and no rules to follow for regulation. In contrast, foreign policy banks have laws to go by. For example, after the war, Japan established Japan Reconstruction Finance Corporation under the Japan Reconstruction Finance Corporation Act, the Japan Policy Bank under the Japan Policy Bank Act, and the SME Credit Insurance Corporation under the SME Credit Insurance Corporation Act. Germany established KfW under the Law Concerning Kreditanstalt für Wiederaufbau. South Korea also established policy-based financial institutions with different functions under the Industrial Bank of Korea Act, the Agricultural Cooperative Act, and the Export–Import Bank of Korea Act. Foreign legislation for policy banks has the following characteristics: first, the establishment of policy banks in accordance with national laws on policy banks, second, independent legislation for different policy banks, and third, the formation of a system of laws on policy banks with characteristics unique to the country.

The long absence of laws on policy (bond) banks in China has led to various problems, such as unclear market positioning, limited choices of business tools, excessive administrative intervention, poor ability to raise capital, and dysfunctional relations with the government. Therefore, legislation for policy banks is a matter of practical necessity and urgency, and should be put on the legislative agenda as soon as possible.

It is recommended that a Policy Bank Law be made by drawing on the successful experience of foreign countries. Several issues should be clarified: The first is the issue of bond credit ratings.it is essential to continue to maintain the rating of sovereign bonds, whether explicitly or implicitly. Foreign bond-based financial institutions, such as KfW, Korea

Development Bank, and the Development Bank of Japan, maintain zero risk weights. Provide long-term state credit support: clarify the long-term sovereign credit ratings of policy banks through institutional arrangements, ensure that policy banks better fulfill their strategic duty to serve the country, and maintain the smooth operation of financial markets. The second is the issue of tax breaks. The state should give policy banks tax breaks, so that all their operating profits can be used to replenish their capital to make development occur on a rolling basis. The third is the issue of regulation. The regulation of bond banks in foreign countries is different from that of commercial banks. For example, the capital requirements for bond banks are lower than those for commercial banks. Implement regulatory standards for policy banks and enjoy equal regulatory policies: Given the unique and strategic nature of policy banks, it is only logical that regulatory standards for policy banks should be applied, rather than policy banks requiring "differential regulation". The fourth is the issue of business performance evaluation. The state's guidance for evaluating the business performance of policy banks should be different from that for state-controlled commercial banks, and evaluation shall be implemented on a category-by-category basis. Implement evaluation criteria for policy banks: Given policy banks' task of serving national strategies, as well as the unique nature of their fundraising and business activities, policy banks should be given equal treatment in performance evaluation. As a single piece of legislation regulating bond banks, the Policy Banking Law must be clear and unambiguous on the above issues, so as to provide a legal safeguard for the healthy and stable development of bond banks.

4.3 Speeding Up the Building of A "Green Finance" System with Chinese Characteristics

As an effective financial instrument in general use, "green finance" has been widely implemented in economically developed countries. Building an all-round "green finance" credit system that integrates finance and taxation is an effective means to establish a market-based mechanism for attracting social capital to ecological and environmental protection and upgrade China's economy, and a historic mission to realize the sustainable development strategy (Chen and Liu 2015).

4.3.1 *The Urgency of Building A "Green Finance" System*

At present, China's ecological situation is grim, and it is urgent to build a "green finance" system. As the world's second largest economy and a heavily polluted country, China is severely constrained by environmental factors in its economic development. In 2014, only eight out of 74 major cities in China met the air quality standards, 75% of drinking water sources exceeded limits for impurities, and over 19% of cultivated land exceeded pollution limits. The Central Economic Work Conference pointed out that China's "environmental carrying capacity has reached or is approaching the upper limit". Faced with such a grim environmental situation, we urgently need to promote the development of an all-round "green finance" system that integrates finance and taxation, and unleash the power of the market. This is a major issue for China in the process of industrial structure upgrading and economic restructuring. Given the financial industry's role in allocating credit resources, building a "green finance" system to guide the withdrawal of funds from highly polluting and energy-intensive industries can have the effect of "extracting the firewood from under the cauldron".

There is a significant gap in funding for environmental protection, which requires the support of a "green finance" system. According to relevant data, during China's 13th Five-Year Plan period, at least two trillion yuan will be invested in green industries annually, and in the next five years, the investment needed for air pollution control is about 1.7 trillion yuan, of which only 10%-15% can be provided by government funds. The large funding gap needs to be supported by a financial channel. At the same time, supporting the energy conservation and environmental protection industry opens up a new growth point for China's economy and provides an effective way for China to achieve its macro goals of "dual objectives, dual combinations and twin engines".

In the process of building a "green finance" system, there are still some problems. First, a policy synergy has not yet been formed, and overlap of responsibilities between government departments coupled with a lack of responsibilities makes it difficult to form a policy synergy in financial support for ecological and environmental protection projects; second, the capacity building-deficient "green finance", weak government supervision over the environmental impact of projects and lax law enforcement cannot support innovation in "green finance" products such as carbon emissions trading and pollution rights trading; third, the current policy system ignores environmental externalities and distorts price signals, making it difficult to activate and guide the flow of private capital to green industries; fourth, there is a lack of incentives for financial regulation, regulatory authorities do not give preferential policies to "green finance" projects in terms of capital usage, deposit reserves and loss provisions, risk tolerance, etc., and when it comes to fiscal and tax policies, no interest discounts or tax breaks are provided for ecological and environmental protection projects, resulting in a lack of motivation on the part of financial institutions to promote "green finance"; fifth, information asymmetry makes it difficult for financial institutions to timely and accurately grasp enterprises' environmental protection information and environmental law enforcement results; sixth, ecological and environmental protection projects are scattered, poorly regulated and small, there is a lack of proven business models, the economic benefits of projects are insignificant, enterprises lack initiative, and financial support is difficult to obtain.

4.3.2 The Basic Architecture of the "Green Finance" System

Promoting ecological progress requires the support of a complete and well-functioning "green finance" system with sound mechanisms and supporting policies. We should do a good job of top-level design and promote the building of a "green finance" system architecture with complete institutions, policies, financial infrastructure and legal infrastructure.

Building of "green finance" institutions and organizations. First, we should set up new financial institutions specializing in "green finance" business, or set up "green finance" business departments in banks, insurance companies, funds, securities companies, guarantee companies and loan companies among existing financial institutions. Second, we should formulate China's "green finance rules by drawing on the Equator Principles and the Global Compact, and lead financial institutions to be more conscious about going green and protecting the environment, fulfill their social responsibilities, and conduct financial business in accordance with the "green finance" rules. Third, we should develop new "green finance" service products, provide green credit, green bonds, green insurance and green funds, and innovate investment and financing models to support the development of green industries. At present, banks play a prominent role in social financing. We can give full play to the professional capabilities, economics of scale, and risk control advantages of green banks in green credit and investment by establishing a green banking system. We can try the PPP model to promote the development of green industries and lever private equity investment with limited government funds. Fourth, we should strengthen collaboration with the World Bank, the Asian Development Bank and other organizations, work to ensure that the Silk Road Fund, the Asian Infrastructure Investment Bank, the New Development Bank and other outbound investment and development institutions led by China or in which China is a participant meet the requirements of the "green finance" guidelines, and establish a high-standard environmental risk management system for international financial operations.

Improve fiscal and financial policies. First, we should improve the mechanism of efficient financial subsidies for green loans; second, we should issue guidelines on green bonds through competent authorities, allowing and encouraging banks and enterprises to issue green bonds; third, we should strengthen stock market mechanisms that support green enterprises.

The construction of financial infrastructure for green investment. First, we should speed up the development of pollution rights and carbon sink trading markets; second, we should establish a green rating system, establish an environmental cost accounting system and database that serve public good, improve the accessibility of environmental assessment methods and data, and lead local governments to establish a green GDP measurement system and provide third parties with energy conservation and emission reduction benefit measurement and environmental assessment consulting services; third, we should establish a green IPO sponsorship mechanism, promote the development and application of a green stock index to lead capital markets to invest more in green industries; fourth, we should establish a green investment network to lead social investors to invest in green industries.

Building a legal and regulatory system and guarantee mechanism for "green finance". First, we should implement mandatory green insurance in more areas, using insurance market mechanisms to restrict polluting investments and provide environmental remediation; second, we should clarify the legal responsibility of banks for the environment, and allow pollution victims to sue financial institutions that provide funds for pollution projects and are jointly and severally liable; third, the CSRC and stock exchanges should establish a mandatory environmental information disclosure mechanism for listed companies to provide a basis for assessing the environmental risk posed by and accurately judging the value of listed companies.

4.3.3 *Concentrating Efforts on Building A "Green Finance" System*

Introduce special supportive policies to promote the development of "green finance" as soon as possible. This is the policy basis for cooperation between local governments and financial institutions, and will help mobilize the enthusiasm and initiative of local governments and financial institutions. To this end, the state should introduce relevant supportive policies and special development plans as soon as possible, set up a "green finance development" category in the annual government investment budget, increase the state's investment in "green finance", and create a good policy environment for local governments and financial institutions to carry out various types of cooperation.

Explore cooperation between the government and financial institutions in setting up "green finance" development funds. First, the government and large financial institutions can cooperate in setting up policy-oriented "green finance" guidance funds. As funds of funds, these funds provide equity and debt financing support to various commercial "green finance" development funds (companies) on the principle of capital preservation and appropriate profits. Second, the government and large financial institutions can jointly set up joint-stock government-financial institution cooperation funds that operate on a commercial basis, or specialized and commercial funds can be set up jointly by domestic banks, insurance companies, investment companies and other financial institutions with the support of preferential policies provided by the government. Through the establishment and development of various policy-based and commercial "green finance" development funds, efforts will be made to alleviate the bottleneck problem of shortage of funds for the development of "green finance".

Move faster to build the ability of the government and financial institutions to cooperate with each other. First, we should encourage local governments with the necessary conditions to speed up the establishment of government investment and financing platforms (companies) for promoting the development of "green finance", build lawful and compliant loan acceptance entities for local governments to cooperate with financial institutions and accept loans from financial institutions, and promote the standardization of credit cooperation between the government and financial institutions. Second, we should actively promote the reform of the fiscal system, establish a stable source of tax revenue for the government, and increase the government's share in the existing tax sharing system, so as to enhance the government's ability to invest public money in the development of "green finance". Third, we should integrate the sources of funds for "green finance" from the government, integrate the development funds for "green finance" from the state and governments at all levels, infrastructure construction funds, industrialization loans, and relevant funds used to support the development of environmental protection, make unified arrangements for and centralize the use of these funds, and effectively strengthen grants, allowances, interest subsidies and other policy inputs for accepting loans directly from financial institutions or encouraging or leading financial institutions to issue loans to small and medium-sized environmental protection enterprises engaged in the development of "green finance".

References

Chen and Liu. Speeding Up the Building of A "Green Finance" System with Chinese Characteristics, Guangming Daily (September 30, 2015, page 15)

Guo and Liu, Theoretical Dynamics, Party School of the CPC Central Committee, Theoretical Trends, February 20, 2015, Issue 2022.

Liu. Suggestions for Speeding Up the Development of China's Medium- and Long-Term Financing System, Study Times, Party School of the CPC Central Committee, November 2011.

Liu. Global Financial Changes and China's Monetary Policy in the New Era, People's Forum—Academic Frontier, late February 2018.

References

[Foundation Project] A General Program of the National Natural Science Foundation of China, Research on Incomplete Exchange Rate Transmission and Monetary Policy: Issues and Challenges in the Process of Economic Globalization (71773085).

A Comparative Study of the Development Paths of China and Major Economies, China Development Bank Research Institute and Institute of World Economics and Politics, Chinese Academy of Social Sciences, November 2013.

Albert. The Strategy of Economic Development, Beijing: Economic Science Press, 1991.

Bian. A Study of Monetary Policy Rules in the Transition Period, Beijing: People's Publishing House, 2006.

Bian. Empirical Issues Relating to Taylor's Rule and Its Test in China. Journal of Financial Research, 2006, (8): 56–69.

Bian. Inflation Targeting: Theory, Practice, and Its Test in China. Journal of Financial Research, 2007, (9): 42–54.

Caceres C, Carriere-Swallow Y, Demir I, Gruss B. U.S. Monetary Policy Normalization and Global Interest Rates. IMF Working Paper, WP/16/195, 2016.

Cao. A Study of Inflation Targeting, Beijing: China Finance Press, 2006: 184–196.

Chen and Ma. A Study of U.S. Quantitative Easing Policy and Exit Effects and Their Impact on China. World Economy Study, 2016, (6).

Chen and Pan. Theoretical Analysis of and Insights from Monetary Policy in Financial Crisis. South China Finance, 2009, (9).

L. Weiping, *American Monetary Policy Adjustment and Its Impacts*,
https://doi.org/10.1007/978-981-99-7810-6

Chen and Sun. An Analysis of the Impact of U.S. Quantitative Easing on China's Macroeconomy. Economic Science, 2012, (1): 12–26.

Chen et al. The History of Theories of Political Economy, Changchun: Jilin People's Publishing House, 1981.

Chen, Yang and Zhao. Analysis of the Effects of China's Fiscal and Monetary Policies Under Different Degrees of Capital Account Liberalization. The Journal of Quantitative & Technical Economics, 2018, 35(3): 96–113.

Chen, Zheng, and Guo. China's Monetary Policy Rules, Optimal Single Rules and Macro Effects. Statistical Research, 2015, 32(1): 41–51

Chen. A Review of Western Traditional Economic Cycle Theory, Research on Financial and Economic Issues, 1996, (6).

Chen. Advanced Econometrics and Stata Applications (Second Edition), Beijing: Higher Education Press, 2014.

Chen. Report on China's Industrialization Process: An Evaluation and Study of the Level of Industrialization in China's Provincial-level Regions from 1995 to 2005, Beijing: Social Sciences Academic Press (China), 2007.

Dai and Zhang. Quantitative Easing Around the World: When to Exit? Xiamen: Xiamen University Press, 2012.

Dai and Zhang. The Exit Mechanism of Non-traditional Monetary Policy in the United States in the Post-Crisis Era. Finance & Economics, 2010, (6).

Ding. Discussion on the Impact of U.S. Quantitative Easing on China and Response Measures. Modern Commerce and Trade Industry, 2012, (1).

Du. A Study of the Transmission Mechanism of U.S. Quantitative Easing Policy, Tianjin: Nankai University Press, 2013.

Fan and Chen. International Liquidity Arrangements and RMB Internationalization. Nankai Journal (Philosophy and Social Science Edition), 2015, (5): 131–139

Fan and Zhao. Contemporary Monetary Policy: Theory and Practice, Shanghai: Shanghai Sanlian Bookstore, 2005.

Fang, He, and Jing. A Study of the Spillover Effects of China-U.S. Trade Frictions on China's Financial Markets. Finance & Trade Economics, 2019, (6).

Fu. Fed Rate Hikes, RMB Exchange Rate and Price Volatility. Journal of International Trade, 2017, (3).

Gao. Econometric Analysis Methods and Modeling: Views Applications and Examples, Beijing: Tsinghua University Press, 2014.

Guo, Chen, and Chen. A Study of the Declining Effectiveness of China's Monetary Policy and Expectation Management. Economic Research Journal, 2016, 51(01): 28–41.

Guo, Xu, and Tong. A Study of the Characteristics of Japanese Quantitative Easing Policy and Its Short-term Impact on the Stock Market—Based on An Event Study Methodology. Studies of International Finance, 2016, (5).

Hu, Wang, and Huang. The Effects of the Fed's Quantitative Easing Policy and Its Implications for China—A Perspective on the Transmission Mechanism of Monetary Policy Based on Tobin's Q Theory. Studies of International Finance, 2013, (12): 4–13.

Huang and Guo. The Impact of the Order in Which Capital Account Liberalization and Interest Rate Liberalization Occur on Macroeconomic Stability. The Journal of World Economy, 2016, 39(9):3–27.

Huang. The Impact of U.S. Expansionary Monetary and Fiscal Policy on China's Inflation, Changchun: Jilin University Press, 2014.

International Monetary Fund (IMF). Policy Support and Vaccines Expected to Lift Activity (2021-1-25).

Jiang and Li. Money Supply Should Continue to Be the Intermediary Target of China's Monetary Policy for the Time Being. China Finance, 2002, (10): 14–18.

Jiang, Liu, and Zhao. An Empirical Analysis of the Effectiveness of the Mechanisms for Transmission Through the Monetary Channel and Credit Channel—And the Choice of Intermediate Target of Monetary Policy, 2005, (5): 70–79.

Jiao. An Analysis of the Market Competition Pattern of China's Banking Industry and the Institutions Behind It. Macroeconomics, 2001, (6).

Jin and Hong. Coordination of Interest Rate Policy and Exchange Rate Policy in the International Monetary Environment. Economic Research Journal, 2015, 50(5): 35–47.

Keynes. General Theory of Employment, Interest and Money, Beijing: Commercial Press, 1983.

Li and Gao. A Study of Spillovers from U.S. Monetary Policy Normalization—A Comparison of Emerging and Developed Economies. Shanghai Journal of Economics, 2019, (6).

Li and Gao. An Analysis and Empirical Test of the Impact of Policy-Based Finance on Economic Growth. Inquiry Into Economic Issues, 2009, (9).

Li and Li. A Re-examination of the Impact of Fluctuations in International Crude Oil Prices on China's Macroeconomy. Economic Review, 2011, 3: 009

Li and Li. A Study of the Impact of Fed Tapering on the Strong Dollar Cycle and Emerging Markets. Forum of World Economics & Politics, 2017, (6).

Li and Shen. The Development Dilemma and Prospect of Student Loans in the Places of Origin of Students—A Case Study of City A in Hubei Province. Tsinghua Journal of Education, 2007, 28(5): 40–45.

Li and Zhang. Has the U.S. Quantitative Easing Policy Affected China's Inflation?—An Empirical Study based on the SVAR Model. Studies of International Finance, 2013, (8).

Li et al. Report on the Development of China's Market Economy in 2003, Beijing: China Foreign Economic and Trade Press, 2003.

Li, Wu, and Tang. Talents in the High-tech Industries of A Knowledge-based Economy—Insights from the Development of the U.S. and Japanese Economies. R&D Management, Vol. 12.

Li. "Forecast and Analysis of China's Economic Development in the 21st Century (2000–2050)"; Zhang Zhuoyuan, editor in chief, Experts on China's Economic Issues in the 21st Century, Zhengzhou: Henan People's Publishing House, 1999.

Li. A Study of the Impact of U.S. Quantitative Easing Policy on the Global Economy, Wuhan: Wuhan University Press, 2013.

Li. A Study of the Theoretical Basis and Impact of U.S. Quantitative Easing Policy and the Strategy Adopted In Response to It, Tianjin: Nankai University Press, 2014.

Li. Poor Students in Colleges and Universities are a Cause for Concern: A Survey Report on the Situation of Poor Students in the Capital's Colleges and Universities. Beijing Statistics, 1999, (8).

Li. Reflections on the Taylor's Rule, the Fed's Monetary Policy and China's Monetary Regulation. Studies of International Finance, 2001, (6): 15–19.

Li. The Choice of Intermediate Target of China's Monetary Policy, The Chinese Banker, 2002, (7).

Liu and Han. An Analysis of the Spillover Effects of Quantitative Easing Policy on Emerging Markets—A Study Based on the Experience of China and Brazil. Management Review, 2014, (6).

Liu and Zhang. Progress in and Insights From Research on Monetary Policy and Its Transmission Mechanism: A Perspective From Contemporary Western Economics. Journal of Peking University (Philosophy and Social Sciences), January 2012, 49(1).

Liu, Guoguang et al. A Study of the Model of China's Economic System Reform, Guangzhou: Guangdong Economic Publishing House, 1998.

Liu, Jia, and Zhang. An Analysis of the Exit Path of Broad Quantitative Easing in the United States: A Central Bank Balance Sheet Perspective. Economic Perspectives, 2014, (12): 21–32.

Liu, Xu, and Liu. Will Fed Rate Hike Expectations Cause Asset Price Volatility in China?—Empirical Evidence based on the Exchange Rate Transmission Path. Journal of Xi'an Jiaotong University (Social Sciences), 2016, (4).

Liu, Zhang, and Zhang. Smoothing the Economic Cycle at a Moderately High Level. Economic Research Journal, 2005, (11).

Liu, Zhang, et al. The "New Economy" in Perspective, Beijing: Social Sciences Academic Press (China), 2001.

Liu. A Study of the Industrial Structure in the Period of Accelerated Industrialization, Beijing: China Renmin University Press, 1995.

Liu. A Study of U.S. Monetary Policy Adjustment and Its Impact, Beijing: Tsinghua University Press, 2017.

Liu. An Empirical Study of the Correlation between Money supply, Output and Prices in China. Journal of Financial Research, 2002, (7).

Liu. The Applicability of Money Supply and Interest Rates As the Intermediate Targets of Monetary Policy. Journal of Financial Research, 2006, (1): 51–63.

Liu. The Feasibility of the Application of Optimal Simple Monetary Policy Rules in China. Journal of Financial Research, 2003, (9): 22–38.

Lu and Fang. A Study of the Impact of U.S. Quantitative Easing Policy Adjustment on Short-Term Capital Flows in China. Macroeconomics, 2015, (2).

Ma and Yu. A Study of the Spillover Effects of U.S. Quantitative Easing Policy on BRICS Countries. Studies of International Finance, 2015, (3): 13–22.

Ma and Yu. A Study of the Spillover Effects of U.S. Quantitative Easing Policy on BRICS Countries, Studies of International Finance, 2015, (3).

Macro Group, China Center for Economic Research, Peking University. Monetary Policy? Fiscal Policy?—Comments on China's Macroeconomic Policy and Suggestions for Growth. Economic Research Journal, 1998, (10).

Macro Group, China Center for Economic Research, Peking University. Research on Preventing Deflation and Maintaining Fast Economic Growth, Beijing: Peking University Press, 2005.

Mao. Has Trade Policy Uncertainty Affected Imports by Chinese Enterprises? Economic Research Journal, 2020, 55(2): 148–164.

National Economic Growth and Accounting Research Center, Peking University. China Economic Growth Report 2007, Beijing: China Economic Press, 2007.

Neely C J. Unconventional Monetary Policy had Large International Effects. Journal of Banking & Finance, 2015, 52.

Nie and Jin. A Study of the Spillover Effects of U.S. Quantitative Easing Policy on the Exports of Chinese Industries. Studies of International Finance, 2015, (3): 3–12.

Nie and Jin. A Study of the Spillover Effects of U.S. Quantitative Easing Policy on the Exports of Chinese Industries. Studies of International Finance, 2015, (3).

Pan and Yan. The Macroeconomic Effects of the Fed's Interest Rate Commitment. Studies of International Finance, 2012, (4)

Peter. Monetary Policy Goals, Institutions, Strategies, and Instruments, Beijing: China Renmin University Press, 2013.

Qi, Cheng, Wang, and Li. The Impact of the Fed's Quantitative Easing Policy on the Chinese Economy and the RMB Exchange Rate. Management Review, 2013, (5).

Sun and Zhang. Time Variance, Fed Rate Hikes and China's Output—An Empirical Analysis Based on the TVP-VAR Model. Studies of International Finance, 2016, (4).

Tang. A Study of the Impact of the Fed's Quantitative Easing Policy on China's Capital Markets. World Economy Study, 2015, (6): 12–23, 127.
Tang. Feldstein and His Supply-Side Economics. Economic Science, 1982, (1): 48–51.
Tomales. Capital in the Twenty-First Century, Beijing, CITIC Press, 2014, pp. 486–487.
Wang and Chen. China-U.S. Economic Relations, Exchange Rate Regime and China's Exchange Rate Policy—An Empirical Analysis Based on the FAVAR Model. The Journal of Quantitative & Technical Economics, 2010, (1).
Wang and Qu. Exchange Rate Pass-through, Currency Mismatch and Optimal Monetary Rules. World Economic Papers, 2018(2): 40–56.
Wang and Xiong. The Effect of U.S. Quantitative Easing Policy and Its Impact on China. Social Science Journal, 2011, (6).
Wang Wang, Peng, and Song. Comparative Analysis of China's Monetary Policy Rules—A Three Rule Perspective Based on the DSGE Model. Economic Research Journal, 2017, 52(9): 24–38.
Wang, Wang, and Chen. Monetary Policy Expectations and Inflation Management: A DSGE Analysis Based on News Shocks. Economic Research Journal, 2016, 51(2): 16–29.
Wang, Xiao, Liu, and Wu Yu. Dollarization and Monetary Policy Spillovers. World Economy Study, 2022, (6).
Wang, Zhou, and Zhang. Interest Rate Shocks, Capital Flows and Economic Volatility—An Analysis from an Asymmetric Perspective. Economic Research Journal, 2019, 54(6): 106–120.
Wang: Professor at the Economics and Management School of Wuhan University, Zhou Shangyao and Zhao Haoquan.
Wei and Zou. An Empirical Analysis of China's Monetary Policy Independence From U.S. Monetary Policy. Journal of International Trade, 2012, (7): 115–124.
Wu and Liu. An Empirical Study of the International Transmission of U.S. Monetary Policy and Its Impact. The Journal of Quantitative & Technical Economics, 2009, (6): 42–52.
Xiao and Lan. The Spillover Effects of the Fed's Monetary Policy Normalization on the Chinese Economy. World Economy Study, 2017(12): 38–49+133.
Xiao and Lan. The Spillover Effects of the Fed's Monetary Policy Normalization on the Chinese Economy. World Economy Study, 2017, (12).
Xiao. A Study of the International Transmission of U.S. Monetary Policy Shocks: An Empirical Analysis of Asian Economies. Studies of International Finance, 2011, (9): 18–29.
Xiao. The Impact of the U.S. Economic Recovery on the Global and Chinese Economies. International Trade, 2015, (2).

Xing and Tang. A Study of the Spillover Effects of U.S. Monetary Policy on China's Monetary Policy. Research on Financial and Economic Issues, 2011, (11): 50–55.

Xu. A Study of the Theory, Practice and Effects of Quantitative Easing Policy (1st Edition), Beijing: Economic Press China, 2013.

Xu. The Impact of the Effects of the Fed's Monetary Policy on China's Economic Growth: An Interprovincial Study Based on the TVP-VAR-SV model. World Economy Study, 2018 (4): 40–48+135–136.

Yang, Xu, and Wang. A Comparative Study of the Two-way Spillover Effects of the Monetary Policy of China and the United States: Based on A Two-Country DSGE Model. Studies of International Finance, 2018, (11): 14–24.

Yin. A Discussion on the Loose Monetary Policies Adopted by China and the United States, Inflation Expectations and Monetary Rules. World Economy Study, 2010 (2).

Yu, Zhang, and Wu. The Impact of the U.S. Exit from QE on the Financial Markets of China and the United States and China's Countermeasures—An Analysis Based on the FAVAR Model. World Economy Study, 2015, (4): 24–32; 127.

Yu. Processing Trade, Firm Productivity and Tariff Reductions and Exemptions—Evidence from the Chinese Product Side. China Economic Quarterly, 2011, 10(4): 1251–1280.

Zhang. Monetary Policy Transmission Mechanism: Theoretical Development and Practical Choice. Chinese Review of Financial Studies, 2011, (1).

Zhu. The Mechanism by Which U.S. Monetary Policy Affects China's Economy, PhD thesis, Changchun: Jilin University Press, 2014.

Zhuang, Cui, Gong, and Zou. Expectations and Economic Volatility—Are Expectation Shocks the Main Force Driving China's Economic Fluctuations? Economic Research Journal, 2012, 47(6): 46–59.

English Section

Aizenman J, Chinn M D, and Ito H. Monetary Policy Spillovers and the Trilemma in the New Normal: Periphery Country Sensitivity to Core Country Conditions. Journal of International Money and Finance, 2016, 68: 298–330.

Akinci Ö, and Chahrour R. Good News is Bad News: Leverage Cycles and Sudden Stops. Journal of International Economics, 2018, 114 (C): 362–375.

Anaya P, Hachula M, and Offermanns C J. Spillovers of U.S. Unconventional Monetary Policy to Emerging Markets: The Role of Capital Flows. Journal of International Money and Finance, 2017, 73.

Apostolou A, and Beirne J. Volatility Spillovers of Unconventional Monetary Policy to Emerging Market Economies. Economic Modelling, 2019, 79.

Bachmeier L J, and Swanson N R. Predicting Inflation: Does the Quantity Theory Help? Economic Inquiry, 2005, 43(3): 570–585.

Bauer and Rudebusch. The Signaling Channel for Federal Reserve Bond Purchases. Federal Reserve Bank of San Francisco Working Paper Series, Working Paper No. 2011–21.

Bauer M D, and Neely C J. International Channels of the Fed's Unconventional Monetary Policy. Federal Reserve Bank of St. Louis Working Paper Series, Working Paper 2012–028A, 2012.

Baumol W J. The Transactions Demand for Cash: An Inventory Theoretic Approach. The Quarterly Journal of Economics, 1952: 545–556.

Bauraeister C, and Benati L. Unconventional Monetary Policy and the Great Recession Estimating the Impact of a Compression in the Yield Spread at the Zero Lower Bound. European Central Bank, Working Paper Series No. 1258, 2012.

Bekaert G, Hoerova M, and Duca M L. Risk, Uncertainty and Monetary Policy. Journal of Monetary Economics, 2013, 60(7): 771–788.

Bekaert, Ehrmann, Fratzscher, and Mehl. Global Crises and Equity Market Contagion. NBER Working Paper No. 17121, 2011.

Benigno P, and Nistico S. Safe Assets, Liquidity and Monetary Policy. American Economic Journal: Macroeconomics, 2017, 9(2): 182–227.

Berentsen A, Huber S, and Marchesiani A. Financial Innovations, Money Demand, and the Welfare Cost of Inflation. Journal of Money, Credit and Banking, 2015, 47(S2): 223–261.

Bernanke and Reinhart. Conducting Monetary Policy at Very Low Short-term Interest Rates. The American Economic Review, 2004, 94.

Bernanke B S, and Blinder A S. Credit, Money, and Aggregate Demand. American Economic Review, 1988, 78(2): 435–439.

Bernanke B S, and Gertler M. Inside the Black Box: The Credit Channel of Monetary Policy Transmission. Journal of Economic Perspectives, 1995: 27–48.

Bernanke B S. Monetary Policy and the Housing Bubble. Speech at the Annual Meeting of the American Economic Association, Atlanta, Georgia. 2010, 3.

Bernanke B S. The Crisis and the Policy Response. Stamp Lecture, London School of Economics, January, 2009, 13.

Bernanke B, and Gertler M. Agency Costs, Net Worth, and Business Fluctuations. American Economic Review, 1989 (1): 14–31.

Bernanke, Reinhart and Sack. "Monetary Policy Alternatives at the Zero Bound: An Empirical Assessment", Brookings Papers on Economic Activity, Vol. 35, 2004, Reserve: Did They Work? Federal Reserve Bank of New York Working Paper No 441, 2011.

Bernanke. Federal Reserve's Exit Strategy. Testimony before the Committee on Financial Services, U. S. House of Representatives, Washington, DC, February 10, 2010.
Bernanke. The Crisis and the Policy Response, Speech at London, 13 January 2009.
Bernankef. "The Federal Reserve's Balance Sheet: An Update", Speech at the Federal Reserve Board Conference on Key Developments in Monetary Policy, Washington, DC, 2009, 10.
Bernaxike. "Semiannual Monetary Policy Report to the Congress." Testimony before the Committee on Financial Services, U.S. House of Representatives, Washington, DC, July 21, 2009.
Bernini F, González J, Hallak J C, Vicondoa A. The Micro-D Classification: A New Approach to Identifying Differentiated Exports. Economía, 2018, 18(2): 59–85.
Betts C, and Devereux M. Exchange Rate Dynamics in a Model of Pricing-to-Market. Journal of International Economics, 2000, 50(1): 215–244.
Bianchi J, and Mendoza E G. Optimal Time-Consistent Macroprudential Policy. Journal of Political Economy, 2018, 126: 588–634.
Bianchi J, and Mendoza E G. Optimal Time-Consistent Macroprudential Policy. NBER Working Paper, No. 19704, 2015.
Bianchi J. Over Borrowing and Systemic Externalities in the Business Cycle. American Economic Review, 2011, 101 (7): 3400–3426.
Blinder A S. Quantitative Easing: Entrance and Exit Strategies. Federal Reserve Bank of St. Louis Review, 2010.
Bloom N, Floetotto M, Jaimovich N, Saporta-Eksten I, and Terry S T. Really Uncertain Business Cycles. Econometrica, 2018, 86(3): 1031–1065.
Bloom N. Fluctuations in Uncertainty. Journal of Economic Perspectives, 2014, 28(2): 153–175.
Bloom N. The Impact of Uncertainty Shocks. Econometrica, 2009, 77(3): 623–685.
Bluedorn J C, Bowdler C. The Empirics of International Monetary Transmission: Identification and the Impossible Trinity. Journal of Money, Credit and Banking, 2010, 42(4): 679–713.
Borio and Disyatat. Unconventional Monetary Policies: An Appraisal. BIS Working Paper No. 292, 2009.
Boz E, Gopinath G, and Plagborg-Moller M. Global Trade and the Dollar. NBER Working Papers, No. 23988, 2017.
Bräuning F, and Ivashina V U S. Monetary Policy and Emerging Market Credit Cycles. Journal of Monetary Economics, 2020, 112.
Bruno V, and Shin H S, Capital Flows and the Risk-Taking Channel of Monetary Policy. Journal of Monetary Economics, 2015, 71: 119–132.

Caldara D, Iacoviello M, Molligo P, Prestipino A, and Raffo A. The Economic Effects of Trade Policy Uncertainty. Journal of Monetary Economics, 2020, 109: 38–59.

Cao D, and L'Huillier J P. Technological Revolutions and the Three Great Slumps: A Medium-Run Analysis. Journal of Monetary Economics, 2014, 96: 93–108.

Carlson, Haubrich, Cherny and Wakefield. Credit Easing: A Policy for a Time of Financial Crisis. Federal Reserve Bank of Cleveland, 2009.

Chang C, Liu Z, and Spiegel M M. Capital Controls and Optimal Chinese Monetary Policy. Journal of Monetary Economics, 2015, 74: 1–15.

Chen Q, Filardo A, He D, et al. Financial Crisis, US Unconventional Monetary Policy and International Spillovers. Journal of International Money and Finance, 2016, 67: 62–81.

Chen, Lei Hou Peng. Quantitative Easing, Liquidity Spillover and Emerging Markets Inflation. Finance & Economics, 2011–10, 2011.

Christiano L J, Motto R, and Rostagno M. Risk Shocks. American Economic Review, 2014, 104(1): 27–65.

Christiano L J, Trabandt M, Walentin K. DSGE Models for Monetary Policy Analysis. Handbook of Monetary Economics, 2010, 3 (7): 285–367, edition 1.

Christiano L J, Trabandt M, Walentin K. Introducing Financial Frictions and Unemployment into a Small Open Economy Model. Journal of Economic Dynamics and Control, 2011, 35(12): 1999–2041.

Christiano L, Ilut C L, Motto R, et al. Monetary Policy and Stock Market Booms. National Bureau of Economic Research, 2010.

Clower R W, and Howitt P W. The Transactions Theory of the Demand for Money: Are Consideration. The Journal of Political Economy, 1978: 449–466.

Cogley T, and Sargent T J. Drifts and Volatilities: Monetary Policies and Outcomes in the Post WWII US. Review of Economic Dynamics, 2005, 8(2): 262–302.

Curdia V, and Woodford M. Credit Spreads and Monetary Policy. Journal of Money, Credit and Banking, 2010, 42(s1): 3–35.

Curdia, and Woodford. Conventional and Unconventional Monetary Policy. CEPR, CEPR Discussion Paper No. 7514, 2009.

D'Amico and King. Flow and Stock Effect of Large Scale Treasury Purchases. Federal Reserve Board Finance and Economics Discussion Series, No. 2010–52.

Davis J S, and Presno I. Capital Controls and Monetary Policy Autonomy in a Small Open Economy. Journal of Monetary Economics, 2017, 85: 114–130.

Dedola L, Rivolta G, and Stracca L. If the Fed Sneezes, Who Catches a Cold? Journal of International Economics, 2017, 108(1): 23–41.

Doh. The Efficacy of Large Scale Asset Purchases at the Zero Lower Bound. Economic Review, Federal Reserve Bank of Kansas City, 2011.

Durdu C B, Nunes R, and Sapriza H. News and Sovereign Default Risk in Small Open Economies. Journal of International Economics, 2013, 91(1): 1–17.

Eggertsson G B, Woodford M, Friedman B M, and Gertler M. The Zero Bound on Interest Rates and Optimal Monetary Policy. Brookings Papers on Economic Activity, Vol. 34, 2003.

Eichanbaum E, and Charles L E. Some Empirical Evidence on the Effects of Shocks to Monetary Policy on Exchange Rate. The Quarterly Journal of Economics, 1995: 975–1009.

Eichengreen B, and Gupta P. Tapering Talk: The Impact of Expectations of Reduced Federal Reserve Security Purchases on Emerging Markets. Emerging Markets Review, 2015, 25: 1–15.

Engel C. Currency Misalignments and Optimal Monetary Policy: A Reexamination. The American Economic Review, 2011, 101(6): 2796–2822.

Faia E, and Monacelli T. Optimal Monetary Policy in a Small Open Economy with Home Bias. Journal of Money, Credit and Banking, 2008, 40(4): 721–750.

Fawley B W, Neely C J. Four stories of quantitative easing. Federal Reserve Bank of St. Louis Review, 2013, 95(January/February 2013).

Field A J. Asset Exchanges and the Transactions Demand for Money, 1919–29. The American Economic Review, 1984: 43–59.

Fisher I. The Purchasing Power of Money, Pickering & Chatto, 1911.

Francois J F, and Martin W. Commercial Policy Variability, Bindings, and Market Access. European Economic Review, 2004, 48(3): 665–679.

Fratzscher M, Duca M L, and Straub R. Quantitative Easing, Portfolio Choice and International Capital Flows. Draft, European Central Bank, Frankfurt, 2012, 22.

Fratzscher M. Capital Flows, Push Versus Pull Factors and the Global Financial Crisis. NBER Working Paper No. 17357, 2011.

Frenkel J A, and Jovanovic B. On Transactions and Precautionary Demand for Money. The Quarterly Journal of Economics, 1980, 95(1): 25–43.

Frenkel J A. The Forward Exchange Rate, Expectations, and the Demand for Money: The German Hyperinflation. The American Economic Review, 1977: 653–670.

Friedman M, and Schwartz A J. A Monetary History of the United States, 1867–1960, Princeton University Press, 2008.

Friedman M. A Theoretical Framework for Monetary Analysis. The Journal of Political Economy, 1970: 193–238.

Friedman M. The Quantity Theory of Money: A Restatement, University of Chicago, 1956, 4(2): 281–308.

Gagnon J, Raskin M, Remache J, et al. The Financial Market Effects of the Federal Reserve's Large-Scale Asset Purchases. International Journal of Central Banking, 2011, 7(1): 3–43.

Georgiadis G, and Schumann B. Dominant-Currency Pricing and the Global Output Spillovers from U.S. Dollar Appreciation. Journal of International Economics, 2021, 133, 103537.

Georgios G, and Ben S. Dominant-Currency Pricing and the Global Output Spillovers from U.S. Dollar Appreciation. ECB Working Paper, N2308, 2019.

Gertler M, and Karadi P. A Model of Unconventional Monetary Policy. Journal of Monetary Economics, 2011, 58(1): 17–34.

Gertler M, Kiyotaki N, and Prestipino A. A Macroeconomic Model with Financial Panics. Review of Economic Studies, 2020, Oxford University Press, 87(1): 240–288.

Gilchrist S, Ortiz A, and Zakrajsek E. Credit Risk and the Macroeconomy: Evidence from an Estimated DSGE Model. Unpublished Manuscript, Boston University, 2009.

Góes C, Kamil H, Imus P D, Garcia-Escribano M, Perrelli R, Roache S K, and Zook J. Spillovers from U.S. Monetary Policy Normalization on Brazil and Mexico's Sovereign Bond Yields. IMF Working Paper, WP/17/50, 2017.

Gomes S, Iskrev N, and Mendicino C. Monetary Policy Shocks: We Got News. Journal of Economic Dynamics and Control, 2017, 74 (1): 108–128.

Gopinath G, Boz E, Casas C, Dies F J, Gourinchas P O, and Plagborg M M. Dominant Currency Paradigm. NBER Working Papers, No. 22943, 2016.

Gopinath G, Boz E, Casas C, Dies F J, Gourinchas P O, and Plagborg-Moller M. Dominant Currency Paradigm. NBER Working Paper, No 22943, 2016.

Gopinath G. The International Price System. NBER Working Papers, 2015, No. 21646.

Gopinath G. The International Price System. Jackson Hole Symposium Model with Financial Panics, NBER Digest, 2016.

Guerrieri L, and Iacoviello M. Collateral Constraints and Macroeconomic Asymmetries. Journal of Monetary Economics, 2017, 90: 28–49.

Hamilton and Wu. The Effectiveness of Alternative Monetary Policy Tools in a Zero Lower Bound Environment. NBER Working Paper No. 16956, 2011.

Han X, and Wei S J. International Transmissions of Monetary Shocks: Between a Trilemma and a Dilemma. NBER Working Papers, No. 22812, 2016.

Handley K, and Limão N. Policy Uncertainty, Trade, and Welfare: Theory and Evidence for China and the United States. American Economic Review, 2017, 107(9): 2731–2783.

Handley K. Exporting Under Trade Policy Uncertainty: Theory and Evidence. Journal of International Economics, 2014, 94(1): 50–66.

Hanisch M. US Monetary Policy and the Euro Area. Journal of Banking and Finance, 2019, 100: 77–96.

Hansen A H. Guide to Keynes, 1953.
Hansen A H. Monetary Theory and Fiscal Policy, 1949.
Hicks J R. Liquidity. The Economic Journal, 1962: 787–802.
Hicks J R. Mr. Keynes and the “Classics”: A Suggested Interpretation. Econometrica: Journal of the Econometric Society, 1937: 147–159.
Ho S W, Zhang J, and Zhou H. Hot Money and Quantitative Easing: The Spillover Effects of U.S. Monetary Policy on the Chinese Economy. Journal of Money, Credit and Banking, 2018, 50(7): 1543–1569.
Iacoviello M, and Navarro G. Foreign Effects of Higher U.S. Interest Rates. Journal of International Money and Finance, 2019, 95: 232–250.
Imbruno M. Importing Under Trade Policy Uncertainty: Evidence from China. Journal of Comparative Economics, 2019, 47(42): 806–826.
Justiniano A, Primiceri G E, and Tambalotti A. Investment Shocks and Business Cycles. Journal of Monetary Economics, 2010, 57(2): 132–145.
Kaketsis A, and Sarantis N. The Effects of Monetary Policy Changes on Market Interest Rates in Greece: An Event Study Approach. International Review of Economics & Finance, 2006, 15(4).
Kalu E, Okoyeuzu C, Ukemenam A, and Ujunwa A. Spillover Effects of the US Monetary Policy Normalization on African Stock Markets. Journal of Economics and Development, 2020, 22(1).
Kapetanios G, Mumtaz H, Stevens I, and Theodoridis K. Assessing the Economy-Wide Effects of Quantitative Easing. Bank of England Working Paper Series No. 443, 2012.
Keynes J M. The General Theory of Interest, Employment and Money, 1936.
Kim M, Nam D, Wang J, and Wu J. International Trade Price Stickiness and Exchange Rate and Pass-Through in Micro Data: A Case Study on US-China Trade. Working Papers, No. 202013, 2013.
Kiyotaki N, Moore J. Credit Cycles. Journal of Political Economy, 1997, 105: 211–248.
Kolasa M, and Wesołowski G. International Spillovers of Quantitative Easing. Journal of International Economics, 2020, 126.
Krishnamurthy A, and Vissing-Jorgensen A. The Effects of Quantitative Easing on Internet Rates: Channels and Implications for Policy. NBER Working Paper Series 17555, 2011.
Liu Z, Wang P, and Zha T. Land-Price Dynamics and Macroeconomic Fluctuations. Econometrica, 2013, 81(3): 1147–1184.
Lucas R E, and Nicolini J P. On the Stability of Money Demand. Journal of Monetary Economics, 2015.
Marshall A. Money, Credit & Commerce, AM Kelley, Bookseller, 1923.
McKinnon R, and Liu Z. Zero Interest Rates in the United States Provoke World Monetary Instability and Constrict the US Economy. Review of International Economics, 2013, 21(1).

Meltzer A H. Monetary, Credit and (Other) Transmission Processes: A Monetarist Perspective. The Journal of Economic Perspectives, 1995: 49–72.

Milani F, and Treadwell J. The Effects of Monetary Policy "News" and "Surprises". Journal of Money, Credit and Banking, 2012, 44(8): 1667–1692.

Neely C J. The Large Scale Asset Purchases had Large International Effects. Federal Reserve Bank of St. Louis, Research Division, 2010.

Neri S, and Nobili A. The Transmission of US Monetary Policy to the Euro Area. International Finance, 2010, 13 (1): 55–78.

Obstfeld M. Trilemmas and Tradeoffs: Living with Financial Globalization. BIS Working Papers, No. 480, 2015.

Ongena S, Schindele I, and Vonnak D. In Lands of Foreign Currency Credit, Bank Lending Channels Run Through? CFS Working Papers, No. 474, 2015.

Ossa R. Trade Wars and Trade Talks with Data. American Economic Review, 2014, 104(12): 4104–4146.

Phillips A W. The Relation Between Unemployment and the Rate of Change of Money Wage Rates in the United Kingdom, 1861–1957. Economica, 1958, 25(100): 283–299.

Pigou A C. The Value of Money. The Quarterly Journal of Economics, 1917: 38–65.

Ragot X. The Case for a Financial Approach to Money Demand. Journal of Monetary Economics, 2014, 62: 94–107.

Reis R. Interpreting the Unconventional US Monetary Policy of 2007–09. National Bureau of Economic Research, 2010.

Rey H. Dilemma Not Trilemma: The Global Financial Cycle and Monetary Policy Independence. NBER Working Papers, No. 21162, 2015.

Ricci O. The Impact of Monetary Policy Announcements on the Stock Price of Large European Banks During the Financial Crisis. Journal of Banking & Finance, 2015, 52: 245–255.

Roosa R V. Interest Rates and the Central Bank. Money, Trade, and Economic Growth: Essays in Honor of John Henry Williams, 1951.

Schmitt-Grohé S, and Uribe M. What's News in Business Cycle. Econometrica, 2012, 80(6): 2733–2764.

Sims C A. Macroeconomics and Reality. Econometrica: Journal of the Econometric Society, 1980: 1–48.

Statement on Longer-Run Goals and Monetary Policy Strategy (2021–1–26).The Federal Reserve System.

Sunderam A. Money Creation and the Shadow Banking System. Review of Financial Studies, 2014: hhu083.

Taylor J B. Discretion Versus Policy Rules in Practice. Carnegie-Rochester Conference Series on Public Policy, North-Holland, 1993, 39: 195–214

Taylor J B. The Robustness and Efficiency of Monetary Policy Rules as Guidelines for Interest Rate Setting by the European Central Bank. Journal of Monetary Economics, 1999, 43(3): 655–679.

Thornton D L. Evidence on The Portfolio Balance Channel of Quantitative Easing, Federal Reserve Bank of St. Louis Working Paper Series 2012–015A, 2012.

Tillmann P. Unconventional Monetary Policy and the Spillovers to Emerging Markets. Journal of International Money and Finance, 2016, 66.

Tobin J, and Brainard W C. Financial Intermediaries and the Effectiveness of Monetary Controls. The American Economic Review, 1963:383–400.

Tobin J. A General Equilibrium Approach to Monetary Theory. Journal of money, credit and banking, 1969, 1(1): 15–29.

Tobin J. Commercial Banks as Creators of "Money." Cowles Foundation for Research in Economics at Yale University, 1964.

Tobin J. Liquidity Preference as Behavior Towards Risk. The Review of Economic Studies, 1958, 25(2): 65–86.

Tobin J. The Interest-Elasticity of Transactions Demand for Cash. The Review of Economics and Statistics, 1956: 241–247.

Tsiang S C. The Precautionary Demand for Money: An Inventory Theoretical Analysis. The Journal of Political Economy, 1969: 99–117.

Wang C, and Zou H F. Optimal Monetary Policy Under a Global Dollar Standard: The Effect of Vertical Trade and Production. Open Economies Review, 2015, 26: 121–137

Wang S, and Guo R F. Asymmetric Exchange Rate Pass-through and Monetary Policy in Open Economy. Annals of Economics and Finance, 2016, 17(1): 33–53.

Werner R A. How to Create a Recovery Through 'Quantitative Monetary Easing'. The Nihon Keizai Shinbun (Nikkei), 2 September 1995 (morning edition), 1995:26.

Wright J H. What does Monetary Policy do to Long-term Interest Rates at the Zero Lower Bound? The Economic Journal, 2012, 122(564): F447–F466.

Wu S, Hu B, and Pan Q. The Impact of the US Interest Rate Hike on Emerging Market Economies and the Belt and Road Initiative. China & World Economy, 2019, 27(3).

Yang Z, and Zhou Y. Quantitative Easing and Volatility Spillovers Across Countries and Asset Classes. Management Science, 2017, 63(2).

Zhang T. Monetary Policy Spillovers through Invoicing Currencies, Working Paper, 2020.

Zhang T. Monetary Policy Spillovers Through Invoicing Currencies. Journal of Finance, 2022, 77: 129–161.

Index

L. Weiping, *American Monetary Policy Adjustment and Its Impacts*, https://doi.org/10.1007/978-981-99-7810-6

SPRINGER NATURE

GPSR Compliance

The European Union's (EU) General Product Safety Regulation (GPSR) is a set of rules that requires consumer products to be safe and our obligations to ensure this.

If you have any concerns about our products, you can contact us on ProductSafety@springernature.com

In case Publisher is established outside the EU, the EU authorized representative is:

Springer Nature Customer Service Center GmbH
Europaplatz 3
69115 Heidelberg, Germany

The manufacturer's authorised representative in the EU is Springer Nature Customer Service Centre GmbH, Europaplatz 3, 69115 Heidelberg, Germany. If you have any concerns regarding our products, please contact ProductSafety@springernature.com

Printed and bound by CPI Group (UK) Ltd, Croydon, CR0 4YY

01/10/2026

02225898-0012